T0384341

The Economics of Optimal Growth Pathways

S. Niggol Seo

The Economics of Optimal Growth Pathways

Evaluating the Health of the Planet's Natural
and Ecological Resources

S. Niggol Seo
Muaebak Institute of Global Warming Studies
Bangkok, Thailand

ISBN 978-3-031-20753-2   ISBN 978-3-031-20754-9   (eBook)
https://doi.org/10.1007/978-3-031-20754-9

This Palgrave Macmillan imprint is published by the registered company Springer Nature Switzerland AG.
The registered company address is: Gewerbestrasse 11, 6330 Cham, Switzerland

PREFACE

The planet we live in is endowed with many kinds of valuable natural resources—including plants, animals, trees, fuels, lands, oceans, and atmosphere—which are relied upon by human beings for their survival and prosperity. It is a central quest of economics to explicate the best ways to utilize these resources, that is, in the manner that maximizes the welfare of people on the planet, over an unforeseeable time horizon. On the other hand, a nation's economy is built crucially on how its people utilize the precious natural resources, in addition to the technological, cultural, and intellectual resources its people advance. The same can be said of the global economy as well.

Can a nation's economy be managed in a way for it to continue to grow along an optimal economic growth pathway over an infinite time horizon? This question has intrigued many intellectuals over the past two centuries. What has intrigued even more intellectuals is the conundrum of whether a nation's economy, or the planet's economy if pertinent, can be managed for it to continue to grow over time, despite the hard reality of the eventually fixed stocks of natural resources on the planet.

This book entitled "The Economics of Optimal Growth Pathways: Evaluating the Health of the Planet's Natural and Ecological Resources" puts forth a lucid answer to these questions of great importance to the future of the planet and its people. It takes an extensive historical approach by tracing the history of economic thoughts during the past two centuries that has engaged the two vital economic questions: managing natural resources efficiently on the one hand and managing national economic growth optimally on the other.

At the core, this book demonstrates that the two questions are interdependent. That is, the first question cannot stand alone without the second question, and *vice versa*. In other words, it is neither rational nor persuasive for a serious thinker to approach the first question relying on one set of principles while approaching the second question relying on another different set of principles.

For an exposition of the natural resource use questions, the present author provides a critical review of the following six literatures: David Ricardo's rent theory applied to croplands in Chap. 2, von Thunen's spatial land use theory in Chap. 3, Martin Faustmann's forest harvest rotation economics in Chap. 4, Harold Hotelling's fossil fuel economics in Chap. 5, a bio-economics of fisheries in Chap. 6, and Irving Fisher's capital assets in Chap. 7.

For an exposition of the national economic growth questions, the present author provides a review of the following five literatures: Irving Fisher's theory of capital and interest rate in Chap. 7, Frank Ramsey's theory of national savings in Chap. 8, Robert Solow's modern economic growth theory as capital accumulation in Chap. 9, Tjalling Koopmans's optimal economic growth path in Chap. 10, and William Nordhaus's optimal trajectory of price of carbon dioxide in Chap. 11.

In common to the two categories of economic inquiries, each of the above ten literatures is concerned with a dynamic trajectory of a primary variable of interest in the respective literature. For the inquiry on fossil fuels, for example, an efficient long-term management of a petroleum well will lead to a dynamic trajectory of the Hotelling rent. For the inquiry of the Koopmans's national economic growth model, a societally welfare optimizing management will lead to a dynamic pathway of the economy's capital accumulation or the society's consumption.

In each chapter of this book from Chap. 2, the chief economic theory selected for the topic addressed in the chapter, elaborated in the above, is first described. This is then followed by a description of one or two major critiques against the theory. These critiques that appear across the ten chapters are then synthesized at the final chapter of this book, Chap. 13. The present author calls them collectively in the final chapter a sub-optimal growth critique or a post-growth critique alternatingly. The sub-optimal or post-growth critiques are in turn classified into three streams of thoughts: a sustainable development critique, an ecological economics critique, a degrowth critique.

Tjalling Koopmans provides the most comprehensive answer to the afore-described questions relating to the concept of optimal economic growth, which was in fact the title of his 1963 article. If the national economy were to be managed in a way that achieves the societal welfare optimum, he clarifies, it should grow at a rate that approximates the rate of population growth plus the discount rate plus the rate of unforeseeable technological progress, all of which again depend, *inter alia*, on market interest rate, social inequality aversion, and consumption patterns.

Koopmans's optimal economic growth pathways are well conceptualized to unfold over a very distant time horizon while simultaneously addressing the resource constraints of the planet as well as the negative side-effects of the economic activities. The former includes, *inter alia*, numerous ecological limits. The latter includes, *inter alia*, environmental pollution and global climate change. The way it does so is well illustrated by, *inter alia*, William Nordhaus's climate and economy model, the topic of Chap. 11.

The resource constraints, limits, availabilities are well clarified in this book *via* the six chapters, from Chaps. 2 to 6, devoted to the natural resource economic questions such as croplands, grazing lands, urban lands, forests, fossil fuels, and fish species. The unintended consequences of the economic activities are extensively addressed in this book in multiple chapters including the chapters on fossil fuels, marine resources, capital growth, and global climate change respectively.

To put Koopmans's conclusion in the context of Irving Fisher's theory on capital and interest, a nation's economy will grow in dependence on individuals' preferences, technological possibilities, and the mutually beneficial exchanges that people strike in marketplaces. This conclusion or insights are surely extendable to the planet's economy as well.

It is the present author's sincere aspiration that this book puts forth a novel contribution to the humanity's understandings of a better management of natural resources and life on the planet as well as a better management of the planet's economy. The present author would also like to express deep gratitude to William Nordhaus, Robert Shiller, and Robert Mendelsohn, through whom the present author was able to get in intimate contacts with the great economists introduced in this book, notably, Tjalling Koopmans, Irving Fisher, and Robert Solow.

Finally, the present author would like to thank the editorial team at Palgrave Macmillan especially Wyndham H. Pain and Ruby Panigrahi for their outstanding teamwork to get this book produced and promoted.

Bangkok, Thailand   S. Niggol Seo

CONTENTS

About the Author

S. Niggol Seo is a natural resource economist who specializes in the study of global warming and globally shared goods. He received a PhD degree in Environmental and Natural Resource Economics from Yale University in May 2006 with a dissertation on microbehavioral models of global warming. Born in a remote rural village in South Korea in 1972, he was invited for a doctoral study at UC Berkeley, University of Oxford, and Yale University. Since 2003, he has worked on various World Bank projects on climate change in Africa, Latin America, and Asia. He held professor positions in the UK, Spain, and Australia from 2006 to 2015. He received an Outstanding Applied Economic Perspectives and Policy Article Award from the Agricultural and Applied Economics Association (AAEA) in Pittsburgh in June 2011. He has published eleven books on climate change, pandemics, and globally shared goods. He is the editor-in-chief of the *Handbook of Behavioral Economics and Climate Change* published in 2022.

LIST OF FIGURES

LIST OF TABLES

CHAPTER 1

An Introduction to the Economics of Optimal Growth Pathways and the Health of Natural and Ecological Resources

1.1 Introduction

If you are a natural resource manager of, say, four acres of cropland or two hectares of forest stand, how would you manage it over your planning time horizon? This is the first and most fundamental question you have to answer in your brain before you get your hands and feet down and dirty. Any reasonable answer would encompass many future time periods, that is, beyond the single present time period, as well as a possibility of converting it to another land use at one future period or even selling it (Ricardo 1817; von Thunen 1826; Faustmann 1849).

The economics of optimal growth pathways, the book in your hands or on your kindle presently, is written to provide a rational answer to this question faced by the respective natural resource manager. The scope of this book is, however, far greater than cropland farming or forest management. This book starts with "four acres" of cropland in Chap. 2, continues to the nation's economy from Chap. 8 onwards, and ends big with the planet's atmosphere and the global economy from Chap. 11. The purview of this book falls on the planet's resources and the economic systems built upon it.

Let me clarify this point from the first question in the above. If you are a national economy's manager, how would you manage it over your time horizon? Can it be managed in a way that it grows at a rate that is optimal for the society? Similarly, if you are a global decision-maker, how would

S. N. Seo, *The Economics of Optimal Growth Pathways*, https://doi.org/10.1007/978-3-031-20754-9_1

1

you manage the planet's atmospheric changes such as global warming over a very long horizon of planning? Can it be managed in such a way that is most beneficial to the planet's citizens and simultaneously protects the nature (Solow 1957; Koopmans 1965; Nordhaus 1994a)?

This is one of the unique contributions of this book. In addressing the question of economic growth, which is the core question of this book entitled "The Economics of Optimal Growth Pathways," which is raised in the literature predominantly in the national economy's context, this book approaches it from the three different vantage points: individual natural resource enterprises, a national economy, and the planet.

Across the three levels of viewpoint, a same fundamental question pervades: how should an "owner" of a respective resource manage the concerned resource over the present and future time periods for the benefit of "oneself" and others? It is the question of dynamic growth pathways with respect to a concerned resource or economy.

In between the two extremities of scale, that is, a plot of cropland at a local scale and a global atmosphere at a planetary scale, a national economy has stood most prominently in the corpus of intellectual inquiries on economic growth dynamics. How should a national economy be managed, that is, under what principles? What should be the ultimate goal in managing a national economy over the present and future time periods? Can it continue to grow, if so, is there an optimal rate of growth? These are some of the questions that still powerfully intrigue many scholars as well as the general public.

Understandably, the questions regarding the national economy appear far more abstract than the questions regarding a cropland farmer or a forest stand manger. In addition, political powers and policy decisions rest mostly within national boundaries based on the concept of national sovereignty, which makes the national economic decisions far more complicated. For these reasons and others, the questions of how the nation's economy should be arranged and managed have been a prominent point of debates and even conflicts among the economists since the very beginning of economic science (Smith 1776; Malthus 1798; Ricardo 1817; Marx 1867).

Economists have long espoused the vital importance of continued economic growth of a nation, given that the economy's aggregate output is the sum of the values of the goods and services produced by all the economic actors of the nation for the consumption by its people. The higher the economy's growth rate, the better. A slower growing economy will fall behind a faster growing economy eventually at some point over the long run, which would be a harbinger of a declining country.

Extending this logic, can we say that a nation's economy should be arranged in such a way that it continues to grow in the manner that maximizes the society's welfare? Put differently, should a nation's economy be managed with the goal of achieving an optimal rate of economic growth? A large majority of economists would agree on this thesis (Ramsey 1928; Fisher 1930; Solow 1957; Friedman 1962; Koopmans 1965; Nordhaus 2008).

Having said that, there are many and diverse groups of economists, semi-economists, and non-economists who would vehemently disagree on the thesis. The antagonists of economic growth place their emphasis on numerous points, including, *inter alia*, the limits of continued economic growth, negative consequences of economic growth, unsustainable development, ecological thresholds and limits, global climate change, social inequalities, and racial injustice (Meadows et al. 1972; Daly 1973; WCED 1987; Costanza 2010). To them, the pursuit of continued economic growth is by and large a misguided endeavor. The most extreme of these critiques referred to as degrowth theorists would argue unequivocally that the national economy is better off by a zero growth or even a negative growth (PDED 2008).

The essential question that this book addresses is this: Which growth pathways should the nation, or the globe if appropriate, pursue in "managing" its economy? This book will present the concept of optimal economic growth established in the economics literature. This concept will be elucidated against the backdrop of the alternatives which espouses suboptimal economic growth or post-growth pathways in one way or another.

Although the question of the national economy's growth appears far more abstract and complex, the inquiry of managing a plot of cropland or a hectare of forest stand does not appear to be that way. On the contrary, it appears, at least at the first glance, to be rather concrete and straightforward. If that is indeed the case, why the question of the whole economy appears so difficult to handle while the questions regarding the individual natural resource sectors which constitute the national economy appear to be so straightforward to take on? An important message that this book delivers, which is hoped, is that the question regarding the national economy cannot be answered successfully independently of addressing the questions of the individual sectors and enterprises in the economy, and *vice versa*.

Of the component sectors of the economy which are diverse, this book puts a spotlight on those that hinge critically on natural and ecological resources. This is because, among other reasons, the aforementioned critiques against the pursuit of optimal economic growth path are formulated on the concept of limits, thresholds, critical values regarding these resources that were made available by the planet (Meadows et al. 1972). The individual sectors to be covered in this book are cropland agriculture, spatial land uses including grasslands and cities, forest resources, fossil fuels such as coal, crude oil, and gas, marine resources including fishes in the oceans. The financial sector whose exposition comes after the expositions of these resources will offer bridges to and across all these sectors (Ricardo 1817; von Thunen 1826; Faustmann 1849; Hotelling 1931; Gordon 1954; Fisher 1930).

The analysis of the nation's macro economy will follow the chapters on the individual natural resource sectors. It begins again with the financial sector where the concepts of capital and interest rate are defined, which is followed in sequence by a theory of national saving rate, a modern economic growth theory through capital accumulation, a theory of optimal economic growth pathway, and a theory of a globally harmonized carbon tax (Fisher 1906, 1930; Ramsey 1928; Solow 1957; Koopmans 1965). The last of these is explicitly concerned with the global economy and the planet's resources, that is, beyond the national economy (Nordhaus 1991, 1994a).

The expositions from Chap. 2 to Chap. 11 will pave the way for the present author to offer a general description of the economics of optimal economic growth pathways in Chap. 12 synthesizing all the theories in the preceding chapters. This again will be reviewed in the milieu of the fervor in today's societies across the planet toward non-optimal as well as post-growth pathways whose synthesis will appear in Chap. 13.

1.2   NATURAL RESOURCES AND LIFE ON EARTH

The host of theories on how a nation should pursue its economy's growth, many of which were mentioned above, has much to do with natural resources on the planet as well as marine and terrestrial life on Earth. The reason is straightforward: It would be extremely hard, if not impossible, for one to find any economically productive work produced without any reliance on some natural resources or sentient animals. Final products of the economic production processes, whether they be foods, clothes, houses, medical products, vehicles, art works, temple tankas, or others, should come from some combinations of the resources and animals that nature provides.

That being the case, it is not surprising that at the heart of the countless debates and conflicts regarding an appropriate economic growth pathway of a society lies the concern on the wellbeing of at least one of the planet's natural resources and animals cherished by people. It may be as grand as monarch butterflies, Asian tigers, or California redwood. Alternatively, it may be as unnoticeable as mountain frogs, soils, or grasses to common people.

In describing and analyzing the various theories of economic growth in this book, the present author gives a spotlight to the health and wellbeing of natural resources as well as of marine and terrestrial life that the planet is endowed with or nourished by the planet. Coupling the relevant economic theories with the biological stock and flow data of some of the most concerned resources, this book will lay out a framework for evaluating the present status of these resources against the milieu of the critics' deep concerns.

The natural resources examined in Chap. 2 are croplands where a large portfolio of different kinds of crops are cultivated worldwide. Major staple crops are most familiar to people, such as wheat, rice, corn, and soybeans. But, a list of the crops that are essential for the humanity's consumption and wellbeing is very long, to mention major categories of them only, cereals, vegetables, tubers and root crops, pulses and beans, tree crops such as coffee, non-timber forest products such as mushrooms, fibers such as cotton and flax, and cash crops such as tobacco (Seo 2016a, b, c).

Croplands have always been a hotbed for fierce debates among concerned people as far as we can remember, whose core point of disagreements is centered around the term "food security" (Malthus 1798; Ricardo 1817). Will the croplands on Earth continue to be as fertile and abundant as to feed the planet's citizens whose number has increased over sevenfold since the beginning of the twentieth century? This debate kicked off at a global scale by the famed Rome Club Report entitled the "Limits to Growth" in as early as 1972, but has not relented at all since then (Meadows et al. 1972; World Bank 2008, 2009). The recent battle field in the planet's food security debate lies around the concern on the impacts of global climate change on food security (IPCC 1990, 2014; Seo 2014, 2015; Schlenker and Roberts 2009).

The natural resources given a spotlight in Chap. 3 are other types of land use than croplands, especially grasslands and urban lands (von Thunen 1826). The grasslands are often forgotten lands in the minds of critics who are concerned about food security. To the eyes who are keen on fertile croplands, grasslands tend to appear as a wasted land, that is, a land of no worth. To them, the grasslands are von Thunen's wilderness.

This is an uninformed perception of the grasslands. The land surface of the planet is in fact dominated by the grasslands, the fact which eludes most people's perception. To be specific, the grassland biome is the largest land biome of Earth, covering about 40% of the land surface (WRANGLE 2020). Readers may have not been to one of the world's most sublime grasslands, but I am quite sure that you have heard much during your life about various legends from there. Some of the most famed are the Pampas grasslands in South America, the Steppe grasslands in Mongolia and Eurasia, the Prairie in North America, the Savannah grasslands of Africa, the outback rangelands of Australia and New Zealand, and the Tibetan Plateau grasslands on the Himalayas (Seo 2021a, b).

The grassland biome of Earth is richly endowed with natural and ecological resources. A large variety of grasses live or are grown by people there. The biome is also perhaps the favorite homes of many animal species and plants. As for the humanity, it has long been a place for animal raising for human consumption and trades (Seo 2006; Seo and Mendelsohn 2008). The animals that can feed on rich grassland resources are favored by people who are keen on economic utilizations, the most salient of which are horses, cattle, yaks, buffaloes, sheep, and goats. For example, the Pampas grasslands are the biggest producer and exporter of cattle on the planet (Lanfranco et al. 2022).

In a major contrast, urban lands are located at the opposite side of the grasslands across the fertile croplands. People perceive urban lands as precious lands as the value of urban lands far exceeds, on average, that of rural lands. Urban lands are largely dominated by commercial land uses as well as residential land uses. Instead of plants and animals, urban lands are populated densely by humans and large man-made structures, but also where largest markets are located for exchanges of goods and services.

Forests are the next natural resources on the planet this book examines in Chap. 4. No one would be doubtful of the value and benefits of trees and forests to humans and other life forms, but only a small fraction of the people would be in a position to manage a large number of trees and a still smaller fraction of the people on Earth in a position to manage a forest-land for many decades.

Trees are one of the most valuable resources for humanity. Timbers are used as building materials. Pulps are used for paper making. For rural areas, trees offer many types of food and health resources, to name just some, coconuts, apples, persimmons, mushrooms, gums, and numerous medicinal plants (Vedeld et al. 2007; Seo 2010, 2016b). Until the expansion of fossil fuels at the beginning of the twentieth century, trees had been the most important fuel for heating and cooking. For the beings on the planet other than *Homo sapiens*, trees also offer favorite habitats to them, say, birds and animals.

An examination of the forest management practices that were popular historically offers an intriguing example of the debates among economists and practitioners on the dynamic management methods of natural resources (Samuelson 1976; Mendelsohn and Neumann 1999). Trees are renewable resources, as such, the point of dynamic management is to find the years at which the stand of trees should be cut for sale. Multiple theories of forest management which have been practiced by foresters world-wide for centuries would offer a refreshing insight on the society's dynamic management of the economy. An economically optimal management of forest resources over time is referred to as the Faustmann rotation, which is the main theory to be explored in Chap. 4 (Faustmann 1849).

Chapter 5 shifts the focus of analysis to non-renewable resources, also called exhaustible resources, specifically the fossil fuels such as coal, crude oil, and natural gas. These energy sources collectively and individually are strictly limited in its available quantity for human consumption (Hubbert 1956). Given the total stock that is fixed, an elucidation of the dynamic extraction pathways that are most beneficial to humanity has long been one of the most fascinating areas of economics and policy studies during the twentieth century (Hotelling 1931; Devarajan and Fisher 1981). An advance in new technologies may "drastically" increase the amounts of recoverable fossil fuels for a limited period of time, as evidenced in the hydraulic fracture technology at the beginning of the twenty first century which led to the natural gas boom in the US and elsewhere (Joskow 2013).

The fossil fuels are resources of exceptional importance to the human civilization. Unlike any other fuels such as fuel woods, bio fuels, wind energy, or solar energy, the energy density of the fossil fuels is exceedingly high, which enables the functioning of the present global economy via a massive supply of energy and electricity every day. As of 2022, the planet consumes nearly 1 billion drums of crude oil equivalent every day (BP 2021; US EIA 2021).

As for the fossil fuels, two questions are burning the global community for the past half-century. The first is whether the planet can find sufficient amounts of the fossil fuels to sustain the current global economy and, if so, for how long. The second is the environmental cost of burning fossil fuels for energy generations, including climate change. A combustion of the fossil fuels results in the emissions of numerous air pollutants such as carbon monoxide (CO), sulfur dioxide (SO_2), nitrogen oxides (NO_x), nitrous oxides (N_2O), fine particulate matter (PM_x), methane (CH_4), and carbon dioxide (CO_2) (US EPA 1990; IPCC 1990).

In view of these two pressing concerns, what are the societally optimal extraction pathways for the fossil fuels? This question ultimately leads to the question of a transition into alternative fuels (Nordhaus 1973; Heal 2010). The alternatives are an array of renewable fuels including solar energy, hydro energy, wind energy, thermal energy, wave energy, and biogas energy (NREL 2020). Alternative energy generation, storage, or saving technologies also include nuclear fission, nuclear fusion, novel battery technologies, and new lighting technologies (Seo 2020, 2021a; EC 2022).

Departing from the land-based resources, Chap. 6 brings a close look to the readers at what the oceans of the planet offer. The planet's oceans occupy two thirds of its surface areas and offer habitats for roughly a quarter of all species of life on the planet (Mora et al. 2011). In fact, the deepest ocean floor, which is located at the Mariana Trench in the Pacific Ocean, is as deep as 11 km below the surface, far "higher" than the highest mountain peak on the land, that is, Mount Everest whose peak is about 8 km high.

The oceans are an unmatched provider of food resources to humanity *via* mostly a large variety of fish. In 2018, the total production of fish amounted to 180 million tons globally, of which 84 million tons were from marine fisheries and 12 million from inland capture fisheries. Each citizen of the planet consumes 20.5 kg of fish annually on average (FAO 2020). Fish accounts for 17% of the animal protein consumed by people and as much as 50% of it in many least-developed countries (UN 2017).

A significant fraction of the human population is engaged in a variety of fisheries. As in the land-based resources, can we define an optimal pathway to manage a fishery over its planning time horizon? A big difference of the fisheries is that the fishes in the oceans are open access resources, which means that anyone with a boat and needed skills can freely catch fishes and other marine resources for free (Gordon 1954; Scott 1955). This might indeed have been the case in many ocean regions until 1976 when the 200-mile offshore limit was established by the international community (UN 1982). Even within the 200-mile limit off the coasts of a nation, the oceans do not belong to any individual or nation, as such, the open access problem persists. A host of economic instruments to deal with it is rooted in creating private property rights on related goods, for example, individual tradable quota (ITQ) and fishing licenses (Hartwick and Olewiler 1997).

A salient issue in the open access fisheries is over-fishing or over-exploitation which may cause extinction of certain marine species, for example, blue whale during the twentieth century (Clark 1973). In the economics of fish catch, therefore, it is of vital importance to capture biological features of the fish species concerned, such as growth and regeneration which vary drastically across fish species, which has led to the development of a bioeconomic model of fisheries (Clark 1985; Hartwick and Olewiler 1997; Seijo et al. 1998).

Let's expand our outlook even further to the planet itself. The resources that are shared by the entire global community are referred to as globally shared goods, which are also known as global commons or global public goods (Seo 2020). A commons is literally everywhere, that is, any rural village will have a shared space by all the people in the village (Ostrom 1990). However, a commons at the scale of the planet itself is extremely rare. A global atmosphere or a global climate system is such a rare example, which was first recognized by William Nordhaus in his "How fast should we graze the global commons?" (Nordhaus 1982). This is owing to the unique characteristics of carbon dioxide which, once released by someone somewhere on the planet, quickly mixes in the atmosphere and stays there for over a hundred years. Besides the global warming caused by carbon dioxide, globally shared goods include a worldwide pandemic, a killer asteroid collision, a high-risk physics experiment, an artificial intelligence singularity (Seo 2018, 2022a).

How the global community should manage the global warming and climate change problem has been extensively investigated by researchers over the past four decades (Seo 2020). Conspicuously, an international climate change policy negotiation led by the United Nations Framework Convention on Climate Change (UNFCCC) since its inception in 1992 has showcased to the global community the crux of the challenges in any attempt to provide the globally shared good (UNFCCC 1992). Specifically, after three decades of fierce negotiations among the 200 or so member parties, there is still not a legally binding climate treaty adopted by the global community (UNFCCC 2015; Seo 2017).

In addition to building a consensus among a large number of stakeholders with conflicting views and objectives (Nordhaus 2010, 2015; Seo 2012), at the heart of the economics of climate change is a projection of an optimal dynamic trajectory of a policy variable or another over a centuries-long time horizon. The most essential of them is that of carbon price/tax (Nordhaus 1991, 1992c). An implementation of a carbon tax trajectory across the globe would induce a trajectory of carbon dioxide emissions abatement by the planet's community over the centuries.

The globally shared goods are distinct from the other planet's resources introduced thus far in this section for the provisions of which there are multiple prices determined at respective markets upon which relevant economic agents make supply and demand decisions. In the case of global climate change, nobody in the markets knows the price of carbon dioxide. Neither does anyone know the correct price of the global atmosphere. The price of carbon dioxide should be calculated by economists who would integrate changes in the global climate system, changes in the ecological systems, and changes in the economies. The integrated assessment model (IAM) should then put in the framework of the dynamic social welfare optimization to determine the social cost of carbon dioxide (Nordhaus 2013, 2015).

1.3   Financial Assets

The natural resources introduced in the preceding section are referred to by many as natural capital of the planet (NRC 1999). Another type of capital, with which in fact people are more familiar, is a financial capital. A financial capital refers to a large basket of financial assets people own, for example, currencies, equities, bonds, funds, savings accounts, insurances, mortgages, foreign exchanges, options, derivatives, and crypto currencies (Shiller 2004; Fabozzi et al. 2009). As will be made clear in this book, the financial system in which these assets are traded is a pivotal bridge from the natural capital of the planet to the economic system thereof, and *vice versa*.

A profit-maximizing dynamic management or investment is fundamental to the financial manager who trades a very large pool of financial assets. S/he will switch away from low-return assets to high-return assets while constantly evaluating the fluctuations of the potential returns from the financial assets. Without a sound understanding of the ways that these assets are created, managed, and traded and how their prices are determined in the financial markets, it will be nearly futile to attempt to explicate the national economy or the optimal growth pathways of the economy (Tobin 1958; Sharpe 1964; Fama 1970; Black and Scholes 1973; Shiller 2005).

From the financial markets, the following economic concepts of vital importance to this book most clearly emerge: an interest rate, a discount rate, capital, and value of capital (Fisher 1906, 1907). These concepts are by themselves indispensable to those who are concerned about the dynamic pathways of the economy. In fact, the establishments of these concepts have played a key role in the development of the economic growth theories (Solow 1957; Koopmans 1965).

Even more importantly, these core financial variables link natural resource managers' decisions to the national economic decisions, and *vice versa*. Without an explicit account of these variables, the decisions to manage certain natural resources or even ecological resources cannot be made any reasonably (Faustmann 1849; Hotelling 1931; Hartwick and Olewiler 1997).

In Chap. 7, the present author takes on Irving Fisher's theory of interest rate as well as his definitions of the nature of capital and income, which laid the foundation for the financial economics of the twentieth century, which is even perhaps an understatement (Fisher 1906, 1930; Samuelson 1994). To understand the determination of the interest rates in the economy, one needs to look into debt (lending) markets where buyers (borrowers) and sellers (lenders) of money make trades. A borrower of the money shall pay the interest, in addition to the principal (borrowed money), to the lender at the termination date of the lending agreement, through which mechanism the market interest rate is determined. The market participants' willingness to trade in turn relies on their preferences as well as the technological possibilities of the economy (Fisher 1930).

The interest rate thus determined is, therefore, the price of time. It is paid for holding the borrowed money for the time period between the borrowing date and the termination date. It is not hard to understand, then, why the interest rate is so crucial in the economics of optimal growth pathways which are the economy's trajectories over the time horizon of concern, as such, must account for the interest rate (Koopmans 1963). The interest rate is the discount rate of future consumptions and values in the market decisions.

For a natural resource manager, say, of natural gas, the decision to extract the fuel from an underground well today *versus* in a future date hinges on the market interest rate. If he puts off an extraction of a ton of gas by one period, s/he will have to forego the interest to be earned if s/he were to extract that amount today. In this market, the resource rent, that is, the profit to be earned, from the natural gas extraction should rise at the rate of interest in the competitive market, which is Hotelling's rule (Hotelling 1931).

The basket of financial assets is also referred to as a financial capital or simply a capital individually as well as collectively. The concept of capital was defined by Fisher simply as the asset which gathers a stream of incomes today and in future time periods (Fisher 1906). So, we can say that a forest stand is a natural capital or nature's capital, so is a natural gas reservoir. The same for the plot of cropland, the plot of grasslands, or the fish stock (NRC 1999; Dasgupta 2008). The other type of capital is a physical capital such as a factory, for example, a Ford vehicle assembly line, or a machinery, for example, a farm tractor.

An investor in financial assets will decide how she will allocate her capital into different assets with a goal of achieving the highest return from the investment. She will choose her portfolio in which a large number of assets are held with a different size for each asset. She will increase her investment into high-return assets and decrease it into low-return assets. The future returns are uncertain when she makes the decision, for which reason she will make a portfolio decision in consideration of a possibility of a shock (Markowitz 1952; Modigliani and Pogue 1974). The more risk averse she is, the more she will put her capital into safer assets (Arrow 1971).

The national economy's growth can be understood with the same framework as the financial investor's decisions. In this, the goal of the national economy can be set as the achievement of the highest possible discounted sum of net returns or social welfare improvements in its future periods. To give an example, in the Ramsey model, this is achieved simply by a determination of the optimal saving rate in the economy. New productions in the economy are either reinvested or consumed by the citizens. The determination of the saving rate determines the investment rate of the economy. The optimal saving rate would guarantee the economy's best possible growth where the economic growth is specified *via* the nation's utility function, according to Ramsey (1928).

It would be unreasonable to economists, however, to argue that a simple determination of the national saving rate will put the national economy on the best possible path. Economists would want to know how the national economy would select high-return projects and deselect low-return projects, as in the financial sector, in the economic system itself. Put differently, the economics of economic growth should explain how the capital in the economy is allocated within the system itself away from lower return projects to higher return projects, both private and public.

1.4 An Optimal Economic Growth Pathway for the Nation

Having considered the economic decisions in managing the vital natural resources and financial assets, can we conclude that a national economy or a global economy should be managed with the same decision rules and the objectives? Further, is it possible to conceptualize the "optimal" growth pathway of the economy as a whole? Even further, is there an optimal growth pathway of the economy that can be measured as an optimal rate of growth in each time period?

From a critic's perspective, these questions can be stated alternatively as follows. Are the national economy's evolvements subject to completely different decision rules and objectives from those applied in the afore-described individual sectors? Is there a need for continued economic growth at all? How can the economy's performance be measured given many unmeasurable things in people's lives and nature's wellbeing? Should the government then have a different set of priorities or objectives determined by itself from the priorities determined in the market sectors?

To begin with in disentangling these questions, it can be recognized that a theory of economic growth needs to encompass more than a size of capital accumulation or a determination of a national savings rate (Paul Romer 1990; Aghion and Howitt 2009; David Romer 2018; Seo 2022a). There are many ineluctable dynamics unfolding in a macroeconomy. In this regard, two such dynamics would immediately come to mind: population growth and technological growth (Solow 1957; Griliches 1979, 1998). The stock of human resources, also referred to as human capital, such as education and training is also a pivotal dynamic in the economy (Nelson 1959; Mankiw et al. 1992).

The concept of capital, as defined by Irving Fisher, proves essential, perhaps indispensable, in the conceptualizations of the nation's economic growth (Fisher 1906; Solow 1957). The productions of the entire national economy can be measured simply as the new capital created in the economy. The capital is then reinvested, excluding the capital set aside for consumption by its people, into new production activities. Therefore, the capital in this framework is also an input into the economy.

If an economic growth theory should measure the progresses in the economy's total production each year, the size of population and its growth is another essential variable, in addition to the capital. A change in population means a change in labor supply which is another input in the production function of the economy.

To continue, a form of the national economy's production function should be specified. It is quite common in the literature to adopt a Cobb-Douglas production function with a constant elasticity of output in response to each factor (Solow 1957). The specification of the production function reflects the economy's technology at one point in time.

It is the case that a new technology emerges in the economy once in a while, which largely alters the direction of the economy as well as its productivity. To mention just some of them, personal computers during the 1990s, internal combustion engines during the 1920s, or petroleum extractions and electricity generations during the late nineteenth century have fundamentally changed the growth path of the world economy (Nordhaus 1994b, 2007).

Once these factors are well arranged into an economic model, we get to Robert Solow's modern economic growth theory. Solow's economic growth theory, which is explained in Chap. 9, was based on the economy's production function with the above three factors: capital, labor, and technology. In his model, a process of technological breakthroughs or growth is added exogenously, which is referred to as the Total Factor Productivity (TFP) in the literature. It is a model of capital accumulation because the capital stock is the output of the production function, which grows over time in pace with changes in the three inputs: capital, labor, and technology (Solow 1957).

So, the Solow model is a recursive model, rather than an optimization model, which depicts a pathway for the economy. The pathway depends on the changes in the three inputs as well as assumed functional relationships and parameters in the model. It is a dynamic model, but notably not a societal welfare optimization model. The production function can be derived from the producer's profit maximization problem, which means that Solow's growth model is a supply-side theory of economic growth (Mas-Colell et al. 1995).

It is a very abstract model, truthfully. The countless economic decisions of the economy are put into a single function of production. It assumes that the countless decisions are organized in such a way that maximizes the national economy's profit. This is where the expositions of the individual resource sectors and enterprises, whose expositions are provided in Chaps. 2–7 of this book, come to light. Underneath the nation's production function of the economy, innumerable decisions are made in each of these enterprises with an objective of a dynamic profit maximization. These decisions are implicit in Solow's growth model.

However, without an explicit integration of the demand side of the national economy into the model, Solow's growth model would remain incomplete. At the demand side are consumers of the nation who are, in other words, individual citizens. Can the nation's economic growth be explained as a utility maximization of the consumers, that is, a consumers' welfare maximization over a time horizon? If that were to be possible, what would such a model say about the economy's growth over time?

Integrating Fisher's, Ramsey's, and Solow's growth models and key concepts, Tjalling Koopmans provides a comprehensive exposition of the concept of optimal economic growth pathway in an extensive article entitled "On the Concept of Optimal Economic Growth" published in 1963 (Koopmans 1963, 1965). In beginning his article, Koopmans noted that it is always fascinating for the economists to ask whether there is an optimal rate of economic growth to be pursued in the economy. His article was as long as 75 pages including the proofs of the propositions in the article. So, it was way more than a single article.

Koopmans's article provides the most direct answer to the question of whether the nation or the globe should pursue the path of economic growth in an optimal manner, which is the core question of this book. Along with William Nordhaus's global warming economic model, Koopmans's article reflects the central idea of this book. William Nordhaus was a doctoral student of Robert Solow at MIT and a colleague of Tjalling Koopmans when he joined the Yale economics department in the late 1960s (Nordhaus 1994a).

Unlike the previously explained economic growth models, Koopmans's model is truly a dynamic societal welfare optimization model of the economy over an infinite time horizon of its future. The social welfare is defined as the sum of individuals' utilities. An individual's utility function at each time period is defined as a function of consumption where a functional form is specified in dependence on the inequality aversion of the society.

The societal welfare is the discounted sum of the societal welfare at each time period where the social rate of time preference determines the discounting rate.

The consumption of each individual at each time period is determined by the production side of the economy, setting aside a fraction for new investments. The total production is allocated to consumption and new investments. The production function is specified as above as Solow's production function.

Unlike the previously explained models, Koopmans's model explicitly accounts for a population growth function which is assumed to grow at a constant rate over time. The model also explicitly accounts for the discounting rate as well as changes in the preferences of individuals. Further, a rate of technological growth is explicitly incorporated into the model exogenously.

He provided a rigorous proof of concept of the optimal economic growth path with a conclusion that in such an economy, the rate of economic growth should approximate the rate of population growth plus the social rate of time preference plus the rate of unforeseeable technological growth, all of which in turn depend on preferences, interest rate, and consumption. This is explained in depth in Chap. 10.

Koopmans's model did not appear to have received great attention by his peers during the mid-1960s, as far as the present author's literature review can reveal. Koopmans was awarded the Nobel Prize in Economics in 1975, shared with Leonid Kantorovich, for their contributions to the theory of the optimum allocation of resources. They were the developers of the linear and mathematical programming models of economics (Kantorovich 1939, 1959; Koopmans 1949, 1951).

However, after three decades since the aforementioned Koopmans's publication, his conceptual model might have begun to leave a big influence on economics when Nordhaus published a climate change policy model named the "Dynamic Integrated Climate and Economy (DICE)" model during the early 1990s (Nordhaus 1991, 1994a). In another two and a half decades later, Nordhaus was also awarded the Nobel Prize in Economics in 2018 for "integrating climate change into long-run macroeconomic analysis."

What Nordhaus did was to build a dynamic integrated assessment model of climate and economy, known widely as the DICE, to explicate in economic terms one of the greatest challenges faced by the global community, that is, climate change (Nordhaus 1991, 1992c). The DICE model was founded on Koopmans's model of optimal economic growth but expanded it by linking an economic system with a natural system on the one hand and by revising the model for the global economy on the other hand. The natural system, which may also be called a biogeophysical system, comprised very strange concepts then such as radiative forcings, carbon cycle, carbon reservoirs, thermal inertia, climate normals, temperature anomalies, and equilibrium temperature sensitivity (IPCC 1990; UNFCCC 1992; Nordhaus 1994a).

Koopmans's model was a purely theoretical one, so abstract that only a handful of people might have found the intrigue in it to read it through. Nordhaus, through his DICE model, made it a real-life model that "everyone" had a reason or another to go eagerly after to comprehend it. The DICE model is composed of a large number of functional relationships, parameters, and variables for representing the economic system as well as the nature system. Nordhaus specified all the functional relationships for the DICE model and then calibrated all the parameters. That was a monumental work, given that such specifications and calibrations must not break the basic economics fundamentals, neither the biophysical fundamentals.

Nordhaus agrees with Koopmans on the framework of a dynamic social welfare optimization as a conceptual apparatus for comprehending the nation's economic growth. However, it should be clear that Nordhaus's social welfare is quite different from Koopmans's social welfare. Nordhaus's is a "generalized" social welfare in which increased leisure activities as well as outdoor nature activities are added while environmental pollution and climate change damages are treated as negative social welfare, more precisely, negative consumption incurred by economic activities (Nordhaus 1992a, 2000, 2006; Muller and Mendelsohn 2009; Muller et al. 2011).

A dynamic trajectory of carbon price is a primary outcome of the DICE model which is presented to the global community. In the societally optimal economic growth path put forth by Koopmans, the price of carbon dioxide should be set in accordance with Nordhaus's carbon price at each time period. To give you an idea, the price of carbon dioxide, which can be implemented as a national carbon tax across the planet, may start at 30 US\$ per ton of carbon (tC) in 2025, which rises to 60 US\$/tC by the middle of this century, and to 240 US\$/tC by the end of this century (Nordhaus 2008, 2013, 2017).

The carbon price/tax is referred to alternatively as the social cost of carbon. Can Nordhaus's carbon price trajectory be adopted as a global policy instrument by the global community to deal with global climate change? It is nearly an impossibility, considering the last 40 years of policy experience. First of all, people disagree widely on the carbon tax trajectory with some people arguing for a substantially higher price trajectory while others for a substantially lower trajectory (Tol 2009; Weitzman 2009). The optimal carbon dioxide price trajectory depends on behaviorally efficient adaptations, forward looking behaviors, and greenhouse technological options that people employ in addressing the climate change challenges (Mendelsohn and Neumann 1999; Seo 2020, 2021a). These behavioral responses should be learned by going back to the decisions of individual sectors and enterprises (Seo 2022b).

Second, a global climate policy *via* a globally harmonized carbon tax as suggested by the DICE model will have largely disparate monetary impacts on participating nations (Nordhaus 2010; Seo 2012). The same is true of the monetary impacts of climate change on the nations across the planet (Mendelsohn et al. 2006). Given this, countries will have a strong incentive to free ride. That is, countries will hope that others will pay the cost of combatting climate change (Samuelson 1954; Buchanan 1968; Barrett 1994; Seo 2017, 2019a; Nordhaus 2015). A globally agreed treaty will be very difficult to achieve. Again, the incentives of the nations for a global climate treaty depend on the three behavioral responses: efficient adaptations, forward looking behaviors, and greenhouse technological options (Seo 2019b, 2020, 2021a, 2022b).

It should be emphasized that the optimal carbon tax transition pathway is not incompatible at all with the three behavioral responses. An optimally growing economic pathway will have a well-functioning system in which accurate carbon prices are well reflected in addition to efficient adaptations, forward looking behaviors, and greenhouse technological options unfolding over time.

1.5   POST-GROWTH AND SUB-OPTIMAL GROWTH CRITIQUES

The closure of the last section with Nordhaus's social welfare leads us seamlessly to the discussion of the many critiques against the pursuit of economic growth. Unlike Nordhaus who maintains the social welfare dynamic optimization framework while at the same time fully incorporating the side effects of economic growth, detractors argue that because of the unintended negative side effects of economic growth, the social welfare dynamic optimization framework in the pursuit of economic growth should be discarded. More precisely speaking, they argue that the goal of continued economic growth adopted by the nations around the globe should be abandoned (Nordhaus 1992a; Costanza 2010; Speth 2012; Kallis et al. 2018).

The critiques against economic growth end up pushing for a sub-optimal growth pathway relative to the socially optimal growth pathway described in the above section. There are quite a few cohorts of critics against the pursuit of economic growth. As mentioned before, these groups will be referred to as a sub-optimal growth critique or a post-growth critique. The term post-growth is widely used by these groups (Speth 2012; Paech 2012).

Broadly speaking, the post-growth critiques can be classified into three separate groups. The first is a sustainable development critique. This movement began during the early 1970s with notable international events such as the United Nations Conference on Human Environment in Stockholm and the Rome Club Report entitled "Limits to Growth" by the United Nations (UN 1972; Meadows et al. 1972). With the United Nations' numerous initiatives since then, for example, the Millennium Development Goals in 2000, the sustainable development group wields strong influence in global affairs (UN 2000, 2015; Bartelmus 2012).

The second post-growth group is an ecological economics critique. Given that the members of this group do not consider themselves as a traditional economist, it can be more properly called an ecological critique against the goal of economic growth. This group considers that the pursuit of economic growth is misguided because of the ecological thresholds. That is, natural resources and ecological capacities on the planet are strictly limited (Georgescu-Roegen 1971; Daly 1973; Daly and Farley 2003; Costanza 2010).

The third group against the optimal economic growth is a degrowth critique. Degrowth is a zero growth or a negative growth to this group which prefers to define it as the economic theory of "managing without economic growth" declaratively (Victor 2008; Kallis et al. 2018). Protagonists of this group diagnose that the economic growth during the past two centuries or more has not reduced the poverty, therefore, not turned out to be beneficial for the people and the planet. On the other hand, they argue the global economy is already past the ecologically sustainable limits. They argue that the global economy should pursue "sustainable degrowth" which would mean ecological sustainability, social equity, and so on (PDED 2008).

Of the three post-growth groups, the degrowth critique is perhaps most vehemently against the economic theory of optimal growth. However, the deeper you take a look at the three critiques, the more obscure, you will find, are the distinctions between the three groups (Speth 2012; Kallis et al. 2018). They all rely on interrelated concepts such as limits to growth, ecological thresholds, steady-state economy, natural resource limits, sustainability, and equity.

Underneath the three critiques against the pursuit of economic growth is a common thread of skepticism on a continued growth of the economy: How can the economy possibly continue to get bigger as measured by the stock of new productions if the natural and ecological resources gifted to the planet are all strictly limited? A paradigm-setting work in this line of skepticism was certainly the report by the Club of Rome entitled "The Limits to Growth" in the early 1970s which issued a grim prediction that the world will suffer from mass poverty and hunger by the year 2000 owing to a rapid increase in global population and a declining land productivity coupled with a decrease in arable lands (Meadows et al. 1972; Nordhaus 1992b).

We all witnessed that the Rome Club Report's fateful predictions had not materialized by the gate of the new millennium, which was attributable, among other things, to the high yield variety (HYV) crop developments and many revolutions in farming practices, as far as poverty and hunger are concerned (Ruttan 2002; Evenson and Gollin 2003; Seo 2019b; Chankrajang and Talerngsri-Teerasuwannajak 2022). These innovations and ingenuity of people resulted in a significant reduction of poverty across the planet, contrary to the Rome Club predictions (World Bank 2008, 2009)

This, however, has not deterred the spread of the post-growth critics during the past five decades, to the contrary, they flourished. Some of the most notable initiatives and proclamations are the Brundtland Report by the World Commission on Environment and Development in 1987 (WCED 1987), the Agenda 21 adopted at the Rio Earth Summit convened by United Nations Conference on Environment and Development in 1992 (UN 1992), the declaration of the UN Millennium Development Goals (UN 2000), and the UN 2030 Agenda for Sustainable Development (UN 2015). The Rome Club itself has continued to be thriving until today.

In line with the Rome Club Report, all three post-growth critiques have as their priority an end of poverty and hunger globally, but their agendas reach far beyond that concern. They each have a long list of priority issues and goals, including healthy lives for all, equitable education, empowering women, water and sanitation for all, energy for all, decent works for all, reducing inequalities across the countries, sustainable cities, sustainable consumption and production, climate change, protecting oceans, biodiversity loss, terrestrial ecosystems, access to justice, and global partnership (UN 2015).

The first degrowth conference held in Paris in 2008 defined it as a group calling for "a voluntary transition towards a just, participatory, and ecologically sustainable society." It was named, expressing succinctly the top priorities of the group, the International Conference on Economic Degrowth for Ecological Sustainability and Social Equity (PDED 2008).

1.6   THE COMMON CONCERN OF ALL: A HEALTH OF NATURE AND LIFE ON EARTH

Up to this point, the present author has introduced a large number of major scholars and organizations, both economists and scientists, who elaborated their views on the matter of economic growth in a society. From them, a range of groups of people was identified, whose views are distinct. As explained, the views of some groups are diagonally opposite to those of the other groups.

Having acknowledged that, is there any common concern enthusiastically shared by the whole range of scholars and organizations introduced in this book? Rather remarkably and in an intriguing way, there is such a shared concern common to all parties. That can be summed up as the concern on the health of natural systems and life on the planet.

It is notable that the three post-growth or sub-optimal growth advocates share the common concern among them and in fact the languages: limits to growth, ecological limits/thresholds, natural and ecological limits. At the heart of their critiques against the pursuit of economic growth lies the misgivings that the world is approaching the limits of the natural and ecological systems, if not it has already run past them.

The proponents of the optimal economic growth are also deeply concerned about the limited natural and ecological resources of the planet

(Solow 1974, 1993; Nordhaus 1992a; Seo 2021a). The economics of fossil fuel extractions, for example, is an economics theory of how best the humanity and the enterprises can utilize such resources that have clear limits in their stocks (Hotelling 1931). Consider, for another example, a forest harvest! The essence of an optimal forest management is to harvest the trees in a way that it can be both sustainable and the best for the owner of a forest stand over a long-term time horizon (Faustmann 1849).

For this book as well as to the present author, this is a brilliant observation. If that is the shared concern by all theorists introduced in this book who express divergent and disparate views, the present author can approach them by way of the analyses and evaluations pertinent to the criteria of that common concern. From this vantage point, the individual chapters devoted to a single natural resource sector, from Chap. 2 to Chap. 6 as well as Chap. 11, each of which deals with croplands, grasslands/cities, forests, fossil fuels, fisheries, and global atmosphere respectively, will offer a nice battle ground of ideas among the family of theorists appreciated in this book.

To give a cursory glimpse of this approach, the present author will evaluate whether the economically optimal forest management rule is better or worse than a socially just or ecologically sustainable management rule of a forest stand. The two forest management practices can be compared in terms of the economic outcomes as well as the ecological/sustainability outcomes which are expected from each thereof (Solow 1974; Newman 1988, 2002).

In line with this approach, each chapter of the book is presented with the contrasts of the two opposing views pertinent to the chapter's main topic. Each chapter will elucidate a description of an economically optimal management of the concerned resource, which will be followed by an exposition of a primary critique against the economic theory. For example, the chapter on forest management, Chap. 4, will be presented with a rejoinder from a deforestation critique (Myers 1979; Repetto and Gillis 1988; Curtis et al. 2018). For another, the chapter on Solow's modern growth theory, Chap. 9, will be described with a rejoinder from a sustainable development critique (Molina and Rowland 1974; Likens and Bormann 1974; WCED 1987; UN 1992; Bartelmus 2012).

1.7   STRUCTURE OF THE BOOK

The book is structured with five parts and thirteen chapters, as presented in Fig. 1.1. The five parts are in the following sequence: Introduction (Part I), Natural Resource Sectors (Part II), National Economy (Part III), Planetary Economy (Part IV), A Synthesis and Critical Evaluations (Part V).

Part I, which is Chap. 1, provides an overview of the book outlining the major inquiries and approaches as well as the natural and ecological resources, economies, and theories explained in this book.

Part II is composed of the five ensuing chapters from Chap. 2 to Chap. 6 in which the five major natural resources are of concern: cropland agriculture, grasslands/cities, forests, fossil fuels, and fisheries.

Part III deals with the national economic questions, which consists of the four chapters from Chap. 7 to Chap. 10. Chapter 7 is a bridge chapter

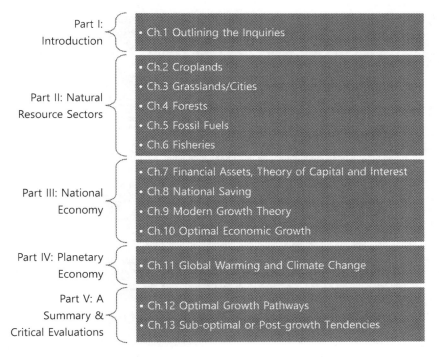

Fig. 1.1   Structure of the book

from Part II to Part III in that it deals with the financial sector and assets and at the same time the economy-wide concepts of capital and interest rate. This is followed by a theory of national saving rate, a modern economic growth theory, and a theory of optimal economic growth. The theories in Part III are highly pertinent to an analysis of the global economy.

Part IV addresses the planetary economy in Chap. 11. It introduces the theories of global warming and climate change economics in which an optimal carbon price trajectory is calculated as an economics solution to the planetwide problem. As will be clarified, the economics of climate change has taken a form of an extended theory of the optimal economic growth model (Koopmans 1965; Nordhaus 1994a).

Part V is a set of concluding chapters where a synthesis of the preceding chapters is provided with critical evaluations of the opposing viewpoints. Chapter 12 provides a synthesis of the economic theories linking the natural resource sector questions to the national and global economic questions. Chapter 13 provides a review of the critiques against the economics of optimal growth where the sub-optimal and post-growth economic theories that appeared in preceding chapters are synthesized.

This concludes Chap. 1, an introduction to the book. I wish you a marvelous journey into the fascinating economics of natural resources, life, and economies on the planet so pleasant and endeared by her residents.

References

Aghion, P., and P. Howitt. 2009. *The Economics of Growth*. Cambridge, MA: MIT Press.

Arrow, K.J. 1971. *Essays in the Theory of Risk Bearing*. Chicago, IL: Markham Publishing Co.

Barrett, S. 1994. Self-enforcing International Environmental Agreements. *Oxford Economic Papers* 46: 878–894.

Bartelmus, Peter. 2012. *Sustainability Economics*. London, UK: Routledge.

Black, F., and M. Scholes. 1973. The Pricing of Options and Corporate Liabilities. *Journal of Political Economy* 81: 637–654.

British Petroleum (BP). 2021. *Statistical Review of World Energy 2021*. London, UK: The BP.

Buchanan, J.M. 1968. *The Demand and Supply of Public Goods*. Chicago, IL: Rand McNally & Co.

Chankrajang, T., and K. Talerngsri-Teerasuwannajak. 2022. Climate Change and Historical Changes in Rice Yield in Thailand. In *Handbook of Behavioural Economics and Climate Change*, ed. S.N. Seo. Cheltenham, UK: Edward Elgar.

Clark, C.W. 1973. The Economics of Over Exploitation. *Science* 181: 630–634.

———. 1985. *Bioeconomic Modelling and Fisheries Management*. New York, NY: Wiley.

Costanza, R. 2010. What is Ecological Economics? *Yale Insights*. Yale School of Management, New Haven, CT. https://insights.som.yale.edu/insights/what-is-ecological-economics.

Curtis, P.G., C.M. Slay, N.L. Harris, A. Tyukavina, and M.C. Hansen. 2018. Classifying Drivers of Global Forest Loss. *Science* 361 (6407): 1108–1111.

Daly, H.E. 1973. *Toward a Steady-state Economy*. New York, NY: W.H. Freeman and Company.

Daly, H.E., and J. Farley. 2003. *Ecological Economics: Principles and Applications*. 1st ed. Washington, DC: Island Press.

Dasgupta, P. 2008. Natural Capital and Economic Growth. *Encyclopedia of Earth*. http://editors.eol.org/eoearth/wiki/Natural_capital_and_economic_growth.

Devarajan, S., and A.C. Fisher. 1981. Hotelling's "Economics of Exhaustible Resources": Fifty Years Later. *Journal of Economic Literature* 19: 65–73.

European Commission (EC). 2022. *EU Taxonomy: Commission Presents Complementary Climate Delegated Act to Accelerate Decarbonization*. Brussels, Belgium: The EC.

Evenson, R., and D. Gollin. 2003. Assessing the Impact of the Green Revolution 1960–2000. *Science* 300: 758–762.

Fabozzi, F.J., F.G. Modigliani, and F.J. Jones. 2009. *Foundations of Financial Markets and Institutions*. 4th ed. New York, NY: Prentice Hall.

Fama, E.F. 1970. Efficient Capital Markets: A Review of Empirical Work. *Journal of Finance* 25: 383–417.

Faustmann, Martin. 1849. On the Determination of the Value Which Forest Land and Immature Stands Pose for Forestry. In *Martin Faustmann and the Evolution of Discounted Cash Flow*, ed. M. Gane. 1968, Paper 42. Oxford, UK: Oxford Institute.

Fisher, Irving. 1906. *The Nature of Capital and Income*. New York, NY: Macmillan.

———. 1907. *The Rate of Interest*. New York, NY: Macmillan.

———. 1930. *The Theory of Interest*. New York, NY: Macmillan.

Food and Agriculture Organization (FAO). 2020. *The State of World Fisheries and Aquaculture 2020*. Rome, Italy: FAO.

Friedman, M. 1962. *Capitalism and Freedom*. Chicago, IL: The University of Chicago Press.

Georgescu-Roegen, N. 1971. The Steady State and Ecological Salvation: A Thermodynamic Analysis. *BioScience* 27: 266–270.

Gordon, H.S. 1954. The Economic Theory of a Common-property Resource: The Fishery. *The Journal of Political Economy* 62: 124–142.

Griliches, Zvi. 1979. Issues in Assessing the Contribution of Research and Development to Productivity Growth. *Bell Journal of Economics* 10: 92–116.

———. 1998. *Patents and Technology.* Cambridge, MA: Harvard University Press.

Hartwick, J.M., and N.D. Olewiler. 1997. *The Economics of Natural Resource Use.* 2nd ed. New York, NY: Pearson.

Heal, G. 2010. Reflections: The Economics of Renewable Energy in the United States. *Review of Environmental Economics and Policy* 4: 139–154.

Hotelling, H. 1931. The Economics of Exhaustible Resources. *Journal of Political Economy* 39: 137–175.

Hubbert, M. King. 1956. Nuclear Energy and the Fossil Fuels. Presented at the Spring Meeting of the American Petroleum Institute, San Antonio, TX.

Intergovernmental Panel on Climate Change (IPCC). 1990. *Climate Change: The IPCC Scientific Assessment.* Cambridge, UK: Cambridge University Press.

———. 2014. *Climate Change 2014: Impacts, Adaptation, and Vulnerability.* Cambridge, UK: Cambridge University Press.

Joskow, P.L. 2013. Natural Gas: From Shortages to Abundance in the United States. *American Economic Review* 103: 338–343.

Kallis, G., V. Kostakis, S. Lange, B. Muraca, S. Paulson, and M. Schmelzer. 2018. Research on Degrowth. *Annual Review of Environment and Resources* 43: 291–316.

Kantorovich, Leonid V. 1939. Mathematical Methods of Organizing and Planning Production. *Management Science* 6: 366–422.

———. 1959. *The Best Use of Economic Resources.* Cambridge, MA: Harvard University Press.

Koopmans, Tjalling C. 1949. Optimum Utilization of the Transportation System. *Proceedings of the International Statistical Conferences* 5: 136–145.

———., ed. 1951. *Activity Analysis of Production and Allocation.* New York, NY: Wiley.

———. 1963. *On the Concept of Optimal Economic Growth.* The Cowles Foundation Discussion Paper # 163, Yale University, New Haven, CT.

———. 1965. On the Concept of Optimal Economic Growth. *Pontificiae Academiae Scientiarum Scripta Varia* 28 (1): 1–75.

Lanfranco, B., E. Fernández, B. Ferraro, and J.M.S. de Lima. 2022. Historical Changes in the Pampas Biome, Land Use, and Climate Change. In *Handbook of Behavioural Economics and Climate Change.* Cheltenham, UK: Edward Elgar.

Likens, G.E., and F.H. Bormann. 1974. Acid Rain: A Serious Regional Environmental Problem. *Science* 184: 1176–1179.

Malthus, Thomas R. 1798. *An Essay on the Principle of Population.* London, UK: J. Johnson.

Mankiw, N.G., D. Romer, and D.N. Weil. 1992. A Contribution to the Empirics of Economic Growth. *The Quarterly Journal of Economics* 107: 407–437.

Markowitz, H. 1952. Portfolio Selection. *Journal of Finance* 7: 77–91.

Marx, Karl. 1867. *Das Kapital. Kritik der politischen Oekonomie.* Hamburg, Germany: Verlag von Otto Meisner.

Mas-Colell, A., W.D. Whinston, and J.R. Green. 1995. *Microeconomic Theory.* Oxford, UK: Oxford University Press.

Meadows, D.H., D.L. Meadows, J. Randers, and W.W. Behrens III. 1972. *The Limits to Growth: A Report for the Club of Rome's Project on the Predicament of Mankind.* New York, NY: Universe Books.

Mendelsohn, R., and J. Neumann. 1999. *The Impact of Climate Change on the United States Economy.* Cambridge, UK: Cambridge University Press.

Mendelsohn, R., A. Dinar, and L. Williams. 2006. The Distributional Impact of Climate Change on Rich and Poor Countries. *Environment and Development Economics* 11: 1–20.

Modigliani, F., and G.A. Pogue. 1974. An Introduction to Risk and Return: Concepts and Evidence. *Financial Analysts Journal* 30: 68–80.

Molina, M.J., and F.S. Rowland. 1974. Stratospheric Sink for Chlor-ofluoromethanes: Chlorine Atom-catalysed Destruction of Ozone. *Nature* 249: 810–812.

Mora, C., D.P. Tittensor, S. Adl, A.G.B. Simpson, and B. Worm. 2011. How Many Species Are There on Earth and in the Ocean? *PLoS Biology* 9 (8): e1001127. https://doi.org/10.1371/journal.pbio.1001127.

Muller, N.Z., and R. Mendelsohn. 2009. Efficient Pollution Regulation: Getting the Prices Right. *American Economic Review* 99: 1714–1739.

Muller, N.Z., R. Mendelsohn, and W.D. Nordhaus. 2011. Environmental Accounting for Pollution in the United States Economy. *American Economic Review* 101: 1649–1675.

Myers, Norman. 1979. *The Sinking Ark: A New Look at the Problem of Disappearing Species.* Oxford, UK: Pergamon Press.

National Renewable Energy Laboratory (NREL). 2020. Perovskite Solar Cells. Washington, DC: The NREL, Department of Energy. https://www.nrel.gov/pv/perovskite-solar-cells.html.

National Research Council (NRC). 1999. *Nature's Numbers: Expanding the National Economic Accounts to Include the Environment.* Washington, DC: The National Academies Press. https://doi.org/10.17226/6374.

Nelson, R.R. 1959. The Simple Economics of Basic Scientific Research. *Journal of Political Economy* 67: 297–306.

Newman, D.H. 1988. The Optimal Forest Rotation: A Discussion and Annotated Bibliography. *General Technical Report 48.* Southeastern Forest Experiment Station, Forest Service, USDA.

————. 2002. Forestry's Golden Rule and the Development of the Optimal Forest Rotation Literature. *Journal of Forest Economics* 8: 5–28.

Nordhaus, W.D. 1973. The Allocation of Energy Resources. *Brookings Papers on Economic Activity* 1973: 529–576.

————. 1982. How Fast Should We Graze the Global Commons? *American Economic Review* 72: 242–246.

————. 1991. To Slow or Not to Slow: The Economics of the Greenhouse Effects. *Economic Journal* 101: 920–937.

————. 1992a. The Ecology of Markets. *Proceedings of the National Academy of Sciences* 89: 843–850.

————. 1992b. Lethal Model 2: The Limits to Growth Revisited. *Bookings Papers on Economic Activity* 1992: 1–59.

————. 1992c. An Optimal Transition Path for Controlling Greenhouse Gases. *Science* 258: 1315–1319.

————. 1994a. *Managing the Global Commons*. Cambridge, MA: MIT Press.

————. 1994b. *Do Real Output and Real Wage Measures Capture Reality? The History of Lighting Suggests Not.* Cowles Foundation Discussion Papers 1078, Cowles Foundation for Research in Economics, Yale University.

————. 2000. New Directions in National Economic Accounting. *American Economic Review* 90: 259–263.

————. 2006. Principles of National Accounting for Nonmarket Accounts. In *A New Architecture for the U.S. National Accounts*, ed. D.W. Jorgenson, J.S. Landefeld, and W.D. Nordhaus. Chicago, IL: The University of Chicago Press.

————. 2007. Two Centuries of Productivity Growth in Computing. *Journal of Economic History* 67: 128–159.

————. 2008. *A Question of Balance: Weighing the Options on Global Warming Policies*. New Haven, CT: Yale University Press.

————. 2010. Economic Aspects of Global Warming in a Post-Copenhagen Environment. *Proceedings of the National Academy of Sciences* 107: 11721–11726.

————. 2013. *The Climate Casino: Risk, Uncertainty, and Economics for a Warming World*. New Haven, CT: Yale University Press.

————. 2015. Climate Clubs: Overcoming Free-Riding in International Climate Policy. *American Economic Review* 105: 1339–1370.

————. 2017. Revisiting the Social Cost of Carbon. *Proceedings of the National Academy of Sciences* 114: 1518–1523.

Ostrom, E. 1990. *Governing the Commons: The Evolution of Institutions for Collective Action*. Cambridge, UK: Cambridge University Press.

Paech, N. 2012. *Befreiung vom Ü̈berfluss: Auf dem Weg in die Postwachstumsö̈konomie*. Mü̈nchen: Oekom Verlag.

Paris Declaration on Economic Degrowth (PDED). 2008. Degrowth Declaration of the Paris 2008 Conference. The Conference on Economic Degrowth for Ecological Sustainability and Social Equity, on 18–19 April 2008, Paris, France.

Ramsey, F.P. 1928. A Mathematical Theory of Savings. *Economic Journal* 38: 543–559.

Repetto, R., and M. Gillis. 1988. *Public Policy and the Misuse of Forest Resources.* Cambridge, UK: Cambridge University Press.

Ricardo, D. 1817. *On the Principles of Political Economy and Taxation.* London, UK: John Murray.

Romer, Paul M. 1990. Endogenous Technical Change. *Journal of Political Economy* 98: S71–S102.

Romer, David. 2018. *Advanced Macroeconomics.* 5th ed. New York, NY: McGraw Hill.

Ruttan, V.W. 2002. Productivity Growth in World Agriculture: Sources and Constraints. *Journal of Economic Perspectives* 16: 161–184.

Samuelson, Paul A. 1954. The Pure Theory of Public Expenditure. *Review of Economics and Statistics* 36: 387–389.

———. 1976. Economics of Forestry in an Evolving Society. *Economic Inquiry* 13: 466–492.

———. 1994. Two Classics: Böhm-Bawerk's Positive Theory and Fisher's Rate of Interest through Modern Prisms. *Journal of the History of Economic Thought* 16: 202–228.

Schlenker, W., and M. Roberts. 2009. Nonlinear Temperature Effects Indicate Severe Damages to Crop Yields under Climate Change. *Proceedings of the National Academy of Sciences* 106: 15594–15598.

Scott, A. 1955. The Fishery: The Objectives of Sole Ownership. *Journal of Political Economy* 63: 116–124.

Seijo, J.C., O. Defeo, and S. Salas. 1998. *Fisheries Bioeconomics. Theory, Modelling and Management.* FAO Fisheries Technical Paper (No. 368). Rome, Italy: FAO.

Seo, S.N. 2006. Modeling Farmer Responses to Climate Change: Climate Change Impacts and Adaptations in Livestock Management in Africa. Ph.D. diss., Yale University, New Haven.

———. 2010. Managing Forests, Livestock, and Crops under Global Warming: A Microeconometric Analysis of Land Use Changes in Africa. *Australian Journal of Agricultural and Resource Economics* 54: 239–258.

———. 2012. What Eludes Global Agreements on Climate Change? *Economic Affairs* 32: 73–79.

———. 2014. Adapting Sensibly When Global Warming Turns the Field Brown or Blue: A Comment on the 2014 IPCC Report. *Economic Affairs* 34: 399–401.

———. 2015. Helping Low-latitude, Poor Countries with Climate Change. *Regulation* (Winter 2015–2016): 6–8.

———. 2016a. Modeling Farmer Adaptations to Climate Change in South America: A Microbehavioral Economic Perspective. *Environmental and Ecological Statistics* 23: 1–21.

———. 2016b. The Micro-behavioral Framework for Estimating Total Damage of Global Warming on Natural Resource Enterprises with Full Adaptations. *Journal of Agricultural, Biological, & Environmental Statistics* 21: 328–347.

———. 2016c. *Microbehavioral Econometric Methods: Theories, Models, and Applications for the Study of Environmental and Natural Resources.* Amsterdam, NL: Academic Press.

———. 2017. *The Behavioral Economics of Climate Change: Adaptation Behaviors, Global Public Goods, Breakthrough Technologies, and Policy-making.* Amsterdam, Netherlands: Academic Press.

———. 2018. *Natural and Man-made Catastrophes: Theories, Economics, and Policy Designs.* Hoboken, NJ: Wiley-Blackwell.

———. 2019a. *The Economics of Global Allocations of the Green Climate Fund: An Assessment from Four Scientific Traditions of Modeling Adaptation Strategies.* Cham, Switzerland: Springer Nature.

———. 2019b. Will Farmers Fully Adapt to Monsoonal Climate Changes through Technological Developments? An Analysis of Rice and Livestock Production in Thailand. *Journal of Agricultural Science* 157: 97–108.

———. 2020. *The Economics of Globally Shared and Public Goods.* Amsterdam, Netherlands: Academic Press.

———. 2021a. *Climate Change and Economics: Engaging with Future Generations with Action Plans.* London, UK: Palgrave Macmillan.

———. 2021b. Sublime Grasslands: A Story of the Pampas, Prairie, Steppe, and Savannas Where Animals Graze. In *Climate Change and Economics: Engaging with Future Generations with Action Plans.* London, UK: Palgrave Macmillan.

———. 2022a. *The Economics of Pandemics: Exploring Globally Shared Experiences.* London, UK: Palgrave Macmillan.

———., ed. 2022b. *Handbook of Behavioral Economics and Climate Change.* Cheltenham, UK: Edward Elgar.

Seo, S.N., and R. Mendelsohn. 2008. Measuring Impacts and Adaptations to Climate Change: A Structural Ricardian Model of African Livestock Management. *Agricultural Economics* 38: 151–165.

Sharpe, W.F. 1964. Capital Asset Prices: A Theory of Market Equilibrium under Conditions of Risk. *Journal of Finance* 19: 425–442.

Shiller, R.J. 2004. *The New Financial Order: Risk in the 21st Century.* Princeton, NJ: Princeton University Press.

———. 2005. *Irrational Exuberance.* 2nd ed. Princeton, NJ: Princeton University Press.

Smith, Adam. 1776. *The Wealth of Nations.* London, UK: W. Strahan and T. Cadell.

Solow, R.M. 1957. A Contribution to the Theory of Economic Growth. *Quarterly Journal of Economics* 70: 65–94.

———. 1974. The Economics of Resources or The Resources of Economics. *American Economic Review* 64: 1–14.

———. 1993. An Almost Ideal Step toward Sustainability. *Resources Policy* 19: 162–172.

Speth, G. 2012. Manifesto for a Post-growth Economy. *YES! Magazine*, WA. https://www.yesmagazine.org/new-economy/Manifesto-for-a-post-growth-economy-james-gustavesspeth.

Tobin, J. 1958. Liquidity Preference as Behavior Toward Risk. *Review of Economic Studies* 25: 65–86.

Tol, R. 2009. The Economic Effects of Climate Change. *Journal of Economic Perspectives* 23: 29–51.

United Nations (UN). 1972. Report of the United Nations Conference on Human Environment. Stockholm, Sweden.

———. 1982. United Nations Convention on the Law of the Sea. https://www.un.org/depts/los/convention_agreements/texts/unclos/unclos_e.pdf.

———. 1992. Agenda 21. United Nations Conference on Environment & Development. Rio de Janeiro, Brazil.

———. 2000. United Nations Millennium Declaration. New York, NY: UN.

———. 2015. Transforming Our World: The 2030 Agenda for Sustainable Development. New York, NY: UN.

———. 2017. Our Ocean, Our Future: Call for Action. Resolution Adopted by the General Assembly on 6 July 2017. The Ocean Conference. New York, NY: UN.

United Nations Framework Convention on Climate Change (UNFCCC). 1992. United Nations Framework Convention on Climate Change. New York, NY: UNFCCC.

———. 2015. The Paris Agreement. New York, NY: UNFCCC.

United States Energy Information Administration (US EIA). 2021. Annual Energy Outlook 2021. The US EIA, Department of Energy, Washington, DC.

United States Environmental Protection Agency (US EPA). 1990. *The Clean Air Act Amendments*. Washington, DC: The US EPA.

Vedeld, P., A. Angelsen, J. Bojø, E. Sjaastad, and G.K. Kobugabe. 2007. Forest Environmental Incomes and the Rural Poor. *Forest Policy and Economics* 9: 869–879.

Victor, P.A. 2008. *Managing Without Growth: Slower by Design, Not Disaster*. Cheltenham, UK: Edward Elgar.

von Thunen, J.H. 1826. The Isolated State. Trans. CM Wartenberg. Oxford/New York: Pergamon. [1966]

Weitzman, M.L. 2009. On Modeling and Interpreting the Economics of Catastrophic Climate Change. *Review of Economics and Statistics* 91: 1–19.

World Bank. 2008. *World Development Report 2008: Agriculture for Development.* Washington, DC: World Bank.

———. 2009. *Awakening Africa's Sleeping Giant: Prospects for Commercial Agriculture in the Guinea Savannah Zone and Beyond.* Washington, DC: World Bank and FAO.

World Commission on Environment and Development (WCED). 1987. *Our Common Future.* Oxford, UK: Oxford University Press.

World Rangeland Learning Experience (WRANGLE). 2020. North American Short Grass Prairie. Tucson, AZ: College of Agriculture and Life Sciences, University of Arizona.

CHAPTER 2

Ricardo's Rent

2.1 Agriculture for Food and Nutrition

Today, agriculture is still a primary provider of food and nutrition to people on the planet. It brings to the home kitchen tables such staples as, to name just several, jasmine rice, wheat bread, corn chowder, tomatoes, lettuce, beef, and chickens. In addition, it gives to humanity calorie and protein, as well as numerous micronutrients, essential for the health and wellbeing of individual citizens of Earth (Zilberman 1998; WB 2008; FAO 2022).

A form of agriculture practiced by farmers varies considerably from place to place, but the most common form of agriculture comprises crop farming, livestock management, and management of non-timber forest products such as, to name just some, mushrooms, gum, coffee, and rubber. A majority of farmers on the planet, especially small farm businesses, practice the three activities jointly (Seo 2016a, b, c).

In addition, an agricultural sector employs a large number of people. Although a large majority of the economic population during the nineteenth century and before identified themselves as a farmer, the agricultural sector accounts for about 2–3% of the national GDP in developed countries as of 2020 (USDA 2021; World Bank 2021). This, however, does not include the manufacturing, marketing, and service activities related to food consumption. Notwithstanding, the sector still employs over 50% of the economic population in many sub-Saharan African and Latin American countries (World Bank 2008).

© The Author(s), under exclusive license to Springer Nature Switzerland AG 2023
S. N. Seo, *The Economics of Optimal Growth Pathways*,
https://doi.org/10.1007/978-3-031-20754-9_2

In the world's least developed countries (LDCs), the problem of poverty and hunger among their populations remains one of the biggest challenges faced (World Bank 2009). The problem gets exacerbated further when failures in crop farming are caused and sustained for multiple years by extreme weather events or a multi-decadal climatic shift. It leads to high malnutrition and mortality rates among infants, children, and pregnant women. This is a big concern of the respective countries but also of the global community as a whole (Ravallion and Chen 2004).

For these reasons and situations, agriculture and food production have remained as one of the top priority areas in the numerous global policy agendas, either *via* international organizations' efforts such as the World Food Programme (WFP), the United Nations Development Progamme (UNDP), or the World Bank, or *via* individual countries' outreach efforts such as the USAID (United States Agency for International Development) and the JAICA (Japan International Cooperation Agency) (UN 2001, 2015; WFP 2019; Seo 2019; GCF 2022).

The international concern for agriculture and food production is not limited to poverty, hunger, and malnutrition in the least developed countries. A planetwide catastrophe of not being able to feed the world population in a not far away future is often predicted by analysts. One factor that many such predictions are rooted in is a rapid population increase on the planet (Malthus 1798). The global population has indeed grown steeply from about 1 billion at the beginning of the twentieth century to over 7 billion as of 2022 (IIASA 2007; Lutz et al. 2014). The limited arable lands which are available in a fixed quantity to the planet coupled with the declines in land qualities through various routes add weight to the food security concern expressed by many attributable to a population increase (Ehrlich 1968; Meadows et al. 1972).

Another factor that propels such grim predictions is a potentially big disruption in the world's climate system (IPCC 1990; Le Treut et al. 2007; Seo 2013, 2014, 2015a). Many analysts reported that the changes in the climate system as predicted by scientists will impact inputs and conditions for agriculture such as temperature, precipitation, carbon dioxide concentration, and solar radiation, resulting in a severe loss in the global crop production (Reilly et al. 1996; Schlenker and Roberts 2009). According to many of them, the number of people in hunger will increase by hundreds of millions of people by the middle of this century owing to the climate change disruptions (Rosenzweig and Parry 1994).

To elaborate and address these concerns by disentangling the complex interactions involved, this chapter approaches it with an exposition of how a farmer manages her croplands over a time horizon. At the heart of this is the theory of rent developed by David Ricardo in the early nineteenth century (Ricardo 1817). The rent of a cropland is the profit or net revenue earned from the cropland each year by managing it efficiently by the farmer. A marginal land with poor soil quality will command no rent. The stream of rents earned over the time horizon determines the value of the cropland.

In Ricardo's rent theory, a cropland is managed by a farmer over a long period of time in an optimal way. A salient capacity of the rent theory is that it can account for a long list of activities that the farmer can do in an effort to overcome numerous obstacles and constraints faced in the cropland (Seo 2016a, b, c). To give an example, if the atmospheric temperature at the farmland should rise by a degree or two Celsius, a farmer would reshuffle her portfolio by switching to another set of crops that do better in the changed climate condition (Seo et al. 2005, 2008). For another, if the South Asian monsoon season should be shifted owing to the global climate change, a farmer could adjust her planting and harvesting dates, for example, plant the seeds or crop earlier than the "normal" season (Kala 2015).

This unique characteristic makes the rent theory a solid platform from which numerous agriculture and food security concerns and predictions, some of which described above, can be evaluated (Mendelsohn et al. 1994; Seo 2016a). Unlike a range of other methodologies, a rent-based evaluation will make it possible to capture the behavioral responses of farmers to external factors and conditions that affect crop farming (Adams et al. 1990; Reilly et al. 1996; Seo 2015b).

2.2   David Ricardo's Rent Theory

The development of the concept of a rent by David Ricardo was originated from his effort to explain the rise in farmland rent during his time. According to Ricardo, a rent is "that portion of the produce of the earth, which is paid to the landlord for the use of the original and indestructible powers of the soil." The level of the rent on a specific plot of cropland is determined by the difference in the soil quality of the plot from that of the marginal cropland, that is, the plot at the margin of croplands (Ricardo 1817). According to him, if the land were unlimited in quantity or all lands were uniform in soil fertility, there will be no difference in the rents to be paid for the use of a cropland.

Let's imagine that there are in the society three degrees of croplands which cultivate corn which was the focus of Ricardo's analysis and is also called maize internationally. The first degree is the most fertile cropland, the second degree is the second most fertile cropland, and the third degree is the least fertile cropland. Let's call them Cropland No. 1, Cropland No. 2, and Cropland No. 3, respectively. The three croplands are of the same size. There are croplands No. 4, No. 5, No. 6, and so on with the lesser degrees of cropland, but they are not utilized for corn farming.

If there is abundance of fertile lands to produce the corn for the population and the lands are uniform in soil quality, there would exist no rent. If a population increase in the country necessitates the use of the croplands of the second quality, then the rent is formed. In this situation, the Cropland No. 2 is the marginal land. If the population increase is such that the Cropland No. 1 and No. 2 are insufficient to feed the population, then the Cropland No. 3 will be cultivated. Again, the Cropland No. 3 becomes the marginal land in that case.

Let's imagine again that, with the employment of the same amount of capital and labor, each of which is of equal quality across the croplands, Cropland No. 1 yields the produce of 100 quarters of corn "after supporting the labourers," Cropland No. 2 the produce of 90 quarters of corn, and Cropland No. 3 the produce of 80 quarters of corn. The yield differences are resulted from the land quality differences only.

The rent of a specific plot is determined by the land quality difference between that plot and the marginal land plot. At the marginal land, the rent to be paid is zero. This is because, by the definition of a marginal land, the entire harvest from the marginal land, 80 quarters of corn in our example, is only sufficient to cover the cost of production there. In other words, net revenue is zero.

A higher quality land yields the rent. The rent paid at the Cropland No. 2 is 10 quarters of corn, that is 90 quarters minus 80 quarters of corn. The rent paid at the Cropland No. 1 is 20 quarters of corn, that is, 100 quarters minus 80 quarters of corn. The rent is generated because of higher fertility of the lands. The higher the fertility, the higher the rent. This is summarized in Table 2.1.

The value of, that is, the price of corn is regulated by the amount of labor and capital employed at the marginal land. In the example, it produces 80 quarters of corn for the farmer. If we expand Ricardo's example

Table 2.1 Ricardo's rent from land fertility differences

	Land fertility	Capital	Labor	Produce	Rent
[1] Rent from land quality differentials					
Cropland No. 1	1st degree	£1000	φ hours	100 quarters	20 quarters[a]
Cropland No. 2	2nd degree	£1000	φ hours	90 quarters	10 quarters
Cropland No. 3	3rd degree	£1000	φ hours	80 quarters	0

[a]A quarter weighed 480 lbs in the port of Liverpool in 1815 (Britannica 2022)

into a competitive market economy where capital and labor are exchanged, the total cost paid to the factors of production at the marginal land would equal the value of the produce.

To summarize, the rent is determined by the marginal land where the land fertility is the lowest of the lands utilized for crop cultivations. At the marginal land, there is no rent payment. At the marginal land, the price of corn is regulated: the cost of production should be equal to the value (price) of the produce. Therefore, Ricardo says that the price of corn is not determined by the size of rent. Alternatively, he states that the rent is not a component of the price of corn.

The analysis by David Ricardo was prompted by the following social concern at the time (Ricardo 1817):

> *Nothing is more common than to hear of the advantages which the land possesses over every other source of useful produce, on account of the surplus which it yields in the form of rent.*

British people at the time wondered why the corn price is so high and whether it is that way because of the high rents set by the landlords. At that time, the UK enforced the Corn Laws which imposed severe restrictions and tariffs on the corn imports from Europe, which resulted in high corn prices in the country (Williamson 1990). In response, Ricardo showed through his analysis that the corn price is not high because of the rent and argued that, on the contrary, the rent is high because the corn price is high. In his own words:

> *The reason then, why raw produce rises in comparative value, is because more labor is employed in the production of the land portion obtained, and not because a rent is paid to the landlord. The value of corn is regulated by the quantity of labour bestowed on its production on that quality of land, or with that portion of capital, which pays no rent. Corn is not high because a rent is paid, but a rent is paid because corn is high.*

The rent from other assets can be explained in the same manner. As will be made clear throughout this book, a variety of rents, including resource rents, exist in the economy (von Thunen 1826; Hotelling 1931; Fisher 1930). It is intriguing that the following statement by Ricardo alluded to the possibilities of air rent, water rent, steam rent, and atmosphere rent (Ricardo 1817):

> *If air, water, the elasticity of steam, and the pressure of the atmosphere, were of various qualities; if they could be appropriated, and each quality existed only in moderate abundance, they, as well as the land, would afford a rent, as the successive qualities were brought into use. With every worse quality employed, the value of the commodities in the manufacture of which they were used, would rise, because equal quantities of labour would be less productive.......A rent would be paid to all those who possessed the most productive [resource].*

2.3   A Marginal Revolution

In the history of economics, Ricardo is famed for the marginal revolution he introduced to the economic thinking. Two centuries later, the idea is still popular, for example, it is the name of one of the most widely read economics blogs on the internet run by professional economists (Cowen and Tabarrok 2022). To be honest with you, Ricardo's marginal revolution was the first idea in economics that fascinated the present author when he just got started learning economics in a college.

With the example introduced above, the present author can explain what a marginal analysis is and means. In brief, it is a method of economic analysis which relies on the quantitative effect of a marginal change in one variable of interest on another variable of interest. A marginal change is a small change which often means one unit change and sometimes means an instantaneous change. A marginal change also most often means the small change from an equilibrium state of the variable of concern.

The contemporary economics is by and large a marginal analysis, which we can handily verify from the economic terms such as marginal utility, marginal consumption, marginal production, marginal revenue, marginal cost, marginal benefit, marginal damage, an equimarginal principle, comparative statics, and so on.

Let's start at the marginal land in the above example. A farmer would earn 80 quarters of corn by cultivating Cropland No. 3. Why does she not cultivate, say, after purchasing it or borrowing it, Cropland No. 2 instead and earn 90 quarters of corn instead? She would have no such motive because she should pay 10 quarters of corn as the rent payment for cultivating Cropland No. 2. At the equilibrium, she is indifferent between farming Cropland No. 2 and farming Cropland No. 3. The same analysis can be applied to the choice by the farmer between Cropland No. 1 and Cropland No. 3 or the choice between Cropland No. 2 and Cropland No. 3.

A marginal analysis can be conducted from the landlord's perspective as well. Let's start from the above equilibrium state in Table 2.1. The landlord of Cropland No. 3 charges no rent, considering the reality in the marginal farmland. The landlord of Cropland No. 2 charges the tenant farmer 10 quarters of corn as a rent payment.

What happens if the land owner lowers the rent payment to 5 quarters of corn? Then, the farmer of Cropland No. 2 will earn an excess profit of 5 quarters of corn, compared with the farmers in Cropland No. 1 and Cropland No. 3. Potential farmers will rush to sign the lease with the land owner of Cropland No. 2, which will push the landlord to increase the rent payment, that is, in response to the increase in demand. This will continue until the rent of Cropland No. 2 reaches 10 quarters of corn. The market in this example will be back to the equilibrium state.

The marginal analysis conducted by David Ricardo as in the above case of corn fields takes place always in reference to the marginal land, more generally speaking, from the last unit of the input employed. The rent payment condition at the marginal land, which equals zero, determines the equilibrium in the market of croplands. The rent payment at a higher quality land should be equal to the difference in the land quality of the land and that of the marginal land. The equilibrium from the marginal analysis is reached when the (marginal) profits from the three croplands are equalized. Put differently, the rents are determined in a way that "there cannot be two rates of profit" across the croplands (Ricardo 1817).

2.4   SHORT-TERM AND LONG-TERM EFFECTS
OF AGRICULTURAL IMPROVEMENTS

What is the effect of various agricultural improvements on the Ricardian land rent? Many improvements in agriculture have occurred, including a modern chemical fertilizer; a high-yield variety (HYV) of rice, wheat, and corn; an application of a modern farm tractor; and an advanced storage facility (Borlaug 1958; Ruttan 2002; Zilberman 1998; Evenson and

Gollin 2003). How does each of these major improvements affect the cropland rent?

Ricardo distinguishes two types of agricultural improvements. The first type is that which improves the productive powers of the land. The examples he cited are a more skillful rotation of crops by which he means a turnip-based husbandry of sheep along the croplands. It saves the land previously devoted to sheep raising. Another example is a better choice of manure, whose modern equivalent is a chemical fertilizer.

The second type of agricultural improvements is labor-saving improvements to produce the same output, instead of affecting land productivity. He cites "plough and thrashing machine, economy in the use of horses employed in husbandry, and a better knowledge of the veterinary art." The modern equivalents are agricultural machines such as a farm tractor that reduces labor input.

An analysis of short-term and long-term effects of an agricultural improvement of the first type is provided by Ricardo, which is summarized in Table 2.2. Before the agricultural improvement, to support a given population, four croplands with differing land qualities are cultivated. The cropland of the first degree produces 100 quarters of corn, that of the second degree produces 90 quarters of corn, that of the third degree produces 80 quarters, and that of the fourth degree produces 70 quarters.

Table 2.2 The short-term and long-term effects of agricultural improvements

	Land fertility	Capital	Labor	Produce	Rent	Analysis of effects
[1] Before improvements						
Cropland no. 1	1st degree	£1000	φ hours	100 qu	30 qu	Production = 340 qu;
Cropland no. 2	2nd degree	£1000	φ hours	90 qu	20 qu	Rent = 60 qu.
Cropland no. 3	3rd degree	£1000	φ hours	80 qu	10 qu	
Cropland no. 4	4th degree	£1000	φ hours	70 qu	0	
[2] After improvements: long term with demand increase 440 qu						
Cropland no. 1	1st degree	£1000	φ hours	125 qu	30 qu	Production = 440 qu;
Cropland no. 2	2nd degree	£1000	φ hours	115 qu	20 qu	Rent = 60 qu.
Cropland no. 3	3rd degree	£1000	φ hours	105 qu	10 qu	
Cropland no. 4	4th degree	£1000	φ hours	95 qu	0	
[3] After improvements: short term with population (demand) fixed						
Cropland no. 1	1st degree	£1000	φ hours	125 qu	20 qu	Production = 345 qu;
Cropland no. 2	2nd degree	£1000	φ hours	115 qu	10 qu	Rent = 30 qu.
Cropland no. 3	3rd degree	£1000	φ hours	105 qu	0	

Note: qu = quarters

The total production is 340 quarters of corn which is sufficient to feed the population, say, of the nation. The rent generated is 60 quarters of corn as calculated in the top panel of Table 2.2.

Let's assume that the agricultural improvements increase the productivity of each cropland to 125 quarters for Cropland No. 1, to 115 quarters for Cropland No. 2, to 105 quarters for Cropland No. 3, and to 95 quarters for Cropland No. 4. If all croplands are cultivated, it will produce 440 quarters of corn, as such, an oversupply of corn to the nation. Therefore, the Cropland No. 4 will be withdrawn from the cultivation. In total, the three croplands produce 345 quarters of corn, sufficient to feed the population. The rent is decreased to 30 quarters. These short-term effects are summarized at the bottom panel of Table 2.2.

A long-term impact analysis is shown at the middle panel of Table 2.2, with an assumption that the corn demand increases to 440 quarters in the long term. Then, under the new agricultural practices and technologies, the first three croplands cannot feed the population. As a consequence, the Cropland No. 4 is brought into cultivation again, with whose production the total production reaches 440 quarters to meet the demand of the nation.

In the long-term scenario, the rent to Cropland No. 3 increases to 10 quarters, Cropland No. 2 to 20 quarters, and Cropland No. 1 to 30 quarters. The total rent for the four croplands is back to 60 quarters, the level before the agricultural improvements.

What is the mechanism in the long term that increases the population and the corn demand to 440 quarters? According to Ricardo, the agricultural improvements lead to "accumulation" since the same amount of capital and labor results in additional 25 quarters of corn production at each cropland. The accumulation leads to an increased demand for labor, which then leads to a higher wage, which again leads to increased population and increased demand (Ricardo 1817).

2.5   THE OPTIMAL PATHWAYS OF LAND VALUE AND RENT

A modern economic explanation of Ricardo's rent theory would involve the market and prices of agricultural commodities. To continue, let's take for a further analysis the long-term impact analysis explained above. If a new agricultural technology is introduced, say a modern fertilization, it would increase the yield of corn significantly with the same amount of labor and capital employed on the same land. The short-term effect would be an increase in the supply of corns to the corn market, which would result in a reduction in the sale price of corn, given the fixed demand for corn in the short term. This will push some corn farmers out of the corn farming as they cannot meet the cost of production with the reduced sale price. Such farmers will search for and switch to another productive activity to be performed on the farmland without making a loss.

In the long term, let's say that the farmers who opted out of corn farming switch to sheep raising for the sale of sheep wool and meat to the market. As a result, the supply of the sheep products will increase in the society. An economy-wide production will increase due to an increased sheep production and consumption. This can lead to increased labor demands, higher wages, and a larger population in the economy as a whole. As a result, the demand for corn would also increase, which again will force some farmlands to be brought in to produce corn.

Let's define formally the rent at farmland i at year t, of a fixed land size, as follows:

$$\pi_{it} = TR_{it} - TC_{it}, \qquad (2.1)$$

where TR is total revenue or total income and TC is total cost of production which includes labor cost and the cost of capital employed.

The rent will be different across the arable lands in the nation, with more fertile croplands generating higher rents. Following Ricardo's classification in Tables 2.1 and 2.2 of the four types of croplands with different qualities, the rents across the four lands satisfy the following inequalities attributable to the differences in land fertility:

$$\pi_{1t} > \pi_{2t} > \pi_{3t} > \pi_{4t}. \qquad (2.2)$$

The rent at the marginal land is zero:

$$\pi_{4t} = 0. \qquad (2.3)$$

The Eqs. (2.1), (2.2), and (2.3) are subscripted by time variable t, which means that the rent received at one year may not be the same as the rent received at another year. Further, as was in the case of Cropland No. 4 in the above long-term analysis, the land may be used for one productive activity at one point in time, for example, corn farming, and for another productive activity at another point in time, for example, millet farming. In other words, there may be a land use change at each cropland over time.

If the rent is the profitability of the cropland at one specific year, how can we define the profitability of the land across the years, that is, over present and future time periods? Put differently, what is the long-term profitability of the land? We can think of it as the sum of yearly rents earned over this year and future years:

$$V_i = \sum_{t=0}^{\infty} \varphi_t \pi_t. \tag{2.4}$$

In the above, V is the long-term profitability of the land, which is the value of the land in the competitive market, φ is a discount factor for future incomes. In the competitive market for private lands, the discount factor is determined by the market interest rate (γ) (Fisher 1906, 1930):

$$\varphi_t = (1+\gamma)^{-t}. \tag{2.5}$$

In Fig. 2.1, the values of the croplands in the US are drawn from the United States Department of Agriculture (USDA) survey data made available by the USDA National Agricultural Statistics Service (NASS) (USDA 2021). The data shown are from the two agriculture-heavy States: Iowa and Nebraska. The value is expressed in dollars per acre of cropland inflation adjusted *via* 2020 US dollars.

The State of Iowa is where some of the prime croplands of the country, sometimes dubbed the "Field of Dreams," are located whereas the State of Nebraska is where the nation's largest livestock industry is located relying on the grasslands of the Great Plains. The value of the croplands more than doubled over the time period shown in the figure in both States, that is, from 1998 to 2021. The value of the croplands per acre is higher in Iowa than that in Nebraska because of the more fertile croplands overall in Iowa, which agrees with Ricardo's explanation of the rent differentials, although the values are not calculated at a farm level or at a specific plot level.

In Fig. 2.2, the land value of the US farmlands from 1980 to 2009 is drawn (Nickerson et al. 2012; USDA 2021). This is the average of all the US farmlands. Overlaid to the figure is the farm net income for the same time period, again for all US farmlands. The relationship between the farm

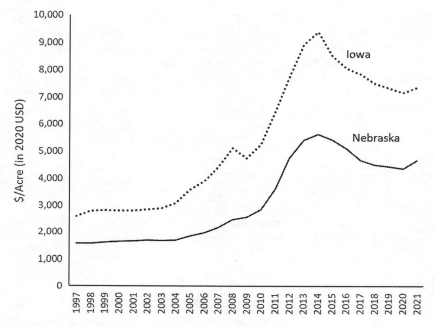

Fig. 2.1 Value of the US Croplands in two states: Iowa and Nebraska. (Source: USDA National Agricultural Statistics Service (USDA 2021))

net income and the farmland value should exhibit the relationship in Eqs. (2.4) and (2.5). The farm net income is the rent, both of which are calculated per acre of land. It fluctuated between 30 US dollars to 90 US dollars per acre of land. The farmland value is the sum of the stream of discounted future rents, which fluctuated between 1200 US dollars to 2000 US dollars per acre of farmland.

2.6   THE ROME CLUB CRITIQUE

Will the optimal pathways in agricultural profits, farm net incomes, and farmland values, likely similar to those presented in Figs. 2.1 and 2.2, guarantee that there will be sufficient foods for consumption by people on Earth over an infinite time horizon, barring any planet-wrecking catastrophe? Granted that the optimal trajectories are the results of the best decisions by countless individual farmers and individuals, how can we be sure

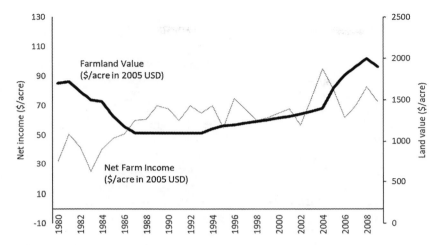

Fig. 2.2   Land value versus net income in the US farmlands. (Source: USDA National Agricultural Statistics Service (USDA 2021))

that such utilizations by individuals of the planet's farmlands will guarantee food security for the humanity over its future? To address this question, the present author will resort to the famed report, known to the world as the Rome Club Report, which asked the same question and arrived at a starkly negative conclusion.

The Rome Club Report was published in 1972 with a title "The Limits to Growth: A Report for the Club of Rome's Project on the Predicament of Mankind." The analysis was conducted by a team of researchers at the Massachusetts Institute of Technology (MIT) in response to the request by the Club of Rome. A 20-year anniversary edition with a title "Beyond the Limits" was published in 1992 (Meadows et al. 1972, 1992).

The Club of Rome, founded in 1968 in Rome, Italy, has 100 members who are notable scientists, economists, business leaders and former politicians, selected from, among other groups of people, current and former heads of state and government, United Nations administrators, high-level politicians from around the globe (Club of Rome 2021).

The Report was a dire warning against a catastrophic consequence from the rate of economic growth that had been observed during the latter half of the twentieth century. It warned against many dire consequences such as depletions of fossil fuels and other precious minerals, inability to meet food demands, carbon dioxide emissions heating the Earth, nuclear power disasters. The Rome Club Report has had much, if not overwhelming, influence on the movements of sustainable development, climate change regulations, ecological economics, and degrowth critiques, all of which will be reviewed for analysis throughout this book (WCED 1987; Meadows et al. 1992; UN 1992, 2000, 2015).

The Report was, however, not an economic analysis. The analyses were conducted by a team of scientists at the MIT, owing to which and many other reasons their analyses were in essence various simulation models relying on the observed trends and the assumptions about the future trends of the variables included in the Report (Nordhaus 1992).

In this chapter, the present author sets eyes on the Report's predictions with regard to the future food security of the planet. The key variable in the Report's predictions on the world's food security was the total population of the planet. As shown in Fig. 2.3 which replicates the trajectory presented in the Report, the world population exhibited an astoundingly high rate of growth since the end of World War II. The rapid increase in

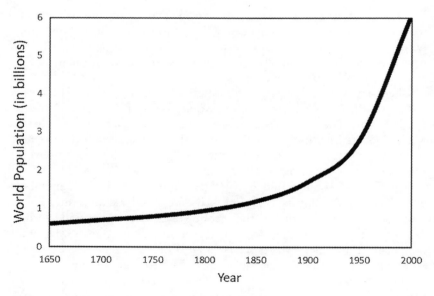

Fig. 2.3 World population explosion presented by the Rome Club Report

the world population began from the middle of the nineteenth century spurred by the Industrial Revolution. Before the nineteenth century, the world population was rather static fixed at around 1 billion people. During the first half of the twentieth century, it reached 2 billion people. By year 2000, the Report predicted that it would reach 6 billion people (Ehrlich 1968; Meadows et al. 1972).

There might have been a widespread concern at that time regarding whether the planet can sustain such a large number of people on the planet by the dawn of the twenty-first century. For your reference, the world population did reach 6 billion and in fact reached 7 billion by the decade of the 2010s (Lutz et al. 2014). Underneath the concern lied the observation that the planet has only, and will have only, a fixed amount of arable lands from which foods can be produced.

This concern was not new. It had been recognized for centuries *via* the Malthus's prediction known as the Malthusian trap. The publication of "An Essay of the Principle of Population" by Malthus coincided approximately with the publication of Ricardo's "On the Principle of Political Economy and Taxation" in 1817 (Malthus 1798; Ricardo 1817).

To simulate a variety of future trends that determine food insecurity, the authors of the Report relied on such past trends as the economic growth rates during the twentieth century, the food consumption per people, and the productivity of arable lands, in addition to the population growth rate.

What was forecast by the Report regarding the planet's food security is similar to the various trajectories shown in Fig. 2.4 which the present author replicated from the Report's. First, the stock of arable lands on the planet is fixed at 3.2 billion hectares (HA). For your reference, 1 HA is the size of the square land which is 100 meters long and 100 meters wide, roughly 4 acres. The size of arable lands on the globe available for agriculture, which is drawn with a thin black line, had remained fixed until the beginning of the nineteenth century. Since then, it started to decline at an increasing rate of loss owing to the conversion of arable lands to other land uses, for example, urban development.

The arable land needed at the present productivity level is drawn with a thick black line in the figure, which assumes the present level of consumption per person as well as the present productivity of arable land, that is, the crop yield per HA. Here, note that the "present" was the early 1970s when the Report became public. The needed arable land increases

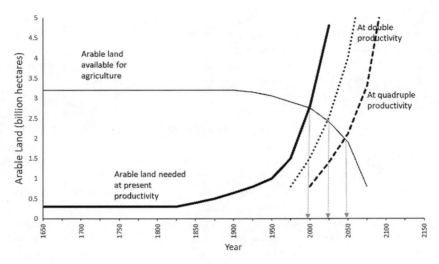

Fig. 2.4   The food security problem in the Rome Club Report

exponentially in the figure, which is again an approximation of the world population growth trajectory shown in Fig. 2.3.

When the two lines cross, the world can no longer support the food consumption of all the world citizens. This occurs conveniently, according to the Report, by around year 2000 when the two aforementioned trend lines cross. At the time of this prediction, the year 2000 might have felt far away into the future to the modelers. To the readers, the year 2000 may feel again far away into the past: we ran past the year 2000 quite a while ago. A natural question to arise is this: Did the Rome Club Report's prediction on food insecurity of the planet come to realize by the year 2000 or not?

It did not materialize, which we all know 20 years past the predicted cross time. On the contrary, the global community has achieved a remarkable reduction of the population under extreme poverty and hunger, despite the population growth which has unfolded as forecast by the Report (World Development Report 2008; World Bank 2009). Over a billion people escaped from poverty, hunger, and malnutrition since the Rome Club Report, which is attributable to many reasons.

The Report's writers, however, also presented alternative paths, as drawn in Fig. 2.4. They showed the needed land trajectory assuming a doubling of land productivity as well as a quadrupling of land productivity from the reference level of productivity. Two alternative trajectories are presented with dotted lines in the figure. Assuming the doubling of land productivity, the cross of the two lines was predicted to occur around 2025. Assuming the quadrupling of land productivity, the cross of the two lines was predicted to occur around 2050.

Since we are at around the year 2025, we can also evaluate the Report's prediction based on the doubling land productivity scenario. The planet does not have a global food shortage problem as of today attributable to a shortage of croplands, although local production failures and food shortages at some regions occur every year. The reality as of 2023 is that the consumption of food per capita is still on the increase globally while the number of people at hunger is still on the decrease planetwide, as will be discussed shortly.

2.7   Evaluating Food Security of the Planet

What went wrong for the Rome Club Report's dire predictions on the food insecurity of the planet? The crosses in Fig. 2.4, that is, in 2000 and 2025, have never come to pass. If such crosses had happened, the number of people at hunger would have increased markedly globally since the predicted cross years. On the contrary, a World Bank statistic, to cite one example, on the number of people under hunger in Thailand shows that it has halved over the past 20 years in the country (World Bank 2021).

To understand what actually happened, a crop production index of Thailand is drawn in Fig. 2.5 drawn from the World Bank data compiled in the World Development Indicators (World Bank 2021). The crop production of the country has increased over 550% from 1960 to 2018, that is, more than a quintuple of the crop production in 1960. The production index stood at around 20 in 1960, which has linearly increased to nearly 110 in 2018. The linear trend line shows that the crop production has increased at the rate of 1.6% points per year for the six decades, that is, as large as 16% points per decade. Even more strikingly, there is no sign of slowing down in the crop production index.

What explains the remarkable quintupling of the crop production in Thailand over the past six decades? On the one hand, the size of the aggregate lands used for crop productions has increased substantially. On the other hand, the productivity of the cropland, as measured in the yield per Ha of cropland, has increased significantly. The two trajectories over the

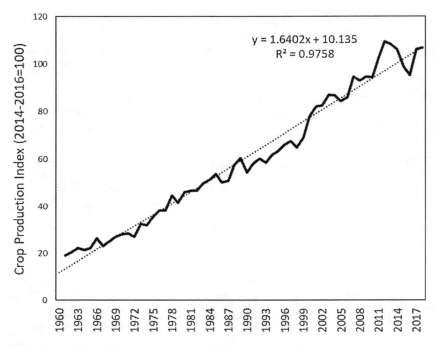

Fig. 2.5 A pathway of crop production index, Thailand

same time period used in Fig. 2.5 are overlaid in Fig. 2.6 (World Bank 2021).

The cereal yield in kg per hectare of cropland has more than doubled, from 1600 kg/ha in 1960 to 3200 kg/ha in 2018. The cereal refers to a plant with edible grains such as rice, maize, wheat, millet, sorghum, and so on. In Thailand which is the largest global exporter of rice, rice is the most important of all cereals (World Bank 2009).

The land used for the cereal production has also doubled, from around 6.4 million hectares in 1960 to around 13.3 million hectares in 2013, before the dips in recent years right before the COVID-19 pandemic outbreak in 2020 (Seo 2022).

How could Thailand achieve such a notable growth in the cereal yield? There are two primary factors that caused it. One is the advances of agricultural technologies, most notably, chemical fertilizers (Ruttan 2002). The other is the development of high-yield varieties (HYVs) of cereals,

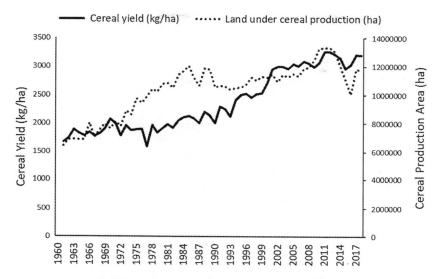

Fig. 2.6 Pathways of cereal yield and production area, Thailand

known as the Green Revolution, including semi-dwarf wheat and rice (Borlaug 1958; Evenson and Gollin 2003).

The effects of the two advances are clearly exhibited by the recent work from Thai researchers (Seo 2019; Chankrajang and Talerngsri-Teerasuwannajak 2022). There are two types of rice in the country: traditional jasmine rice and high-yield variety (HYV) rice. The researchers show that the yield of the traditional jasmine rice was about 1500 kg/ha in 1980, which has increased to about 3000 kg/ha in 2020. On the other hand, with the introduction of the HYV rice, the yield of the HYV rice was about 4000 kg/ha in 1980, which has increased to about 4500 kg/ha in 2020 (OAE 2021).

The yield increase by the introduction of the HYV rice can be attributed to the development of new high-yield varieties of rice. On the other hand, the yield doubling that occurred in the traditional jasmine rice can be attributed to agricultural technological developments, most notably, chemical fertilizers and an expansion of the irrigation infrastructure, in addition to efficient land use decisions (Schoengold and Zilberman 2007; Seo 2011).

The increase in the cereal yield such as the one that occurred in Thailand depicted in Fig. 2.6 has been unfolding even more remarkably in traditionally food insecure countries such as India and some Sub-Saharan African countries such as Mali (World Bank 2008; Seo 2021). Has there been any impact of such increases in the crop yield and production observed in many regions of the planet on the global community's ability to feed the population in it?

In Fig. 2.7, the present author puts together the trajectory of rice yield in India and the trajectory of poverty rate in the country over the period from 1960 to 2018 (World Bank 2021; Seo 2021). The rice yield trajectory in dark bullets shows a remarkable increase from about 1300 kg/ha in 1960 to about 4000 kg/ha in 2018. It has nearly tripled in a linear trend with no sign of slowing down.

As for the poverty rate of the country shown in asterisks, it has declined in a nonlinear fashion. The poverty line used for the figure is 1.9 US dollars per day. It declined from 62% of the population in 1977 when the measure was first calculated to 21% in 2011. This reduction in poverty in India is largely attributable to the increase in the crop production (Ravallion and Chen 2004; World Bank 2008). Another contributing factor to the declining trend is a revolution in the Indian dairy sector which

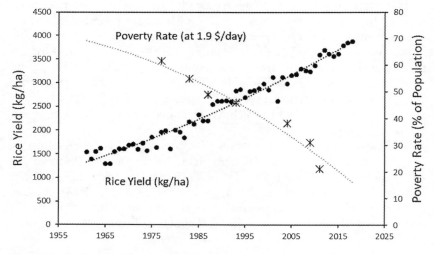

Fig. 2.7 Pathways of food production and poverty rate in India

provides milk to Indian people, a primary source of calories and protein to Indian people (World Bank 1998; Seo 2016d).

One might ask whether the cross in Fig. 2.7 is only observable in India. That is not the case. A very similar figure can be drawn from the historical Thailand data as well. In many sub-Saharan African countries, the cross of the crop yield trajectory and the poverty rate trajectory is also found (Byerlee and Eicher 1997). As far as the yield increase over the past half-century is concerned, China has outpaced all these countries (World Bank 2008).

2.8   Conclusion

To analyze the challenges of food security for the planet's rapidly growing population, it is not sufficient to focus on the crop production, nor Ricardo's rent theory. This is because food can be obtained from many other sources than crops. The most notable non-crop foods are obtained from livestock production and fish catch (Seo 2006; Nin et al. 2007; FAO 2020; Lanfranco et al. 2022). The former is the topic of the next chapter of this book while the latter is the topic of Chap. 5 of this book. Another is forest products called the non-timber forest products (NTFP), for example, mushrooms, coconuts, coffee, to name only a few, which is the main topic of Chap. 4 (Faustmann 1849).

In this sense, Ricardo's rent theory laid down the foundation stones, but did not complete it. A rent theory must account for changes in land use from one type to another, that is, beyond the corn farming, which is the topic of the next chapter where we discuss von Thunen's spatial land use theory (von Thunen 1826).

References

Adams, R., C. Rosenzweig, R.M. Peart, J.T. Ritchie, B.A. McCarl, J.D. Glyer, R.B. Curry, J.W. Jones, K.J. Boote, and L.H. Allen. 1990. Global Climate Change and US Agriculture. *Nature* 345: 219–224.

Borlaug, Norman E. 1958. The Impact of Agricultural Research on Mexican Wheat Production. *Transactions of the New York Academy of Sciences* 20: 278–295.

Britannica. 2022. Corn Law. https://www.britannica.com/event/Corn-Law-British-history.

Byerlee, D., and C.K. Eicher. 1997. *Africa's Emerging Maize Revolution*. Boulder, CO: Lynne Rienner Publishers Inc.

Chankrajang, T., and K. Talerngsri-Teerasuwannajak. 2022. Climate Change and Historical Changes in Rice Yield in Thailand. In *Handbook of Behavioural Economics and Climate Change*, ed. S.N. Seo. Cheltenham, UK: Edward Elgar.

Club of Rome. 2021. About Us. https://www.clubofrome.org/about-us/.

Cowen, T., and A. Tabarrok. 2022. Marginal Revolution: Small Steps Toward a Much Better World. https://marginalrevolution.com/about.

Ehrlich, Paul L. 1968. *The Population Bomb*. New York: NY Sierra Club/ Ballantine Books.

Evenson, R., and D. Gollin. 2003. Assessing the Impact of the Green Revolution 1960–2000. *Science* 300: 758–762.

Faustmann, Martin. 1849. On the Determination of the Value Which Forest Land and Immature Stands Pose for Forestry. In *Martin Faustmann and the Evolution of Discounted Cash Flow*, ed. M. Gane. Oxford: Oxford Institute. [1968, Paper 42].

Fisher, Irving. 1906. *The Nature of Capital and Income*. New York, NY: Macmillan.

———. 1930. *The Theory of Interest*. New York, NY: Macmillan.

Food and Agriculture Organization (FAO). 2020. *The State of World Fisheries and Aquaculture 2020*. Rome, IT: FAO.

———. 2022. *FAO STAT*. UN, Rome, IT: FAO. https://www.fao.org/faostat/en/#home.

Green Climate Fund (GCF). 2022. *Projects + Programmes*. Songdo, South Korea: GCF. https://www.greenclimate.fund/what-we-do/projects-programmes.

Hotelling, H. 1931. The Economics of Exhaustible Resources. *Journal of Political Economy* 39: 137–175.

Intergovernmental Panel on Climate Change (IPCC). 1990. *Climate Change: The IPCC Scientific Assessment*. Cambridge, UK: Cambridge University Press.

International Institute of Applied Systems Analysis (IIASA). 2007. Probabilistic Projections by 13 World Regions, Forecast Period 2000–2100, 2001 Revision. http://www.iiasa.ac.at/Research/POP/proj01/.

Kala, N. 2015. *Ambiguity Aversion and Learning in A Changing World: The Potential Effects of Climate Change from Indian Agriculture*. PhD dissertation, Yale University, New Haven, CT.

Lanfranco, B., E. Fernández, B. Ferraro, and J.M.S. de Lima. 2022. Historical Changes in the Pampas Biome, Land Use, and Climate Change. In *Handbook of Behavioural Economics and Climate Change*, ed. S.N. Seo. Cheltenham, UK: Edward Elgar.

Le Treut, H., R. Somerville, U. Cubasch, Y. Ding, C. Mauritzen, A. Mokssit, T. Peterson, and M. Prather. 2007. Historical Overview of Climate Change. In *Climate Change 2007: The Physical Science Basis. The Fourth Assessment Report of the IPCC*, ed. S. Solomon et al. Cambridge, UK: Cambridge University Press.

Lutz, W., W. Butz, and K.C. Samir, eds. 2014. *World Population and Global Human Capital in the 21st Century.* Oxford, UK: Oxford University Press.

Malthus, Thomas R. 1798. *An Essay on the Principle of Population.* London, UK: J. Johnson.

Meadows, D.H., D.L. Meadows, J. Randers, and W.W. Behrens III. 1972. *The Limits to Growth: A Report for the Club of Rome's Project on the Predicament of Mankind.* New York, NY: Universe Books.

Meadows, D.H., D.L. Meadows, and J. Randers. 1992. *Beyond the Limits.* Chelsea: VT Chelsea Green Publishing.

Mendelsohn, R., W. Nordhaus, and D. Shaw. 1994. The Impact of Global Warming on Agriculture: A Ricardian Analysis. *American Economic Review* 84: 753–771.

Nickerson, C., M. Morehart, T. Kuethe, J. Beckman, J. Ifft, and R. Williams. 2012. *Trends in U.S. Farmland Values and Ownership.* EIB-92. Economic Research Service, U.S. Department of Agriculture, Washington, DC.

Nin, A., S. Ehui, and S. Benin. 2007. Livestock Productivity in Developing Countries: An Assessment. In *Handbook of Agricultural Economics,* ed. R. Evenson and P. Pingali, vol. 3. Oxford, UK: North Holland.

Nordhaus, W.D. 1992. Lethal Model 2: The Limits to Growth Revisited. *Bookings Papers on Economic Activity* 1992: 1–59.

Office of Agricultural Economics (OAE). 2021. *Agricultural Statistics.* OAE, Government of Thailand.

Ravallion, M., and S. Chen. 2004. How Have the World's Poorest Fared Since the Early 1980s? *The World Bank Research Observer* 19: 141–169.

Reilly, J., W. Baethgen, F. Chege, et al. 1996. Agriculture in a Changing Climate: Impacts and Adaptations. In *Climate Change 1995: Impacts, Adaptations, and Mitigation of Climate Change.* Cambridge, UK: Cambridge University Press.

Ricardo, D. 1817. *On the Principles of Political Economy and Taxation.* London, UK: John Murray.

Rosenzweig, C., and M. Parry. 1994. Potential Impact of Climate Change on World Food Supply. *Nature* 367: 133–138.

Ruttan, V.W. 2002. Productivity Growth in World Agriculture: Sources and Constraints. *Journal of Economic Perspectives* 16: 161–184.

Schlenker, W., and M. Roberts. 2009. Nonlinear Temperature Effects Indicate Severe Damages to Crop Yields Under Climate Change. *Proceedings of the National Academy of Sciences* 106: 15594–15598.

Schoengold, K., and D. Zilberman. 2007. The Economics of Water, Irrigation, and Development. In *Handbook of Agricultural Economics,* ed. R. Evenson and P. Pingali, vol. 3. Amsterdam, NL: Elsevier.

Seo, S.N. 2006. *Modeling Farmer Responses to Climate Change: Climate Change Impacts and Adaptations in Livestock Management in Africa.* PhD dissertation, Yale University, New Haven.

———. 2011. An Analysis of Public Adaptation to Climate Change using Agricultural Water Schemes in South America. *Ecological Economics* 70: 825–834.

———. 2013. An Essay on the Impact of Climate Change on US Agriculture: Weather Fluctuations, Climatic Shifts, and Adaptation Strategies. *Climate Change* 121: 115–124.

———. 2014. Adapting Sensibly When Global Warming Turns the Field Brown or Blue: A Comment on the 2014 IPCC Report. *Economic Affairs* 34: 399–401.

———. 2015a. Helping Low-latitude, Poor Countries with Climate Change. *Regulation* (Winter 2015–2016): 6–8.

———. 2015b. *Micro-Behavioral Economics of Global Warming: Modeling Adaptation Strategies in Agricultural and Natural Resource Enterprises.* Cham, CH: Springer.

———. 2016a. *Microbehavioral Econometric Methods: Theories, Models, and Applications for the Study of Environmental and Natural Resources.* Amsterdam, NL: Academic Press.

———. 2016b. Modeling Farmer Adaptations to Climate Change in South America: A Microbehavioral Economic Perspective. *Environmental and Ecological Statistics* 23: 1–21.

———. 2016c. The Micro-behavioral Framework for Estimating Total Damage of Global Warming on Natural Resource Enterprises with Full Adaptations. *Journal of Agricultural, Biological, and Environmental Statistics* 21: 328–347.

———. 2016d. Untold Tales of Goats in Deadly Indian Monsoons: Adapt or Rain-retreat under Global Warming? *Journal of Extreme Events* 3: 1650001. https://doi.org/10.1142/S2345737616500019.

———. 2019. Will Farmers Fully Adapt to Monsoonal Climate Changes through Technological Developments? An Analysis of Rice and Livestock Production in Thailand. *Journal of Agricultural Science* 157: 97–108.

———. 2021. Indian Monsoon: A Tale of Indian Water Buffaloes, Goats, and High-Yield Rice. In *Climate Change and Economics: Engaging with Future Generations with Action Plans*, ed. S.N. Seo. London, UK: Palgrave Macmillan.

———. 2022. *The Economics of Pandemics: Exploring Globally Shared Experiences.* Cham, CH: Palgrave Macmillan.

Seo, S.N., R. Mendelsohn, and M. Munasinghe. 2005. Climate Change and Agriculture in Sri Lanka: A Ricardian Valuation. *Environment and Development Economics* 10: 581–596.

Seo, S.N., R. Mendelsohn, A. Dinar, R. Hassan, and P. Kurukulasuriya. 2008. *Differential Adaptation Strategies of African Cropland across Agro-Ecological Zones.* World Bank Policy Research Working Paper 4601, World Bank, Washington, DC.

United Nations (UN). 1992. *Agenda 21.* Rio de Janeiro, Brazil: United Nations Conference on Environment & Development.

————. 2000. *United Nations Millennium Declaration*. New York, NY: UN.

————. 2001. *Road Map Towards the Implementation of the United Nations Millennium Declaration*. New York, NY: UN.

————. 2015. *Transforming Our World: The 2030 Agenda for Sustainable Development*. New York, NY: UN.

United States Department of Agriculture (USDA). 2021. *National Agricultural Statistics Service*. USDA, Washington, DC. https://www.nass.usda.gov/.

von Thunen, J.H. 1826. *The Isolated State* (C.M. Wartenberg, trans.). Oxford/ New York: Pergamon. [1966].

Williamson, J.G. 1990. The Impact of the Corn Laws Just Prior to Repeal. *Explorations in Economic History* 27: 123–156.

World Bank. 1998. *India's Dairy Revolution*. World Bank Operations Evaluation Department, #168, The World Bank, Washington, DC.

————. 2008. *World Development Report 2008: Agriculture for Development*. Washington, DC: World Bank.

————. 2009. *Awakening Africa's Sleeping Giant: Prospects for Commercial Agriculture in the Guinea Savannah Zone and Beyond*. Washington, DC: World Bank and FAO.

————. 2021. *World Development Indicators*. Washington, DC: World Bank.

World Commission on Environment and Development (WCED). 1987. *Our Common Future*. Oxford, UK: Oxford University Press.

World Food Programme (WFP). 2019. *Annual Performance Report for 2019*. Rome, IT: WFP. https://www.wfp.org/funding/2019.

Zilberman, D. 1998. *Agricultural and Environmental Policies: Economics of Production, Technology, Risk, Agriculture and the Environment*. Oswego, NY: The State University of New York.

CHAPTER 3

Von Thunen's Spatial Land Use: Grasslands and Cities

3.1   INTRODUCTION

The theory of rent by David Ricardo explained in Chap. 2 was the first theoretical model on the determination of land rent. His analysis was motivated by the contemporaneous events in England where the Corn Laws were enforced and the corn price was high on the political agenda of the country. In short, he showed that the rent of the cornland is determined by the productivity of the marginal land and the differences in soil fertility across the different plots of corn lands (Ricardo 1817).

One may naturally be curious about what would happen beyond the marginal land where the rent is zero. Will this be a wasted land in which no productive activity is performed? That is certainly not the case, which we can state from our common experiences. The lands beyond the marginal land of corn may turn out to be utilized for other staple grains such as wheat, millet, or sorghum, or other types of crops such as vegetables, root crops, tree crops, or even other cash crops (Seo 2016a). That being the case, one can easily imagine an extended theory of rent from Ricardo's corn land rent, which encompasses a wide variety of crops.

In such an extended rent model encompassing all the crops, the rent will be determined again at the marginal land just like Ricardo analyzed it. What will then happen beyond the new marginal land? Will there be again a wasted land in which no productive activity is performed? That is certainly not the case, either. Many other productive activities than

S. N. Seo, *The Economics of Optimal Growth Pathways*, https://doi.org/10.1007/978-3-031-20754-9_3

cultivating numerous crops can be imaged in those lands beyond the newly defined marginal land, to mention just a few, pasturelands for livestock management, energy lands for a large array of solar panels, woodlands for timber and pulpwood (Seo 2016a, b, c).

This line of reasoning leads us to a general theory of rent, and more importantly, a general theory of land use across space. A spatial land use theory would explain how the lands of different soil qualities on the planet are utilized for a multitude of different purposes, which would look like a gigantic mosaic of different land uses if viewed from the sky, say, with a bird's-eye view (Seo 2010b, 2012b). The general theory would be capable of explaining how one land use type dominates one spatial location while another land use type dominates another spatial location. Such a transition from one land use type to another must be explained by the rent theory in David Ricardo, that is, the difference in the rents earned from the two land use types at a specific location.

The first spatial land use theory is known eponymously as the von Thunen model which was developed by a German economist and a landowner, Johann Heinrich von Thunen in 1826, nine years after Ricardo's Principles was published (von Thunen 1826). Notwithstanding, his magnum opus entitled "The Isolated State" had not been translated into English until 1966.

Von Thunen's spatial land use theory is the main topic of this chapter, which is apposite because it allows us to account for the other types of land use than the cropland, especially, the vast grasslands on the planet and, to some degree, urban land uses. Untrained eyes may encounter a large stretch of grasslands perceiving it as no man's land or even a wasteland, that is, the land that is lifeless and worthless. It might surprise many of those to be told that the grassland is the largest terrestrial ecosystem, that is, the largest land-based biome, on the planet, far greater than croplands, or urban lands, or forested lands (Seo 2021a).

That being the case, it is not surprising that the planet's biggest grasslands are each renowned among people for its sublime landscape, tall history, and deep culture (Wilder 1932; Rosner 2012). To mention some of them, the Pampas in South America, the Prairie in North America, the Steppe in Eurasia, the African Savannas, and Tibetan grasslands (Lanfranco et al. 2022a).

Moreover, unlike its initial impression to untrained eyes, each of these famed grasslands is rich in natural resources and wildlife, upon which an unmeasurable array of anthropogenic economic and non-economic activities is occurring all the time (World Bank 1998; Delgado et al. 1999; Nin et al. 2007; Seo and Mendelsohn 2008). Of those, what stands out most in economic terms, as least up to this point in time, is livestock management. For example, the Pampas grasslands, also referred to as the Rio de la Plata Grasslands in the region, is the planet's largest producer and exporter of beef cattle (Steiger 2006; Seo 2010a, 2016b; Lanfranco et al. 2022b).

Starting with the spatial land use theory, this chapter goes on to explain a variation in land use across space which is observable. It then introduces a set of critiques which treats, *albeit* unintentionally, non-croplands and especially grasslands as barren lands or wasted lands, which is referred to by the present author as a wasteland critique. This chapter responds to the critics by demonstrating that the grasslands are neither wasted lands nor valueless lands for the human society and in fact a tremendous store of value and economic wealth.

3.2 VON THUNEN'S SPATIAL LAND USE

Von Thunen's land use model described in his 1826 publication entitled "The Isolated State" is the first and oldest spatial land use theory (von Thunen 1826). He made a number of simplifying assumptions, to be described shortly, to conceptualize the simplest model of land use variations across space. The von Thunen model became a basis from which more realistic models have sprung up over time one after another, including the concentric zone model, the Hoyt model, the multiple nuclei model, hybrid models, the land market model, and cellular automata models (Hartwick and Olewiler 1997; Malamis et al. 2016).

The original version of the von Thunen model is explained most often graphically with a figure such as Fig. 3.1. An examination of the original edition of the Isolated State preserved at Stanford University libraries reveals that Fig. 3.1 was not in the edition, but a concentric semicircle version of Fig. 3.1 was inserted at the end of the book, which is available online via Google Play (von Thunen 1826; Hartwick and Olewiler 1997). That was the only figure in the book. He instead relied on numerical explanations throughout the book for establishing his model.

He began with an assumption of an isolated state. What it meant was that the state is self-sufficient and not influenced by external forces. Further, it is separated by a vast area of wilderness from the neighboring states. The wilderness is depicted in Fig. 3.1 as the area outside the

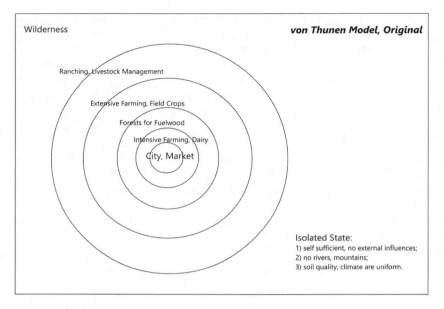

Fig. 3.1   The von Thunen model, original

concentric circles. He most likely meant by wilderness the wastelands where no economic value is produced. In the early nineteenth century, wilderness meant wastelands, well ahead of Aldo Leopold's wilderness theory which gave a special meaning to the concept of wilderness as appreciated today (Leopold 1949).

Modern readers of the twenty-first century might feel that the assumption was too restrictive to reflect the reality. To the contrary, it strikes the present author as a brilliant device without which the spatial land use theory by von Thunen might have not come to be realized because of many real-life complexities. As will be made clear, these assumptions, including the ones to be described below, can be easily relaxed within the model to replicate the reality.

The second major assumption was that there is no river or mountain in the state. This assumption also simplifies the theory dramatically as rivers as well as mountains are important variables to consider in people's decisions on land use. Rivers and mountains largely determine water runoffs and flows, more generally, accessibility to water resources (Strezepek and McCluskey 2006; Seo 2012a).

The third major assumption was that there is no variation in soil quality across the state. Neither is there any variability in the climate across the state. These assumptions are again remote from the reality where soil types, soil quality, and the climate vary widely across the landscape, as such, are crucial variables in people's land use decisions (FAO 2003; Le Treut et al. 2007). Soils and climate variables are particularly crucial in a large-scale economic analysis such as a planetary climate change, for example, an analysis of land use choices of Latin American farmers or African farmers in response to the global climate change (Seo 2010b, 2012a, 2016a, b, c).

With these assumptions, let the city be located at the center of the state, that is, the smallest circle in the figure. The city is where the market is located to which people of the state bring their produces to sell and buy the goods of others. In the concentric semicircle version of the von Thunen diagram, the city would be located at the base of the diagram.

In the nearest concentric circle outside the city, von Thunen observed that intensive farming and dairy production will be the land use of choice. The intensive farming includes such activities as vegetable production and horticulture. According to von Thunen's observation, the nearest areas to the city should be used for these production activities because the produces such as milk and vegetables should be quickly brought to the market. Otherwise, these produces will be easily rotten to be unsaleable. Note that there was no modern refrigerator at that time.

This brings us to a discussion of transportation in the economics of land use. In the von Thunen model, the only transportation method is an oxcart, that is, a cart carried by an ox. Von Thunen's time preceded, *albeit* only by 15 years, the proposals and defense in 1841 by economist Friedrich List on the development of a national railway system in Germany (Lalor 1881). Because of the absence of a steam engine locomotive in the von Thunen model, the transportation cost plays a pivotal role in his model.

The concentric circle beyond the intensive farming circle is utilized for forests and woodlands. Modern readers would wonder why? The reason was that the forests offered people fuelwoods which were the primary energy source at von Thunen's time. It was before the first commercial drilling of petroleum at Erie, Pennsylvania, in 1859 (USEIA 2015). The commercial extractions of crude oil have turned out to have a lasting big impact on the planet by causing, among other things, lighting and transportation revolutions during the twentieth century.

The concentric circle beyond the forest circle is utilized for an extensive farming of which a cultivation of field crops is most prominent. A field crop, which includes wheat, rice, maize, and soybeans, can only be cultivated on a sufficiently large cropland. These crops do not rot for months after a harvest if well stored, as such, can be carried by oxcarts to the city market even for days.

The concentric circle beyond the extensive farming circle is utilized for ranching or livestock management. A commercial livestock management requires an even more extensive land than the field crops do. Cattle and other farm animals can be walked to the city market even without any transportation vehicle, but fouls such as chickens, turkeys, ducks, and so on should be carried by oxcarts.

The livestock management that von Thunen imagined for this model, or rather observed during his time in Germany, is an extensive grassland-based management of animals. These animals would be kept in cowsheds or cattle pens but are allowed to roam freely to feed on natural grasses or managed pastures (Lanfranco et al. 2022b).

Another type of livestock management is an intensive management in which farm animals are kept in cowsheds and feedlots. The animals are fed grains produced or purchased from the market from the field crop farmers, for example, of corns (Seo and Mendelsohn 2008, Lanfranco et al. 2022b). This intensive livestock management is certainly not what von Thunen imagined in his model.

Beyond the livestock management circle is wilderness. Contemporary readers would think of wilderness as a tremendous store of wildlife and valuable resources. In von Thunen's time in Europe, the wilderness was simply a wasteland where no economic value is existent or created. This change in perception was perhaps inevitable. Today, there are many wilderness societies as well as wildlife societies including the World Wildlife Fund (WWF) and the Wilderness Society. The founder of these societies is often cited as Aldo Leopold who wrote a classic book entitled "A Sand County Almanac" in which he describes why wilderness or wildlife is more valuable than the economic value for which he meant the tradable value in the market (Leopold 1949; Seo 2018).

The point I am making here is that the wilderness is another type of land use deliberately chosen by the people of the state. To reflect this point, in Fig. 3.1, we could modify the figure by creating another concentric circle outside the ranching circle to clarify that the wilderness is another

land use type just like the other land use types identified in the figure by
von Thunen.

Von Thunen developed the land use pattern across space in Fig. 3.1
from the concept of marginal productivity in a numerical way, which corresponds to the concept of rent in the Ricardo model. His land rent per
unit of land, say, an acre of land, can be defined as follows:

$$\pi = y \bullet (p-c) - y \bullet Fr \bullet D. \qquad (3.1)$$

In Eq. (3.1), π is land rent per acre of land, y yield from the land, p sale
price of the yield at the market, c production cost, Fr is freight rate per
unit of freight and unit distance, D is the distance from the land to
the market.

Relying on the von Thunen rent, the land use pattern across space in
Fig. 3.1 can be explained by the rent distributions of different land use
types, as depicted in Fig. 3.2. Since Fig. 3.2 incorporates the spatial rent
distributions, it is more common, than Fig. 3.1, in the economics literature as well as the economic geography literature (Hartwick and Olewiler
1997; Dauphiné 2017). The bottom panel of Fig. 3.2 replicates Fig. 3.1.
The top panel explains the changes from one land use to another across
space shown in the bottom panel with a linear land rent function for each
type of land use: residential, dairy, forest, field crops, livestock.

Let's first focus on the linear land rent function for the residential land
use. The land rent function is assumed to be linear but can be a nonlinear
as long as it is monotonically decreasing from the left. The rent declines,
the farther apart are the lands from the city center. These two features are
present in all the five land rent functions drawn in Fig. 3.2.

Now focus on the residential land rent function and the dairy farming
land rent function. At the intersection of the two linear lines, the land use
shifts from the residential land use to the dairy farming land use. At the
city, the residential land use is chosen because it yields a higher rent, which
is depicted at the bottom panel of the figure.

Next, focus on the dairy land rent function and the forest land rent
function. Again, the farther apart is the land from the city, the lower the
land rent, which is true of the two types of the land use. At the intersection
of the two functions, the land use shifts from the dairy farming to the forest. In the areas where the dairy land use is chosen, the land use type is
marked at the bottom panel as the dairy land use. Further, we can verify

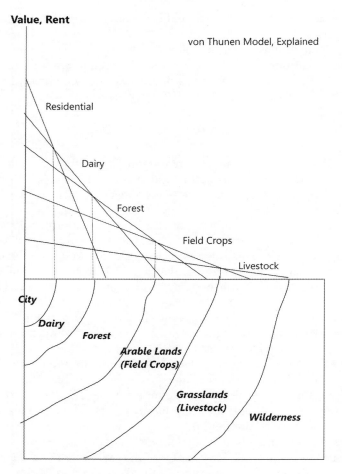

Fig. 3.2 The von Thunen model, explained

easily from the figure that the dairy land rent is greater in the places where the dairy production is chosen than the land rent possibly earned from any other land use type.

The same reasoning can be repeated to the shift of land use from the forest land to the field crops as well as to the shift from the field crops to the ranching. There is no land rent function in Fig. 3.2 for the wilderness.

Further, it is represented by a horizontal line in the figure. Von Thunen might have considered the horizontal line to mean zero land rent that can be generated from the wilderness. However, as mentioned above, the horizontal line is not certainly zero value line, rather it should be set at some positive value. In the today's economics, there should be another land rent function added to the figure for the wilderness.

As noted above, the von Thunen model has expanded ever since and been recreated with modifications of the simple assumptions in the model (Malamis et al. 2016). In the agricultural land use, one of the most prominent modifications is an inclusion of rivers and mountains in the model. When such geographical features are added, the city will be formed at a riverside location and the dairy and intensive farming will be located "along" the river line owing to the easy access to water and transportation. Outside the dairy and intensive farming, other land use types will emerge again in consideration of accessibility to water which can be also obtained from high mountains in addition to rivers. In addition, there may emerge a secondary city at the foot of the mountain, thereby giving birth to a multiple-market state (Rodrigue 2020).

3.3   A WASTELAND CRITIQUE

The theory of spatial land use is an important conceptual tool in a host of economic analyses of major policy issues. The theory is unavoidable in an analysis of the impact of a certain external disturbance on a specific group of agricultural producers or the impact of a policy intervention to support a certain group of producers. To explain this point, the present author will review two sets of analyses on the impact of global climate change on food security, one with a spatial land use model and the other without it.

Let's start with the latter, specifically, an analysis of the impact of climate change on agriculture without a spatial land use modeling. For this, I introduce two models. The first is an agronomic model (Rosenzweig and Parry 1994; Butt et al. 2005) and the second is a statistical yield model (Schlenker and Roberts 2009).

Both models concentrate on cereal productions, thereby leaving out the impacts of climate change on other agricultural activities such as intensive farming, dairy production, forestry, grassland management, livestock management, and wilderness (Seo 2015a, 2019a). Since the two models treat, *albeit* unintentionally, these other activities as if of zero value, the present author will call the two models as a wasteland critique. That is, the two models treat non cereal production areas as a wasteland. This is like the von Thunen model in Figs. 3.1 and 3.2 where the wilderness was treated like a wasted land with no meaningful value.

An agronomic model developed to measure the impact of climate change on agriculture focuses on major staple grains of the globe: wheat, rice, and corn (Adams et al. 1990). The impact of climate change on each crop is measured first by a crop yield simulation conducted in a laboratory setting (Tubiello and Ewert 2002). In the second stage, the agronomic results obtained from the laboratory are extrapolated, one crop at a time, to the national economy and then to the global economy. For an extrapolation to the national economy, a national profile of the concerned crop such as production areas, soils, and water access is relied upon. For an extrapolation to the global economy, a global trade model and trade scenarios, for example, a Basic Linked System (BLS), is developed and applied (Rosenzweig and Parry 1994; Hillel and Rosenzweig 2010; Parry et al. 2004).

The predictions on the impact of climate change on agriculture by the modelers are as follows. Based on the UKMO (United Kingdom Met Office) scenario and assuming no adaptation by farmers, the authors predicted by 2060 a decline of cereal production by 12%, a spike of cereal price by 140%, and an additional number of people at risk of hunger of 380 million people worldwide. This was a pretty dire prediction at that time (Rosenzweig and Parry 1994). All figures are for developing countries. The 2060 is the time assumed for a global carbon dioxide concentration doubling.

The authors also offered alternative predictions for when "reasonable" adaptation activities are taken into account. By the same time period and the same climate scenario, the authors predicted a decline of cereal production by 12%, a spike of cereal price by 100%, an additional number of people at risk of hunger at 300 million people worldwide (Rosenzweig and Parry 1994).

The statistical modeling approach of measuring the impact of climate change on crop yields is the second of the wasteland critiques. The statistical model estimates the relationship between the yield of a selected crop and climate variables while controlling other covariates. It carefully takes into account the crop growing phases, for example, vegetative, reproductive, and ripening phases. Selected crops are major staple grains such as wheat, rice, maize, and soybeans (Schlenker and Roberts 2009; Welch et al. 2010; Lobell et al. 2011).

The predictions of the impact of climate change on crops by a representative statistical yield model are as follows for the time period of 2070–2099 and for the UKMO climate models, specifically UKMO's Hadley III model. Under the Hadley III B1 scenario, the authors predicted about 43% decrease in corn yield, about 35% reduction in soybean yield, and about 38% reduction in cotton yield. Under a severe climate change scenario A1F1 of the same model (Nakicenovic et al. 2000), the authors predicted about 82% decrease in corn yield, about 72% decrease in soybean yield, and about 72% decrease in cotton yield (Schlenker and Roberts 2009).

The predictions were a dire warning against the impact of climate change on agriculture, which stood out by far even among the large number of studies on the impact of climate change surveyed by the Intergovernmental Panel on Climate Change (IPCC)'s signature report (Porter et al. 2014).

Again, the salient weakness of this study and other statistical yield models is that the agricultural and rural areas that are not growing a selected crop at the time of the modeler's calibration are treated as wasted lands with no value. Specifically speaking, the statistical model assumes, *albeit* implicitly, the yield of zero for the selected crop in the areas that are not utilized for the crop at the present (Seo 2014b, 2015b). This finer insight can be obtained from the literature of selection bias in the econometric studies as well as from the microbehavioral economic models of climate change (Heckman 1979; Dubin and McFadden 1984; Seo 2016a, 2022).

3.4   Optimal Pathways of Land Use Changes

In response to the dire predictions regarding the impact of climate change on agriculture, Mendelsohn and his coauthors developed an economic model in which the possibility of land use changes in response to a shift in the climate is captured in the final estimates of the climate change impact. They argued that the predicted impacts of climate change by the above-described models are so severe in large part because these models do not account for the possibility of land use changes (Mendelsohn et al. 1994).

The authors named it a Ricardian model after David Ricardo's rent theory. Their hypothesis was presented graphically in the paper, which is recreated in Fig. 3.3. There are four land value functions: wheat, corn, grazing, and retirement home. The authors hypothesized that as the degree of climate change increases, people will switch land use from wheat

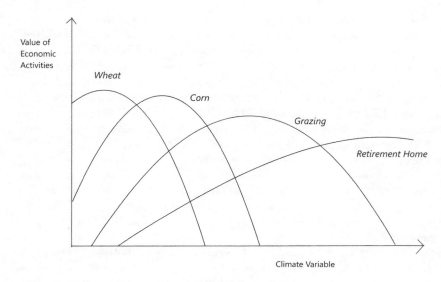

Fig. 3.3 A hypothesis of land use changes versus climate change

to corn, corn to grazing, grazing to retirement home. If such transitions in the land use of the society are taken into account, they argued that the impact will be not as severe as the above-described models predicted. They argued further that the impact of climate change on agriculture may turn out to be beneficial if a mild climate change scenario were to materialize in the future.

Readers will have noticed the similarity of Fig. 3.3 to that in the top panel of Fig. 3.2. A notable difference is a quadratic land value function in Fig. 3.3 instead of a linear function in Fig. 3.2. Alternatively, Fig. 3.2 can be drawn without any loss of the von Thunen land use model with a quadratic land value function for each type. The authors named the model a Ricardian model but could have named it a Ricardo-von Thunen model.

Notice that the Ricardian theory of rent does not explain a change in land use: it was explained in the context of a single crop, that is, corn. On the other hand, the von Thunen model does not explain the changes in land use owing to differentials in soil quality or climate variables. Von Thunen assumed these factors are invariable across the isolated state. By contrast, in Fig. 3.3, land values are assumed to vary across the climate variable, that is, the degree of climate warming, in a non-linear fashion, specifically, a quadratic fashion.

After its publication, the Ricardian analysis set the literature of climate change impact analysis ablaze, significantly altering the climate change economics as well as global policy designs. According to one citation measure, it was the most influential paper among all climate change economics publications by the mid-2010s. The paper was also recognized as the Publication of Enduring Quality (PEQ) by the Association of Environmental and Resource Economists in 2019 (AERE 2019).

Are there in fact such land use value functions and land use changes across the climate variables as those depicted in Fig. 3.3 and hypothesized by the Ricardian modelers? People asked. The problem with the authors was that the Ricardian model was a black box model, that is, the inside content of it cannot be revealed until an actual crash event occurs.

The efforts to develop an "explicit" model in which land use choices are explicitly modeled and predicted across the range of the global climate system ensued and resulted in a new economic modeling framework (Seo 2006, 2010a, 2016a; Seo and Mendelsohn 2008). It can be called a microbehavioral economic model (Seo 2022) because (1) it relies on micro decisions of individual farms, that is, instead of a county-level decision data or a national-level decision data; (2) it directly models choices of individual farms based on a range of probabilistic models (Train 2003); (3) the dollar consequences of such choices are revealed by estimating the land value functions after selection bias corrections (Heckman 1979; Dubin and McFadden 1984). The publication received an Outstanding Applied Economic Perspectives and Policy Award from the Agricultural and Applied Economics Association (AAEA) in 2011.

A presentation of some of the notable results from the microbehavioral economic model will clarify what are stated in the last paragraph as well as the core arguments of this chapter. Figure 3.4, which is recreated from one of the microbehavioral economic analyses, illustrates the choices of Sub-Saharan African farmers and how their choices have changed in response to climate change (Seo 2012a).

In the figure, there are three systems of agriculture: a crops-only, a livestock-only, and a mixed crops-livestock system. Through a survey of over 10,000 farms in Africa, each farm is asked what crops and livestock species it manages. From the answers given, an agricultural system is identified. Applying the discrete choice models to the data, the probability of each agricultural system to be chosen is estimated. Therefore, the vertical axis in the figure is the probability of choice which ranges from 0 to 1 (Seo 2016a).

The horizontal axis is a climate variable, specifically, a measure of long-term rainfall risk to farming. Concretely, it is the coefficient of variation in annual precipitation (CVP) "measured" at the locations of farms. The CVP is a measure of variation independent of the rainfall size in each location, meaning it only measures a percentage variation.

The figure shows that as the precipitation risk increases, African farmers increase adoption of a mixed crops-livestock system. By contrast, they decrease a specialized crops-only system when the CVP increases. The livestock-only system is also increasingly chosen when the CVP increases up to some point, after which it is less frequently chosen.

The figure confirms the hypothesis of Fig. 3.3 to some extent. That is, the observed choices of African farmers show that farmers do indeed switch from crops such as corn and wheat to grazing for livestock management. A similar result to that shown in Fig. 3.4 is obtained when another

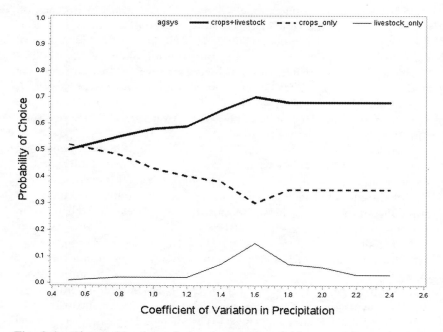

Fig. 3.4 Observed land use choice changes from field crops to livestock versus climate change

climate variable, such as temperature normal, is chosen as the horizontal axis variable (Seo 2010b, 2014b).

Another microbehavioral research conducted at a farm animal species level is presented in Fig. 3.5, that is, instead of an analysis at the agricultural system level. With the same data collected from Africa, the authors examined African farmers' choices of livestock species across the range of temperature normal in the continent. Five livestock species are most widely adopted: beef cattle, dairy cattle, goats, sheep, and chickens (Seo 2006; Seo and Mendelsohn 2008).

As the temperature normal gets hotter, the figure shows that African farmers increasingly adopt certain species. The hotter the region, the less frequently beef cattle and dairy cattle are adopted. By contrast, the hotter the region, the more frequently goats and sheep are adopted by farmers. The response function for chickens shows a hill-shape one (Seo and Mendelsohn 2008).

Figures 3.4 and 3.5 confirm, to a large extent, the insight of the land use change hypothesis by Mendelsohn and coauthors. What is then the accurate impact of climate change on agriculture if such land use change decisions were fully taken into consideration? Studies in Africa and Latin

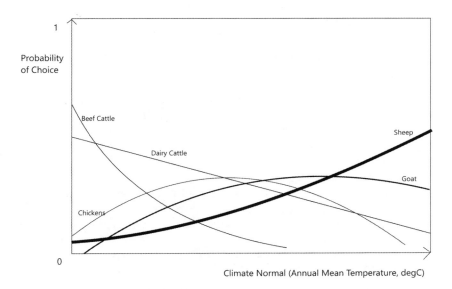

Fig. 3.5 Choice probabilities of farm animals versus climate change

America did indeed show that the impact of climate change on agriculture will be modest, if not very minor, by the middle of this century (Seo et al. 2009, Seo 2014b, 2016b, c).

In Africa, a hotter and more arid climate brought about by the ongoing climate change will increase an integrated crop and livestock system of agriculture as well as adoptions of goats, sheep, and cattle by farmers, which would replace reduced crop productions in the continent (Seo et al. 2009; Seo 2014b). In Latin America where a grassland-based livestock management is a dominant form of agriculture in many grassland biomes of the continent, to be explained in the next section, a hotter and more arid climate will make the currently successful livestock operations to prosper even more by negatively affecting crop yields and revenues in a significant manner (Baethgen 1997; Magrin et al. 2005; Seo 2016a, b).

The key take-home message is that the land use choice decisions do matter in a policy analysis of climate change and other major policy issues, which in turn tells that the spatial land use model first put forth by von Thunen remains an important intellectual device for policy analysts, that is, with proper extensions of the initial model. The lesson to policy analysts is that any type of land use we observe today, how insignificant they may look from contemporary standpoints, should not be treated as a wasteland in the policy model.

3.5   Evaluating the Health of Grasslands on the Planet

What is the status of health of the planet's grasslands? It is not widely known to the public that the grassland is the largest land-based biome on the planet (Seo 2021b). It is far larger than the other biomes such as arable lands, forestlands, woodlands, shrublands, desert, and tundra.

A biome is defined as a community of plants and animals with many commonly shared characteristics. An ecosystem is a similar concept, which is derived from the concept of a biome after putting an emphasis on climate and soil characteristics (Box and Fujiwara 2005). Economic activities in rural areas of the planet are conditioned, among other things, on the dominant ecosystems thereof (Seo 2012a, 2014a).

Major grasslands of the planet are depicted in Fig. 3.6, overlaid on the two-dimensional map of the globe. The figure is based on the NASA (National Aeronautics and Space Administration)'s land cover and land use data (Matthews 1983, 1999). The major grasslands can be seen in every continent and in fact dominate many of them. The grasslands are marked in black while the deserts which adjoin the grasslands are marked in gray.

In South America, there are three major grasslands: the Pampas, the Llanos, the Cerrado (Lanfranco et al. 2022a). The Llanos is a highland grassland while the other are lowland grasslands. In North America is the Prairie. Notably, you can see the grasslands even on the high mountain ranges of the Andes, that is, along Peru and Chile.

Africa is predominantly occupied by deserts and Savanna zones. The Savanna is defined as the landscape that has a continuous grass cover, interrupted occasionally by trees and shrubs (WRANGLE 2020). The largest Savanna biome is found in sub-Saharan Africa, including the Sahel, the Sudanian Savanna, and the Veld grasslands in the south of the continent (Seo 2014a).

Australasia is predominantly covered by grasslands. The rangelands, which are referred to as the outback, cover about 81% of Australia. The Australian rangelands are arid and semi-arid regions of the country, whose biomes are dominantly grasslands, savannas, and shrublands. Across the rangelands, the amount of rainfall is scarce, below 30 mm/month, about 350 mm/year (ACRIS 2008; Seo 2011). As can be seen in Fig. 3.6, New Zealand is by and large grasslands. A pastoral farming employs 60% of the economically active population of the country.

From Asia to the edge of Europe, there is the Eurasian Steppe. The belt of the Steppe extends 8000 kilometers east to west, from Mongolia and Manchuria in the east, Ukraine and Central Asia in the middle to Hungary in the west. The Steppe, which is a Russian word meaning a flat grassy plain, is an ecological zone characterized by a grassland plain without trees where the grasses are short grasses.

In the figure, it can be seen that grasslands are found in unexpected places as well. You can see grasslands marked in Alaska, for example. These are regions of forbs, that is, wildflowers. You can also see grasslands in Tibetan plateau in the Himalayas. The grasses are short grasses and meadows, similar to those in the Andes Mountains.

The figure reveals that the grasslands are too big a part of the planet to ignore in an analysis of any policy issues pertinent to the globe. Nonetheless, there is a tendency among researchers and the general public to set aside the grasslands as the lands of no value. Further, it is hard to find a researcher who is concerned about deteriorating grasslands due to some policy or

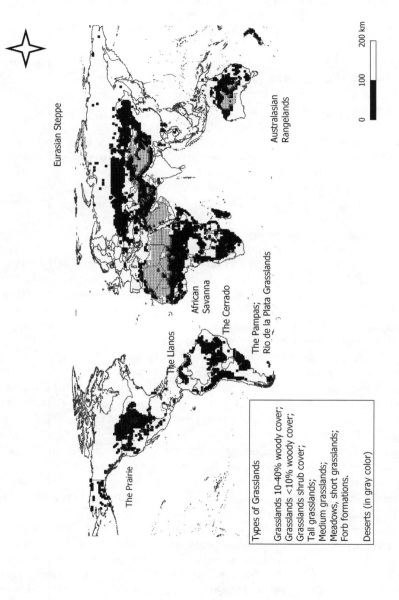

Fig. 3.6 Major grasslands of the planet

natural factors while those who are concerned about deteriorating crop-lands are easily encountered.

In fact, the researches that predict a loss or deterioration of arable crop-lands owing to some factors tend to predict an increase of grasslands at the expense of the croplands: as croplands become less profitable, people will turn the crop farming to grassland-based economic activities. An active conversion of the land from crop farming to grassland-based activities can occur *via* an increase in grass quantity and quality owing to some factors (Shaw et al. 2002; Chan and McCoy 2010).

To sum up, the planet's grassland biome continues to be an overwhelm-ing presence on the surface of the planet. Notwithstanding, the human society's efforts to utilize the grassland resources seem to have been very limited or not appreciated properly. As the human society faces numerous challenges, just one of which is climate change, it is right time for the planet's communities to reconsider the biology and economics of grass-lands (Seo 2021b).

3.6   Conclusion

This chapter began with the exposition of von Thunen's spatial land use theory and how land use decisions are made optimally with a goal of mak-ing the best use of the land resources. Efficient land use choices and deci-sions are a major component in the optimal economic growth trajectory over time. In the efficient land use pathways, the land resources of the planet are best utilized by individual owners, both private and public, for the maximum benefit. In the inefficient land use pathways, the land resources are wasted, that is, not utilized to gain the full benefit, becoming a hindrance to the pursuit of an optimal growth of the economy over time.

The discussion in this chapter clarifies how efficient land use change decisions are critical in the society's growth in the face of grand or unprec-edented challenges such as climate change. Critics argue that climate change will severely harm agriculture in the coming century owing to cli-matic shifts, population growth, and other correlated factors. However, such assessments do not heed to the possibilities that farmers may switch their current land use types to different ones in responding to such chal-lenges. Two examples of such microbehavioral changes of farmers are explained in this chapter drawing from the study of African and Latin American agriculture: changes in the adoption of agricultural systems and changes in the choice of livestock species.

78 S. N. SEO

REFERENCES

Adams, R., C. Rosenzweig, R.M. Peart, J.T. Ritchie, B.A. McCarl, J.D. Glyer, R.B. Curry, J.W. Jones, K.J. Boote, and L.H. Allen. 1990. Global Climate Change and US Agriculture. *Nature* 345: 219–224.

Association of Environmental and Resource Economists (AERE). 2019. *Publication of Enduring Quality*. AERE. https://www.aere.org/publication-of-enduring-quality.

Australian Collaborative Rangeland Information System (ACRIS). 2008. *Rangelands 2008—Taking the Pulse*. Canberra, AU: Department of Environment.

Baethgen, W.E. 1997. Vulnerability of Agricultural Sector of Latin America to Climate Change. *Climate Research* 9: 1–7.

Box, E.O., and K. Fujiwara. 2005. Vegetation Types and Their Broad-scale Distribution. In *Vegetation Ecology*, ed. E. van der Maarel. New York, NY: Wiley Blackwell.

Butt, T.A., B.A. McCarl, J. Angerer, P.T. Dyke, and J.W. Stuth. 2005. The Economic and Food Security Implications of Climate Change in Mali. *Climatic Change* 68: 355–378.

Chan, K.Y., and D. McCoy. 2010. Soil Carbon Storage Potential Under Perennial Pastures in the Mid-north Coast of New South Wales, Australia. *Tropical Grasslands* 44: 184–191.

Dauphiné, A. 2017. *Geographical Models with Mathematica*. Amsterdam, NL: ISTE Press—Elsevier.

Delgado, C., M. Rosegrant, H. Steinfeld, S. Ehui, and C. Courbois. 1999. *Livestock to 2020: The Next Food Revolution*. Washington DC: International Food Policy Research Institute, Food, Agriculture, and the Environment Discussion Paper 28.

Dubin, J.A., and D.L. McFadden. 1984. An Econometric Analysis of Residential Electric Appliance Holdings and Consumption. *Econometrica* 52 (2): 345–362.

Food and Agriculture Organization (FAO). 2003. *The Digital Soil Map of the World (DSMW) CD-ROM*. Rome, IT: FAO.

Hartwick, J.M., and N.D. Olewiler. 1997. *The Economics of Natural Resource Use*. 2nd ed. New York, NY: Pearson.

Heckman, J. 1979. Sample Selection Bias as a Specification Error. *Econometrica* 47: 153–162.

Hillel, D., and C. Rosenzweig, eds. 2010. *Handbook of Climate Change and Agroecosystems: Impacts, Adaptation and Mitigation*. London, UK: Imperial College Press.

Lalor, John J., ed. 1881. *Cyclopaedia of Political Science, Political Economy, and of the Political History of the United States by the Best American and European Authors*. New York, NY: Maynard, Merrill, & Co.

Lanfranco, B., E. Fernández, B. Ferraro, and J.M.S. de Lima. 2022a. Historical Changes in the Pampas Biome, Land Use, and Climate Change. In *Handbook of Behavioural Economics and Climate Change*, ed. S.N. Seo. Cheltenham, UK: Edward Elgar.

———. 2022b. Sustainable Intensification of Agriculture and Economy in the Pampas Grasslands Under Climate Change. In *Handbook of Behavioural Economics and Climate Change*, ed. S.N. Seo. Cheltenham, UK: Edward Elgar.

Le Treut, H., R. Somerville, U. Cubasch, Y. Ding, C. Mauritzen, A. Mokssit, T. Peterson, and M. Prather. 2007. Historical Overview of Climate Change. In *Climate Change 2007: The Physical Science Basis. The Fourth Assessment Report of the IPCC*, ed. S. Solomon et al. Cambridge, UK: Cambridge University Press.

Leopold, Aldo. 1949. *A Sand County Almanac: And Sketches Here and There.* Oxford, UK: Oxford University Press.

Lobell, D., W. Schlenker, and J. Costa-Roberts. 2011. Climate Trends and Global Crop Production Since 1980. *Science* 333: 616–620.

Magrin, G.O., M.I. Travasso, and G.R. Rodriguez. 2005. Changes in Climate and Crop Production During the 20th Century in Argentina. *Climatic Change* 72: 229–249.

Malamis, S., E. Katsou, V.J. Inglezakis, S. Kershaw, D. Venetis, and S. Folini. 2016. Chapter 5—Urban Environment. In *Environment and Development: Basic Principles, Human Activities, and Environmental Implications*, ed. S.G. Poulopoulos and V.J. Inglezakis. Amsterdam, NL: Elsevier.

Matthews, E.G. 1983. Global Vegetation and Land Use: New High-Resolution Data Bases for Climate Studies. *Journal of Climate and Applied Meteorology* 22 (3): 474–487.

———. 1999. *Global Vegetation Types, 1971–1982 (Matthews)*. Oak Ridge, TN: Oak Ridge National Laboratory. https://doi.org/10.3334/ORNLDAAC/419.

Mendelsohn, R., W. Nordhaus, and D. Shaw. 1994. The Impact of Global Warming on Agriculture: A Ricardian Analysis. *American Economic Review* 84: 753–771.

Nakicenovic, N., O. Davidson, G. Davis, A. Grübler, T. Kram, E.L. La Rovere, B. Metz, T. Morita, W. Pepper, H. Pitcher, A. Sankovski, P. Shukla, R. Swart, R. Watson, and Z. Dadi. 2000. *Emissions Scenarios. A Special Report of Working Group III of the Intergovernmental Panel on Climate Change*. Geneva, CH: The IPCC.

Nin, A., S. Ehui, and S. Benin. 2007. Livestock Productivity in Developing Countries: An Assessment. In *Handbook of Agricultural Economics*, ed. R. Evenson and P. Pingali, vol. 3. Oxford, UK: North Holland.

Parry, M.L., C.P. Rosenzweig, A. Iglesias, M. Livermore, and G. Fischer. 2004. Effects of Climate Change on Global Food Production Under SRES Emissions and Socioeconomic Scenarios. *Global Environmental Change* 14: 53–67.

Porter, J.R., L. Xie, A.J. Challinor, K. Cochrane, S.M. Howden, M.M. Iqbal, D.B. Lobell, and M.I. Travasso. 2014. Food Security and Food Production

Systems. In *Climate Change 2014: Impacts, Adaptation, and Vulnerability*, ed. C.B. Field et al. Cambridge, UK: Cambridge University Press.

Ricardo, D. 1817. *On the Principles of Political Economy and Taxation*. London, UK: John Murray.

Rodrigue, J.-P. 2020. *The Geography of Transport Systems*. 5th ed. New York, NY: Routledge.

Rosenzweig, C., and M. Parry. 1994. Potential Impact of Climate Change on World Food Supply. *Nature* 367: 133–138.

Rosner, H. 2012. *Dreaming of a Place Where the Buffalo Roam*. New Haven, CT: Yale Environment 360.

Schlenker, W., and M. Roberts. 2009. Nonlinear Temperature Effects Indicate Severe Damages to Crop Yields Under Climate Change. *Proceedings of the National Academy of Sciences* 106: 15594–15598.

Seo, S.N. 2006. *Modeling Farmer Responses to Climate Change: Climate Change Impacts and Adaptations in Livestock Management in Africa*. PhD dissertation, Yale University, New Haven, CT.

———. 2010a. A Microeconometric Analysis of Adapting Portfolios to Climate Change: Adoption of Agricultural Systems in Latin America. *Applied Economic Perspectives and Policy* 32: 489–514.

———. 2010b. Managing Forests, Livestock, and Crops Under Global Warming: A Microeconometric Analysis of Land Use Changes in Africa. *Australian Journal of Agricultural and Resource Economics* 54: 239–258.

———. 2011. The Impacts of Climate Change on Australia and New Zealand: A Gross Cell Product Analysis by Land Cover. *Australian Journal of Agricultural and Resource Economics* 55: 220–239.

———. 2012a. Decision Making Under Climate Risks: An Analysis of Sub-Saharan Farmers' Adaptation Behaviors. *Weather, Climate, & Society* 4: 285–299.

———. 2012b. Adaptation Behaviors Across Ecosystems Under Global Warming: A Spatial Micro-econometric Model of the Rural Economy in South America. *Papers in Regional Science* 91: 849–871.

———. 2014a. Adapting Sensibly When Global Warming Turns the Field Brown or Blue: A Comment on the 2014 IPCC Report. *Economic Affairs* 34: 399–401.

———. 2014b. Evaluation of Agro-Ecological Zone Methods for the Study of Climate Change with Micro Farming Decisions in Sub-Saharan Africa. *European Journal of Agronomy* 52: 157–165.

———. 2015a. *Micro-Behavioral Economics of Global Warming: Modeling Adaptation Strategies in Agricultural and Natural Resource Enterprises*. Cham, CH: Springer.

———. 2015b. Helping Low-latitude, Poor Countries with Climate Change. *Regulation* (Winter 2015–2016): 6–8.

————. 2016a. *Microbehavioral Econometric Methods: Theories, Models, and Applications for the Study of Environmental and Natural Resources*. Amsterdam, NL: Academic Press.

————. 2016b. Modeling Farmer Adaptations to Climate Change in South America: A Microbehavioral Economic Perspective. *Environmental and Ecological Statistics* 23: 1–21.

————. 2016c. The Micro-behavioral Framework for Estimating Total Damage of Global Warming on Natural Resource Enterprises with Full Adaptations. *Journal of Agricultural, Biological, and Environmental Statistics* 21: 328–347.

————. 2018. *Natural and Man-Made Catastrophes: Theories, Economics, and Policy Designs*. Wiley-Blackwell, Hobokken, NJ.

————. 2019a. *The Economics of Global Allocations of the Green Climate Fund: An Assessment from Four Scientific Traditions of Modeling Adaptation Strategies*. Cham, CH: Springer Nature.

————. 2021a. Indian Monsoon: A Tale of Indian Water Buffaloes, Goats, and High-Yield Rice. In *Climate Change and Economics: Engaging with Future Generations with Action Plans*, ed. S.N. Seo. London, UK: Palgrave Macmillan.

————. 2021b. Sublime Grasslands: A Story of the Pampas, Prairie, Steppe, and Savannas Where Animals Graze. In *Climate Change and Economics: Engaging with Future Generations with Action Plans*, ed. S.N. Seo. London, UK: Palgrave Macmillan.

————., ed. 2022. *Handbook of Behavioral Economics and Climate Change*. Cheltenham, UK: Edward Elgar.

Seo, S.N., and R. Mendelsohn. 2008. Measuring impacts and adaptations to climate change: A structural Ricardian model of African livestock management. *Agricultural Economics* 38, 151–165.

Seo, S.N., R. Mendelsohn, A. Dinar, R. Hassan, and P. Kurukulasuriya. 2009. A Ricardian Analysis of the Distribution of Climate Change Impacts on Agriculture Across Agro-Ecological Zones in Africa. *Environmental and Resource Economics* 43: 313–332.

Shaw, M.R., E.S. Zavaleta, N.R. Chiariello, E.E. Cleland, H.A. Mooney, and C.B. Field. 2002. Grassland Responses to Global Environmental Changes Suppressed by Elevated CO_2. *Science* 298 (5600): 1987–1990.

Steiger, C. 2006. Modern Beef Production in Brazil and Argentina. *Choices* 21: 105–110.

Strezepek, K., and A. McCluskey. 2006. *District Level Hydroclimatic Time Series and Scenario Analyses to Assess the Impacts of Climate Change on Regional Water Resources and Agriculture in Africa*. CEEPA Discussion Paper No. 13, Centre for Environmental Economics and Policy in Africa, University of Pretoria, Pretoria, Republic of South Africa.

Train, K. 2003. *Discrete Choice Models with Simulation*. Cambridge, UK: Cambridge University Press.

Tubiello, F.N., and F. Ewert. 2002. Simulating the Effects of Elevated CO_2 on Crops: Approaches and Applications for Climate Change. *European Journal of Agronomy* 18: 57–74.

United States Energy Information Administration (USEIA), 2015. Energy Explained. US EIA, Department of Energy, Washington, DC.

United States Energy Information Administration (US EIA). 2022. Energy Explained. US EIA, Department of Energy, Washington, DC.

von Thunen, Johann Heinrich. 1826. *Der isolirte Staat in Beziehung auf Landwirtschaft und Nationalökonomie.* Wirtschaft & Finan. [*The Isolated State* (trans. C.M. Wartenberg). Oxford/New York: Pergamon Press, 1966]. https://play.google.com/store/books/details?id=K-M2AQAAMAAJ&rdid=book-K-M2AQAAMAAJ&rdot=1.

Welch, J.R., J.R. Vincent, M. Auffhammer, P.F. Moya, A. Dobermann, and D. Dawe. 2010. Rice Yields in Tropical/subtropical Asia Exhibit Large but Opposing Sensitivities to Minimum and Maximum Temperatures. *Proceedings of the National Academy of Sciences* 107: 14562–14567.

Wilder, L.I. 1932. *Little House on the Prairie.* New York, NY: Harper & Brothers.

World Bank. 1998. *India's Dairy Revolution.* World Bank Operations Evaluation Department, #168, The World Bank, Washington, DC.

World Rangeland Learning Experience (WRANGLE). 2020. *North American Short Grass Prairie.* Tucson, AZ: College of Agriculture and Life Sciences, University of Arizona.

CHAPTER 4

Faustmann's Forest Harvest Rotation

4.1   INTRODUCTION

From the analyses of croplands and grasslands offered in the previous chapters, let's refocus our attention to another valuable as well as much cherished resources by the people on the planet: trees and forests. As in the previous chapters, the primary inquiry is how the global community should manage forest resources in the best way for humanity dynamically. The present author hopes to describe a dynamically optimal pathway over the course of a forest management by its manager.

A forest is a large land area covered predominantly by trees and their undergrowth. A forest biome on the planet comprises more than a dozen different forest types whose distributions in turn depend on, among other things, regional climates. To simplify, there are rainforests on the tropics such as the Amazon, the Congo River, and the Java Island; boreal forests in the high latitude regions such as the cold-deciduous forest hosting, *e.g.*, Douglas fir and Norwegian spruce; austral forests in the Southern Hemisphere such as the sclerophyllous (thick-leaved) forest hosting, *e.g.*, Eucalyptus (snow gum) and Fig (Banyan); the xerophytic (dry plant) forest in the arid zones hosting, *e.g.*, Joshua tree and the Saguaro (Joyce et al. 1995, 2014; Seo 2021b).

A forest, which is a big community of many different trees, has been a valuable resource to humanity from the very beginning of human civilizations, more precisely stated, even before that. The value of a forest

S. N. Seo, *The Economics of Optimal Growth Pathways*, https://doi.org/10.1007/978-3-031-20754-9_4

originates from many components and aspects of the resources thereof. The most valued forest component, including for those seeking solitude, has evolved over the course of the planet's history, which further is varied across the regions of the planet at the present time (Thoreau 1854; Peters et al. 1989; Holliday 2002).

Before the commercial extraction of fossil fuels in late nineteenth century, the value of a forest largely originated from its usage as fuelwoods, as in von Thunen's time in Europe (von Thunen 1826). Since the first arrivals of Europeans in North America until the mass production of steel, to mark the specific date, the birth of the US Steel Company in 1901, the vast forest resources that had stood in the new world largely unmanaged for thousands of years had been of great economic value to the emerging nation, especially as a provider of timber for the constructions of residential houses, railways, and shipbuilding (Misa 1995). From another historical perspective, forest resources have long been cherished for their provisions of edible and medicinal forest products to the rural communities, for example, the Sri Lankan forests and the Amazon rainforests (Peters et al. 1989; Vedeld et al. 2004; Seo et al. 2005).

Since the establishment of the United Nations Framework Convention on Climate Change (UNFCCC) in 1992, a novel concept of forest value as a store of carbon dioxide absorbed from the planet's atmosphere has been created incrementally and at the present time traded among various parties through international agreements, *e.g.*, the Reducing Emissions from Deforestation and Forest Degradation in Developing Countries (REDD+) scheme or the Green Climate Fund (GCF) (Schlesinger 1997; UNFCCC 2016; Seo 2019; Lanfranco and Seo 2022).

If you owned a forest stand, you will need to determine the best practices with which you could manage the stand (Ashton and Kelty 2018). In particular, you need to decide when you should cut the trees of the stand for sale at the market. In other words, you ought to determine a forest rotation, *i.e.*, a harvest schedule. The forest rotation is the key decision variable in forest management because trees, unlike crops, grow over many decades to many hundred years. Some trees in fact live up to a thousand years. The economic value that is generated from a forest stand hinges critically on the forest rotation. This point was first elucidated by a German forester Martin Faustmann who defined an economically optimal forest rotation (Faustmann 1849). This concept of an efficient forest rotation is central to the economics of forest management as well as a wide range of policy analyses regarding the forest economic activities (Sohngen and Mendelsohn 1998, 2003; Seo 2010).

When Gifford Pinchot learned the art of forestry in Europe, including Faustmann's, and returned home to become the first Chief of the US Forest Service at the beginning of the twentieth century, he was certainly aware of the vast forest resources of the United States when he coined the term "conservation of natural resources" which is among the most popular keywords in the environmental literature. At the same time, he was skilled in the best ways to manage them in an economically optimal manner (Pinchot 1901).

As a matter of fact, forests are, by and large, not privately owned resources. In developing countries, over 80% of forests are on public lands (Repetto and Gillis 1988; Mendelsohn 1994). These forests are the properties of the government of the respective nations and are managed by the public sector such as the US Forest Service. The public sector would endeavor to manage the forest resources in a 'socially' optimal manner which should include, among other things, the conservation value of a forest in its calculation of the benefits of a forest.

The conservation value of a forest, which arises from its function as habitats for animal species or from the ecological value of the forest, is likely greater in a mature forest, also called the old growth forest in the literature, left unmanaged for centuries by people, like the North American forests before the European conquests (Hartman 1976; Chang 1981; Pearce 1998; Laurance et al. 2012).

The Faustmann rule, to be explained in this chapter, can be applied to the management of the old growth forest by, *e.g.*, adding such conservation and ecological values to the economic value. In a similar manner, the Faustmann rotation can be applied to the management of a public forest.

The Faustmann rotation, which is an economically efficient rotation in managing forest harvests, has long been known to foresters. Nonetheless, foresters still determine the forest rotation based on physically based measures, more specifically, a biological growth function of a forest (Newman 1988, 2002; Hartwick and Olewiler 1997). The simplest such rule is cutting trees at the time when they are tallest, more precisely, at the time when the volume of the tree is at its maximum. The rule used by the US Forest Service is referred to as the Culmination of Mean Annual Increment (CMAI) which is also called the biologically Maximum Sustained Yield (MSY). These alternative rotations are inferior to the Faustmann rotation for the society, which will be clarified shortly (Samuelson 1976; Mitra and Wan Jr 1985, 1986).

On the other hand, many critics, including the conversationists, have argued that the economic forest harvest rule is a primary cause of the rapid deforestation problem of the planet (Myers 1979; Curtis et al. 2018). By cutting trees on the basis of economic benefits, they argue, the forests of the planet are shrinking at a fast rate, which they argue can be verified by various forest watch databases (FAO 2022). In responding to the critiques, this chapter will review the global forest databases and trends, which will certainly show ups and downs in the forest coverage over the past century.

This chapter will also examine the literature that seeks to clarify the factors that cause deforestation. The literature reveals that the deforestation, that is, a loss of forest areas, in developing countries occurs mostly by a conversion of forested lands into croplands (Barbier et al. 1991; Barbier and Burgess 2001). A widespread lack of private property rights on forested lands in developing countries is another key factor for harvesting trees over and beyond the economically optimal harvest (Mendelsohn 1994; Deacon 1994).

4.2   Economics of Renewable Resources

In the economics which endeavors to find the best ways to utilize the planet's natural resources for the benefit of the society and its members, it is imperative to distinguish between renewable resources and non-renewable resources from a very large basket of valued natural resources on the planet. Non-renewable resources are also referred to as exhaustible or depletable resources. The economic problems of the two categories of natural resources are much different, as will be expounded presently.

The economics of forestry, to be elaborated in this chapter, holds much importance to economists because it encapsulates the economic problems of managing renewable natural resources. A forest stand will regrow once it is cleared by a forester at one day. Therefore, the question of forest management is not to exhaust the forest stand over the course of its life but rather to harvest it at right times. Crops as well as pasturelands, explained in the previous two chapters, are also such renewable resources. But, the economic problems of managing renewable resources were not conspicuous in the expositions of the two chapters because harvest times of crops depend critically on seasons, *e.g.*, once a year in the fall.

Contrast the economics of forestry against the economics of exhaustible resources, for example, fossil fuels! The economics of fossil fuels, say, crude oil, is that of finding an optimal extraction trajectory for the depletion of the non-renewable resource whose quantity is fixed (Hotelling 1931). The stock of it is fixed 'forever,' as such, one more unit of current consumption by the society means one fewer unit of future consumption of the crude oil. The economic decision is to determine the amount of consumption for each year until the year of exhaustion, *i.e.*, the terminal year. Since alternatives to fossil fuels exist such as solar Photovoltaic (PV) technologies and nuclear fusion technologies, the exhaustion date of fossil fuels can be interpreted as the transition date to alternative fuels (Nordhaus 1973). The economics of non-renewable resources is the subject of the next chapter, Chap. 5, where the economic problems of fossil fuels are explained.

The economics of fisheries is also concerned with renewable resources, that is, fishes in the oceans. Once a certain amount of a fish species in a region is caught in one year, the fish population will regenerate and grow again as long as there are sufficient number of the fish left in the ocean region. As in the forestry, a biological growth function of a fish species is an important variable in the fishery management. However, the fishery economic problems are quite different from the forestry economic problems because of the lack of property rights in the fish harvests. Fishes are, barring any governmental regulation and international laws, harvested under open access in the oceans (Gordon 1954; Clark 1973). The fishery decision is the topic of Chap. 6.

4.3   A Forester's Harvest Rotation

Humans have utilized forest resources for a variety of uses such as timber for constructions, pulpwood for papermaking, fuelwoods for energy, fruits for food, and numerous products for medicinal benefits. These forest products are sold in the market in exchange for dollars, but some of which are consumed by the harvesters themselves. There are millions of species of trees on the planet while there are trillions of individual trees.

What is the best way to manage or utilize these forest resources? Broadly speaking, we can distinguish between a forester's harvest rule of forest products and an economist way of harvesting them. The forester's way is determined by maximizing the physical volume of the trees harvested. On the other hand, the economist's way is determined by maximizing the economic benefit from the trees harvested over an infinite time horizon. Although both groups make their decisions considering the series of harvests to be made over time during the course of the forest's life, they do so in different senses.

This section explains the forester's harvest rule with a focus on timber products. Let's begin with a forest stand growth function. A forest stand is a community of trees where individual trees are sufficiently uniform and continuously located. A forest is a collection of forest stands. In the forest stand growth function, the volume of a forest stand (V) can be expressed as a function of time (t):

$$V = V(t). \tag{4.1}$$

A typical forest stand growth function, which is a volume-age schedule, is drawn in Fig. 4.1 (Newman 1988). It assumes that the trees are planted on bare ground at time zero, which grow at the same rate and are cut at the same time. So, the growth function in Fig. 4.1 is that of a tree planted on the area as well. The V in Eq. (4.1) is more exactly the volume of wood

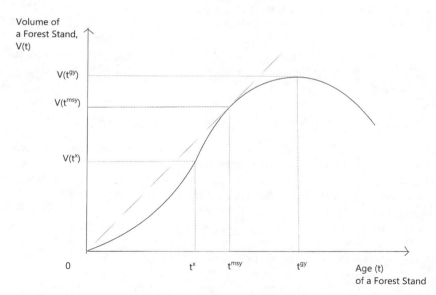

Fig. 4.1 A typical forest stand growth and a forester rotation

in the stand measured in cubic meters. Another type of a forest stand is an old growth forest which will be clarified in the next section.

Once the trees are planted on the plot, the wood volume of the stand grows at an increasing rate until time t^x. From that point on, the volume continues to grow but at a decreasing rate, up to the point t^{msy}. The wood volume reaches the maximum at that point. Thenceforth, the volume of wood in the stand decreases owing to various reasons such as old age, decay, and diseases.

For the interval between t^x and t^{msy}, the following holds:

$$V_t > 0 \text{ and } V_{tt} < 0, \tag{4.2}$$

where the subscripts denote the first-order partial derivative in the former (dV/dt) and the second-order partial derivative in the latter with regard to age t.

The tree volume function of the forest stand in Fig. 4.1 can be shifted up or down by human efforts (E). A range of forest management practices, also known as silviculture practices, affects the growth function, which includes a choice of tree density on the stand, fertilizer applications, thinning trees, clearing out dead trees, pest control, and fire control (Ashton and Kelty 2018). The stand tree volume is, incorporating the human efforts,

$$V = V(t,E). \tag{4.3}$$

Knowing that once the trees are harvested, they will start growing again following the growth function in Fig. 4.1, when should a forester cut the trees? In other words, what is the forester's rotation? The rotation refers to the time period between the formation and the harvest of the forest stand in the sense that once it is determined, it is repeated over and over again. Or, it can be referred to as the rotation interval. There are two rotations shown in Fig. 4.1 which are relied upon by foresters historically: t^{gy}, t^{msy}.

The first rotation, t^{gy}, relying on the criterion of a Maximization of the Gross Yield (MGY) is called the MGY rotation. This rotation had been used historically in some countries (Newman 1988). As shown in Fig. 4.1, the rotation is determined at the time when the growth of the stand volume is at its maximum. Formally, the MGY rotation (V^{gy}) is derived from the following decision:

$$V^{gy} = \max_t pV(t).$$

(4.4)

In the equation, p is the price per unit volume of wood. It is a constant in the model, so does not affect the decision in Eq. (4.4). The solution is obtained when the stand is atop its growth:

$$\frac{dV}{dt} = 0.$$

(4.5)

This rotation was relied upon when the objective of the decision-maker is to maximize the stock of wood in the nation. The rationale behind it may be a reduction of wood imports from other nations or just the maximization of natural capital in the nation as enthusiastically pursued by contemporary ecologists. This practice was common, in one form or another, in the forestry of Germany and other European countries before the twentieth century (Thomson 1942).

The forester's rotation relied upon by today's foresters is denoted by t^{msy} in Fig. 4.1. It is referred to as a Maximum Sustainable Yield (MSY) rotation and also a Culmination of Mean Annual Increment (CMAI) rotation. This is the criterion upon which the US Forest Service manages its timber production (Newman 1988).

Let me clarify the names. First, this rotation is called the MSY rotation because it produces the greatest physical volume of wood from the forest permanently managed. It maximizes the average annual physical yield per unit area. This rotation results in the greater production than that from the MGY rotation because the trees would grow after the harvest. Second, as shown in Fig. 4.1, the rotation is determined at the point where the straight line from the origin touches the forest stand growth function. This means that the rotation maximizes the mean annual growth of a forest stand which corresponds to the slope of the straight line, i.e., $\frac{V}{t}$. This rotation is determined at the point of CMAI, which is illustrated in Fig. 4.2.

Formally, the MSY rotation is derived from the following decision:

$$V^{msy} = \max_t \frac{pV(t)}{t}.$$

(4.6)

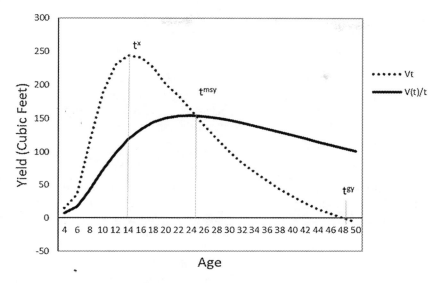

Fig. 4.2 Maximum Sustainable Yield (MSY) rotation

The first-order condition (FOC) for the solution for Eq. (4.5) is that the derivative of Eq. (4.5) with respect to t equals zero, which occurs when the marginal growth equals average growth of the forest stand:

$$V_t = \frac{V(t)}{t}.$$ (4.7a)

$$\frac{V_t}{V(t)} = \frac{1}{t}$$ (4.7b)

The Maximum Gross Yield rotation (MGY) and the Maximum Sustainable Yield (MSY) rotation are compared in Fig. 4.1. The MSY rotation is shorter than the MGY rotation. The MSY rotation is determined at the tangency between the stand volume growth function and the straight line from the origin.

The MGY rotation and the MSY rotation are compared in Fig. 4.2 as well. The dotted line is the marginal growth of the forest while the black line is the average growth of the forest, both of which are plotted against the age. The MGY rotation occurs when the marginal growth hits the horizontal axis. The MSY rotation occurs when the average growth reaches its peak, at which point the marginal growth and the average growth are equal.

In both Figs. 4.1 and 4.2, the rotation that maximizes the annual rate of growth, that is, the marginal growth of the forest stand volume, which is clear in Fig. 4.2, is marked as t^x. This is neither a theoretical nor an actually practiced rotation, as such, marked for the heuristic purpose only.

4.4   Faustmann's Optimal Harvest Rule

Faustmann formulated an economically optimal rotation of the forest stand which is superior to the foresters' rotations described in the previous section. The Faustmann rotation takes into account renewability of the forest stand. That is, according to his formulation, a forest harvest decision today is made in consideration of the fact that the first harvest affects all succeeding harvests in the future indefinitely.

Faustmann derived the rotation in 1849 in order to determine the right compensation to forest-land owners when their lands were appropriated by the government for the purpose of conversion to agriculture, which is known to foresters by such terms as soil rent, land expectation value (Newman 1988).

The objective of the Faustmann rotation is to maximize the present value obtained from the series of net incomes to be generated indefinitely into the future from the forest stand:

$$V^* = \max_t \left\{ \left[pV(t)e^{-\gamma t} - \omega E \right] \left(1 + e^{-\gamma t} + e^{-2\gamma t} + e^{-3\gamma t} + \bullet \bullet \bullet \right) \right\} \qquad (4.8a)$$

$$= \max_t \left\{ \left[pV(t)e^{-\gamma t} - \omega E \right] / \left(1 - e^{-\gamma t} \right) \right\}. \qquad (4.8b)$$

In the above equations, the total effort, E, is an index of the range of forestry efforts and practices introduced in Eq. (4.3) while ω is the cost of each unit of the effort. The efforts and the cost of the efforts occur today while the forest income is earned at the time of harvest, t, both of which explain the terms inside the bracket in Eqs. (4.8a) and (4.8b). The cost structure, however, can be modified without any loss of generality of the above equations. A possible modification can be, to give an example, that there is a fixed cost of planting at the initial time period and the cost of harvesting at the harvest time.

In the Faustmann formulation, the rotation thus found determines all future harvest times, that is to say, not just a single harvest time: t, $2t$, $3t$, and so on. The future revenues and costs are discounted back to their values at the present time using a market interest (discount) rate, γ. This is so because the rotation decision is made at the present time.

What does the Faustmann rotation look like? To explain this, let's start with the first-order condition (FOC) for the optimal solution with regard to the problem in Eq. (4.8a):

$$dV^*\!\!\Big/\!\!_{dt} = \frac{\left\{\left(1-e^{-rt}\right)\left[pV_t - \gamma pV(t)\right] - \gamma\left[pV(t)e^{-rt} - \omega E\right]\right\}}{\left(1-e^{-\gamma t}\right)^2} = 0. \quad (4.9)$$

$$\frac{V_t}{\left[V(t) - \omega E\!\Big/\!_{p}\right]} = \gamma\!\!\Big/\!\!_{\left(1-e^{-rt}\right)} \quad (4.10)$$

Equation (4.10) is a rearrangement of the FOC in Eq. (4.9). The Faustmann rotation can be calculated by applying the formula in Eq. (4.10) to the empirical data, for example, on the Loblolly pine in Southern United States or Douglas fir (Schumacher and Coile 1960). In Fig. 4.3 below, the Faustmann rotation will be compared with the foresters' rotations using the empirical forestry data on the Southern pine.

Before that, let me clarify the optimality condition. A further rearrangement of Eq. 4.10 reveals the economic implications of the Faustmann rotation:

$$pV_t = \gamma\left(pV(t) - \omega E\right)/\left(1-e^{-rt}\right) \quad (4.11)$$

$$pV_t = \gamma pV(t) + \gamma\left\{\left[pV(t)e^{-\gamma t} - \omega E\right]/\left(1-e^{-rt}\right)\right\} \quad (4.12)$$

Note that the term inside the parentheses on the right-hand side (RHS) of Eq. (4.12) is the same as the maximand in Eq. (4.8b). Replacing it with V^*,

$$pV_t = \gamma pV(t) + \gamma V^*. \quad (4.13)$$

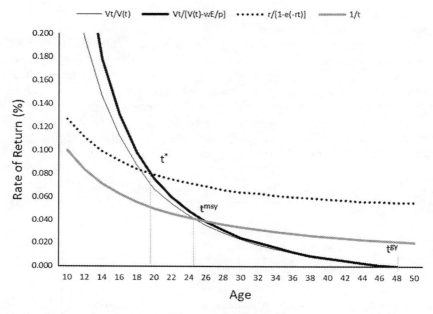

Fig. 4.3   The Faustmann rotation versus the Forester's rotations

Equation (4.13) states that the value of waiting for one more period (left-hand side) is equal to the cost of waiting for one more period (right-hand side) at the optimal solution. The left-hand side (LHS) is the value of waiting one more period because the forest stand grows by V_t whose sale price is p per unit.

The right-hand side (RHS) is the cost of waiting one more period which has two components: the cost of holding the trees and the cost of holding the land. The first component is the cost of holding the forest stand, which is the first term on the RHS of Eq. (4.13), that is, $\gamma p V(t)$. This is the amount of interest that can be earned by cutting the trees at the present period, selling them, and reinvesting the revenue thus generated at the market interest rate for one period (Fisher 1930).

The second component is the cost of holding the land on which the forest stand stands, which is the second component of the RHS of Eq. (4.13). This is the rent you can earn by leasing the land in exchange for the land rent for one period, that is, γV^*, which would become possible if the trees were removed from the stand today.

How does the Faustmann rotation compare with the two forester's rotations explained in the preceding section? The three rotations are shown in Fig. 4.3, relying on the Southern pine data mentioned above (Schumacher and Coile 1960; Newman 1988). There are four nonlinear lines in the figure, the exact functional relation of each of which is explained in the figure legend.

The Maximum Gross Yield (MGY) rotation is marked by t^{gy}, which occurs at the point where marginal growth is zero. The Maximum Sustainable Yield (MSY) rotation is marked by t^{msy}, which occurs when Eq. (4.7b) is satisfied. The Faustmann rotation is marked by t^*, which occurs when Eq. (4.10) is satisfied.

Note that, for the Southern pine data, the MGY rotation is roughly 48 years, the MSY rotation is roughly 25 years, and the Faustmann rotation is roughly 20 years. The following relationship holds for the Southern pine forestry but also broadly across different types of forest management:

$$t^* < t^{msy} < t^{gy}. \tag{4.14}$$

Equation (4.14) states that the Faustmann rotation interval is shorter than the other physically based rotations relied upon by foresters. The Faustmann rotation is superior because it allows the manager to harvest the trees earlier than the other rotations, which again makes it possible for her/him to invest the revenue into an interest-earning financial asset on the one hand and to regrow the cut trees in the stand at a higher growth rate on the other hand.

The gap between the Faustmann rotation and the forester's rotation (specifically, the MSY rotation) becomes larger, the higher the market interest rate. The lower the interest rate, the smaller the gap between the Faustmann rotation and the forester's rotation. Put differently, the relationship in Eq. (4.14) holds even under variable interest rates.

4.5   Extensions of the Faustmann Rotation

4.5.1   An Old Growth Forest

The above-described Faustmann model may not appear to be realistic to you if you are a forester or grew up in a forested region. First of all, it is a model of a bare land upon which individual trees are planted at the same time. Therefore, all trees are of the same age when they are cut according to the Faustmann rotation. In a real-life forest management, the trees on the forest stand can be well past the Faustmann rotation interval, for example, a mature forest. The mature forest in which trees have been left unmanaged for a very long time by people, say, for centuries, is called an old growth forest. In the old growth forest, individual trees are of different ages and also of different species.

The simple Faustmann model described in the preceding section is still applicable to the old growth forest management. Let's consider two scenarios. The first scenario is a clear cutting of the stand, after which the forestland is managed according to the Faustmann rotation. The second scenario is a selective harvesting, beginning from the older trees, which is known as a selective logging in forestry (Chang 1981; Ashton and Kelty 2018).

For the sake of simplicity, let me explain the clear-cutting scenario further. In this scenario, the trees are clear cut at the initial time period, from which the income is earned at that single time period. Let's say that the net revenue is US$ K. Since the future rotations are independent of the one-time net revenue, the future rotations are not affected by the clear cutting. Mathematically, it is equivalent to adding US$ K to the objective function in Eq. (4.8a), which leads to the following modified objective function of the Faustmann model:

$$V^* = \max_{s}\left\{K + \left[pV(s)e^{-\gamma s} - \omega E\right]\left(1 + e^{-\gamma s} + e^{-2\gamma s} + e^{-3\gamma s} + \bullet \bullet \bullet\right)\right\}. \quad (4.15)$$

4.5.2   Non-Timber Forest Products (NTFPs)

The second weakness of the simple Faustmann model is that it is a timber-based model. In reality, a forest offers more than the timber including sawlogs and pulpwood. The forest products other than the timber are referred to collectively as the Non-Timber Forest Products (NTFPs) in the literature. The NTPFs include edible fruits such as, to mention just some, cacao, Brazil nut, and persimmon; wild foods such as, to name just some, mushrooms, birds, honey, and spices. The NTPFs also include fuel woods, fodder for animals, medicinal plants, oils, fibers, and latex for rubber (Peters et al. 1989).

The value of the NTFPs that a forest stand offers can be thought of as a function of time from a harvest to the next harvest. Let's assume that a forester can earn US$ F(n) at year n from the sale of NTFPs from the forest stand. Then, the present value (PV) of the revenues from the NTFPs at time t can be calculated as follows in Eq. (4.16a), which is then inserted to the original Faustmann model in Eq. (4.8b) to yield Eq. (4.16b) (Hartman 1976):

$$PV\_ntfp = \int_0^t F(n)e^{-\gamma n}dn. \tag{4.16a}$$

$$V^* = \max_t \left\{ \left[pV(t)e^{-\gamma t} - \omega E + \int_0^t F(n)e^{-\gamma n}dn \right] / \left(1 - e^{-\gamma t}\right) \right\}. \tag{4.16b}$$

4.5.3   Climate and Ecological Value

Other than the NTFPs, there are many valuable forest services that are not traded in the market, *ergo* not valued. These are referred to as the non-market value of forest services. An often-cited example is the value of a forest as a species habitat. Forests offer a habitat for many species of animals, especially birds (Pearce 1998; Laurance et al. 2012).

Another example of the non-market value of the forest is its function as a carbon sink. It absorbs carbon dioxide from the atmosphere *via* the photosynthesis of the trees, which removes the Earth-heating greenhouse gases (Schlesinger 1997). The carbon sink value of the forest is not valued in the market while regional as well as global institutions are attempting to establish a carbon price system in which these forest services are valued and paid to the owners (CARB 2019; UNFCCC 2016). A compensation scheme also emerged *via* the Green Climate Fund, *e.g.*, to the Brazil's Amazon rainforests (Seo 2019; Lanfranco and Seo 2022).

The simple Faustmann model can be modified to include the non-market value of the forest services in the same way as the NTFP value of the forest is incorporated *via* Eqs. (4.16a) and (4.16b). Having said that, a major challenge arises in the case of the non-market value, which is onerous to fully address: there are no market prices that can be applied to put a value on each of these non-market services offered by a forest (Peters et al. 1989). Economists have strived for over four decades to develop a variety of methods for putting a value on the non-market services (Mendelsohn and Olmstead 2009). Broadly speaking, economists rely on either revealed preferences in the market or stated preferences in a survey (Hanemann 1994). Therefore, the value of a non-market forest service derived from an application of one of these economic valuation techniques is only an indirect value also with large uncertainty (Freeman III et al. 2014).

How would an inclusion of the non-timber value of the forests, both the NTPFs and the carbon/ecological value, affect the optimal forest rotation interval in the Faustmann model? If the share of the non-timber value in the total forest value is small, the optimal rotation interval in the modified model will approach the initial Faustmann rotation (Calish et al. 1978).

If the share is large, on the other hand, the optimal rotation interval in the modified model will become either longer or shorter than the initial Faustmann rotation. Why does the large share of the non-timber value not always result in a longer forest rotation interval? One of the reasons is that, although an optimal timber-based rotation interval tends to be many decades long, many non-timber forest products are appropriated multiple times per year or once every two years. The value of these services can reach a peak rather quickly, that is, before the optimal timber-based rotation. Another reason is that, when there are multiple forest stands managed by a forester or another in the same region, the non-timber value of a single forest stand as a species habit is minimal as long as birds can nest on adjacent forest stands (Calish et al. 1978). An inclusion of the carbon dioxide storage value would certainly lengthen the optimal forest rotation if the carbon storage depends on the age but not if it depends on the volume growth rate.

4.6   A Deforestation Critique

Critics of the economically optimal forest rotation such as the Faustmann rotation argue that the economic incentives-driven forest management have resulted in a rapid rate of deforestation in the tropics. This is especially so when the numerous forest services other than the timber supply are not valued in the market, they argue. This leads to a shorter forest rotation as well as an easier conversion of a forestland into another economic activity, most notably, crop cultivation or cattle ranching (Hartman 1976; Repetto and Gillis 1988; Pearce 1998; Laurance et al. 2012; Curtis et al. 2018).

Tropical deforestation began to receive international attention from the late 1970s and the early 1980s. Scientists called the world's attention on the potential negative consequences of a tropical forest destruction, which included biodiversity loss, climate change, and loss of traditional livelihoods by indigenous peoples (Myers 1979; Peters et al. 1989; Barbier et al. 1991).

During the 1980s, the loss of forests observed in the tropics was striking. According to the Food and Agriculture Organization (FAO)'s Global Forest Resource Assessment, the forest cover loss amounted to 41 million hectares in Africa, 39 million hectares in Asia Pacific, and 74 million hectares in Latin America and the Caribbean during 1980–1990 period (Barbier and Burgess 2001; FAO 2022). For that decade alone, roughly 10% of the tropical forest cover was lost.

In response, economists analyzed the various survey data collected from the tropical regions to uncover the reasons for the rapid tropical deforestation. Scientists similarly analyzed the satellite data on land use as well as biome changes in the tropics. Both groups observed that tropical forests are converted primarily to crop cultivation as well as animal ranching (Barbier and Burgess 2001; Margulis 2004; Curtis et al. 2018). Underneath these apparent observations of changes lied the several leading causes such as ill-defined property rights, public sector forests, and unaccounted non-market values (Repetto and Gillis 1988; Peters et al. 1989; Mendelsohn 1994; Pearce 1998).

By the decade of the 2010s, tropical deforestation gained renewed attention from the international community owing to the international climate change negotiations led by the United Nations Framework Convention on Climate Change (UNFCCC) (UNFCCC 1992). A harvest of trees is a source of greenhouse gas emissions (GHGs), specifically carbon dioxide, which again contributes to the heating of the planet. During the 1990s, the net amount of greenhouse gas emissions released from the land use changes, which is largely from forest emissions and forestland conversions, was estimated to be as large as 6 giga tons of CO_2 annually ($gtCO_2$), which accounted for a quarter of the total greenhouse gas emissions during that decade (Houghton 2008; Houghton et al. 2012). The gross amount of greenhouse gas emissions from the deforestation during the 1990s, that is, without carbon dioxide sink by forests, was most likely in the range of 10–14 gt CO_2 per year, roughly about a half of the total greenhouse gas emissions during that decade (GCP 2021).

The deforestation critics of the economically optimal forest harvest rail against the economic incentives-driven conversions of forestlands into commercial lands such as industrial logging, agriculture, cattle ranching, and the roads built to connect the products and people to the market.

One of such critics can be found in the "Glasgow Leaders' Declaration on Forests and Land Use" which was signed during the 2021 Conference of Parties (COPs) of the United Nations Framework Convention on Climate Change (UNFCCC 2021). The declaration called for a complete halt to deforestation by 2030. The New York Declaration on Forests (NYDF) which was initiated in 2014 called for the same (NYDF 2021).

4.7   The Pathways of the Planet's Forest

Many questions arise regarding the deforestation critiques. Why do the deforestation critics such as the Glasgow Leaders' Declaration and the New York Declaration push for a halt in deforestation? Is it a rational conclusion expected from the influential international organizations? On the contrary, should the planet pursue an economically optimal forest harvest and utilization while fully recognizing the afore-described renewable nature of forest resources?

It is not a small task in any way to tackle these questions comprehensively. Here the present author will approach them from three plus one angles: recent deforestation rates, recent carbon dioxide emissions trends, and the current distributions of the planet's forests. The fourth angle is the recent tree planting movement and initiatives, which will be covered in the next section.

Although the deforestation concerns emerged during the 1980s and 1990s when the rate of deforestation was high, recent deforestation trends are rather different from those early trends. This is depicted in Fig. 4.4 which shows four trends, based on the FAO's Global Forest Resource Assessment: global forests, Brazilian forests, Indonesian forests, and global woodlands (FAO 2022). The global forest cover is at around 4 billion hectares globally, which has been rather stable during the past 3 decades since 1990. Additionally, the global woodland cover is at around 1 billion hectares globally, which has also been rather stable during the same period.

The only big change revealed in the figure is found in the Amazon (Brazilian) rainforest cover. It declined substantially from roughly 600 million hectares in 1990 to roughly 500 million hectares in 2010. Even the Amazon rainforest cover, however, appears to have stopped its decline by 2010. During the most recent decade, the forest cover appears to be stable from 2010 to 2020.

The coverage of another tropical rainforest shown in the figure is that of the Indonesian rainforest. Its forest coverage is roughly 100 million

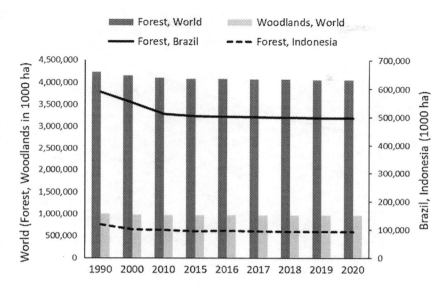

Fig. 4.4 Trajectories of global deforestation over the past 30 years. (Note: FAO's Global Forest Resource Assessment 2022)

hectares. During the 1990s, its coverage declined but not as much as the Amazon rainforest's shrinking during the decade. Thenceforth, it appears to have stabilized as well.

The examination in Fig. 4.4 of the forest coverage provided by the FAO's Global Forest Resource Assessment tells us that the concern on global deforestation in 2020 should not be as serious as those put forth during the 1980s and 1990s by concerned scientists (Myers 1979; Barbier et al. 1991; Pearce 1998).

Neither do the international forest data illustrated in Fig. 4.4 render a rationale for a vehement push by the global community for a complete halt to global deforestation. However, we should not ignore the possibility that the concerns and works by the early pioneers on this issue may have contributed to a slowdown in the rate of deforestation during the recent decade.

The second response to the deforestation critique is illustrated in Fig. 4.5 which shows the trajectory of net land use emissions of carbon dioxide during the past four decades. The net land use emissions is defined as "the difference between the carbon dioxide emissions, primarily from

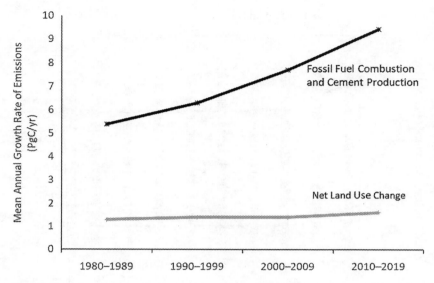

Fig. 4.5 A trajectory of carbon dioxide emissions from deforestation. (Note: IPCC 2021)

deforestation, and the carbon dioxide removals, primarily from abandonment of agricultural land" in the Global Carbon Project (GCP) report (GCP 2021). The carbon dioxide emissions from land use change have been stable during this time period at roughly 1.5 PgC per year. For your reference, the Peta gram of Carbon (PgC) is equivalent to a giga ton of carbon (gtC). It is the net emissions, that is, the amount of carbon dioxide emissions minus the amount of carbon dioxide absorption. The data in the figure is what is presented in the most recent Intergovernmental Panel on Climate Change report (IPCC 2021).

The trajectory of land use emissions shown in the figure is striking when it is compared with the trajectory of the carbon emissions from the fossil fuel combustion and cement production (FFCCP). The latter has nearly doubled during the four decades from roughly 5 PgC/yr to 10 PgC/yr.

The contrast between the two trajectories is even more remarkable when the data period is extended further back to the 1960s. According to the Global Carbon Project (GCP), the carbon emissions from the FFCCP stood at about 2 PgC/yr in 1960, which has continued to increase to about 10 PgC/yr in 2020. By contrast, the net carbon emissions from the land use change stood at about 2 PgC/yr in 1960, about the same amount of carbon emissions as the FFCCP emissions, which has steadily declined to about 1 PgC/yr in 2020 (GCP 2021).

The analysis of the IPCC estimates and the GCP estimates reveals that the concern on the carbon dioxide emissions from deforestation driven by the economic motives such as that in the Faustmann forest rotation is somewhat overblown. Instead, the GCP data shows that the land use accounts for about 9.9 $gtCO_2$ absorption, not emissions, annually from the atmosphere (GCP 2021).

The third response to the deforestation critique is to show how forests and woodlands on the planet are flourishing in a variety of types under a wide range of soil, climate, and water conditions (Matthews 1983, 1999). Figure 4.6 illustrates the distribution of the three types of rainforests: tropical, subtropical, and temperate. Figure 4.7 illustrates the distribution of other types of forests than the rainforests.

The equatorial zones of the planet are covered by the three famed tropical rainforests: Amazon rainforests in South America, Indonesian rainforests in South Asia, and Congo rainforests in Sub-Saharan Africa. Subtropical rainforests are found in the border regions among Argentina, Paraguay, Uruguay, and Brazil, as well as in Australia. Temperate rainforests are located in New Zealand, Australia, and southern Chile.

The distributions of the other types of forests, shown in Fig. 4.7, reveal many different types of forests: broad-leaved forests, cold-deciduous forests, needle-leaved forests, drought-deciduous forests, xeromorphic forests, and woodlands. Noticeable is that even the world's coldest zones, *e.g.*, Siberia, have different types of boreal (meaning "of the North") forests such as cold-deciduous forests and needle-leaved forests. North American forests are also largely evergreen needle-leaved forests and different types of deciduous forests.

Drier zones of the world are covered by drought-deciduous forests in India, xeromorphic (meaning "water conserving") forests in southern Brazil, and woodlands in Sub-Sahara and northern Australia.

The forests in Australia, an austral (meaning "of the South") forest, are broad-leaved forests, *e.g.*, sclerophyllous (thick-leaved) forests, and woodlands. Broad-leaved forests are also seen in subtropical regions such as Southeast Asia and southern China.

The diversity of the forest biomes across the planet means that the forest resources are highly likely resilient against the global scale climate

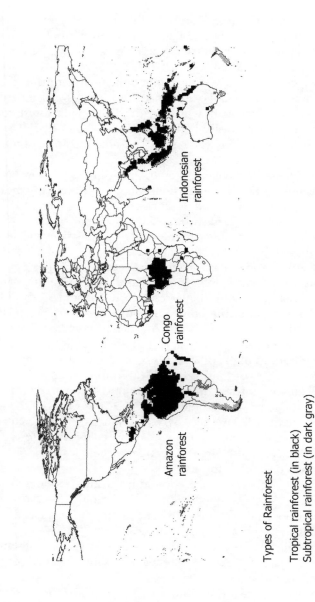

Types of Rainforest

Tropical rainforest (in black)
Subtropical rainforest (in dark gray)
Temperate/subpolar rainforest (in gray)

Fig. 4.6 Rainforests of the planet

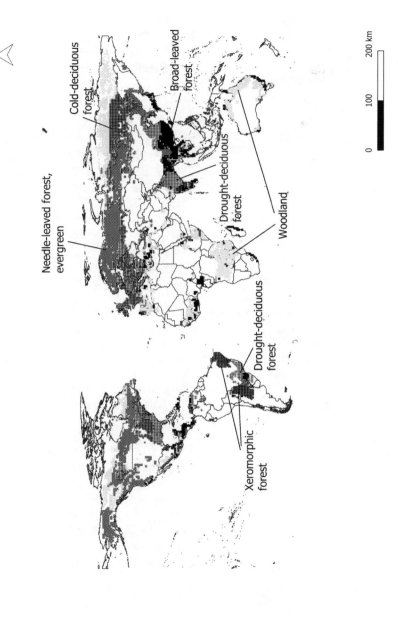

Fig. 4.7 Forests and woodlands of the planet

change. A forest biome may disappear from one region but another forest biome may spring up in that region if the global climate system were to shift in a gradual way over the coming centuries (Sohngen and Mendelsohn 1998). Picturesquely speaking, red maple may disappear from New England but may reemerge in Canada if the climate were to warm in North America (Joyce et al. 2001).

4.8   Concluding Remarks: Tree Planting Initiatives

The fourth rejoinder to the deforestation critique is, given here as the conclusion of this chapter, on the recent various initiatives to plant trees nationwide undertaken by different countries (Seo 2021a).

In July 2019, it was reported that Ethiopia planted 350 million trees in a single day as a nationwide tree planting initiative (UNEP 2019). This was a forest coverage reclamation project as well as a climate policy action. The country's forest land has shrunk from 30% of the country at the beginning of the twentieth century to less than 4% today. Through the Warsaw Framework of the United Nations, developing countries such as Ethiopia can ask for a financial payment for the increased forest coverage and forest carbon stocks (UNFCCC 2016).

Similarly, in August 2019, the State of Uttar Pradesh, the most populous State of India, planted 220 million trees in a single day (USA Today 2019). It was reported one million people participated in the tree planting from about 60,000 villages. This was a climate policy action by the country whose one of the commitments to the Paris Climate Agreement in 2015 was to keep one-third of the country land areas under tree cover (UNFCCC 2015; Seo 2019).

Finally, the Trillion Trees Vision is a joint venture by the three conservation agencies—BirdLife International, World Wildlife Fund, Wildlife Conservation Society—which has a goal of planting one trillion trees by 2050 as a climate action. It connects donors to forest ventures (Trillion Trees 2022). Notably, then President Trump announced in 2020 that the US would join this effort (The Hill 2020).

For our reference, how many trees are on the planet? According to one study, there are roughly 3 trillion trees on Earth, of which 1.3 trillion trees are in tropical and subtropical regions (Crowther et al. 2015). Although the range of uncertainty around this estimate is large, it indicates that planting one trillion additional trees by 2050 is an ambitious project.

A tree planting initiative may not be a novel phenomenon. Neither is it planned on private lands. Notwithstanding, it can be an effective program for maintaining a forest cover of a nation in certain circumstances. For example, the forest areas lost by wildfire or the mountainous regions with the dense trees lost by a war or civil conflicts can be restored rather 'speedily' through such a national tree planting effort. Similarly, as in the case of Ethiopia, the lost forest lands due to multi-decadal climate and weather fluctuations can be restored by such an effort (Janowiak 1988).

It takes multiple years for the planted trees to survive in the soil and climate conditions of the planting areas. It may be worthwhile for developing countries to designate one day in early Spring time as a national tree planting day. A tree planting in the autumn is not effective because the planted trees will not have time to take roots before a harsh winter. A tree planting program may be developed as a school program for the elementary and secondary schools. For the program, one day may be devoted to the education of tree and plant ecology as well as the care of trees. A well-developed program would be able to achieve many benefits, including schoolchildren education, forest landscape management, and material benefits that mature trees give.

References

Ashton, Mark S., and M.J. Kelty. 2018. *The Practice of Silviculture: Applied Forest Ecology.* Hoboken, NJ: John Wiley & Sons.

Barbier, E.B., and J.C. Burgess. 2001. The Economics of Tropical Deforestation. *Journal of Economic Surveys* 15: 413–433.

Barbier, E.B., J.C. Burgess, and A. Markandya. 1991. The Economics of Tropical Deforestation. *Ambio* 20: 55–58.

California Air Resources Board (CARB). 2019. *Assembly Bill (AB) Compliance Offset Program.* Sacramento, CA: ARB. https://ww3.arb.ca.gov/cc/capandtrade/offsets/offsets.htm.

Calish, S., R.D. Fight, and D.E. Teeguarden. 1978. How do Nontimber Values Affect Douglas-fir Rotations? *Journal of Forestry* 76: 217–222.

Chang, S.J. 1981. Determination of the Optimal Growing Stock and Cutting Cycle for an Uneven-aged Stand. *Forest Science* 27: 739–744.

Clark, C.W. 1973. The Economics of Over Exploitation. *Science* 181: 630–634.

Crowther, T.W., H.B. Glick, K.R. Covey, C. Bettigole, D.S. Maynard, S.M. Thomas, J.R. Smith, et al. 2015. Mapping Tree Density at a Global Scale. *Nature* 525 (7568): 201–205.

Curtis, P.G., C.M. Slay, N.L. Harris, A. Tyukavina, and M.C. Hansen. 2018. Classifying Drivers of Global Forest Loss. *Science* 361 (6407): 1108–1111.

Deacon, R.T. 1994. Deforestation and the Rule of Law in a Cross-section of Countries. *Land Economics* 70: 414–430.

Faustmann, Martin. 1849. On the Determination of the Value Which Forest Land and Immature Stands Pose for Forestry. In *Martin Faustmann and the Evolution of Discounted Cash Flow*, ed. M. Gane. Oxford, England: Oxford Institute. [1968, Paper 42].

Fisher, Irving. 1930. *The Theory of Interest*. New York, NY: Macmillan.

Food and Agriculture Organization (FAO). 2022. *Global Forest Resource Assessment*. Rome: FAO. https://fra-data.fao.org/.

Freeman, A.M., III, J.A. Herriges, and C.L. Cling. 2014. *The Measurements of Environmental and Resource Values: Theory and Practice*. Washington, DC: RFF Press.

Global Carbon Project (GCP). 2021. Global Carbon Budget 2021. www.globalcarbonproject.org/carbonbudget/index.htm.

Gordon, H.S. 1954. The Economic Theory of a Common-property Resource: The Fishery. *The Journal of Political Economy* 62: 124–142.

Hanemann, W.M. 1994. Valuing the Environment Through Contingent Valuation. *Journal of Economic Perspectives* 8: 19–43.

Hartman, R. 1976. The Harvesting Decision When the Standing Forest Has Value. *Economic Inquiry* 14 (1): 52–58.

Hartwick, J.M., and N.D. Olewiler. 1997. *The Economics of Natural Resource Use*. 2nd ed. New York, NY: Pearson.

Holliday, I. 2002. *A Field Guide to Australian Trees*. 3rd ed. Australia: New Holland Publishers.

Hotelling, H. 1931. The Economics of Exhaustible Resources. *Journal of Political Economy* 39: 137–175.

Houghton, R.A. 2008. Carbon Flux to the Atmosphere From Land-use Changes: 1850–2005. In *Compendium of Data on Global Change*, ed. A. Trends. Oak Ridge, TN: Carbon Dioxide Information Analysis Center. Oak Ridge National Laboratory, U.S. Department of Energy.

Houghton, R.A., J.I. House, J. Pongratz, G.R. van der Werf, R.S. DeFries, M.C. Hansen, C. Le Quéré, and N. Ramankutty. 2012. Carbon Emissions from Land Use and Land-cover Change. *Biogeosciences* 9 (12): 5125–5142.

Intergovernmental Panel on Climate Change (IPCC). 2021. Chapter 5: Global Carbon and Other Biogeochemical Cycles and Feedbacks. In *Climate Change 2021: The Physical Science Basis, The Sixth Assessment Report of the IPCC*. Cambridge, UK: Cambridge University Press.

Janowiak, J.E. 1988. An Investigation of Interannual Rainfall Variability in Africa. *Journal of Climate* 1: 240–255.

Joyce, L.A., J.R. Mills, L.S. Heath, A.D. McGuire, R.W. Haynes, and R.A. Birdsey. 1995. Forest Sector Impacts from Changes in Forest Productivity Under Climate Change. *Journal of Biogeography* 22: 703–713.

Joyce, L.A., J. Amber, S. McNulty, V. Dale, A. Hansen, L. Irland, R. Neilson, and K. Skog. 2001. Potential Consequences of Climate Variability and Change for the Forests of the United States. In *National Assessment Synthesis Team Climate Change Impacts on the United States: The Potential Consequences of Climate Variability and Change*. Cambridge: Cambridge University Press.

Joyce, L.A., S.W. Running, D.D. Breshears, V.H. Dale, R.W. Malmsheimer, R.N. Sampson, B. Sohngen, and C.W. Woodall. 2014. Ch. 7: Forests. In *Climate Change Impacts in the United States: The Third National Climate Assessment*, ed. J.M. Melillo, T. Richmond, and G.W. Yohe, 175–194. U.S. Global Change Research Program.

Lanfranco, B., and S.N. Seo. 2022. An Analysis of Biogas, Biomass, Forest Credits, and Renewable Energy Programs in Brazil and Argentina Supported by the Green Climate Fund. In *Handbook of Behavioural Economics and Climate Change*, ed. S.N. Seo. Cheltenham, UK: Edward Elgar.

Laurance, W.F., D.C. Useche, J. Rendeiro, et al. 2012. Averting Biodiversity Collapse in Tropical Forest Protected Areas. *Nature* 489: 290–294.

Margulis, S. 2004. *Causes of Deforestation of the Brazilian Amazon*. World Bank Working Paper No. 22, The World Bank, Washington, DC.

Matthews, E. 1983. Global Vegetation and Land Use: New High-resolution Data Bases for Climate Studies. *Journal of Climate and Applied Meteorology* 22 (3): 474–487.

———. 1999. *Global Vegetation Types, 1971–1982* (Matthews). Oak Ridge, TN: Oak Ridge National Laboratory. https://doi.org/10.3334/ORNLDAAC/419.

Mendelsohn, R. 1994. Property Rights and Tropical Deforestation. *Oxford Economic Papers* 46: 750–756.

Mendelsohn, R., and S. Olmstead. 2009. The Economic Valuation of Environmental Amenities and Disamenities: Methods and Applications. *Annual Review of Environment and Resources* 34 (1): 325–347.

Misa, T.J. 1995. *A Nation of Steel: The Making of Modern America, 1865–1925*. Baltimore, MD: Johns Hopkins University Press.

Mitra, T., and H.Y. Wan Jr. 1985. Some Theoretical Results on the Economics of Forestry. *Review of Economic Studies* 52 (2): 263–282.

———. 1986. On the Faustmann Solution to the Forest Management Problem. *Journal of Economic Theory* 40 (2): 229–249.

Myers, Norman. 1979. *The Sinking Ark: A New Look at the Problem of Disappearing Species*. Oxford, UK: Pergamon Press.

New York Declaration on Forests (NYDF). 2021. https://forestdeclaration.org/resources/the-new-york-declaration-on-forests/.

Newman, D.H. 1988. *The Optimal Forest Rotation: A Discussion and Annotated Bibliography.* General Technical Report 48, Southeastern Forest Experiment Station, Forest Service, USDA.

———. 2002. Forestry's Golden Rule and the Development of the Optimal Forest Rotation Literature. *Journal of Forest Economics* 8: 5–28.

Nordhaus, W.D. 1973. The Allocation of Energy Resources. *Brookings Papers on Economic Activity* 1973: 529–576.

Pearce, D. 1998. Can Non-market Values Save the Tropical Forests? In *Tropical Rain Forest: A Wider Perspective*, ed. F.B. Goldsmith. Dordrecht: Springer.

Peters, C.M., A.W. Gentry, and R.O. Mendelsohn. 1989. Valuation of an Amazonian Rainforest. *Nature* 339 (6227): 655–656.

Pinchot, Gifford. 1901. *The Profession of Forestry: An Address to Yale University Students.* The Forest History Society. https://foresthistory.org/wp-content/uploads/2017/01/Pinchot_Forestry_.pdf.

Repetto, R., and M. Gillis. 1988. *Public Policy and the Misuse of Forest Resources.* Cambridge, UK: Cambridge University Press.

Samuelson, Paul. 1976. Economics of Forestry in an Evolving Society. *Economic Inquiry* 13: 466–492.

Schlesinger, W.H. 1997. *Biogeochemistry: An Analysis of Global Change.* 2nd ed. San Diego, CA: Academic Press.

Schumacher, F., and T. Coile. 1960. *Growth and Yields of Natural Stands of the Southern Pines.* Durham, NC: T.S. Coile Inc.

Seo, S.N. 2010. Managing Forests, Livestock, and Crops Under Global Warming: A Microeconometric Analysis of Land Use Changes in Africa. *Australian Journal of Agricultural and Resource Economics* 54: 239–258.

———. 2019. *The Economics of Global Allocations of the Green Climate Fund: An Assessment from Four Scientific Traditions of Modeling Adaptation Strategies.* Cham, CH: Springer Nature.

———. 2021a. *Climate Change and Economics: Engaging with Future Generations with Action Plans.* London, UK: Palgrave Macmillan.

———. 2021b. Giving Forests: A Tale of Amazon Rainforests and Congo River Forests. In *Climate Change and Economics: Engaging with Future Generations with Action Plans.* London, UK: Palgrave Macmillan.

Seo, S.N., R. Mendelsohn, and M. Munasinghe. 2005. Climate Change and Agriculture in Sri Lanka: A Ricardian Valuation. *Environment and Development Economics* 10: 581–596.

Sohngen, B., and R. Mendelsohn. 1998. Valuing the Impact of Largescale Ecological Change in a Market: The Effect of Climate Change on US Timber. *American Economic Review* 88: 686–710.

———. 2003. An Optimal Control Model of Forest Carbon Sequestration. *American Journal of Agricultural Economics* 85: 448–457.

The Hill. 2020, January 21. *Trump Announces the US Will Join 1 Trillion Tree Initiative*. Washington, DC: The Hill.

Thomson, Roy B. 1942. *An Examination of Basic Principles of Comparative Forest Valuation*. Bulletin 6, Duke University School of Forestry, Durham, NC. 99 pp.

Thoreau, H.D. 1854. *Walden; Or, Life in the Woods*. Boston, MA: Ticknor and Fields.

Trillion Trees. 2022. Why Trillion Trees. https://trilliontrees.org/why-trillion-trees/.

United Nations Environment Programme (UNEP). 2019. *Ethiopia Plants over 350 Million Trees in a Day, Setting New World Record*. Nairobi, KE: UNEP. Published on August 2, 2019.

United Nations Framework Convention on Climate Change (UNFCCC). 1992. *United Nations Framework Convention on Climate Change*. New York, NY: UNFCCC.

———. 2015. *The Paris Agreement*. New York, NY: UNFCCC.

———. 2016. *Key Decisions Relevant for Reducing Emissions from Deforestation and Forest Degradation in Developing Countries (REDD +)*. New York, NY: UNFCCC.

———. 2021. *Glasgow Leaders' Declaration on Forests and Land Use*. Glasgow, UK: COP 26, UNFCCC.

USA Today. 2019. Indians Plant 220 Million Trees in Single Day to Combat Climate Change. August 12.

Vedeld, P., A. Angelsen, E. Sjaastad, and G.K. Berg. 2004. *Counting on the Environment. Forest Incomes and the Rural Poor*. Environmental Economics Series #98, World Bank, Washington, DC.

von Thunen, J.H. 1826. *The Isolated State* (C.M. Wartenberg, trans.). Oxford/New York: Pergamon. [1966].

CHAPTER 5

Hotelling's Fossil Fuel Economics

5.1 Introduction

This chapter turns to non-renewable resources, alternatively called exhaustible resources or depletable resources. The previous three chapters were all concerned with renewable resources: crop farming in Chap. 2, land uses and grasslands in Chap. 3, and forest management in Chap. 4. Of a multiplicity of depletable resources of the planet, this chapter focuses on fossil fuels. There are many other non-renewable resources, including some rare earth minerals (Haxel et al. 2002).

Fossil fuels refer to coal, petroleum, and natural gas collectively, all of which come from fossils of dead animals or phytoplankton (FERC 2015). They are of great value to the human society because they are the fuels burned to generate the energy, primarily electricity, that humanity consumes for countless economic and non-economic activities (Griffin and Puller 2005). More specifically, nearly 80% of the energy consumed in the US come from fossil fuels (USEIA 2021). It is not an exaggeration to say that the present human civilization is built on and sustained by the plentiful energy and electricity generated from burning of the fossil fuels.

Unlike the pre-fossil fuel energy sources such as fuelwoods discussed in Chap. 3, or other biomass fuels such as dried cow dung, or other biological energy sources such as donkey and horsepower, the fossil fuels have a far superior energy density (USEIA 2022). Plainly speaking, only a gallon

© The Author(s), under exclusive license to Springer Nature Switzerland AG 2023
S. N. Seo, *The Economics of Optimal Growth Pathways*,
https://doi.org/10.1007/978-3-031-20754-9_5

of petroleum can carry a heavy-duty truck for a hundred miles, although it may require a hundred donkeys to do the same work.

Unlike the forest resources, the total stock of each fossil fuel on the planet is limited, that is, fixed invariably at some quantity. Therefore, a ton of petroleum consumed by humanity means a ton fewer stock of the fossil fuel left on Earth. In the case of a forest stand, a harvest of the stand at one time means that the forest owner should wait for the trees on the stand to grow again until the next harvest time (Faustmann 1849). A forest harvest after another can continue in this way indefinitely.

The economics of fossil fuels is therefore a theory of optimal extractions until exhaustion or a theory of an optimal depletion of the fixed stock over time (Hotelling 1931; Devarajan and Fisher 1981; Fisher 1981). A societally optimal trajectory of extractions of a fossil fuel would maximize the value of the fuel extracted over its lifetime to the society. So, the economics thereof would inform us of how many tons of the fossil fuel should be extracted at each time period from today to the date of exhaustion.

The question of the end date, that is, the period of exhaustion, is where alternative energy sources enter the scene. There are a host of alternative energy sources, which are often referred to as renewable energy or green energy, that are available to humanity at the present time or will become available in the near future, which has fascinated all those who are intrigued by the energy economics and politics of the global community (IPCC 2011; Heal 2010). The renewable energy sources include solar energy, wind energy, geothermal, wave energy, hydro energy, and nuclear energy. Nuclear energy and nuclear fusion energy are increasingly categorized by the nations as a green energy, for example, by the European Union (DW 2022).

In the context of the society's full portfolio of energy sources, therefore, the question of the end date is not a question of exhaustion, but a question of transition from one energy source to another (Nordhaus 1973). Considering that there are not a few alternative energy sources but none of which is widely adopted at this point as a dominant energy source at the society level, a transition from one energy source to another will occur repeatedly, that is, one transition followed by another.

When does the repeated process of transitions end? This inquiry leads us to wonder whether there is the ultimate source of energy, referred to as a backstop energy or technology in the energy literature (Nordhaus 1973). When the idea was first conceived during the early 1970s, a nuclear fusion technology appeared to hold such a promise, but half a century later, the global community is yet without a practical nuclear fusion technology (ITER 2022).

Critics against the efficient energy uses and optimal transitions thus far described argue that the fossil fuels are sources of numerous pollutants that damage the nature and human health. The most prominent of such negative consequences is, they argue, global climate change which is primarily caused by the emissions of, *inter alia,* carbon dioxide from the burning of fossil fuels (IPCC 2021; Le Treut et al. 2007). Critics further contend that the consequences of the continued fossil fuel consumptions by humanity as prescribed by the economic models will be catastrophic to the Earth's civilizations owing to climate disruptions (Lenton et al. 2008; Weitzman 2009).

The calls and initiatives for ending the energy generations from fossil fuels are plentiful, which have been gathering steam for many decades since the early 1970s. Some call for a complete divestment by companies and institutions from fossil fuel industries (Stand.Earth 2021). Some national policies were designed to completely shut down the energy generations from coal-fired power plants, like the US Clean Power Plan (USEPA 2014). Some international policies target for a net-zero emissions of carbon dioxide by 2030 *via* stopping all new coal-, oil-, gas-fired power plant operations, like the Green New Deal in the US or the EU's energy plan (US House of Representatives 2019; EC 2022).

Taking into consideration in a balanced way of the extraordinary benefits to humanity of fossil fuel-fired energy generations as well as the environmental and health consequences of such activities, what is the society's or the planet's best strategy regarding the fossil fuels? The question has intrigued the economists for long time, perhaps since the 1960s during which widely acclaimed environmental classics were published, for example, *The Problem of Social Cost* by Ronald Coase and *Silent Spring* by Rachel Carson, which helped establish the Environmental Protection Agency (EPA) in the US (Coase 1960; Carson 1962).

On another track, critics trumpeted the idea of an impending end of the fossil fuels, known widely as the peak oil hypothesis (Hubbert 1956; Deffeyes 2001). To them, the end of fossil fuels means an end of continued economic growth (Daly and Farley 2003; Heinberg 2011; Kallis et al. 2018). The idea of an end of fossil fuels is neither unreasonable nor avoidable to the economists as well who view them as an exhaustible resource. However, economists often differ from the critics on how much fossil fuels are left underground, that is, how many years are left until their exhaustions. Further, economists do not equate the end of fossil fuels to the end of economic growth.

5.2   Fossil Fuels as Non-renewable Resources

Coal, crude oil, and natural gas are collectively referred to as fossil fuels. They are called "fossil" fuels because they come from the remains of animals and plants that lived many millions of years ago. These fuels were formed *via* anaerobic (oxygen-free) decompositions of dead carbon-based animals, plants, and phytoplankton underground or under the seas for millions of years (FERC 2015).

For the petroleum which means rock oil in Latin, dead bodies of tiny phytoplankton in the seas had accumulated on the sea floor for millions of years, covered by layers of sand, silt, and rock, in an oxygen-free environment. A solid rock of finely decomposed bodies was formed in this way over the long period. Then, the heat and pressure from the layers turned the solid remains of phytoplankton into hydrocarbons, that is, liquid carbon (USEIA 2022).

Crude oil is another term for petroleum. The etymology of the term "crude" oil is interesting, considering that it is also referred to as "light sweet crude" oil. The term oil originally meant vegetable oils such as corn oil, sunflower oil, and canola oil. The term oil began to be used for lighting fuels such as castor oil and whale oil. In contrast to the vegetable oils, the dark black material that spurts from the ground was called "crude" oil.

Fossil fuels became a dominant source of energy for humanity at the beginning of the twentieth century through a series of landmark moments such as, to name some, the first commercial extraction of crude oil in Erie, Pennsylvania, inventions of light bulbs and AC (Alternating Current) motors for electricity supply to the mass public, and the invention of an Internal Combustion (IC) engine vehicle.

By 2019, roughly 90 million barrels of crude oil are produced per day, as shown in Fig. 5.1, which is roughly three times the total production in 1965 (BP 2021). The production of crude oil was heavily dominated by the US until the mid-twentieth century through the discoveries of oil fields in Pennsylvania, Oklahoma, Texas, and so on. Since the discovery of the Gharwar oil field in Saudi Arabia in 1951 whose size is as large as 280 km by 30 km, Middle East countries gradually became a dominant producer of crude oil. The Organization for the Petroleum Exporting Countries (OPEC) was formed in 1960.

The consumption of fossil fuels by humanity has increased dramatically since the beginning of the twentieth century, especially after the discovery of the Gharwar oil field in Saudi Arabia. Figure 5.2 shows the trajectory of

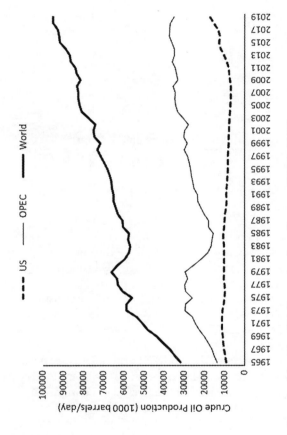

Fig. 5.1 Trajectories of crude oil daily production. (Source: OWID 2022)

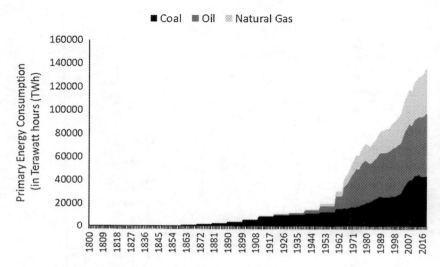

Fig. 5.2 Global primary energy consumption by fossil fuels. (Source: OWID 2022)

global energy consumption since 1800, which is broken down by the type of fossil fuels. The energy is measured in the figure by terawatt hours (TWh). For your reference, the Three Gorges Dam in Yangtze River, the largest hydroelectric dam on the planet, produces roughly 100 TWh of energy per year. As of 2019, the global total energy consumption amounts to 130 thousand TWh, of which coal accounts for 44 thousand TWh, crude oil 54 thousand TWh, and natural gas 40 thousand TWh (OWID 2022).

Before the discoveries of the Middle East oil fields, coal was the primary source of energy of the global community. The share of crude oil rapidly increased during the latter part of the twentieth century, surpassing that of coal. Entering the twenty-first century, the share of natural gas started to increase in the energy consumption mix. This was due to the advances in a hydraulic facture technology through which deep shale gas wells could be pumped (Joskow 2013; Mason et al. 2015).

Critics have argued that the planet will "soon" run out of crude oil. By the end of the twentieth century, many scientists predicted that the global crude oil production would peak during the first decade of the twenty-first century. How much crude oil is left underground and under the seas? Figure 5.3 shows the current estimate of crude oil proven reserve as well as the historical current estimates since 1980 by the British Petroleum (BP 2021). By 2019, the proven reserve is about 1.7 trillion barrels of crude oil, of which 1.2 trillion barrels are located in the OPEC. Canadian oil sands are about 200 billion barrels.

The figure tells us that the global community will run out crude oil in about 50 years. Dividing the proven reserve in Fig. 5.3 by the daily production, or consumption, in Fig. 5.1 results in about 50 years, that is, assuming the current level of consumption henceforth as well as the current estimate of the proven reserve.

What about the other fossil fuels? Table 5.1. summarizes the estimates of proven reserves of the three fossil fuels and the current production levels in 2019 by the Statistical Review of World Energy by the British Petroleum (BP 2021). Dividing the former by the latter, the table presents the estimates of the years left to drill for each fossil fuel. It is about 50 years

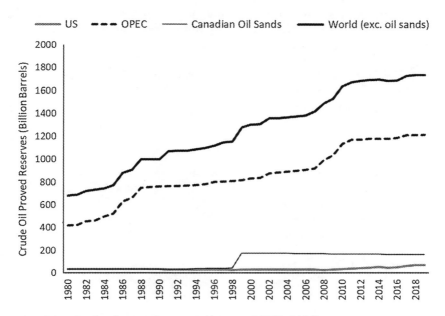

Fig. 5.3 Crude oil proved reserve. (Source: OWID 2022)

Table 5.1 Fossil fuel proven reserves and years left to drill

	Coal	Oil	Gas
Proven reserve in 2019	1074 billion tons	1734 billion barrels	190 trillion cubic meters
Production in 2019	7.7 billion tons	95 million barrels/day	3.976 trillion cubic meters
Years left to drill	139	50	48

again for natural gas. For coal, it is 139 years. Again, the years-left-to-drill estimates are based on the several assumptions mentioned in the previous paragraph.

5.3   Economics of Crude Oil Extractions

Let's start with a simple model of an owner of a reservoir of crude oil. S/he should decide how much crude oil to extract at each period and further how many periods in the future to extract from the reservoir. Let's assume for the time being that the market price of the crude oil remains constant in real dollars. Let's also assume that the owner knows the exact amount of the crude oil in the well.

Let the total stock of crude oil be S_0, the quantity extracted at time t be q_t, the stock at time t be S_t. Then, the extraction path should satisfy the following stock equation:

$$S_t - S_{t+1} = q_t. \tag{5.1}$$

The oil-well owner would determine the trajectory of the extracted amount in each period over the lifetime of the well in a way to maximize the profit to be earned from it. The profit at time t is the revenue earned from the sale of crude oil minus the total cost. Let's assume that the cost is an increasing function of the amount of extraction, that is, $c(q_t)$, and the unit price of oil is p. Then, the profit earned from the extraction at the present period is:

$$pq_0 - c(q_0). \tag{5.2}$$

The crude oil-well owner's profit from the extractions for the life of the well (T) is the sum of the present value of each period profit across all periods, with γ the discount rate:

$$\pi = \left[pq_0 - c(q_0) \right] + \left(\frac{1}{1+\gamma} \right) \left[pq_1 - c(q_1) \right] + \left(\frac{1}{1+\gamma} \right)^2 \left[pq_2 - c(q_2) \right]$$
$$+ \ldots + \left(\frac{1}{1+\gamma} \right)^T \left[pq_T - c(q_T) \right]. \tag{5.3}$$

The owner's problem is to find q_t for each period and the final period T to maximize the profit in Eq. 5.3. It is a complicated dynamic optimization problem, the solution of which is not easily obtainable (Arrow and Intriligator 1981; Dixit 1990). Economists, as always ingenious, solve this optimization problem by two conditions without any computer's assistance. One is the intertemporal no-arbitrage condition and the other is the terminal condition.

An optimal solution should satisfy the intertemporal condition in which the marginal profit from the extraction of one ton of crude oil should be equal across the time periods:

$$\left(\frac{1}{1+\gamma} \right)^t \left[p - c'(q_t) \right] = \left(\frac{1}{1+\gamma} \right)^{t+1} \left[p - c'(q_{t+1}) \right] \tag{5.4}$$

Rearranging the equation,

$$\frac{\left[p - c'(q_{t+1}) \right] - \left[p - c'(q_t) \right]}{\left[p - c'(q_t) \right]} = \gamma. \tag{5.5}$$

The intertemporal condition in Eq. 5.5 says that the $p - c'(q_t)$ should increase at the rate of γ from one period to the next over the lifetime of the well. This quantity, the difference between the price and the marginal cost from one ton of crude oil, is called rent (Ricardo 1817):

$$p - c'(q_t) \tag{5.6}$$

The rent is also referred to in the energy literature as user cost, royalty, dynamic rent, and the Hotelling rent (Gray 1914; Hotelling 1931). So, the intertemporal condition is thus: the Hotelling rent should increase at the rate of γ, the market interest (discount) rate (Fisher 1930). This condition is called the γ percent rule.

At what time period does the extraction end? The terminal condition determines the terminal period, that is, T. The terminal period is the period in which the total stock, S_0, is exhausted. As such, if we know the q_0 and apply the γ percent rule to obtain q_1, q_2, and so on, we will be able to figure out the terminal period, T. The problem with this approach is that we do not know q_0 in the first place because q_0 can be only known when q_1 is known, that is, through the intertemporal condition in Eq. 5.5.

So, we need to start at the final period (T), from which the amount of extraction in the preceding period $(T\text{-}1)$ is obtained. This is called backward induction, which is the analytic method of working backward from the final period. How do we determine the amount of extraction of the terminal period? It should be "as small as possible," which means near-zero extraction at the final period. The other way of stating it is that the Hotelling rent at the final period, $p - \acute{c}(q_T)$, should be "as large as possible." This is because the price in this simplest model is assumed to be constant.

The backward induction determines the crude oil extraction trajectory, as in Fig. 5.4. The extraction at the final period is determined by the terminal condition. From the extraction at the terminal period, the extraction at the immediately preceding period is determined by relying on the

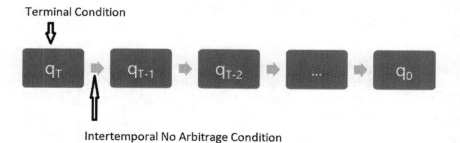

Fig. 5.4   Backward induction

intertemporal condition. This process continues until the present period, that is, the initial period. The well owner does an incredible job of backward induction! The method is a standard procedure in economics for finding a solution in a non-cooperative game (Selten 1965).

From this point on, let's expand the simple model of a single crude oil-well owner to the crude oil industry. Let's assume a competitive oil industry in which each individual well owner is a price taker. The price is determined at the industry level. Unlike the assumption in the above simple model, the price of crude oil will increase over time as ever smaller amounts of crude oil will be left in the crude oil fields, which would make it increasingly harder for the firms to extract. The price of crude oil may also fall, albeit temporarily, if the supply of oil were to suddenly spike for a political reason, for example. The price of oil is determined by the demand force and the supply force in the market.

Let the price schedule of a competitive oil industry is $\{p_0, p_1, p_2, \ldots, p_T\}$. An individual oil-well owner will rely on this schedule to determine the levels of extractions over time in her well. In the competitive market, each and every producer of crude oil makes the same prediction about the price schedule. Once every firm relies on the same price schedule, then the price schedule will become the observed, that is, the realized price path in the market. This is the consequence of rational expectation in the competitive market, which is referred to as the assumption of perfect foresight (Friedman 1968; Lucas 1972).

Let Q_t be the industry production of crude oil at time t, which is the sum of the productions of individual firms at that time. With the competitive oil industry model, an individual firm's extraction is now determined by the following intertemporal no-arbitrage condition:

$$\frac{\left[p_{t+1} - c'(q_{t+1})\right] - \left[p_t - c'(q_t)\right]}{\left[p_t - c'(q_t)\right]} = \gamma. \tag{5.7}$$

The crude oil industry's optimal extraction decision at each time period, that is, Q_t, is marked by a societal welfare optimization. How so? Let the market price of crude oil is a function of the market demand/supply, $p_t = p(Q_t)$. The cost of extraction depends on the level of extraction linearly, $c_t = cQ_t$ where c is the unit cost. Let $B(Q_t)$ be the gross consumer surplus at the society level. The net consumer surplus at the society level is thus $B(Q_t) - cQ_t$. Then, the societal welfare optimization can be written as follows, which is also the crude oil industry's optimization problem (Hotelling 1931):

$$W = \left[B(Q_0) - cQ_0 \right] + \left(\frac{1}{1+\gamma} \right) \left[B(Q_1) - cQ_1 \right]$$

$$+ \left(\frac{1}{1+\gamma} \right)^2 \left[B(Q_2) - cQ_2 \right]$$

$$+ \ldots + \left(\frac{1}{1+\gamma} \right)^T \left[B(Q_T) - cQ_T \right]. \tag{5.8}$$

The optimal solution to this societal problem is determined again by the intertemporal no-arbitrage condition:

$$\left(\frac{1}{1+\gamma} \right)^t \frac{d}{dQ_t} \left[B(Q_t) - cQ_t \right] = \left(\frac{1}{1+\gamma} \right)^{t+1} \frac{d}{dQ_{t+1}} \left[B(Q_{t+1}) - cQ_{t+1} \right]. \tag{5.9}$$

Recalling that $\dfrac{d}{dQ_t} B(Q_t) = p(Q_t)$, we get

$$\frac{\left[p(Q_{t+1}) - c \right] - \left[p(Q_t) - c \right]}{\left[p(Q_t) - c \right]} = \gamma. \tag{5.10}$$

From the social welfare optimization, the Hotelling rent, $p_t - c$, rises at the rate of γ percent. Each firm earns the Hotelling rent for each ton of crude oil produced. The social welfare optimization solution in Eq. 5.10 is the same as the individual firm's optimization solution in Eq. 5.7, except the variable price of oil.

The production at the terminal period for the industry would be determined in the same manner as the individual oil-well's exhaustion decision. The production at the final period should be near zero. The oil price at the final period is so large that the demand of crude oil is practically zero. However, if there is an alternative energy, for example, nuclear energy, which replaces crude oil at some point, the terminal condition needs to be revised. The crude oil price at the final period is determined by the price of the alternative energy, which is the topic of the next section.

5.4   Backstop Energy

The terminal condition plays a critical role in the determination of the optimal extraction path of the crude oil, as explained above. The Hotelling model, though, did not take into account the possibility that alternative energy sources to fossil fuels exist, and one of them may take over as a dominant energy source at some point in the future, replacing the crude oil (Hotelling 1931). Such potential alternatives are solar photovoltaic (PV) energy, wind energy, nuclear fission energy, nuclear fusion energy, hydroelectric energy, and biogas energy (MIT 2003, 2015; Seo 2021a; Lanfranco and Seo 2022).

When such alternative energy technologies are incorporated into the Hotelling model, the terminal condition in the preceding section does not hold, neither does the backward induction from the terminal condition. More concretely, the terminal condition should be restated as a transition condition. That is, crude oil doesn't have to be exhausted at the final period of extraction, but rather has to be transitioned away to an alternative energy. In the revised model, the transition from crude oil to an alternative energy source will be followed by another transition to still another alternative energy source. Thenceforth, this process will continue.

What does the transition condition look like? Under the intertemporal no-arbitrage condition in Eq. 5.10, the price of crude oil will keep rising from one period to another. Let's express the price of energy in the unit of 1 kilowatt-hour (KWh) of electricity generated. If the price of crude oil needed to generate 1 KWh of electricity exceeds the price of the alternative energy source needed to generate 1 KWh of electricity, energy consumers would be willing to switch from the petroleum-fired energy to the alternative energy.

Figure 5.5 illustrates this energy transition from a fossil fuel energy to an alternative energy. In the figure, the price of energy generated by a fossil fuel, that is, crude oil as per our discussion so far, keeps up rising per unit of energy generated, for example, 1 KWh of electricity. A transition occurs when the price of energy generated by an alternative energy source, say, solar PV technology, becomes cheaper than the price of energy generated by crude oil.

Once the transition to the solar PV energy happens, the price of solar PV-generated energy will keep rising again. Why so? Solar radiation, which is inexhaustible, which is the source of solar PV energy generation will not

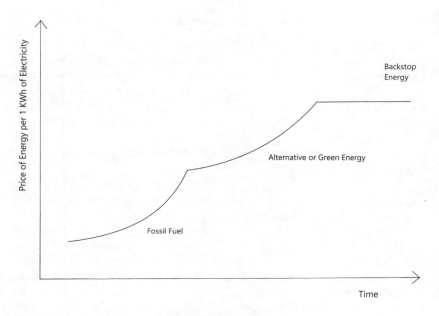

Fig. 5.5   Energy transitions and backstop energy

change over time. Also, a more efficient way to convert solar radiation into electricity may be developed in the future, lowering the cost of solar energy.

Many of the inputs needed for a solar energy generation are, however, limited and scarce resources. The solar panel should be made of such scarce inputs. The larger the demands for such inputs, the higher their prices would get. The most important input in a solar energy generation is the land upon which solar arrays are built. When the demand for solar energy is below a certain level, the solar arrays will be built selectively in inexpensive lands such as, for example, Mojave Desert in California. When the demand cannot be met by the productions in inexpensive lands, solar energy generators need to build their solar panels in increasingly more expensive lands. A nation without abundant lands will have to sacrifice its high-value lands, for example, major agricultural lands or forestlands. As the lands devoted to solar arrays expand, the chances of natural disasters caused by solar panel constructions, for example, landslides, will increase significantly. Further, the cost of maintenance will increase nonlinearly owing to external factors such as birds' excretions onto the solar panels or storm damages (MIT 2015).

The figure also depicts a transition to a backstop energy. The transition from the alternative energy to the backstop energy would occur in the same way as the preceding transition from the fossil fuel energy to the alternative energy. When the price of the alternative energy exceeds the price of the backstop energy, energy consumers will likewise switch from the former to the latter.

Why is it called a backstop energy? This term was coined in the early 1970s to refer to an ultimate energy source (Nordhaus 1973). At that time, nuclear fusion held a high promise as an ultimate energy technology, from which the term emerged. The exact definition of the backstop energy is the energy, generated either from a specific source or technology, that can be used by humanity indefinitely at a constant price. As depicted in Fig. 5.5, the price of the backstop energy does not rise over time.

It may feel to some readers that the existence of a backstop energy strictly defined is a myth than a fact. However, many scientists are also optimistic about finding such an ultimate source or technology given that, for example, solar radiation is an "eternal" energy source to humanity. To them, what needs to be accomplished is to find a way to convert solar radiation into energy and electricity more efficiently and store it for a long period of time. The example of the former is solar PV perovskite cells while that of the latter is a solid-state battery (Reisch 2017; Tian et al. 2020; NREL 2020). For another, the nuclear fusion physics is exactly that of the Sun: Hydrogen atoms combine *via* which solar radiation is emitted (MIT 2003; ITER 2022).

Since the term "backstop energy" emerged, it has passed five decades. Has the scientists' search for it succeeded? It has not. The largest nuclear fusion energy project is the ITER (meaning "the way" in Latin) located in Southern France, which is a collaboration of 35 countries. The project aims to achieve the output-input ratio of 10 ($Q = 10$), that is, to produce 500 Megawatts (MW) of energy from the input of 50 MW of energy. However, the current record Q ratio is only 0.67 set by the European tokamak JET (Joint European Torus), meaning that the input energy exceeding the output energy (ITER 2022). For your reference, the 500 MW of output is only 2% of the energy output of the Three Gorges Dam hydroelectric plant at Yangtze River in China which is 22,500 MW of installed capacity, or the Itaipu Dam in the Parana River in the border of Brazil and Paraguay (IHA 2018; Seo 2021a; Grijsen 2022).

5.5   A PEAK OIL CRITIQUE

The economics of fossil fuels described thus far has been the target of severe criticisms from many fronts. The most prominent of them are a peak oil critique, an environmental and health critique, and a global warming critique. I will address the first two critiques in this chapter and the third critique in Chap. 11 when the economics of global warming and climate change is explained.

The peak oil critique has long been prominent in the literature of fossil fuels ever since the presentation by K. Marion Hubbert in 1956 about an impending peaking of the US oil production at around 1965–1971, known thenceforth as the Hubbert's peak (Hubbert 1956). The upshot of the critique was that the stock of petroleum, that is, crude oil, in the US as well as the global stock has a strict limit and, as such, will run out in the near future owing to the humanity's excessive and exploding consumption of it driven by the pursuit of economic growth. It was widely predicted that a global crude oil production would peak at around the threshold between the twenty-first century and the twentieth century (Deffeyes 2001).

The peak oil critique, however, does not stop there. It is applicable to "everything" in life, according to the followers of this critique. The peak oil theory applies to every resource according to the ecological economics critics who are anchored at the concept of ecological limits and thresholds (Daly and Farley 2003; Costanza 2010). To them, the peak oil means the end of oil, gas, and coal. It means the end of food security. It means the end of climate stability. It means the end of economic growth. It means the end of fresh water. It means the end of rare and precious minerals and ores such as copper and platinum (Heinberg 2011).

The peak oil critique as first put forth by Hubbert is valid. In fact, neither scientists nor economists argue that the peak oil theory or hypothesis is false. However, the theory is interpreted widely differently by the two groups. At the one end of the extremes, pessimism and doom reign: the end of oil is "the ultimate end of everything" and the world will enter into a rapid decline or collapse soon after the peak.

At the other end of the interpretations is that of transition supported by a large majority of economists. This is well captured in Fig. 5.5. Given the limited stock of fossil fuels underground and under the seas, there is no way that they can be relied upon forever by the human society. On the other hand, the end of fossil fuels does not mean the end of the planet's prosperity, but rather points to a transition to the next best energy source, for example, solar radiation, hydropower, nuclear energy, and nuclear fusion.

From another point of analysis, notwithstanding the peak oil predictions by many scholars in the past, the production of crude oil, natural gas, or coal each has not peaked as of 2020 according to Fig. 5.1 above. The production of each of these fossil fuels is still continuing to increase. The trends contradict the peak oil hypothesis, at least for now.

On the other hand, the current predictions of the proven reserves of the fossil fuels summarized in Table 5.1.. indicate that the fossil fuels, especially crude oil and natural gas, will be depleted in about five decades in this century. The statistics in the table appear to yield support for the peak oil hypothesis.

To understand why Fig. 5.1 contradicts the peak oil theory while Table 5.1. supports it, we need to understand the definition of the proven reserve. It is defined as the estimated quantity of crude oil which is, by a geologic and engineering analysis, recoverable profitably with the existing equipment, technology, and operating conditions. Therefore, the estimate of the crude oil proven reserve has been rising over the past 50 years (BP 2021). The proven reserve estimate depends on the current technology as well as the economic conditions.

In this regard, the recovery of shale gas is notable. Readers can see in Fig. 5.2 that the share of natural gas has been rising since the late 1990s. This was due to the advances in the drilling technology called the hydraulic fracturing, commonly known as the fracking. Through this technology, previously unrecoverable gas deep beneath the ground and in between the rocks, referred to as shale gas, became recoverable, resulting in a shale gas boom in the US and then elsewhere on the planet (Joskow 2013; Mason et al. 2015).

5.6   An Environmental and Health Critique

An environmental and health critique *vis-à-vis* fossil fuels lays its aim at the environmental damage that fossil fuel combustions cause, of which the harmful human health effect on people is at the core of their concern.

Fossil fuel-fired power plants release various air and water pollutants, so do the motor vehicles run by the internal combustion engine. The major pollutants are sulfur dioxide (SO_2), nitrogen oxides (NO_x), carbon dioxide (CO_2), carbon monoxide (CO), fine particulate matters (PM_x), ozone (O_3), and volatile organic compounds (VOCs) (USEPA 1990, 2010).

These pollutants individually or jointly cause major environmental events such as acid rain, smog, a brown cloud, an ozone layer depletion, and a PM pollution (Likens and Bormann 1974; Molina and Rowland 1974).

The economic cost of these pollutants is substantial *via* the damages they inflict on natural ecosystems and human health (Mendelsohn 1980; Cropper and Oates 1992). Economic valuation studies show that the human health cost dominates the other costs incurred by the environmental pollution, which also depends critically on the value of a statistical life (VSL) (Viscusi and Aldy 2003; Muller and Mendelsohn 2009; USEPA 2011). They also show that the emissions from coal-fired power plants account for a dominant share of the total cost of pollution. Of a variety of pollutants, fine PM ($PM_{2.5}$) pollution is most harmful to human health (Muller et al. 2011; Mendelsohn and Olmstead 2009).

Early critics portrayed the environmental pollution as the inevitable byproduct of the pursuit of economic growth. These researchers concluded that the aforementioned air, water, and vehicle pollutants would cause a large number of human mortalities as well as many diseases from which people would suffer chronically. Many critics argued that the economic growth is an obsolete idea given the severe negative consequences, albeit unintentionally, of it (Refer to Nordhaus and Tobin 1972 for the earliest economic response). The detractors argued for a most stringent policy and regulation against the pollution-causing economic activities, for example, a zero emissions whatsoever policy, a complete ban of certain chemical substances, or a strict quantity threshold on emissions of a pollutant (Baumol and Oates 1971; Arrow et al. 1996; Sandel 2000).

By the decade of the 2020s, the environmental pollution has lost its status as the most salient environmental challenge of the society (GCF 2011; UN 2015; UNFCCC 2015). The pollution problems, for example, smog, acid rain, vehicle pollution, drinking water pollution, and toxic chemicals, have largely been solved in developed nations, whose successes are being replicated in developing countries such as India, China, Brazil, and elsewhere. On the other hand, policymakers and environmental activists have largely moved on to the global environmental challenges, that is, global warming, numerous global green initiatives, worldwide pandemics (Seo 2019, 2020, 2021b, 2022).

Setting aside the problem of global warming for the moment since it is the primary topic to be addressed in Chap. 11, readers might wonder how developed countries have been able to successfully, even if not completely, address the severe environmental problems such as acid rain, smog,

PM-covered dark skies, and so on (USEPA 2010, 2011). It may have turned out to be true that as people get richer, they demand clean environment, air, and water more (Grossman and Krueger 1995). In the following, the present author lists several key reasons for the ongoing success from an economic perspective.

The first reason for the success is a possibility of mutual bargaining between the polluters and the victims. Many local pollution issues, for example, downstream victims from upstream factories, can be negotiated away between the involved parties in ways to improve the concerned environmental quality (Coase 1960; Friedman 1962). It appears that many local pollution disputes are resolved between both parties as far as developed countries are concerned.

The second reason was the innovative idea of creating a market where each ton of pollution is traded with a price, which is called an emissions allowance and trading system (Montgomery 1972; Tietenberg 1980). It was recognized that the air pollution is not a local problem but involves a large number of polluters as well as an even larger number of pollution victims. In such a case, mutual negotiation is too costly to rely on to resolve the problem. It is a publicly consumed good, in short, a public good (Samuelson 1954; Seo 2020). For a public good problem, a mutual bargaining approach is less effective and can even be ineffective in certain cases.

To address the air pollution problem as a public good, an emission allowance and trading system can be created in which one permit may entitle the owner of the permit one ton of emissions of an air pollutant of concern. A polluter is required by law to purchase the permit for each ton of emissions. The polluters are allowed to trade their permits each other from which a market for the emission permit is created. The market transactions will in turn result in the market price of the permit.

The market price of the permit in a competitive market will end up being equal to the marginal damage of each ton of the air pollutant, which again will be equated to the marginal cost of abating one ton of the emissions of, say, sulfur dioxide (SO_2). This holds only when the total number of the permit is controlled by the environmental authority of a nation which sets it at the efficient level, that is, at the socially optimal level (Seo 2020).

The emissions allowance and trading system as an environmental policy tool may have contributed to a successful control of air pollution considerably in the US and Europe. One example, most often cited in the literature, is the SO_2 allowance trading program implemented in the northeastern United States since 1995 (Stavins 1998; Schmalensee and Stavins 2013; USEPA 2010).

5.7   Energy and Technology Revolutions in the Fossil Fuel Economics

The third reason for the success is perhaps the most critical one: energy and technology revolutions that have taken place since the early 1970s when the Clean Air Act (CAA) and the Clean Water Act (CWA) were signed into law in the US (USEPA 1990, 2010). The technological advances in energy generations, pollution control, and other related technologies have contributed significantly to addressing major pollution problems in developed countries. In the following, the present author offers seven such advances.

The first is an automobile revolution. An ever higher mileage vehicle has been developed while older automobiles have been replaced with newer more efficient ones at an increasing pace by individual automobile owners (Portney et al. 2003; McConnell 2013). Further, lower-emission vehicles such as natural gas vehicles, hybrid vehicles, and electric vehicles (EVs) have enjoyed a big success in the past two decades (NRC 2013; IEA 2020).

The second is a lighting revolution. The search for a more efficient way to produce light for personal and commercial uses has resulted in an ongoing transition from an old incandescent light bulb to a compact fluorescent lamp (CFL) and to a light-emitting diode lamp (LED) (Nordhaus 1994). The LED lamp produces the same amount of light as the incandescent lamp but can last ten times longer and do so with a far smaller amount of input electricity (Akasaki et al. 2014). The transition significantly contributes to the reduction of fossil fuel burning for the production of energy and electricity, *ceteris paribus.*

The third is a transition to cleaner fossil fuels. Compared with low-quality coals (lignite or sub-bituminous coal), a high-quality coal (anthracite coal) emits a much smaller amount of air pollutants in producing the same amount of electricity. Again, compared with high-quality coals, an oil-fired power plant emits a far smaller amount of air pollutants. Still again, compared with a crude oil-fired power plant, a gas-fired power plant emits a far smaller amount of air pollutants (USEIA 2021).

The fourth is an advance in clean energy or green energy. This includes a hydro power, solar PV energy, wind energy, geothermal energy, and wave energy (MIT 2003, 2015; Heal 2010; Graziano and Gillingham 2015). Further, nuclear fission energy is increasingly recognized as a green energy by the international community, for example, the European Union's Complimentary Climate Delegated Act of 2022 (EC 2022). An increasing share of these alternative energy generation systems leads to a reduction in air pollution, *ceteris paribus*.

The fifth is an advance in an energy transmission and monitoring technology. A smart meter, for example, allows a consumer of energy to be aware of her real-time consumption of electricity, gas, or water at home as well as any leakage of electricity, which is communicated to both the consumer and the energy supplier. This allows the consumer to conserve energy more effectively (Joskow 2012).

The sixth is an advance in a power plant construction. A power plant used to be built near a major city where a large population is concentrated, which also reduces the transmission cost from the supplier's viewpoint. New power plants are strategically built as farther away as possible from major population centers. Further, they are built in consideration of a plume analysis. That is, they are built so that the plume from the power plants flows away from population centers, that is, in the downwind direction from the city centers (Mendelsohn 1980).

The seventh is an advance in pollution control inside a power plant. This is commonly referred to as a scrubber. In the case of fine PM ($PM_{2.5}$) pollution which is the most harmful air pollutant, multiple technologies are available to reduce the PM pollution leakage to outside the power plants such as a cyclone separator, a Venturi scrubber, a wet scrubber, electrostatic filters, and baghouses (USEPA 2008).

5.8   Conclusion

Crude oil, coal, and natural gas are some of the most valuable non-renewable resources of the planet. In a socially optimal extraction trajectory of these fuels, the aggregate of the series of net revenues discounted properly from the extractions over the lifetime of the reservoirs will be maximized. In such a trajectory, the resource rent will rise at the rate of the market interest rate. Eventually, fossil fuels will be replaced by an alternative energy source and then by a backstop energy technology. Such alternative energy sources and technologies include a solar PV energy, nuclear energy, nuclear fusion energy, new battery technologies, and new lighting technologies.

The reliance on fossil fuels by humanity will end at some point in the future, on which both critics and economists would largely agree. The critique regarding the harmful environmental and health consequences of burning fossil fuels poses a formidable challenge to humanity. Notwithstanding, the seven novel advances in science and technology as well as the two economic mechanisms explained in the preceding section have helped address this critical challenge in rich countries. It remains to be seen whether developing countries can replicate the success in rich countries and whether these solutions will be further advanced. The question of global warming and climate change that arises, *inter alia*, from the heavy reliance on fossil fuels has yet to be addressed in this book, which is indeed the primary topic of Chap. 11.

REFERENCES

Akasaki, Isamu, Hiroshi Amano, and Shuji Nakamura. 2014. *Blue LEDs: Filling the World with New Light. Nobel Prize Lecture.* Stockholm, SE: The Nobel Foundation. http://www.nobelprize.org/nobel_prizes/physics/laureates/2014/popular-physicsprize2014.pdf.

Arrow, Kenneth J., and Michael D. Intriligator. 1981. *Handbook of Mathematical Economics: Volume 1.* Amsterdam, NL: North-Holland.

Arrow, K.J., M.L. Cropper, G.C. Eads, R.W. Hahn, L.B. Lave, R.G. Noll, et al. 1996. Is There a Role for Benefit-cost Analysis in Environmental, Health, and Safety Regulation? *Science* 272: 221–222.

Baumol, W.J., and W.E. Oates. 1971. The Use of Standards and Prices for Protection of the Environment. *Swedish Journal of Economics* 73: 42–54.

Carson, Rachel. 1962. *Silent Spring.* Boston, MA: Houghton Mifflin Harcourt.

Coase, Ronald. 1960. The Problem of Social Cost. *Journal of Law and Economics* 3: 1–44.

Costanza, R. 2010. *What Is Ecological Economics? Yale Insights.* Yale School of Management, New Haven, CT. https://insights.som.yale.edu/insights/what-is-ecological-economics.

Cropper, Maureen L., and Wallace E. Oates. 1992. Environmental Economics: A Survey. *Journal of Economic Literature* 30: 675–740.

Daly, H.E., and J. Farley. 2003. *Ecological Economics: Principles and Applications.* 1st ed. Washington, DC: Island Press.

Deffeyes, Kenneth S. 2001. *Hubbert's Peak: The Impending World Oil Shortage.* Princeton, NJ: Princeton University Press.

Deutsche Welle (DW). 2022. *European Commission Declares Nuclear and Gas to be Green.* Published on February 2, 2022. https://www.dw.com/en/european-commission-declares-nuclear-and-gas-to-be-green/a-60614990.

Devarajan, Shantayanan, and Anthony C. Fisher. 1981. Hotelling's 'Economics of Exhaustible Resources': Fifty Years Later. *Journal of Economic Literature* 19: 65–73.

Dixit, A.K. 1990. *Optimization in Economic Theory.* 2nd ed. Oxford, UK: Oxford University Press.

European Commission (EC). 2022. *EU Taxonomy: Commission Presents Complementary Climate Delegated Act to Accelerate Decarbonization.* Brussels, BE: EC.

Faustmann, Martin. 1849. On the Determination of the Value Which Forest Land and Immature Stands Pose for Forestry. In *Martin Faustmann and the Evolution of Discounted Cash Flow,* ed. M. Gane. Oxford, England: Oxford Institute. [1968, Paper 42].

Federal Energy Regulatory Commission (FERC). 2015. *Energy Primer: A Handbook of Energy Market Basics.* Washington, DC: The FERC.

Fisher, Irving. 1930. *The Theory of Interest.* New York, NY: Macmillan.

Fisher, Anthony C. 1981. Exhaustible Resources: The Theory of Optimal Depletion. In *Resource and Environmental Economics,* ed. A.C. Fisher. Cambridge, UK: Cambridge University Press.

Friedman, Milton. 1962. *Capitalism and Freedom.* Chicago, IL: The University of Chicago Press.

———. 1968. The Role of Monetary Policy. *American Economic Review* 58: 1–17.

Gray, L.C. 1914. Rent under the Assumption of Exhaustibility. *Quarterly Journal of Economics* 28: 466–489.

Graziano, M., and K. Gillingham. 2015. Spatial Patterns of Solar Photovoltaic System Adoption: The Influence of Neighbors and the Built Environment. *Journal of Economic Geography* 15: 815–839.

Green Climate Fund (GCF). 2011. *Governing Instrument for the Green Climate Fund.* Songdo City, South Korea: GCF.

Griffin, J.M., and S.L. Puller. 2005. *Electricity Deregulation: Choices and Challenges.* Chicago, IL: University of Chicago Press.

Grijsen, J.G. 2022. Rapid Climate Risk Assessment Methodologies for Hydropower Projects: Concepts and Theory. In *Handbook of Behavioral Economics and Climate Change,* ed. S.N. Seo. Cheltenham, UK: Edward Elgar.

Grossman, G.M., and A.B. Krueger. 1995. Economic Growth and the Environment. *Quarterly Journal of Economics* 110: 353–377.

Haxel, G.B., J.B. Hedrick, and G.J. Orris. 2002. *Rare Earth Elements: Critical Resources for High Technology.* Reston, VA: The US Geological Survey.

Heal, G. 2010. Reflections: The Economics of Renewable Energy in the United States. *Review of Environmental Economics & Policy* 4: 139–154.

Heinberg, R. 2011. *The End of Growth: Adapting to Our New Economic Reality*. British Colombia, Canada: New Society Publishers.

Hotelling, H. 1931. The Economics of Exhaustible Resources. *Journal of Political Economy* 39: 137–175.

Hubbert, M. King. 1956. *Nuclear Energy and the Fossil Fuels*. Presented at the Spring Meeting of the American Petroleum Institute, San Antonio, TX.

Intergovernmental Panel on Climate Change (IPCC). 2011. *Special Report on Renewable Energy Sources and Climate Change Mitigation*. Cambridge, UK: Cambridge University Press.

———. 2021. *Climate Change 2021: The Physical Science Basis, The Sixth Assessment Report of the IPCC*. Cambridge, UK: Cambridge University Press.

International Energy Agency (IEA). 2020. *Global EV Outlook 2020: Entering the Decade of Electric Drive?* Paris, FR: IEA.

International Hydropower Association (IHA). 2018. *Hydropower Status Report*. London, UK: IHA.

International Thermonuclear Experimental Reactor (ITER). 2022. ITER: The World's Largest Tokamak. https://www.iter.org/proj/inafewlines

Joskow, P.L. 2012. Creating a Smarter U.S. Electricity Grid. *Journal of Economic Perspectives* 26: 29–48.

———. 2013. Natural Gas: From Shortages to Abundance in the United States. *American Economic Review* 103: 338–343.

Kallis, G., V. Kostakis, S. Lange, B. Muraca, S. Paulson, and M. Schmelzer. 2018. Research on Degrowth. *Annual Review of Environment and Resources* 43: 291–316.

Lanfranco, B., and S.N. Seo. 2022. An Analysis of Biogas, Biomass, Forest Credits, and Renewable Energy Programs in Brazil and Argentina Supported by the Green Climate Fund. In *Handbook of Behavioural Economics and Climate Change*, ed. S.N. Seo. Cheltenham, UK: Edward Elgar.

Le Treut, H., R. Somerville, U. Cubasch, Y. Ding, C. Mauritzen, A. Mokssit, T. Peterson, and M. Prather. 2007. Historical Overview of Climate Change. In *Climate Change 2007: The Physical Science Basis. The Fourth Assessment Report of the IPCC*, ed. S. Solomon et al. Cambridge, UK: Cambridge University Press.

Lenton, T.M., H. Held, E. Kriegler, J.W. Hall, W. Lucht, W.S. Rahmstorf, et al. 2008. Tipping Elements in the Earth's Climate System. *Proceedings of the National Academy of Science* 105: 1786–1793.

Likens, G.E., and F.H. Bormann. 1974. Acid Rain: A Serious Regional Environmental Problem. *Science* 184: 1176–1179.

Lucas, Robert. 1972. Expectations and the Neutrality of Money. *Journal of Economic Theory* 4: 103–124.

Mason, C.F., L.A. Muehlenbachs, and S.A. Olmstead. 2015. *Economics of Shale Gas Development*. RFF, Washington DC: Resources for the Future Discussion Paper.

Massachusetts Institute of Technology (MIT). 2003. *The Future of Nuclear Power: An Interdisciplinary MIT Study*. Cambridge, MA: The MIT.

———. 2015. *The Future of Solar Energy: An Interdisciplinary MIT Study*. Cambridge, MA: The MIT.

McConnell, Virginia. 2013. *The New CAFE Standards: Are They Enough on Their Own? The Resources for the Future Discussion Paper 13-14*. Washington, DC: The RFF.

Mendelsohn, R. 1980. An Economic Analysis of Air Pollution from Coal-fired Power Plants. *Journal of Environmental Economics and Management* 7: 30–43.

Mendelsohn, R., and S. Olmstead. 2009. The Economic Valuation of Environmental Amenities and Disamenities: Methods and Applications. *Annual Review of Environment and Resources* 34 (1): 325–347.

Molina, M.J., and F.S. Rowland. 1974. Stratospheric Sink for Chloro fluoromethanes: Chlorine Atom-catalysed Destruction of Ozone. *Nature* 249: 810–812.

Montgomery, W.D. 1972. Markets in Licenses and Efficient Pollution Control Programs. *Journal of Economic Theory* 5: 395–418.

Muller, N.Z., and R. Mendelsohn. 2009. Efficient Pollution Regulation: Getting the Prices Right. *American Economic Review* 99: 1714–1739.

Muller, N.Z., R. Mendelsohn, and W.D. Nordhaus. 2011. Environmental Accounting for Pollution in the United States Economy. *American Economic Review* 101: 1649–1675.

National Renewable Energy Laboratory (NREL). 2020. *Perovskite Solar Cells*. Washington, DC: The NREL, Department of Energy. https://www.nrel.gov/pv/perovskite-solar-cells.html.

National Research Council (NRC). 2013. *Transitions to Alternative Vehicles and Fuels*. Washington, DC: The National Academies Press.

Nordhaus, W.D. 1973. The Allocation of Energy Resources. *Brookings Papers on Economic Activity* 1973: 529–576.

———. 1994. *Do Real Output and Real Wage Measures Capture Reality? The History of Lighting Suggests Not*. Cowles Foundation Discussion Papers 1078, Cowles Foundation for Research in Economics, Yale University.

Nordhaus, W.D., and J. Tobin. 1972. *Is Growth Obsolete?* Cambridge, MA: National Bureau of Economic Research.

Our World in Data (OWID). 2022. Energy. https://ourworldindata.org/fossil-fuels.

British Petroleum (BP). 2021. *Statistical Review of World Energy 2021*. London, UK: The BP.

Portney, P.R., I.W.H. Parry, H.K. Gruenspecht, and W. Harrington. 2003. The Economics of Fuel Economy Standards. *Journal of Economic Perspectives* 17: 203–217.

Reisch, Mark S. 2017. Solid-state Batteries Inch Their Way Toward Commercialization. *Chemical and Engineering News, American Chemical Society* 95 (46): 19–21.

Ricardo, D. 1817. *On the Principles of Political Economy and Taxation.* London, UK: John Murray.

Samuelson, Paul A. 1954. The Pure theory of Public Expenditure. *Review of Economics and Statistics* 36: 387–389.

Sandel, Michael J. 2000. It is Immoral to Buy the Right to Pollute (with Replies). In *Economics of the Environment: Selected Papers,* ed. R. Stavins, 4th ed. New York, NY: W.W. Norton & Co.

Schmalensee, R., and R.N. Stavins. 2013. The SO2 Allowance Trading System: The Ironic History of a Grand Policy Experiment. *Journal of Economic Perspectives* 27: 103–122.

Selten, R. 1965. Spieltheoretische Behandlung eines Oligopolmodells mit Nachfragetragheit. *Z. fu¨r Gesamte Staatsivissenschaft* 121: 301–324.

Seo, S.N. 2019. *The Economics of Global Allocations of the Green Climate Fund: An Assessment from Four Scientific Traditions of Modeling Adaptation Strategies.* Cham, CH: Springer Nature.

———. 2020. *The Economics of Globally Shared and Public Goods.* Amsterdam, NL: Academic Press.

———. 2021a. Energy Revolutions: A Story of the Three Gorges Dam in China. In *Climate Change and Economics: Engaging with Future Generations with Action Plans,* ed. S.N. Seo. London, UK: Palgrave Macmillan.

———. 2021b. *Climate Change and Economics: Engaging with Future Generations with Action Plans.* London, UK: Palgrave Macmillan.

———. 2022. *The Economics of Pandemics: Exploring Globally Shared Experiences.* Cham, CH: Palgrave Macmillan.

Stand.Earth. 2021. Invest Divest Report 2021. https://www.stand.earth/divestinvest2021

Stavins, R. 1998. What Can We Learn from the Grand Policy Experiment? Lessons from SO_2 Allowance Trading. *Journal of Economic Perspectives* 12: 69–88.

Tian, X., S.D. Stranks, and F. You. 2020. Life Cycle Energy Use and Environmental Implications of High-performance Perovskite Tandem Solar Cells. Science. *Advances* 6 (31): eabb0055. https://doi.org/10.1126/sciadv.abb0055.

Tietenberg, T.H. 1980. Transferable Discharge Permits and the Control of Stationary Source Air Pollution: A Survey and Synthesis. *Land Economics* 56: 391–416.

United Nations (UN). 2015. *Transforming Our World: The 2030 Agenda for Sustainable Development.* New York, NY: UN.

United Nations Framework Convention on Climate Change (UNFCCC). 2015. *The Paris Agreement.* New York, NY: UNFCCC.

United States Energy Information Administration (USEIA). 2021. *Annual Energy Outlook 2021*. Washington, DC: US EIA.

———. 2022. *Energy Explained*. Washington, DC: US EIA.

United States Environmental Protection Agency (USEPA). 1990. *The Clean Air Act Amendments*. Washington, DC: US EPA.

———. 2008. *Air Pollution Control Equipment. MACT (Maximum Achievable Control Technology) EEE Training Workshop*. Washington, DC: US EPA.

———. 2010. *The 40th Anniversary of the Clean Air Act*. Washington, DC: US EPA. http://www.epa.gov/airprogm/oar/caa/40th.html.

———. 2011. *The Benefits and Costs of the Clean Air Act from 1990 to 2020*. Washington, DC: US EPA.

———. 2014. *Carbon Pollution Emission Guidelines for Existing Stationary Sources: Electric Utility Generating Units*. Washington, DC: US EPA.

Unites States House of Representatives. 2019. *Resolution: Recognizing the Duty of the Federal Government to Create a Green New Deal*. Washington, DC: United States House of Representatives. Published February 7, 2019.

Viscusi, W.K., and J.E. Aldy. 2003. The Value of a Statistical Life: A Critical Review of Market Estimates Throughout the World. *Journal of Risk and Uncertainty* 27: 5–76.

Weitzman, M.L. 2009. On Modeling and Interpreting the Economics of Catastrophic Climate Change. *Review of Economics and Statistics* 91: 1–19.

CHAPTER 6

Fisheries Bioeconomics Under Open Access

6.1 Introduction

Up until now, the present author was concerned with the efficient and socially optimal uses of land-based resources: croplands in Chap. 2, grasslands and urban lands in Chap. 3, forests and woodlands in Chap. 4, and fossil fuels in Chap. 5. This chapter shifts the focus of the book to the resources from the water-based systems such as oceans and rivers. Of the vast resources that the water-based ecosystems support, this chapter lays attention on fish resources and a large variety of fisheries around the planet.

The oceans account for about two-thirds of the Earth surface and may host as many as 2.2 million marine species (Mora et al. 2011; UN 2017). As such, it is impossible to critically analyze the planet's dynamic growth pathways without a careful examination of the oceans and the resources they support. On the other hand, analysts and policy-makers concerned with a planetwide challenge or another tend to focus heavily on the land-based biomes such as arable lands, grasslands, forests, cities, mines, and oil fields. The oceans are more often than not overlooked.

One of the reasons for such a tendency is that the oceans are not as easily observable as the land biomes. Referred to as the last frontier on the planet, not much is as yet known about the creatures, occurrences, and regional geographies in the oceans. To give you an idea, it is much harder to reach the deepest point in the planet's oceans, named the Challenger Deep in the Mariana Trench, than the highest point in the land, the Mt.

© The Author(s), under exclusive license to Springer Nature Switzerland AG 2023
S. N. Seo, *The Economics of Optimal Growth Pathways*,
https://doi.org/10.1007/978-3-031-20754-9_6

Everest in the Himalayas. The former is 11 km deep while the latter is 8 km high. In addition, only roughly 10% of the marine species may have been as of yet described by biologists (Mora et al. 2011; Seo 2021).

The primary question of this chapter is, like those in the preceding chapters, how the fish resources of the oceans should be utilized by human society (Anderson 2002). The present author will describe the economics of optimal harvests of fish resources in which a biological growth function of a fish is carefully balanced against the economic return (Clark 1985; Hartwick and Olewiler 1997). This will be followed by an inquiry on whether there are alternative ways to managing fish resources. For example, an alternative is to keep the concerned fish stock at its biological maximum while another alternative is to harvest the fish at Maximum Sustainable Yield (MSY).

The economics of fisheries or fish catch cannot be successfully described without a thorough exposition of open access resources. In the open ocean, there is no property rights for fishes therein, which leads to an over-exploitation of some fishes (Gordon 1954; Scott 1955; Ostrom 1990). Under the open access to oceans, fishing boats compete with each other to catch the fishes first before others, resulting in an overfishing of some fishes. In an extreme case, extinction of a fish species could happen if, for example, the fish species of concern is not given sufficient time to regenerate.

One way to address the open access over-exploitation of marine resources, although largely unintentionally, was the establishment of a 200 nautical mile limit by the international community, referred to as the Exclusive Economic Zone (EEZ), which resulted in a limited property right, that is, against the fishermen from other countries within the EEZ (UN 1982). An increase in aquaculture is another way to create property rights pertinent to fishing businesses. A range of policy interventions for the same include fish harvest tax, fishing licenses, and individual tradable fishing quota (Scott 1955; Hartwick and Olewiler 1997).

The economics of fish harvests should carefully incorporate a biological characteristic of a fish species of concern. Each species has its own unique biological characteristics. Owing to this, the economics of fisheries is often referred to as a bioeconomic model, that is, a biological plus economic model. In the bioeconomic model of a fishery, the fish species' biological growth and regeneration mechanisms are integrated into the economic model of the benefits and costs of fishing (Clark 1973, 1985; Clark et al. 1979; Seijo et al. 1998).

Another salient feature of the economics of fisheries is that all fishes, both demersal and pelagic, are mobile, especially, the pelagic fishes can swim across a large ocean, however long it may take, to the coasts of other nations. It is thus a matter of cross-boundary economic issue. A large number of international as well as national laws and regulations regulate the fishing activities. Further, many fishes have the adaptive capacity to a local environmental disaster because of this mobility (Seo 2021).

A critique against the economics of efficient harvests of fish resources will be presented later in this chapter from the conservationist's viewpoint on the potential mass extinction of fish species (IUCN 2021). The extinction of a fish species or another has for long time been a concern to many conservationists (Reid and Miller 1989). There are many examples of a conservation movement on a certain marine species, for example, blue whales and coral reefs (Smith 1984). The problem of extinction becomes a salient topic in the economics of fisheries because of the proclivity for overfishing in many fisheries. The overfishing problem in turn arises from, among other things, the open access characteristic of, especially, open ocean fisheries (Clark 1973).

6.2   A BIOECONOMIC MODEL OF FISHERIES

A fishery refers to the activity of harvesting fish or raising to harvest them. It is differentiated by the types of fish. Also, it is differentiated by the locations of fishing activity (FAO 2020). Thirdly, it is also differentiated by the types of vessels and gear used (Hartwick and Olewiler 1997). For the discussion in this chapter, we can define a fishery, without loss of generality, as a particular region where one type of fish is harvested.

Here, the fish in this chapter is a reference to all marine animals whether they are fish (e.g., croaker, mackerel, cod, salmon, catfish, etc.), crustaceans (e.g., crabs, lobsters, shrimp, etc.), molluscs (soft-bodied invertebrate such as clams, oysters, mussels, squids, etc.), or sea mammals (e.g., whales, dolphins, seals, etc.).

A classification of the fishes into two major classes depending on their mobility is of much use to both biologists and economists: demersal and pelagic (Daw et al. 2009; Cheung et al. 2010; FAO 2020). Demersal fish are dwellers: they feed on ocean or lake bottoms and do not range over long distance in the ocean. Pelagic fish are tourists: they swim over and migrate over a wide area in the ocean. The examples of the former are oysters, flounder, cod, and so on. The examples of the latter are tuna, herring, whales, and so on.

Let's consider, for our analysis, a lobster fishery in the coast of Maine in the US. The fish are renewable resources: they reproduce, grow, and die. The stock of the fish at one point in time can be measured by the number of the fish or by the total biomass, that is, the aggregated weight of the fish population. The latter is a more accurate measure in some sense but not always. The flow of the fish at one point in time is the change in the stock of the fish over an interval of time.

A change in the stock of fish occurs both biologically and economically. An entry of a new fish by birth, growth of an existing fish, and natural death are biological factors. Raising and harvesting fish through aquaculture is an economic factor. Migration of the fish owing to an ocean change brought about by global climate change is both a biological and an economic factor (Daw et al. 2009; Feely et al. 2020).

Let $X(t)$ be the stock of the fish, that is, the lobster population in the Maine coast, at time t. A change in the stock over a very short time interval is an instantaneous rate of growth of the fish population, $F(X)$:

$$F(X) = \frac{d}{dt}(X_t). \tag{6.1}$$

The $F(X)$ is referred to as a biological fish growth function, a typical one of which is drawn in Fig. 6.1. It is the most common shape of a fish growth function, in other words, there can be one with another shape. From the origin to the point marked X_{msy}, the fish stock grows, measured as the amount of biomass, at each time period with an increasingly higher rate of growth. Let's call it Phase I. From the X_{msy} to k, the fish stock still grows at each time period, however, with an increasingly lower rate of growth. Let's call it Phase II. From k onward, the fish stock declines, that is, the rate of growth is negative. Let's call it Phase III.

The X_{msy} point is referred to as the Maximum Sustainable Yield (MSY) while the point k is referred to as the carrying capacity (CC) of the habitat. The CC point is the maximum population or stock of the fish that the habitat can support, so it is called as such. The fish population at the CC point is the biological equilibrium of the fish stock at which point the rate of the fish population growth is equal to zero.

The X_{msy} is the point where the net growth is at a maximum. The largest net growth at that time period is marked F^* in the figure. If we harvest F^*

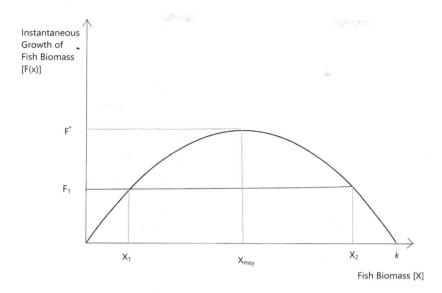

Fig. 6.1 A fish biological growth function

amount of the fish at that time period, the fish biomass will not change at X_{msy}. At the same time, the net growth in the next period will remain at F^*, which is again harvested. Thus, the X_{msy} is the fish stock where the maximum sustainable fish catch occurs. Hence, it is referred to as the MSY stock.

Is the harvest at the MSY stock efficient, that is, economically optimal for the fishery? That is not the case because it does not take into account the cost of fishing effort and the revenue to be generated from the harvest. To start with a simple model that incorporates economic considerations, let's assume a competitive fish industry.

To determine an optimal fishing effort, let's define the harvest function (H) which is a function of fishing effort (E) and the fish stock (X) at one point in time:

$$H_t = H\left(E_t, X_t\right). \tag{6.2}$$

The fishing effort (E) is a composite of numerous factor inputs that are correlated with the level of fishing efforts such as capital, labor, materials, and energy. These factor inputs are aggregated with proper weights to

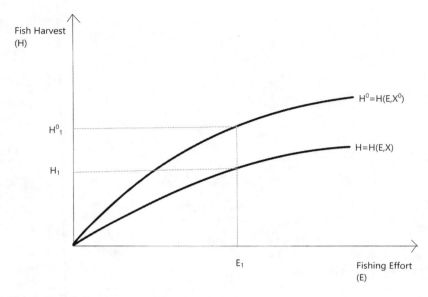

Fig. 6.2   The harvest function

yield a single measure of the fishing effort. In other words, it is an index for a wide range of fishing efforts. In the case of the lobster industry, it can be thought of simply as the number of lobster traps set by the fisherman (Hartwick and Olewiler 1997).

The harvest function is drawn in Fig. 6.2. With the fish stock fixed at X, the harvest increases with the level of fishing effort, which is drawn as the bottom black line. There is a diminishing marginal harvest with the increasing fishing effort. With the effort at E_1, the resultant harvest is H_1. With instead the fish stock fixed at X_0 which is larger than X, the harvest function shifts upward from H to H^0. With the same amount of effort E_1, the resultant harvest is H_1^0 because there are more fish in the region.

6.3   Open Access Fisheries

A distinguishing feature of fisheries from the other natural resources reviewed in this book up until this chapter is that fish are largely open access resources. A fisherman, who has necessary equipment and skills, can go out to a river or an ocean and catch, say, lobsters or tuna. No one owns a certain quantity of lobsters or tuna living on a particular section of the river bed or an ocean. Neither does one have an exclusive right to harvest a certain quantity of lobsters/tuna from the river/ocean. Fish are shared resources or, to put it differently, a commons or a common property resource (Samuelson 1954; Gordon 1954; Ostrom 1990). This means that fishermen will compete without restraint to catch as many as lobsters/tuna before others catch. This will be especially the case in open oceans while there tend to be informal local customs and rules in local rivers and lakes (Ostrom 1990).

From the mid-1970s, the 200-mile offshore limit was established as the Exclusive Economic Zone (EEZ) by the United Nations Convention on the Law of the Sea (UNCLOS) (UN 1982). This gives each nation a control over the EEZ to limit the entry of the fishermen from other countries. The EEZ limits open access fishing by international fishermen, but does little to limit open access fishing by domestic fishermen. Nor does it pertain to the open ocean fisheries.

An open access equilibrium in a fishery is illustrated in Fig. 6.3. To understand the two panels, let's start with the bottom panel. The Total Cost (TC) is a linear function of fishing effort (E) assuming a constant marginal cost per effort. The Total Revenue (TR) is a parabolic function which is defined as the unit price times the harvest amount, which resembles the biological growth function in Fig. 6.1 assuming the constant unit price.

In the open access fishery, fishermen will continue to enter the ocean to catch lobsters as long as there is profit to be earned, in other words, until the TR equals the TC. At the bottom panel, this is illustrated as the intersection of the TR curve and the TC curve, at which point the open access effort (E_{OA}) and the open access TR and TC (TR_{OA}) are determined.

Given the effort level thus determined, the harvest function can be drawn as a function of X, fish biomass, as in the top panel of Fig. 6.3. The open access equilibrium is then illustrated as the intersection of the biological growth function and the harvest function, at which point the open access biomass (X_{OA}) as well as the open access harvest (H) are determined, as shown in the top panel.

The two panels show a graphical analysis of comparative statics. When the marginal cost of effort increases from c to c', the TC curve shifts upward. This leads to a new equilibrium at which the open access effort is E' which is smaller than before, shown in the bottom panel. With the reduction in the effort, the harvest function shifts downward from H to

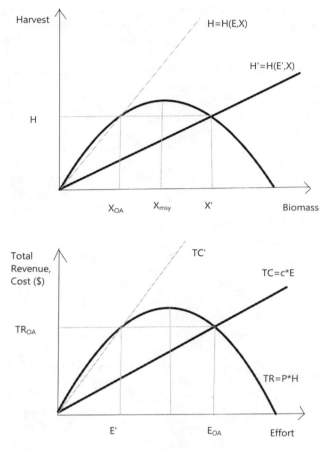

Fig. 6.3 The open access equilibrium

H, as shown in the top panel. With the new harvest function, the open access harvest remains unchanged at H, but the fish biomass increases from X_{OA} to X.

An inefficient outcome of the open access equilibrium is analyzed in Fig. 6.4. From the TR curve and the TC curve in Fig. 6.3, the marginal cost curve (MC), the marginal revenue curve (MR), and the average revenue curve (AR) are derived. The open access equilibrium is shown at the point where the AR equates the MC, which is denoted by E_{OA}.

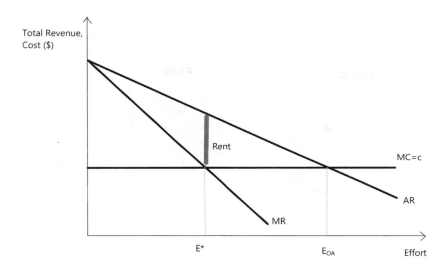

Fig. 6.4   Inefficient fishing effort under open access

An efficient outcome is achieved when the lobster fishery achieves its harvest level at the point where the MR equates the MC, which determines the efficient harvest and effort level of E^*. At that level of effort, the fishery earns the resource rent or royalty equivalent to the thick gray line marked in the figure. The rent equals the difference between the total revenue and the total cost at the efficient level of harvest. Per unit effort, the rent equals the difference between the average revenue and the average cost. Therefore, the open access equilibrium is inefficient, that is, not economically optimal.

The efficient fishing effort, E^* in Fig. 6.4, is achieved under a private property fishery. A comparison between the outcomes of the open access fishery and those of the private property fishery is analyzed in Fig. 6.5 The top panel shows that the fishery rent is the difference between the total revenue and the total cost. It also shows that the efficient effort level is lower than the open access effort level. To put it differently, excess fishing efforts are made under the open access fishery, leading to the problem of over-fishing. That is, $E_{OA} > E^*$ (Clark 1973).

The bottom panel in Fig. 6.5 shows the open access equilibrium at X_{OA} and H_{OA} whose determinations were explained in Fig. 6.3. With the

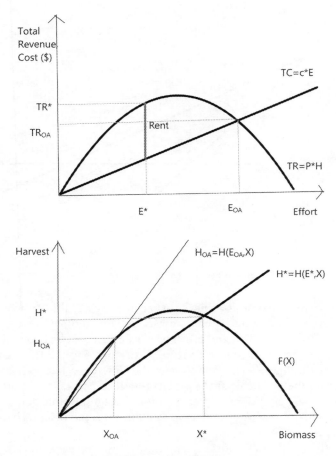

Fig. 6.5 Private property equilibrium versus open access equilibrium

private property fishery, the harvest function shifts downwards from H_{OA} to H^* owing to the reduction in fishing effort in the private property fishery as explained in Fig. 6.4. Under the private property fishery, the fish biomass increases from X_{OA} to X^* while the harvest increases from H_{OA} to H^*. In this figure, the open access equilibrium is inefficient as it leads to a larger effort but a smaller catch. The loss of profit owing to the open access is illustrated in the top panel of Fig. 6.5 as the lost rent at E^* as a thick gray line.

6.4   CREATING PRIVATE PROPERTY RIGHTS

An open access fishery is economically inefficient, that is, socially suboptimal, causing overfishing and in the extreme cases extinction of a species. To correct the inefficiency of the open access fishery, a private property fishery should be established, as is implied in Figs. 6.4 and 6.5 in the previous section.

To explain how a private property fishery may be established, let's start with the mechanics of an optimal tax imposed on the open access fishery, which is illustrated in Fig. 6.6. The open access equilibrium is at the intersection of the TR and the TC, which determines the level of effort, E_{OA}. The goal of a policy intervention is to induce the efficient level of effort, E^*. The imposition of an optimal harvest tax is marked by the vertical thick gray line in the figure. With the imposition of the tax, the TR curve shifts downwards from TR to TR' where $TR' = (P - tax) * H$. With the new TR curve for the fishery after the harvest tax introduction, the fishery earns less revenue, although the amount of harvest is not changed, while the cost of fishing remains unchanged. This forces the fishery to reduce the level of effort to E^*. At the changed level of fishing effort, the

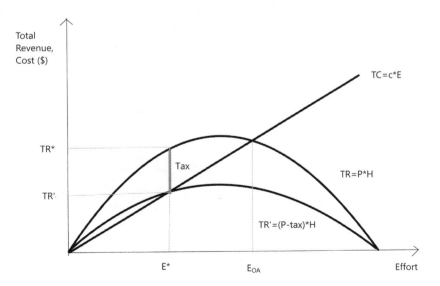

Fig. 6.6 An optimal harvest tax in the open access fishery

fishery earns TR' of total revenue while the government earns the tax revenue equal to the length of the thick gray vertical line.

The optimal taxation on the fish catch illustrated in Fig. 6.6, however, does not create the private property rights explicitly on fish resources. Under this tax scheme, when a fisherman catches the fish in an open ocean which does not belong to any country's EEZ, the tax revenue will be earned by the fisherman's country. This does not render a strong rationale for the optimal fish catch tax as far as the open ocean fish catch is concerned because the open ocean does not belong to the tax colleting government.

Another way to induce the efficient level of fish harvest is to tax the fishing effort directly, whose mechanism is illustrated in Fig. 6.7 The first effort tax is to impose a fee for a fishing license. With the license requirement, the TC curve shifts upwards in parallel by the amount of the license fee marked by the thick gray vertical line in the figure and denoted by *tax*. That is, the $TC = c * E + tax$. With the license fee, every fishing firm is required to purchase the fishing license whose fee is fixed, under which the efficient level of effort is induced, that is, E^*.

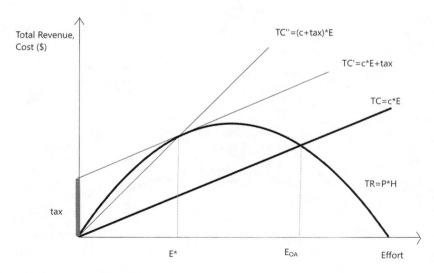

Fig. 6.7 An optimal tax on fishing effort

The second effort tax is a uniform tax on the level of effort, which rotates upward the TC curve to TC'. The new total cost curve is $TC' = (c + tax) * E$. With the imposition of the uniform effort tax, the larger the fishing effort, the larger the tax burden of fishermen become. This again induces the efficient level of effort, E^*.

To remind you, the effort in this model is an index or a composite of all the factor inputs, that is, capital, labor, energy, and materials. For this reason, a uniform effort tax is far more difficult to impose than the fishing license fee because all factor inputs of fishing firms should be known by a regulatory agency. In other words, it is harder to achieve the optimal fishing effort under the uniform effort tax.

All three approaches thus far are a tax instrument, which is also called a price-based instrument. A quantity-based instrument for fishery regulations is an imposition of a fish quota. Under the quota instrument, the total amount of fish catch is assigned and enforced by the government. In Fig. 6.8, the efficient level of fish catch is denoted as H^* and the efficient level of fish biomass is denoted by X^*, whose determinations were explained before multiple times in this chapter. The fishing quota should be set at H^*

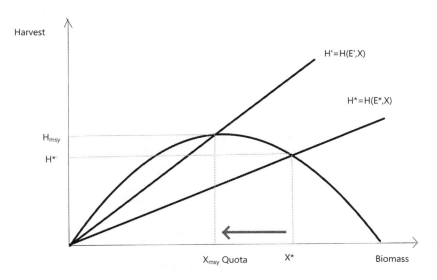

Fig. 6.8 Fish quota

or X^* in order to induce the efficient fishing effort as well as the efficient harvest.

The challenge with the fish quota is, first of all, to place the quota on the right amount of harvest, that is, the efficient harvest level. The government, however, tends to put the fish quota on the MSY harvest level as shown in the figure. At the MSY biomass and harvest, as the figure shows, the problem of overfishing persists, that is, the excessive fishing effort continues. This is indicated in the figure by the shift of the effort level, that is, $E > E^*$.

The MSY harvest under this quota scheme is larger than the efficient level of harvest, that is, $H^{msy} > H^*$.

The fish quota should be allocated to individual fishermen. This brings up another question of how to divide the total fish quota to individual fishermen. A most intuitive way is to divide it equally, so that each fisherman receives the same amount of fish quota. Such an approach is however not easy to implement because, among other reasons, fishermen have all different capacities and characteristics such as years of fishing, skills, and so on.

The individual fish quota, once allocated to individual fishermen, can be made tradable among the fishermen. Each unit quota will be tradable, from which buyers and sellers will emerge. The price of the unit quota will be determined by the market force. This will create the price of the unit permit. This approach is called the individual and transferrable quota (ITQ).

The individual and transferrable quota policy instrument is commensurate conceptually with the emissions allowance and trading system described in the previous chapter, for example, the SO_2 allowance and trading system in the US, the (attempted) carbon dioxide cap-and-trade policy in the US, and the EU Emissions Trading Scheme (ETS). The challenges in successfully designing and implementing this type of policy instrument include, in addition to setting the quota at the correct amount as well as allocating the quota to individual firms, whether the quota should be allocated to individual firms freely, what the correct size of the market for a specific policy should be (Stavins 2007; Schmalensee and Stavins 2013).

6.5   A Species Extinction Critique

Owing to the fact that fish are open access resources especially in the open oceans, overfishing and over-exploitation of fish resources there are unavoidable, which is what the bioeconomic model described thus far tells us (Gordon 1954; Scott 1955). This defining feature of the open access fisheries has long raised a concern about the possibility of extinction of

Table 6.1   Recorded extinctions since 1600

Category	Approximate number of species	Total number extinctions since 1600	Ocean: total number of extinctions since 1600
Mammals	4000	83	2
Birds	9000	113	0
Reptiles	6300	21	0
Amphibians	4200	2	0
Fish	19,100	23	0
Invertebrates	1,000,000+	98	1
Vascular plants	250,000	384	0
Total		724	3

Source: Reid and Miller (1989)

many fish species via over-exploitation driven by the competitive profit-seeking among fishermen (Clark 1973; Reid and Miller 1989).

In the book entitled *Keeping Options Alive: The Scientific Basis for the Conservation of Biodiversity*, Reid and Miller presented their estimates of the numbers of recorded extinctions since 1600, which is summarized in Table 6.1. There was a total of 724 species that had become extinct during that time period, of which were 23 fish species and 3 ocean species.

According to the most recent International Union for Conservation of Nature (IUCN)'s Red List of threatened species updated in 2022, there are roughly 40,000 species that are facing extinction out of 142,000 species assessed by the international organization, as summarized in Table 6.2 Threatened species are of three categories defined by the IUCN: Critically Endangered (CR), Endangered (EN), or Vulnerable (VU) species. According to this, roughly 28% of the total assessed species are threatened.

The number of threatened species is estimated for different categories of marine species: fishes, molluscs, crustaceans, and corals. According to the assessment, 15% of fishes, 26% of molluscs (like mussel, squids), 23% of crustaceans (like lobsters, shrimps), and 27% of corals are at some risk of becoming extinct.

These numbers presented by the IUCN Red List are astounding. However, the list keeps a complexity of ecology, which is also pertinent to economic considerations, hidden, to some degree (Solow 1974; Simpson et al. 1996; Weitzman 1998). Why is that the case? To assess the Red List, we need to know how many species are in fact there on the planet. To our dismay, it is a thorny question to answer. Scientific estimates range from 3

Table 6.2   The number of threatened species by IUCN Red List

Year	Fishes	Molluscs	Crustaceans	Corals	Total (including non-marine species)
Total assessed	22,581	9019	3189	848	142,577
threatened species (N)	3332	2385	743	232	40,084
Threatened species (%)	15%	26%	23%	27%	28%

Source: IUCN (2021)

million species at the low end to 300 million species at the high end. To make things worse, these estimates are largely from opinions of experts, that is, not strictly scientific (Mora et al. 2011). At present, only 1.25 million species, including both marine and non-marine species, are described by biologists and entered into the Linnaean system of classification (Linnaeus 1758).

According to the Census of Marine Life (CML), a worldwide collaborative project, it is estimated that there are 8.74 million eukaryote (an organism whose cell or cells have a nucleus) species on Earth. Of the total 8.74 million species, it is estimated that 6.5 million species are land species and 2.2 million species are marine species (Mora et al. 2011). However, only about 250,000 species (11%) are described by scientists and entered into the catalogue of the Linnaean taxonomy.

Depending on which estimate of the total number of species we adopt, the Red List becomes a more or less serious concern (Seo 2021). If we adopt the CML estimate, the Red List amounts to roughly 0.5% of the total species. In addition, of the Red List, the species classified as the Critically Endangered (CR) may be a better index for the species faced with extinction. The Red List identifies roughly 8400 species as CR.

The CR in the Red List is less than 0.1% of the total number of species estimated by the Census of Marine Life, but still appears to be a very large number. However, this again conceals the fact that there are species that are newly emerging owing to many factors to be elaborated shortly. For one example, scientific studies predict a higher rate of total turnover in species richness in a warmer world. This means that a warmer world leads to a higher rate of extinction of species, but at the same time a higher rate of origination of new species (Dornelas et al. 2018; Blowes et al. 2019). Be reminded that even at the current or pre-industrial climate conditions some species go to extinction and other species are newly originating constantly.

The discussion on extinction up to this point in this section leads us back to the question regarding the bioeconomic model of fisheries: What factors included in the model lead to or explain the mechanism of extinction of a species? There are two factors: biological mechanics and economic characteristics (Hartwick and Olewiler 1997). An important biological mechanic is that of female reproductive capacity. If the female species could give birth to only a few offspring, the risk of extinction of the species will be high. For such a species, the fish biomass (X in the Figs. 6.1–6.8) will easily go below a critical mass needed for the survival of the species. If, on the other hand, one female fish could produce millions of offspring, such as shrimp, the risk of extinction will be miniscule.

Of the economic characteristics, the cost of fishing effort is an important element for a certain species' extinction. If the marginal cost of fishing effort increases, say, nonlinearly, as there are increasingly smaller number of the species left in the ocean with each additional harvest, the fishing effort will come to the point beyond which it is no longer worthy to the fishermen. At that point, the remaining fish will remain unharvested, as such, survive and have the time to regenerate the species population.

Graphically, the increase in the marginal cost of fishing effort corresponds to the shift of the total cost curve upward to the left in Fig. 6.3. This reduces the efficient level of fishing effort, which results in a larger stock of fish biomass (X) and a smaller stock of fish harvest (H).

To explain how these two factors play out in the bioeconomic model of extinction, Hartwick and Olewiler described the case of blue whale which faced near extinction during the latter half of the twentieth century (Hartwick and Olewiler 1997). The blue whale harvest peaked during 1928–1938 after which the number of blue whales harvested declined steadily. By the early 1960s, the species was near extinction. In 1965, an international agreement among whaling nations set a moratorium on whale catching, prohibiting their catch beginning in 1965 (Smith 1984; HSUS 2022).

Authors pointed to a particular characteristic of blue whale fishing that led to its near extinction. In other fisheries, the catch would decline at some point beyond which the cost would rise faster than the value of the catch. Boats would then exit the fishery. However, in the case of whaling, whaling boats do not specialize by species. Whaling boats will therefore go from one species to another species until the aggregate of whale population becomes very low. This means that the marginal cost of fishing the blue whale does not change as long as there are a large number of other species of whales in the ocean. Further, the products of the blue whale which are valuable in the market, such as whale oil, blubber (fat), and meat, are also readily obtainable from other species of whale.

6.6   Conclusion

The economics of fish harvest is distinct in a major way from the other natural resource problems surveyed in this book for its open access analysis. Attributable to the open access characteristic, a central problem in fisheries economics and policy is over-exploitation of fish species which may drive extinction of some species when a combination of the conditions described in this chapter holds simultaneously.

The economics of fish catch relies on the bioeconomic modeling which integrates the biology of fish growth and regeneration to the economics of fish harvest. The biological component describes the fish growth and regeneration which differs markedly from species to species. The economic component describes the profit maximization of fishermen via the fish harvest function of fishing efforts and fish stock.

A shift from open access fisheries to private property rights fisheries, one fishery after another across the planet, can lead to more societally optimal fishing efforts at the planet level. A 200-mile exclusive economic zone, fish catch tax, fishing licenses, individual tradable fish quotas, and private aquaculture are some of the emerging policy instruments that can stimulate the establishments of private property rights in fisheries. These instruments are expected to go a long way in protecting the marine species as well as the health of the oceans.

References

Anderson, L.G., ed. 2002. *Fisheries Economics: Collected Essays*. London, UK: Routledge.

Blowes, Shane A., Sarah R. Supp, Laura H. Antão, Amanda Bates, Helge Bruelheide, Jonathan M. Chase, Faye Moyes, et al. 2019. The Geography of Biodiversity Change in Marine and Terrestrial Assemblages. *Science* 366 (6463): 339–345.

Cheung, William W.L., Vicky W.Y. Lam, Jorge L. Sarmiento, Kelly Kearney, Reg Watson, Dirk Zeller, and Daniel Pauly. 2010. Large-Scale Redistribution of

Maximum Fisheries Catch Potential in the Global Ocean under Climate Change. *Global Change Biology* 16 (1): 24–35.

Clark, Colin W. 1973. The Economics of Over Exploitation. *Science* 181: 630–634.

———. 1985. *Bioeconomic Modelling and Fisheries Management.* New York, NY: Wiley.

Clark, Colin W., Frank H. Clarke, and Gordon R. Munro. 1979. The Optimal Exploitation of Renewable Resource Stocks: Problems of Irreversible Investment. *Econometrica* 47: 25–47.

Daw, T., W.N. Adger, K. Brown, and M. Badjeck. 2009. Climate Change and Capture Fisheries: Potential Impacts, Adaptation and Mitigation. In *Climate Change Implications for Fisheries and Aquaculture: Overview of Current Scientific Knowledge*, ed. K. Cochrane, C.D. Young, D. Soto, and T. Bahri. FAO Fisheries and Aquaculture Technical Paper. No. 530. Rome, IT: FAO.

Dornelas, Maria, Laura H. Antão, Faye Moyes, Amanda E. Bates, Anne E. Magurran, et al. 2018. BioTIME: A Database of Biodiversity Time Series for the Anthropocene. *Global Ecology and Biogeography* 27: 760–786.

Feely, R.A., R. Wanninkhof, P. Landschützer, B.R. Carter, and J.A. Triñanes. 2020. Global Ocean Carbon Cycle [in State of the Climate in 2019]. *Bulletin of the American Meteorological Society* 101 (8): S170–S175.

Food and Agriculture Organization (FAO). 2020. *The State of World Fisheries and Aquaculture 2020.* Rome, IT: FAO.

Gordon, H.S. 1954. The Economic Theory of a Common-Property Resource: The Fishery. *The Journal of Political Economy* 62: 124–142.

Hartwick, J.M., and N.D. Olewiler. 1997. *Ch. 4. The Economics of the Fishery: An Introduction & Ch. 5. Regulation of the Fishery. In: The Economics of Natural Resource Use.* 2nd ed. New York, NY: Pearson.

Humane Society of the United States (HSUS). 2022. *Whaling and the International Whaling Commission.* Washington, DC: The HSUS. Accessed from https://www.humanesociety.org/sites/default/files/archive/assets/pdfs/SWNW_IWCFctsht.pdf.

International Union for Conversion of Nature (IUCN). 2021. IUCN Red List Summary Statistics. https://www.iucnredlist.org/resources/summary-statistics.

Linnaeus, Carolus. 1758. *Systema naturæ per regna tria naturæ, secundum classes, ordines, genera, species, cum characteribus, differentiis, synonymis, locis.* Stockholm, SE: Laurentius Salvius.

Mora, Camilo, Derek P. Tittensor, Sina Adl, Alastair G.B. Simpson, and Boris Worm. 2011. How Many Species Are There on Earth and in the Ocean? *PLoS Biology* 9 (8): e1001127. https://doi.org/10.1371/journal.pbio.1001127.

Ostrom, E. 1990. *Governing the Commons: The Evolution of Institutions for Collective Action.* Cambridge, UK: Cambridge University Press.

Reid, Walter V., and Kenton R. Miller. 1989. *Keeping Options Alive: The Scientific Basis for the Conservation of Biodiversity.* Washington, DC: World Resources Institute.

Samuelson, Paul A. 1954. The Pure Theory of Public Expenditure. *Review of Economics and Statistics* 36: 387–389.

Schmalensee, R., and R.N. Stavins. 2013. The SO2 Allowance Trading System: The Ironic History of a Grand Policy Experiment. *Journal of Economic Perspectives* 27: 103–122.

Scott, A. 1955. The Fishery: The Objectives of Sole Ownership. *Journal of Political Economy* 63: 116–124.

Seijo, J.C., O. Defeo, and S. Salas. 1998. *Fisheries Bioeconomics. Theory, Modelling and Management.* FAO Fisheries Technical Paper (No. 368). Rome, IT: FAO.

Seo, S.N. 2021. A Story of Coral Reefs, Nemo, and Fisheries: On Biodiversity Loss and Mass Extinction. In *Climate Change and Economics: Engaging with Future Generations with Action Plans.* Cham, CH: Palgrave Macmillan.

Simpson, R. David, Roger A. Sedjo, and John W. Reid. 1996. Valuing Biodiversity for Use in Pharmaceutical Research. *Journal of Political Economy* 104 (1): 163–185.

Smith, G. 1984. The International Whaling Commission: An Analysis of the Past and Reflections on the Future. *Natural Resources Lawyer* 16: 543–567.

Solow, Robert M. 1974. The Economics of Resources or the Resources of Economics. *American Economic Review* 64: 1–14.

Stavins, Robert. 2007. *A US Cap-and-trade System to Address Global Climate Change.* Hamilton Project Discussion Paper 2007-13. Washington, DC: The Brookings Institution.

United Nations (UN). 1982. *United Nations Convention on the Law of the Sea.* New York, NY: UN. https://www.un.org/depts/los/convention_agreements/texts/unclos/unclos_e.pdf.

———. 2017. *Our Ocean, Our Future: Call for Action. Resolution Adopted by the General Assembly on 6 July 2017.* The Ocean Conference. New York, NY: UN.

Weitzman, Martin L. 1998. The Noah's Ark Problem. *Econometrica* 66 (6): 1279–1298.

CHAPTER 7

Irving Fisher's Capital and Interest

7.1 INTRODUCTION

From Chaps. 2, 3, 4, 5, and 6, the present author has completed the descriptions of the economics of efficient and socially optimal uses of the major natural resources of the planet, which included croplands in Chap. 2, spatial land uses in Chap. 3, forest resources in Chap. 4, fossil fuels in Chap. 5, and ocean and marine resources in Chap. 6. In these chapters, a discount rate, which was equivalent to an interest rate therein, appeared as a key economic variable in determining the dynamically optimal trajectories of these resources by the global community. This is the right time that the present author gives an exclusive attention to this key economic variable in this chapter.

As for the structure of this book, this chapter on the interest rate and capital is a bridge chapter, as will be made clear shortly, from the preceding chapters to the succeeding chapters of the book. The succeeding chapters provide a set of theories on economy-wide optimal growth pathways, that is, encompassing all the subsectors of the economy. The concepts of a discount rate and capital offer a bridge that connects the set of natural resource sector level analyses presented in the preceding chapters to the set of economy-wide growth analyses presented in the ensuing chapters.

The theory of interest rate was laid out lucidly by Irving Fisher in the early twentieth century (Fisher 1907, 1920, 1930, 1933). Following the pedagogy of Irving Fisher who were known for his knack of explaining

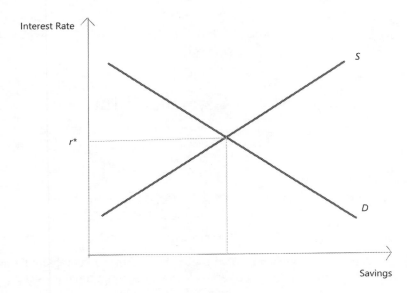

Fig. 7.1 Determination of an interest rate

complicated economic concepts in plain English, the present author will describe his theory in plain terms and graphically with the help of the four diagrams, Figs. 7.1, 7.2, 7.3, and 7.4, in the following sections. Each of these figures will illustrate how different factors interact in the market to settle at a market interest rate. An individual agent's preferences such as impatience on future outcomes, characteristics of production technologies, and trades among market participants are such factors (Samuelson 1994).

The concept of capital as well as the value of capital are not explainable independently of the concept of the interest rate. Irving Fisher was the economist who defined the concept of capital in a way that is still used today by economists, notwithstanding a wider popularity of the Karl Marx's capital among political economists (Marx 1867; Fisher 1896, 1906). There are numerous capital assets in the economy, for example, physical assets like machines and factories, financial assets like equities and bonds, real estate assets like residential houses and commercial buildings, natural capital assets like forests and biological diversity (Shiller 2004, 2005; Fabozzi et al. 2009; Dasgupta 2008; Maler 2013).

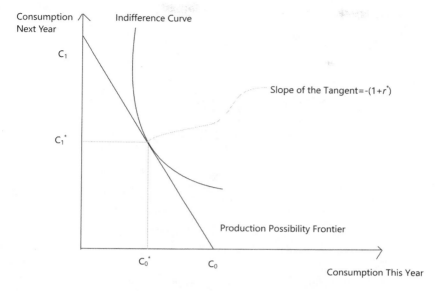

Fig. 7.2 A two-period model: technology determines the interest rate

According to Fisher's theory, the value of each of these capital assets is determined by, most prominently, the interest rate. Without the foundation of the Fisher model of the interest rate, it would be nearly impossible to explain many of the foundational concepts of economics, including those of capital, income, and the value of capital.

According to Fisher, a debt market where a market interest rate is determined is Pareto welfare improving for the society. In other words, the interest rate is determined by the people who seek to borrow money and the people who seek to lend it, through which both parties benefit from the trades (Pareto 1906).

However, suboptimal growth critics have often resorted to the argument of a zero interest rate for a long-term public sector project (Weitzman 1998a; Stern 2007). History tells us that a zero interest policy, for example, immoralizing an interest-attached lending, is neither rational nor enforceable (Shiller 2004). This chapter will respond to the zero discount rate critique in a way that shows that such an arbitrary, or *ad hoc*, application of the interest rate to the public sector projects will lead to suboptimal outcomes only, that is, too little social benefits gained in the future to justify the large monetary sacrifice today.

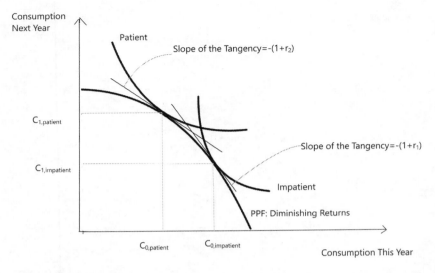

Fig. 7.3 A two-period model: technology and preference determine the interest rate

7.2   CAPITAL

What is capital? Fisher asked this question when he was the first PhD degree recipient in economics from Yale University during the final several years of the nineteenth century and before becoming the first professor of economics at the same institution (Fisher 1896, 1907). He found that there were many different uses of the term as well as many different definitions of it, making it nearly impossible to comprehend it in a consistent manner.

Even today, the term capital is appropriated by different groups of people for different interpretations and purposes. The term is used commonly in such words as financial capital, physical capital, natural resource capital, nature's capital, social capital, human capital, educational capital, and green capital (Table 7.1). Further, it is the term used to refer to the economic system driven by a free market or market interactions of individuals and businesses, that is, capitalism or a capitalist economy (Marx 1867; Friedman 1962; Piketty 2014).

What should be the overarching definition of the term which is appropriated in so many ways? Fisher defined it as follows, which is as simple as

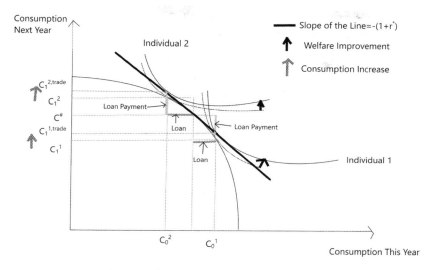

Fig. 7.4 Trade determines the interest rate

Table 7.1 The types of capital assets

Capital	Types of capital assets	Examples
	Physical asset	Land, buildings, machinery, residential houses
	Financial asset	Equities, bonds, savings, options, futures, ETFs, cryptocurrency
	Natural asset	Forests, fossil fuels, minerals (gold, etc.), marine resources, farm animals
	Ecological asset	Biodiversity
	Knowledge/technological asset	Royalties, patents, academic degrees

it gets: Capital is any asset, whether it be a physical, a financial, or a natural asset, that generates a flow of income over a sustained period of time. The income is an earning by a holder of the capital at one period of time. So, Fisher's definition establishes the link between capital and income (Fisher 1896, 1907).

Then, Fisher defined the value of a capital as the present value of the flow of net incomes that are generated from the asset. With π_t being the net income at one period in time and γ being the interest rate, the value of

the capital (V) is as follows in continuous time (above in Eq. 7.1) and in
discrete time (below in Eq. 7.1):

$$V = \int_0^\infty \pi_t e^{-\gamma t} dt;$$

$$= \sum_{t=0}^\infty \frac{\pi_t}{(1+\gamma)^t}. \tag{7.1}$$

The definition of capital and the value of capital, as in Eq. (7.1), by
Fisher bring out the importance of the interest rate, which is the topic of
the next section, in the theory of capital. Further, readers will be quick to
recall the importance of Eq. (7.1) and the interest rate in the analyses of
natural resource sectors such as agriculture, forests, fossil fuels, fisheries,
and so on, that were reviewed in the preceding chapters.

Further, Fisher's definition of a capital asset and its value renders an
expedient way to conceptualize the wealth of an individual, a corporation,
or a nation. That is, the wealth is simply the sum of the value of each capital asset across the range of capital assets that an individual agent holds.
Let V_j be the value of asset j. Then, the wealth of an individual agent is

$$W = \sum_{j=1}^J V_j. \tag{7.2}$$

This definition of wealth encompasses all assets of an individual agent,
inter alia, cash, savings, equities, bonds, buildings, lands, forests, fuels.
This definition is aptly applicable to a nation's wealth or a corporation's wealth.

The present author provides a classification of the five types of capital
assets in Table 7.1: physical, financial, natural, ecological, and knowledge/
technological. The physical asset includes lands, buildings, machinery, and
residential properties (Ricardo 1817; von Thunen 1826; Shiller 2005);
the financial asset includes currencies, equities, bonds, savings, options,
futures, Exchange Traded Funds (ETFs), and cryptocurrency (Shiller
2004; Fabozzi et al. 2009); the natural asset includes forests, fossil fuels,
minerals, marine resources, farm, and animals (NRC 1999; Dasgupta
2008; Daily et al. 2000); the ecological asset includes biodiversity (Perrings
et al. 1992; Simpson et al. 1996; Weitzman 1998b; Arrow et al. 2005;

Maler 2013); the knowledge and technological asset includes royalties, patents, and academic degrees (Griliches 1998).

Fisher's definitions of capital, income, interest rate, and wealth are often explained with the following analogy. Let's imagine a waterfall in a mountain below which is formed a large pond. From the pond, a fraction of water is also flowing downward. The flow of water that falls into the pool at a certain volume at each time unit is income. The flow of water that goes out of the pond is negative income, that is, cost. The pool with a given volume of water at a certain point in time is capital. The volume of water in the pond is the value of the capital (Allen 1993; Tobin 2005).

Fisher's definitions of these fundamental economic concepts are still the standard ways how economists see these variables (Tobin 1958; Sharpe 1964; Black and Scholes 1973; Shiller 2004). Along with the theory of interest rate to be explained presently, Fisher was clearly the pioneer who laid the foundation of modern financial economics and modern financial markets in general (Markowitz 1952; Tobin 1958; Modigliani and Pogue 1974; Fabozzi et al. 2009).

7.3   INTEREST RATE

For the calculation of the value of a capital asset *via* Eq. (7.1), which of the many interest rates available in the market should be inserted into the equation? Before answering this question, a more fundamental question needs to be posed: that is, what is the interest rate at all? An answer to the latter question will largely determine an answer to the former.

The interest rate is the cost of borrowing expressed as a percentage of the loan you get or, equivalently, the price of lending expressed as a percentage of the loan you give. A loan contract will specify the maturation date on which the principal is paid back as well as the interests to be paid periodically. The principal is the amount borrowed or lent. The interest rate on the principal may be specified as an annual rate or a quarterly rate to be paid back in either case on a monthly basis.

The interest rate existed for thousands of years in the human history, along with borrowing and lending money or other valuables between people. What determines the rate of interest? Even further, why do people charge the interest for the loan they provide? According to Shiller, major religions in the West appeared to have prohibited common people from earning an interest from a loan, referred to as "usura" in the Bible (Shiller 2008). These fundamental questions had not been answered in economics until Fisher's publication of the theory of interest during the early twentieth century (Fisher 1907, 1930; Samuelson 1994).

The theory of the interest rate as elucidated by Irving Fisher is explained in this section with Figs. 7.1, 7.2, 7.3, and 7.4. In Fig. 7.1, the interest rate is shown to be determined at the intersection of the demand curve and the supply curve of savings. The demand curve is downward sloping, that is, the lower the interest rate, the higher the demand for the savings, that is, the loan. The supply curve is upward sloping, that is, the higher the interest rate, the higher the supply curve of the savings, that is, the loan. At the intersection of these two forces in the market, the interest rate is determined, which is denoted as γ^* in the figure.

Why are the suppliers willing to provide the loan? The suppliers of the savings would do so for the purpose of earning an interest payment in the future from the loan. Why are the demanders willing to borrow despite the interest cost? The demanders are the investors who want to invest the loan into the productive activities that can generate, although not guaranteed, a stream of profits in excess of a stream of interest payments to the lender. In dependence upon the preferences and production technologies of the borrowers and lenders involved in the loan transaction, the interest rate, the size of the loan, the length of the loan period, and the method to pay back the principal will all be determined. Considering all these variables, although Fig. 7.1 is deceptively simple, we are led to surmise that the mechanisms that underlie the figure may be far more complex.

Heeding to the behaviors of borrowers and lenders, Eugene von Boehm-Bawerk's "Positive Theory" published in 1884 came with three explanations, "in a long verbose manner," for what causes the interest to exist between the borrowers and the lenders of money (von Bohm-Bawerk 1884; Samuelson 1994). The first was technological possibilities. The second was advantages to, what he calls, "roundaboutness." The third was time preference or impatience of individuals.

Fisher, on the other hand, elucidated not only the factors that determine the interest rate but also the complex mechanisms through which the interest rate is determined and further demonstrated that the debt market is Pareto welfare improving for the society. Avoiding the literary approach, Fisher relied for his exposition on the differences in preferences and technologies from which a social welfare-improving trade occurs between the borrowers and the lenders, which results in the interest rate (Fisher 1930; Samuelson 1994; Shiller 2008). His theory was that of mathematical economics in which the effect of a variation in each of the factors on the interest rate can be calculated within the model.

Let me clarify step by step what the preceding paragraph states. For this, the present author draws on Samuelson's work on Irving Fisher and Shiller's lectures at Yale University, in addition to Fisher's The Theory of Interest (Samuelson 1994; Nordhaus 2005; Shiller 2008). Let's start with the simplest two-period model of a lending market: this year and next year. This is graphically analyzed in Fig. 7.2. Further, it is a Robinson Crusoe economy, that is, there is only one person in the economy. He is endowed with a fixed quantity of a grain, say, corn. With this endowment, he should survive or enjoy the two periods in the best possible way.

The decision that this Crusoe faces is how much quantity of the grain he should consume this year and how much of it he should leave for the next year's consumption. More correctly, how much quantity of the grain he should plant during the planting season this year for the next year's consumption.

In Fig. 7.2, the horizontal axis is the consumption this year while the vertical axis is the consumption next year. The initial endowment of the grain is denoted C_0. If he decides to consume all what he has in period 1, owing to his extreme impatience, there will be nothing left over for the next year. So, he will not survive in the next year, which is certainly not the best decision for him.

Each bushel of the grain he leaves and plants, it yields a harvest at the end of this year whose yield is determined according to the technology at the time. The technology is represented by a Production Possibility Frontier (PPF) in Fig. 7.2. In this simple model, the technology is linear, that is, each bushel planted yields a fixed number of bushels of the grain regardless of how many bushels of the grain are planted. This is the slope of the PPF in the figure.

If Mr. Crusoe decides to plant all of the grain owing to, say, extreme patience, he will harvest C_1 bushels of the grain, along the PPF curve in the figure. Of course, he will not be able to survive to see the next year in this case!

Given the technology represented by the linear PPF, how much he will consume today and plant for the next year is determined by his preference. The preference is represented by the indifference curve in the figure, whose shape is determined by his time preference between this year's consumption and next year's (Mas-Colell et al. 1995).

At the tangency between the PPF and the indifference curve is determined the consumption of this year and the consumption of next year, denoted C_0^* and C_1^*. The slope of the tangent line determines the rate of interest. Specifically, the slope is equal to $-(1 + \gamma^*)$. How is this so? It is the ratio between the amount he borrows from the endowment and the amount she earns from the investment, that is, planting.

As readers can see, the slope of the linear PPF, however, never changes in this simple model. The interest rate is always unchanging, regardless of his preference changes, that is, different contours of the indifference curves. In the linear technology case, the technology alone determines the interest rate.

With a more realistic specification of the technology, the Fisher model shows that the interest rate is determined by both technology and preferences. This is illustrated in Fig. 7.3. Notice that the technology is now a diminishing-returns-to-scale technology, which is reflected in the concave PPF curve in the figure. In plain terms, each additional bushel of the grain left and planted for the next period's consumption yields an increasingly smaller quantity of the grain.

The figure shows the two indifference curves: one for a (relatively) patient individual and the other for a (relatively) impatient individual. Since there is only one individual in the model, at least for now in this chapter's exposition, so we are assuming the individual to be either patient or impatient. The impatient one chooses to consume more this year and less next year. The patient one chooses to consume less this year and more next year. That is,

$$C_{0,impatient} > C_{0,patient}; C_{1,impatient} < C_{1,patient}. \tag{7.3}$$

Recalling that the interest rate is determined by the slope of the tangency between the indifference curve and the PPF, we can verify in the figure that the interest rate is dependent on the individual's preference, in addition to the PPF. For the impatient one, the interest rate is high while the interest rate is low for the patient one. To put it in plain terms, for the impatient one, each bushel given up this year must be returned with a "significant" gain next year for him to make the sacrifice today. For the patient one, on the other hand, each bushel given up this year may be returned with a less "significant" gain next year for him to make the sacrifice today.

The slope of the tangency again equals $-(1 + \gamma)$, so determines the interest rate. Two interest rates are shown therefore in the figure, with γ_1 for the impatient one and γ_2 for the patient one, whose relationship is as follows:

$$\gamma_1 > \gamma_2. \tag{7.4}$$

The models in Figs. 7.2 and 7.3 are both a one-person Robison Crusoe economy. Even in this economy, it is important to remember that an interest rate exists. As explained in Fig. 7.1, however, the interest rate exists because of the trade between the suppliers and the demanders of savings, that is, the loan. The parties of the trade take part in such actions because they believe that the trade is mutually beneficial to them.

The two-period trade model of the interest rate determination is illustrated in Fig. 7.4, that is, a two-period two-person trade model. The situation is thus. Let's suppose that there are in this economy two individuals with different preferences on the island: Crusoe 1 and Crusoe 2. They have not yet met, as such, do not know the other's existence. Crusoe 1 is, relative to each other, an impatient one and Crusoe 2 is a patient one. There is only one technology in this economy, that is, a single diminishing-returns-to-scale PPF.

With no discovery of each other, two individuals will consume the grain this year and next year according to the tangency between the indifference curve and the PPF pertinent to each respective individual. The consumption basket for Crusoe 1 is $\left(C_0^1, C_1^1\right)$. The consumption basket for Crusoe 2 is $\left(C_0^2, C_1^2\right)$. The subscripts denote time periods while the superscripts the persons. Each consumption basket is the best for the respective individual, that is, without any trade among them. As such, the two consumption baskets are the best for the society, that is, without any trade among them.

Now, just before the planting season, let's suppose that they discover each other. They soon find out that Crusoe 2 is faced with a large diminishing-returns to planting an additional bushel of grain while Crusoe 1 still enjoys a large return, in relative terms, to planting an additional bushel of the grain.

The realization will lead eventually to striking a deal between the two through which Crusoe 2 will loan a certain quantity of the grain to Crusoe 1 with a loan payment guarantee by Crusoe 1 in the next year who would plant and harvest the loaned grains. In the figure, these transactions are denoted "Loan" and "Loan Payment" for Crusoe 1 and Crusoe 2, respectively.

Once Crusoe 2 gives the loan to Crusoe 1, Crusoe 1 employs his production technology and produces as much grain as $C^\#$ for the next year, as marked in the figure. Of the total production, Crusoe 1 returns the loan payment to Crusoe 2 that is agreed to be $C^\# - C_1^{1,trade}$, which is marked "Loan Payment" in the figure as well as in a thick gray vertical line. After the loan payment, his consumption for period 2 is therefore $C_1^{1,trade}$, which is larger than the period 2 consumption without trade, C_1^1. There is a consumption increase for Crusoe 1 from this trade, that is, the loan contract between the two parties.

For Crusoe 2, after giving the loan to Crusoe 1, her production for period 2 consumption decreases to $C^\#$. But, with the receipt of the loan payment from Crusoe 1 in the second period, her consumption for period 2 increases to $C_1^{2,trade}$. There is a gain of consumption for Crusoe 2 as well from the trade. That is, $C_1^{2,trade} > C_1^2$. There is a gain from this loan contract for Crusoe 2.

In addition to the consumption increase for each individual, the utility of each individual is improved from the loan agreement in the lending market composed of the two parties. As depicted in the figure with a thick black arrow, the indifference curve of Crusoe 1 shifts upwards, so is that of Crusoe 2. This is owing to the increase in the available consumption to each party attributable to the trade.

The market interest rate is again the slope of the tangent line, marked as a thick black line in the figure, that touches both the indifference curve of Crusoe 1 and that of Crusoe 2. Specifically, the slope is equal to $-(1 + \gamma^*)$. The interest rate is also by definition equal to the ratio between the loan amount and the loan payment amount. This is the market interest rate now, that is, not an individual's interest rate as was the case in Figs. 7.2 and 7.3.

The interest rate in the Fisher model thus far described is the real interest rate. The real interest rate (γ) is the real return on an investment, in other words, the real return on a lending. This is defined as the nominal interest rate (i) minus the rate of inflation (π). More formally, Fisher defined the real interest rate in the following relationship which is known as the Fisher equation (Fisher 1907, 1920, 1933; Fabozzi et al. 2009):

$$(1+i) = (1+\gamma)(1+\pi);\qquad\qquad\text{(7.5a)}$$

$$\gamma \cong i - \pi.\qquad\qquad\text{(7.5b)}$$

In the above, i is the nominal interest rate, π the rate of inflation, and γ the real interest rate.

7.4   A ZERO DISCOUNTING CRITIQUE

A pervasive nature of the theory of interest rate into all economic theories has been well emphasized throughout the preceding chapters of this book. With a foundation of the interest rate, any private sector investment is evaluated by the sum of a stream of net incomes properly discounted with an appropriate discount rate over the period of the investment's duration. The same is true of any long-term public sector project. This project evaluation technique was fundamental to the analyses of all the preceding chapters.

Critics against this project evaluation framework emerged during the past three decades over the contentious debates on the global warming challenges faced by the planet and appropriate policy responses (Weitzman 1998a, Stern 2007). At the core of their arguments is that a discounting rationale and application in economics treats future generations unfairly against the present generations when it comes to the evaluation of a long-term public project. The critics argued that this problem particularly looms large in a public sector project whose planning horizon is as long as a century such as a global warming policy (Newell and Pizer 2001). The most severe damage from the greenhouse gas emissions released by today's generations will befall the generations of a distant future, say, at the end of the twenty-first century. The future generations will bear the brunt of the damage, they argue, notwithstanding the damage is inflicted by and large by the present generations.

The critics continue: A reasonable response of the current generations to this long-term challenge is to invest in a century-long global project or treaty in a globally cooperative fashion that purports to reduce the emissions of harmful greenhouse gases now and immediately to thereby reduce, if not eliminate, the potential damage to future generations. The dollar to be spent by the public project should be justified by the avoided damage on future generations from the investment. Discounting the future damages that will only occur in distant future periods will render those future damages nearly negligible in terms of their present values. Thereby, a costly investment for a global warming policy by the present generations will never be justifiable under the discounting rationale.

The critics therefore propose to adopt a near zero discount rate for an evaluation of a long-term public sector project such as a global climate treaty. Many critics in fact chose to adopt a zero-discounting approach in their analysis of one or another international climate policy proposal (Arrow et al. 1996, Weitzman 1998, Stern 2007).

The zero-discounting proposal cannot escape the cold reality of interest rate in the market economy (Nordhaus 2007). All public and private investments in the reality of the market are evaluated with a proper discounting rate (Hartwick and Olewiler 1997; Fabozzi et al. 2009). It would not be justifiable for a rational government or any rational international organization to give exception to a single selected project such as a global warming policy. Even within the public sector projects only, it would be indefensible for any consistent national government to apply a zero interest rate to a certain group of projects and then apply a real market interest rate to another group of projects. Considering a large number of theoretical and real-world problems that would arise, a zero-discounting rule for the evaluations of a long-term public sector project is not an option for economists and policy-makers.

Notwithstanding, when it comes to discounting future damages and benefits from a project, reasonable questions arise regarding whether policy modelers should rely on a constant or variable interest rate for a long-term governmental project. Of particular relevance to our discussion, some researchers demonstrate that, when individuals in the market discount future damages and profits, they discount them in a proportional manner. This alternative discounting method is referred to as a hyperbolic discounting (Ainslie 1991; Laibson 1997; Karp 2004; Jamison and Jamison 2011).

At the core of the hyperbolic discounting is the idea, which, according to the proponents, can be established by the observation of individuals' market behaviors, that the farther the future date one engages with, the lower the discount rate that she applies; the nearer the future date that one engages with, the higher the discount rate that she applies (Ainslie 1991; Laibson 1997). This variable discounting behavior is modelled by a hyperbolic function in which the ratio between two adjacent periods' discounting rates remains constant (Seo 2020).

Let me clarify these statements. For an exponential discounting, the dollar in a future time period (t) is discounted exponentially. Let k be a parameter of the degree of discounting, say, the interest rate. Then, the discount factor is written as follows with an exponential function:

$$f(t) = \$1 * e^{-kt}. \tag{7.6}$$

For the exponential discounting, the discounting at any time period of the next year's dollar remains the same, that is, time-consistent. Put differently, the ratio of the discounting factors between two adjacent time periods remains constant, regardless of how far or near in the future the two periods are located:

$$\frac{f(t+1)}{f(t)} = \frac{e^{-k(t+1)}}{e^{-kt}} = e^{-k}. \tag{7.7}$$

For the hyperbolic discounting, the discount factor is defined by the following hyperbolic function, for which the term hyperbolic discounting is originated:

$$g(t) = \$1 * \frac{1}{1+kt}. \tag{7.8}$$

Note that the discount factor depends hyperbolically on how farther the time period is located, that is, t, for which reason it is called a time-inconsistent discounting. For the hyperbolic discounting, the discounting between the two adjacent time periods depends on how far in the future the two periods are occurring, that is, time-dependent:

$$\frac{g(t+1)}{g(t)} = \frac{\dfrac{1}{1+k(t+1)}}{\dfrac{1}{1+kt}} = \frac{1}{1+\dfrac{k}{1+kt}}. \tag{7.9}$$

At $t = 0$, the hyperbolic discounting and the exponential discounting are equivalent in terms of how much they discount the next year's consumption: $\frac{1}{1+k}$. As t gets farther apart from the present, however, the difference in the degree of discounting becomes ever larger between the two discounting methods. In an unforeseeably distant future, the ratio in Eq. (7.9) gets closer to 1, which means that the hyperbolic discounting leads to near zero discounting of the next year's consumption in those remote future periods.

It is noteworthy that the hyperbolic discounting is reconcilable with the exponential discounting. The hyperbolic discounting can be approximated by an exponential discounting with a variable discount rate, $k(t)$, which declines over time (Seo 2020):

$$\frac{dk}{dt} < 0. \tag{7.10}$$

7.5   Conclusion

The theories on capital, income, and interest rate elaborated by Irving Fisher during the early twentieth century have over time turned out to be one of the finest works in economic science (Samuelson 1994; Nordhaus 2005; Dimand and Geanakoplos 2005; Shiller 2008). The importance and influence of his foundational theories on the literature of economic growth will be amply demonstrated in the ensuing chapters. Readers will be able to see that the concepts of capital and interest rate as defined by Irving Fisher turn up over and again as a key economic variable in the theory of national savings by Ramsey, the modern economic growth theory by Solow, the optimal economic growth theory by Koopmans, and the climate and economy model by Nordhaus (Ramsey 1928; Solow 1957; Koopmans 1965; Nordhaus 1994; Piketty 2014).

References

Ainslie, G. 1991. Derivation of 'Rational' Economic Behavior from Hyperbolic Discount Curves. *American Economic Review* 81: 334–340.

Allen, Robert L. 1993. *Irving Fisher: A Biography*. Hoboken, NJ: Wiley-Blackwell.

Arrow, Kenneth, Bert Bolin, Robert Costanza, Partha Dasgupta, Carl Folke, Crawford S. Holling, Bengt-Owe Jansson, Simon Levin, Karl-Goran Maler, Charles Perrings, and David Pimentel. 1995. Economic Growth, Carrying Capacity, and the Environment. *Ecological Economics* 15: 91–95.

Arrow, K.J., W. Cline, K.G. Maler, M. Munasinghe, R. Squitieri, and J. Stiglitz. 1996. Intertemporal Equity, Discounting, and Economic Efficiency. In *Climate*

Change 1995: Economic and Social Dimensions of Climate Change, Intergovernmental Panel on Climate Change, ed. J.P. Bruce, H. Lee, and E.F. Haites. Cambridge, UK: Cambridge University Press.

Black, F., and M. Scholes. 1973. The Pricing of Options and Corporate Liabilities. *Journal of Political Economy* 81: 637–654.

Daily, Gretchen C., Tore Söderqvist, Sara Aniyar, Kenneth Arrow, Partha Dasgupta, Paul R. Ehrlich, Carl Folke, AnnMari Jansson, Bengt-Owe Jansson, Nils Kautsky, Simon Levin, Jane Lubchenco, Karl-Göran Mäler, David Simpson, David Starrett, David Tilman, and Brian Walker. 2000. The Value of Nature and the Nature of Value. *Science* 289: 395–396.

Dasgupta, P. 2008. *Natural Capital and Economic Growth.* Encyclopedia of Earth. http://editors.eol.org/eoearth/wiki/Natural_capital_and_economic_growth.

Dimand, Roger W., and John Geanakoplos, eds. 2005. *Celebrating Irving Fisher: The Legacy of a Great Economist.* Hoboken, NJ: Wiley-Blackwell.

Fabozzi, F.J., F. Modigliani, and M.G. Ferri. 2009. *Foundations of Financial Markets and Institutions.* 4th ed. Hoboken, NJ: Prentice-Hall.

Fisher, Irving. 1896. What is Capital? *The Economic Journal* 6: 509–534.

———. 1906. *The Nature of Capital and Income.* New York, NY: Macmillan.

———. 1907. *The Rate of Interest.* New York, NY: Macmillan.

———. 1920. *The Purchasing Power of Money: Its Determination and Relation to Credit, Interest and Crises.* New York, NY: Macmillan.

———. 1930. *The Theory of Interest.* New York, NY: Macmillan.

———. 1933. The Debt-deflation Theory of Great Depressions. *Econometrica* 1: 337–357.

Friedman, M. 1962. *Capitalism and Freedom.* Chicago, IL: The University of Chicago Press.

Griliches, Zvi. 1998. *Patents and Technology.* Cambridge, MA: Harvard University Press.

Hartwick, J.M., and N.D. Olewiler. 1997. *The Economics of Natural Resource Use.* 2nd ed. New York, NY: Pearson.

Jamison, D.T., and J. Jamison. 2011. Characterizing the Amount and Speed of Discounting Procedures. *Journal of Benefit-Cost Analysis* 2: 1–53.

Karp, L. 2004. *Global Warming and Hyperbolic Discounting.* CUDARE Working Papers, #934, The University of California, Berkeley.

Koopmans, Tjalling C. 1965. On the Concept of Optimal Economic Growth. *Pontificiae Academiae Scientiarum Scripta Varia* 28 (1): 1–75.

Laibson, D. 1997. Golden Eggs and Hyperbolic Discounting. *Quarterly Journal of Economics* 112: 443–477.

Maler, K.G. 2013. *Environmental Economics: A Theoretical Inquiry.* Washington, DC: The Resources for the Future Press.

Markowitz, H. 1952. Portfolio Selection. *Journal of Finance* 7: 77–91.

Marx, Karl. 1867. *Das Kapital. Kritik der politischen Oekonomie.* Verlag von Otto Meisner, Germany.

Mas-Colell, A., M.D. Whinston, and J.R. Green. 1995. *Microeconomic Theory.* Oxford, UK: Oxford University Press.

Modigliani, F., and G.A. Pogue. 1974. An Introduction to Risk and Return: Concepts and Evidence. *Financial Analysts Journal* 1974: 68–80.

National Research Council (NRC). 1999. *Nature's Numbers: Expanding the National Economic Accounts to Include the Environment.* Washington, DC: The National Academies Press. https://doi.org/10.17226/6374.

Newell, R., and W. Pizer. 2001. *Discounting the Benefits of Climate Change Mitigation: How Much Do Uncertain Rates Increase Valuations?* Washington, DC: The Pew Center.

Nordhaus, W.D. 1994. *Managing the Global Commons.* Cambridge, MA: MIT Press.

———. 2005. Irving Fisher and the Contribution of Improved Longevity to Living Standards. *The American Journal of Economics and Sociology* 64 (1). Special Invited Issue: Celebrating Irving Fisher: The Legacy of a Great Economist: 367–392.

———. 2007. A Review of the Stern Review on the Economics of Climate Change. *Journal of Economic Literature* 55: 686–702.

Pareto, V. 1906. In A. Montesano, A. Zanni, L. Bruni, J.S. Chipman, and M. McLure, ed., *Manual for Political Economy.* Oxford, UK: Oxford University Press. [2014].

Perrings, Charles, Carl Folke, and Karl-Göran Mäler. 1992. The Ecology and Economics of Biodiversity Loss: The Research Agenda. *Ambio* 21: 201–211.

Piketty, Thomas. 2014. *Capital in the Twenty-First Century.* Cambridge, MA: Belknap Press.

Ramsey, F.P. 1928. A Mathematical Theory of Savings. *Economic Journal* 38: 543–559.

Ricardo, D. 1817. *On the Principles of Political Economy and Taxation.* London, UK: John Murray.

Samuelson, Paul A. 1994. Two Classics: Böhm-Bawerk's Positive Theory and Fisher's Rate of Interest Through Modern Prisms. *Journal of the History of Economic Thought* 16: 202–228.

Seo, S.N. 2020. *The Economics of Globally Shared and Public Goods.* Amsterdam, NL: Academic Press.

Sharpe, W.F. 1964. Capital Asset Prices: A Theory of Market Equilibrium Under Conditions of Risk. *Journal of Finance* 19: 425–442.

Shiller, R.J. 2004. *The New Financial Order: Risk in the 21st Century.* Princeton, NJ: Princeton University Press.

———. 2005. *Irrational Exuberance.* 2nd ed. Princeton, NJ: Princeton University Press.

————. 2008. *Financial Markets.* Open Yale Courses, Yale University, New Haven, CT.

Simpson, R. David, Roger A. Sedjo, and John W. Reid. 1996. Valuing Biodiversity for Use in Pharmaceutical Research. *Journal of Political Economy* 104 (1): 163–185.

Solow, R.M. 1957. A Contribution to the Theory of Economic Growth. *Quarterly Journal of Economics* 70: 65–94.

Stern, N. 2007. *The Economics of Climate Change: The Stern Review.* New York, NY: Cambridge University Press.

Tobin, James. 1958. Liquidity Preference as Behavior Towards Risk. *The Review of Economic Studies* 25: 65–86.

————. 2005. Irving Fisher (1867–1947). *American Journal of Economics and Sociology* 64: 19–42.

von Bohm-Bawerk, Eugen. 1884, 1889, 1921. Kapital und Kapitalzins, I: Geschichte und Kritik der Kapitalzins-Theorien, II: Positive Theories des Kapitales, III: Exkurse zur "Positiven Theorie des Kapitales", Wagner, Innsbruck.

von Thunen, Johann Heinrich. 1826. *Der isolirte Staat in Beziehung auf Landwirtschaft und Nationalökonomie.* Wirtschaft & Finan. [*The Isolated State* (trans. C.M. Wartenberg). Oxford/New York: Pergamon Press, 1966]. https://play.google.com/store/books/details?id=K-M2AQAAMAAJ&rdid=book-K-M2AQAAMAAJ&rdot=1.

Weitzman, M.L. 1998a. Why the Far-distant Future Should be Discounted at Its Lowest Possible Rate. *Journal of Environmental Economics and Management* 36: 201–208.

————. 1998b. The Noah's Ark Problem. *Econometrica* 66: 1279–1298.

CHAPTER 8

Frank Ramsey's Optimal Savings

8.1 Introduction

Thus far, the present author has explained a host of the economic theories and models that are concerned with the question of how the society's valuable resources should be utilized over time to maximize the benefits gained from these resources. Some of these were renewable resources while others were exhaustible, non-renewable resources. Some of these were privately owned resources and others were open access resources.

If you are a forest owner, for example, how should you manage it over time if you want to maximize the benefits from the forest? Faustmann grappled with this question during the nineteenth century, putting forth an elegant analysis with a clear optimization solution, which we called a Faustmann rotation in this book (Faustmann 1849).

If you are a crude oil well owner, for another example, how should you extract and sell the petroleum in the reservoir in order to achieve the maximum benefits in a dynamic manner over the course of the well's life? An individual well owner, a petroleum industry, and the society at large would surely pose this question. The Hotelling rule clarified in Chap. 4 provided an analytical answer to this question (Hotelling 1931).

If you are an owner of a financial asset or multiple financial assets, what rate should the asset(s) earn for you at each time period over time? Adding up all the future earnings generated by the asset, what is the value of the capital asset you own? These financial questions were asked by Irving

S. N. Seo, *The Economics of Optimal Growth Pathways*, https://doi.org/10.1007/978-3-031-20754-9_8

Fisher who defined the value of the capital asset, relying on the concept of interest rate, as the sum of the stream of discounted future earnings (Fisher 1906, 1930).

Frank Ramsey grappled with a similar dynamic optimization problem as the above, but with his focus set on the national economy as a whole (Ramsey 1928). As per the national economy, one may ask the following question directly: Can the national economy be managed in an optimal manner over future periods? Or, can the national economy grow in an optimal rate over an infinite horizon of time (Koopmans 1963, 1965)? It is an onerous question to handle considering that there are a large number of various types of assets that comprise the national economy, including forests, croplands, grasslands, urban lands, fossil fuels, marine resources, and financial assets.

Therefore, Ramsey narrowed his question, although unintentionally, to what an optimal saving rate of the economy should be. If the nation's earnings or new productions in each period were either consumed immediately by its citizens or saved (for new investments) for future productions, what should be an optimal rate of saving by the nation? This was Ramsey's inquiry. The savings in his model mean new investments made by the productive sectors of the economy. So, the determination of an optimal rate of savings is equivalent to that of an optimal rate of investment.

When Frank Ramsey published his "A Mathematical Theory of Saving" in 1928, he was only 25 years old. He was encouraged by J.M. Keynes, who was teaching at Cambridge University, to write the article. He died soon afterward at the age of 26 in 1930, probably from a liver infection (Gottlieb 2020). The theoretical contribution widely cited as the "Ramsey equation" still remains a reference to the economists of today. Specifically, when the debates raged among the economists on how the society should discount the future earnings or consumptions in designing a centuries-long global warming policy, the Ramsey argument was given a central spotlight (Stern 2007; Nordhaus 2007; Weitzman 2007).

Is there an optimal economic growth path for the national economy? If so, what does it look like? Is it mathematically solvable, taking into account all the variables and sectors in the economy? Can the optimal growth pathway be derived explicitly from a dynamic optimalization problem of the economy? Then, what should the society's utility function look like? What about the technological advances expected and unexpected? What about uncertain catastrophes natural or man-made? What would be the effects of continued population growth, potentially explosive? How should the national economy be characterized in such an optimization problem? How should the natural resource sectors be accounted for in the economic growth model?

These questions pertain to a broader, encompassing, and essential inquiry on economic growth, which had to be in the wait since Ramsey for another three decades until Tjalling Koopmans published his article in 1963, with rejoinders from the reviewers, entitled "On the Concept of Optimal Economic Growth" for the Cowles Foundation of Economics at Yale University (Koopmans 1963, 1965). Koopmans was a Dutch-American mathematician and economist and received the Nobel Prize in Economic Science in 1975 for his work on the theory of the optimum allocation of resources, more specifically, for the development of mathematical programming (Koopmans 1949, 1951; Kantorovich 1939). That being the case, he has been known well for the latter to economists, but not for the former, that is, the optimal economic growth theory.

What Koopmans described in his lengthy article composed mostly of mathematical equations and proofs had remained incomprehensible to most in the economics profession until a young college student of Koopmans came back to Yale University as a junior Professor in his late 20s, William Nordhaus, around 1970. He started to decode Koopmans's work and 20 years later published one of the best-known economic models of all time. He called it "rolling the DICE," short for Dynamic Integrated model of Climate and Economy (Nordhaus 1991, 1994). Nordhaus was able to wear real economic meaning on Koopmans's model.

These are the stories to be told henceforth up to Chap. 11: the Ramsey model in Chap. 8, Solow's growth model in Chap. 9, Koopmans's optimal growth model in Chap. 10, and Nordhaus's climate and economy model in Chap. 11.

8.2   A Theory of Saving

The significance of Ramsey's sole contribution to the economics literature, the article entitled "A Mathematical Theory of Saving," lies in his attempt to build a dynamic social welfare optimization model of the national economy by way of his search for an optimal saving rate of the economy.

A dynamic optimization framework had long existed in the economics literature but only at the level of a single economic sector or an enterprise. As mentioned in the previous section, Faustmann developed a dynamic optimization model of a forest sector, known as the Faustmann rule (1849). Hotelling provided a dynamic optimization model of a fossil fuel industry (Hotelling 1931). Fisher defined the capital as any asset which generates a flow of net revenues over the course of the asset's life and the value of capital as the sum of the flow of net revenues discounted by the market interest rate (Fisher 1906, 1930).

Unlike these dynamic optimization models, the objective function of the Ramsey model was the social utility or social welfare for which he used as a simple utility function with a constant relative risk aversion (CRRA). In the other aforementioned optimization models, the objective function was the present value of the stream of profits generated over a time horizon.

Right at the start of the article, Ramsey summarized his task as follows (Ramsey 1928):

> THE first problem I propose to tackle is this: how much of its income should a nation save? To answer this a simple rule is obtained valid under conditions of surprising generality; the rule, which will be further elucidated later, runs as follows.

The rule referred to in the above quote for the determination of the economy's optimal saving was stated by the author as follows:

> The rate of saving multiplied by the marginal utility of money should always be equal to the amount by which the total net rate of enjoyment of utility falls short of the maximum possible rate of enjoyment.

The maximum possible rate of enjoyment was referred to as "Bliss" by Ramsey. The optimal condition stated by Ramsey is easy to understand by rearranging it:

$$\left(\text{The rate of saving}\right)^{*}\left(\text{the marginal utility of money}\right) = \begin{pmatrix} \text{the maximum} \\ \text{possible rate} \\ \text{of enjoyment} \\ \text{of utility} \end{pmatrix} - \begin{pmatrix} \text{the total net rate} \\ \text{of enjoyment} \\ \text{of utility} \end{pmatrix}.$$

$$(8.1)$$

The marginal benefit of the society from saving a dollar is the left-hand side (LHS) of the above equation. The marginal cost of the society from saving a dollar is the right-hand side (RHS) of the above equation, which arises from a dollar lost for consumption owing to the saving.

At this point, readers should wonder: Why does the solution to the dynamic optimal saving question, that is, Eq. 8.1, look like a solution to a one-period saving question? Why was the reduction in the social utility from a loss of consumption calculated as the shortfall from the "Bliss"?

This was because Ramsey made several simplifying assumptions which made his model to become in fact a non-dynamic model (Tinbergen 1960; Koopmans 1965). The first was the assumption of no population change in the economy over time (IIASA 2007; Lutz et al. 2014). The second was the assumption of no discounting of future benefits and costs in the model. In his own words as for the first assumption (Ramsey 1928),

> In order to justify this rule it is, of course, necessary to make various simplifying assumptions: we have to suppose that our community goes on for ever without changing either in numbers or in its capacity for enjoyment or in its aversion to labour; that enjoyments and sacrifices at different times can be calculated independently and added; and that no new inventions or improvements in organisation are introduced save such as can be regarded as conditioned solely by the accumulation of wealth.

At the first page of his article, Ramsey made a rather abrupt proclamation with regard to the second assumption, that is, the indefensibility of discounting future consumptions. It was not justified in the article but came to be relied upon broadly among researchers and, especially, actively quoted nearly 80 years after his publication by zero-discounting critics (Stern 2007). Specifically, Ramsey made the following emphatic remark (Ramsey 1928):

> One point should perhaps be emphasised more particularly; it is assumed that we do not discount later enjoyments in comparison with earlier ones, a practice which is ethically indefensible and arises merely from the weakness of the imagination.

8.3   A RAMSEY DISCOUNTING CRITIQUE

Out of his article, the "Ramsey equation" has still been frequently cited by many economists (Hope 2006; Stern 2007; Weitzman 2007). In fact, many consider the "Ramsey equation" to be equivalent to his article.

Although economists frequently cite this as the Ramsey equation, that is to say, without quotation marks, the term Ramsey equation never appeared in the review of the literature by Tjalling Koopmans or his contemporaries (Tinbergen 1960; Koopmans 1963; Inagaki 1963). Moreover, when William Nordhaus referred to it, he always did so with quotation marks, that is, the "Ramsey equation (Nordhaus 2007)." A careful reading of the Ramsey's 1928 article will reveal that the Ramsey equation was not in the article.

The Ramsey optimality condition that actually appeared in his article was that "the rate of saving multiplied by marginal utility of consumption should always equal Bliss minus actual rate of utility enjoyed," specifically, the Eq. 5 in his article (Ramsey 1928).

Anyway, the "Ramsey equation" that is widely relied upon by economists is as follows:

$$\gamma = \delta + \eta g. \tag{8.2}$$

The debates on the discounting of future generations' consumptions and productions that emerged in the context of designing a long-term global warming policy have centered around the above equation (Broome 1994; Weitzman 1998; Newell and Pizer 2001; Karp 2004; Hope 2006; Stern 2007; Seo 2020). The parameters in Eq. 8.2 are γ a real interest rate, δ a pure rate of time preference, η an intergenerational inequality aversion parameter, and g a per capita growth rate of consumption.

The η is the parameter in the social welfare function, more correctly, in the individual's utility function. The utility function is specified as a non-linear function of consumption, referred to as a Bernoulli utility function or aforementioned CRRA social utility function (Weitzman 2009):

$$U(C) = \frac{C^{1-\eta}}{1-\eta}. \tag{8.3}$$

In Eq. 8.3, it is the elasticity of marginal utility (MU) of consumption:

$$\eta = \left| \frac{dMU/MU}{dC/C} \right| = \left| \frac{C}{MU} \frac{dMU}{dC} \right| = \left| \frac{C}{C^{-\eta}} \left(-\eta C^{-\eta-1} \right) \right| \tag{8.4}$$

Although many economists refer to it as the constant relative risk aversion (CRRA) parameter, a more proper interpretation is that of the society's inequality aversion. With $\eta = 1$, the society is neutral to social and intergenerational inequality. With $\eta > 1$, the society is averse to social and intergenerational inequality. With $\eta < 1$, the society is loving social and intergenerational inequality (Nordhaus 2007).

To put the "Ramsey equation" in context, the social rate of time preference should be set at 2% if the real interest is 6% per year, consumption growth rate is 2% per year, and the social inequality aversion parameter is 2 (Table 8.1). The two other calibrations of the "Ramsey equation" are also shown in Table 8.1. The social rate of time preference should be set at 4% if the real interest is 6% per year, consumption growth rate is 2% per year, and the social inequality aversion parameter is 1.

The social rate of time preference (δ) is chosen by the modeler, but the choice must be made in accordance with Eq. 8.2, that is, the "Ramsey equation." In other words, the parameter cannot be determined arbitrarily or independently from the other parameters in Eq. 8.2 (Nordhaus 2007; Weitzman 2009; Seo 2020, 2021). The real interest rates (γ) are obtained from the market data, so is the per capita consumption growth rate (g) (Arrow et al. 1996; Shiller 2019).

The social rate of time preference cannot be set zero independently of the other parameters of the Ramsey equation, whose point will be further clarified in Chap. 10 when Koopmans's model is explained. This is despite the strong objection to a discounting practice by Frank Ramsey as "a practice which is ethically indefensible and arises merely from the weakness of the imagination."

Table 8.1 Determining a pure rate of time preference

	δ	γ	η	g
	Pure rate of time preference	Real interest rate	Social inequality aversion	Per capita consumption growth rate
Calibration I	2%	6%	2	2%
Calibration II	4%	6%	1	2%
Calibration III	2%	4%	1	2%

8.4   Conclusion

This chapter provides a brief review of the mathematical theory of optimal savings by young Frank Ramsey. It dawns on the present author that Frank Ramsey would have had much in store in his life if he had survived the disease at his late 20s. He might have gone on to complete his optimal saving model to the levels that were achieved by Koopmans or Solow four decades later (Solow 1957; Koopmans 1965). From another point of view, he may have had too many interests as well as skills in life such as philosophy, mathematics, economics, among other things, at least at the young age, to focus on a single great subject (Gottlieb 2020).

References

Arrow, K.J., W. Cline, K.G. Maler, M. Munasinghe, R. Squitieri, and J. Stiglitz. 1996. Intertemporal Equity, Discounting, and Economic Efficiency. In *Climate Change 1995: Economic and Social Dimensions of Climate Change, Intergovernmental Panel on Climate Change*, ed. J.P. Bruce, H. Lee, and E.F. Haites. Cambridge, UK: Cambridge University Press.

Broome, J. 1994. Discounting the Future. *Philosophy & Public Affairs* 23: 128–156.

Faustmann, Martin. 1849. On the Determination of the Value which Forest Land and Immature Stands Pose for Forestry. In *Martin Faustmann and the Evolution of Discounted Cash Flow*, ed. M. Gane. Paper 42. Oxford, England: Oxford Institute; 1968. 54 pp.

Fisher, Irving. 1906. *The Nature of Capital and Income*. New York, NY: Macmillan.

———. 1930. *The Theory of Interest*. New York, NY: Macmillan.

Gottlieb, A. 2020. The Man Who Thought Too Fast. New Yorker. May 2020 Issue. https://www.newyorker.com/magazine/2020/05/04/the-man-who-thought-too-fast.

Hope, C. 2006. The Marginal Impact of CO_2 from PAGE2002: An Integrated Assessment Model Incorporating the IPCC's Five Reasons for Concern. *Integrated Assessment Journal* 6: 19–56.

Hotelling, H. 1931. The Economics of Exhaustible Resources. *Journal of Political Economy* 39: 137–175.

Inagaki, M. 1963. *The Golden Utility Path*. Rotterdam, NL: Netherlands Economics Institute.

International Institute of Applied Systems Analysis (IIASA). 2007. Probabilistic Projections by 13 World Regions, Forecast Period 2000–2100, 2001 Revision. http://www.iiasa.ac.at/Research/POP/proj01/.

Kantorovich, Leonid V. 1939. Mathematical Methods of Organizing and Planning Production. *Management Science* 6: 366–422.

Karp, L. 2004. Global Warming and Hyperbolic Discounting. CUDARE Working Papers, #934, The University of California, Berkeley.

Koopmans, Tjalling C. 1949. Optimum Utilization of the Transportation System. *Proceedings of the International Statistical Conference* 5: 136–145.

———., ed. 1951. *Activity Analysis of Production and Allocation.* New York, NY: Wiley.

———. 1963. *On the Concept of Optimal Economic Growth.* The Cowles Foundation Discussion Paper # 163, Yale University, New Haven, CT.

———. 1965. On the Concept of Optimal Economic Growth. *Pontificiae Academiae Scientiarum Scripta Varia* 28 (1): 1–75.

Lutz, W., W. Butz, and K.C. Samir, eds. 2014. *World Population and Global Human Capital in the 21st Century.* Oxford, UK: Oxford University Press.

Newell, R., and W. Pizer. 2001. *Discounting the Benefits of Climate Change Mitigation: How Much Do Uncertain Rates Increase Valuations?* Washington, DC: The Pew Center.

Nordhaus, W.D. 1991. To Slow or Not to Slow: The Economics of the Greenhouse Effects. *Economic Journal* 101: 920–937.

———. 1994. *Managing the Global Commons.* Cambridge, MA: MIT Press.

———. 2007. A Review of the Stern Review on the Economics of Climate Change. *Journal of Economic Literature* 55: 686–702.

Ramsey, F.P. 1928. A Mathematical Theory of Savings. *Economic Journal* 38: 543–559.

Seo, S.N. 2020. *The Economics of Globally Shared and Public Goods.* Amsterdam, NL: Academic Press.

———. 2021. *Climate Change and Economics: Engaging with Future Generations with Action Plans.* London, UK: Palgrave Macmillan.

Shiller, R. 2019. Online Data for Rebert Shiller. New Haven, CT: Yale University. http://www.econ.yale.edu/Bshiller/data.htm.

Solow, Robert M. 1957. A Contribution to the Theory of Economic Growth. *Quarterly Journal of Economics* 70: 65–94.

Stern, N. 2007. *The Economics of Climate Change: The Stern Review.* New York, NY: Cambridge University Press.

Tinbergen, J. 1960. Optimum Savings and Utility Maximization Over Time. *Econometrica* 28: 481–489.

Weitzman, M.L. 1998. Why the Far-distant Future Should be Discounted at Its Lowest Possible Rate. *Journal of Environmental Economics and Management* 36: 201–208.

———. 2007. A Review of the Stern Review on the Economics of Climate Change. *Journal of Economic Literature* 45: 703–724.

———. 2009. On Modeling and Interpreting the Economics of Catastrophic Climate Change. *Review of Economics and Statistics* 91: 1–19.

CHAPTER 9

Robert Solow's Modern Economic Growth

9.1 Introduction

The modern economic growth theory, also referred to as the neoclassical growth theory in contrast to the classical works by Adam Smith, Thomas Malthus, and perhaps Karl Marx, was conceptualized by Robert Solow (Smith 1776; Malthus 1798; Marx 1867). Solow described a simplified model of economic growth over an infinite time horizon from which he derived major predictions on the economy's dynamic progression (Solow 1957).

The Solow model was not a dynamic welfare optimization model of the economy such as the Ramsey model and Koopmans's model (Ramsey 1928; Koopmans 1965). Rather, it was a prediction of the economic growth trajectory based on a simple production function of the economy, which laid the foundation for the modern growth economics. Put differently, his production-based model was extraordinarily popular among the economists during the latter half of the twentieth century (P. Romer 1990, Barro and Sala-i-Martin 1992, Mankiw et al. 1992, Aghion and Howitt 2009, Nordhaus 2014, D. Romer 2018).

What was the reason for the popularity and influence of the Solow model? The heart of it is that he was able to encapsulate successfully a complex economic system into a simple input-output relationship, relying on the core terms of economics which had been being defined and refined up to his time. In Chap. 7, the present author explained the important

S. N. Seo, *The Economics of Optimal Growth Pathways*, https://doi.org/10.1007/978-3-031-20754-9_9

concept of capital elucidated by Irving Fisher (Fisher 1906, 1930). Robert Solow relied on the concept of capital (K), as well as that of labor (L) and technology (A), to capture the complexity of the macro economy.

Based on the core concepts, he specified a representative production function of the economy, that is, a Cobb-Douglas type production function, that explains how endogenous production inputs such as capital (K) and labor (L) determine the total output of the economy in the form of capital (K), in addition to an exogenously determined rate of technical change (A) in the economy.

From this pithy but encompassing model, Robert Solow was able to explain the progress of the macro economy over time. The dynamic model was possible because of the capital accumulation in the model over time, some of which is reinvested for future productions while the rest is consumed by the population at the "present" time. In the model, on the other hand, labor which is treated equivalently to population was assumed to grow exogenously over a time horizon.

He arrived at several key conclusions regarding the macro economy's growth trajectories as inevitable outcomes or predictions of his model. These predictions as well as the Solow model itself have become the subjects of intensive and extensive investigations by the researchers of the twentieth century (To mention just some, P. Romer 1990, Barro and Sala-i-Martin 1992, Mankiw et al. 1992, Aghion and Howitt 2009, Nordhaus 2014, D. Romer 2018).

Of the long list of offshoot studies, a particular emphasis was given to the assumption of the exogenous technical change. In other words, the technological growth ($A(t)$ in the model) was specified by Solow as an independent function from the model's economic variables and the economic growth trajectory itself. The research efforts to specify the dynamic technical change in the economy as an endogenous process within the growth model were one of the major legacies of the Solow model (P. Romer 1990, Aghion and Howitt 1992). For the description of it, readers may refer to the recent publication on the advances in pharmaceutical technologies such as mRNA vaccines in the rich countries which were vital tools against the global responses against the COVID-19 (Corona Virus Disease 2019) pandemic (Pardi et al. 2018; Seo 2022).

For another, the Solow specification of the economy's production function has become a standard way to represent the production side of the macro economy in the dynamic social welfare optimization models of economic growth that came after him such as Koopmans's and Nordhaus's (Koopmans 1965; Nordhaus 1994).

The Solow model has withstood severe critiques ever since its publication, the core of which was that the economic growth espoused by the model is not sustainable (Meadows et al. 1972; Arrow et al. 1995; Bartelmus 2012; UN 1972, 1992). To the critique, Solow himself endeavored to respond in economic terms (Solow 1974a, b, 1993). This chapter will introduce the sustainable development critique then present Solow's response.

9.2   A Solow Growth Model

Following Solow's specification in the seminal 1957 article, let's start with a simple model of capital and labor (Solow 1957, D. Romer 2018). There is one commodity in the economy, output $Y(t)$, at one time period. The amount of capital $K(t)$ and the amount of labor $L(t)$ are two inputs into production:

$$Y = F(K,L). \tag{9.1}$$

The production function (F) which captures the technological possibilities of the economy is assumed to be of a constant-returns-to-scale (CRS) technology. This production function is homogenous of degree 1 with regard to its inputs:

$$cY = F(cK,cL), \forall c. \tag{9.2}$$

The output is the net output after deducting capital depreciation over the previous year. A fraction of the output is saved while the rest is consumed, as was in the Ramsey model discussed in the preceding chapter (Ramsey 1928). Let s be the saving rate of the economy. The saving is immediately reinvested by entrepreneurial spirits (Schumpeter 1942), which increases the capital (input) to the economy. Therefore, the change in capital over time is written as follows:

$$\frac{dK}{dt} \equiv \dot{K} = sY(t). \tag{9.3}$$

Inserting Eqs. (9.1), (9.2), and (9.3),

$$\dot{K} = sF(K,L).$$ (9.4)

Of the two inputs, labor is assumed to grow exogenously, that is, outside the model itself (IIASA 2007, Lutz et al. 2014), with a constant growth rate (n) from the initial labor size (L_0) in the model:

$$L(t) = L_0 e^{nt}.$$ (9.5)

The labor size is nearly equivalent to the population size in the model, which is also the case in Koopmans's and Nordhaus's in the ensuing chapters. Let's define the capital-labor ratio, $r = \dfrac{K}{L}$, which is a per-worker capital. Then, the capital equation is written as follows:

$$K(t) = rL_0 e^{nt}.$$ (9.6)

Differentiating Eq. (9.6) with respect to time, we get

$$\dot{K} = L_0 e^{nt} \dot{r} + nrL_0 e^{nt}.$$ (9.7)

Substituting Eq. (9.7) into Eq. (9.4), we get

$$(\dot{r} + nr) L_0 e^{nt} = sF(K, L_0 e^{nt}).$$ (9.8)

Because of F being a constant-returns to scale technology, we can divide the two inputs by $L_0 e^{nt}$ and then multiply F by the same factor:

$$(\dot{r} + nr) L_0 e^{nt} = sL_0 e^{nt} F\left(K\Big/ L_0 e^{nt}, 1 \right).$$ (9.9)

After dividing both sides by $L_0 e^{nt}$, we get the fundamental equation of the Solow model:

$$\dot{r} = sF(r,1) - nr.$$ (9.10)

In the above, $F(r,1)$ is the total product function from the varying amounts of capital employed with 1 unit of labor. More directly, it is the output per worker as a function of the capital per worker. Eq. (9.10) states that the change in the capital-labor ratio results from two terms: one from the change in capital and the other from the change in labor.

The implication of Eq. (9.10) is illustrated in Fig. 9.1. There are two lines, both as a function of the capital-labor ratio (r) on the horizontal axis. The straight line is nr. The concave function represents the $F(r,1)$ with a diminishing-returns to capital. At the intersection of the two curves, $\dot{r}=0$. That is, there is no change in the capital-labor ratio. When that occurs, the optimal capital-labor ratio is determined, which is denoted as r^*.

What happens at $r_1 > r^*$? At such points, the linear curve is above the concave curve. That is, the population (labor) growth outpaces the capital growth. Therefore, the capital-labor ratio falls. This process continues until r^*.

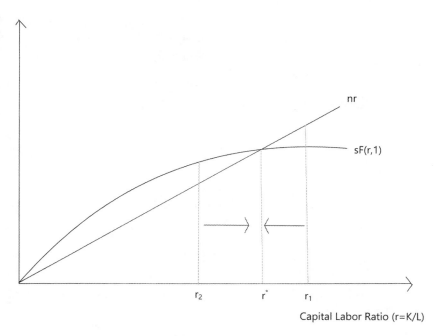

Fig. 9.1 A steady state in the Solow model

What happens at $r_2 < r^*$? At such points, the linear curve is below the concave curve. That is, the population (labor) growth is outpaced by the capital growth. Therefore, the capital-labor ratio increases. This process continues until r^*.

9.3   AN EXOGENOUS TECHNICAL CHANGE

The extended Solow model, which was also in the seminal Solow paper, adds technological changes exogenously to the model. Rewriting Eq. (9.1) with a technical change ($A(t)$) added to a Cobb-Douglas production function which is a constant-returns to scale production function, we get the following. For the sake of introducing the literature on this topic, the present author relies on the specification by the Mankiw, Romer, Weil article (Mankiw et al. 1992):

$$Y(t) = K(t)^\alpha \left(A(t) L(t) \right)^{1-\alpha}. \tag{9.11}$$

The α, $1 - \alpha$ are the elasticities of output with regard to the capital and the "effective labor," respectively. The term "effective labor" came from the notion that the technical change takes the form of reducing the labor needed to produce the same output (Mankiw et al. 1992). The labor variable grows exogenously as before in Eq. (9.5). The technical change variable is assumed by the authors to grow exogenously with the following function:

$$A(t) = A_0 e^{gt}. \tag{9.12}$$

The effective unit of labor, $A(t)L(t)$, grows at a constant rate of $n + g$. Define the capital-labor ratio with the effective labor and the output-labor ratio again with the effective labor as follows:

$$k = K / (A * L); y = Y / (A * L). \tag{9.13}$$

With this model, the evolution of capital is governed by the following, with δ being capital depreciation rate:

$$\dot{k}(t) = sy(t) - (n + g + \delta)k(t).$$ (9.14)

The steady-state capital accumulation converges:

$$k^* = \left[s / (n + g + \delta) \right]^{1/1-\alpha}.$$ (9.15)

Inserting Eq. (9.15) into the production function in Eq. (9.11),

$$\ln\left[\frac{Y(t)}{L(t)}\right] = \ln A_0 + gt + \frac{\alpha}{1-\alpha}\ln(s) + \frac{\alpha}{1-\alpha}\ln(n + g + \delta).$$ (9.16)

Since the capital elasticity of output, α, can be estimated from the empirical market data and the parameters in Eqs. (9.15) and (9.16) are also assumed, that is, estimated, the steady-state capital in Eq. (9.15) as well as the per capita output in Eq. (9.16) are predicted by the extended Solow model (Mankiw et al. 1992).

The technical progress function, $A(t)$ in Eq. (9.11), is referred to as the Total Factor Productivity (TFP) in the literature which is estimated from the empirical data as the residual of the Solow production function in Eq. (9.11) (Hulten 2000; Nordhaus 1994). The present author will further clarify this concept in Chap. 11 for the exposition of a climate and economy model.

A generalized Solow production function incorporates the technical change as a Hicks-neutral process. That is, the technical progress is exogenous, such that it does not affect the balance between the capital and the labor in the production function (Hicks 1932; Nordhaus 2008; Seo 2020). The Solow production function with a Hicks-neutral technical change is specified as follows:

$$Y(t) = A(t)K(t)^\alpha L(t)^{1-\alpha}.$$ (9.17)

9.4   A SUSTAINABLE DEVELOPMENT CRITIQUE

Soon after the publication of the Solow growth model, the economies in the Western nations one after another started to grow exponentially spurred by a post-World War II boom (World Bank 2022). As predicted by the Solow model, the capital accumulation occurred, which spurred the growth in economic output, which further increased the accumulation of capital.

At the same time, the ills of the rapid economic growth post-World War II increasingly became apparent. The publications like Rachel Carson's *Silent Spring* warned the world emphatically that newly developed chemical pesticides and fertilizers are greatly enhancing the economic products, especially crop productions, but are leaving grave harmful consequences on the society, in her own words, a silent spring where birds no longer sing in your village (Carson 1962).

The abundant energy generated by burning fossil fuels were powering the rapidly growing economies in the West, but the negative consequences of the energy abundance for businesses and individuals were emerging. The air pollutants such as sulfur dioxide (SO_2) and nitrogen oxides (NO_x) released into the atmosphere from the powerplants and automobiles were observed by scientists to mix with cloud particles in the atmosphere to eventually fall as wet chemicals on people, animals, and plants, which is referred to as acid rain (Likens and Bormann 1974). The acid rain harms the ecosystems including crops as well as people.

The mass production and application of air-conditioners and refrigerators as a cause for as well as a result of the economic growth were observed to release harmful chemicals, that is, chlorofluorocarbons (CFCs), into the stratosphere, which then destroys the ozone layer thereof of the planet. The ultraviolet (UVB) radiation from the Sun passes through the ozone holes to then leave severe health consequences on people, for example, skin cancer (Molina and Rowland 1974).

The rapid increases in nuclear powerplants as well as the unrestrained pursuits of nuclear arms by the world powers, which were spurred by the advances in nuclear physics during and after World War II, were stoking the fear of the public about a potential life and civilization threatening consequence of nuclear disasters and/or nuclear wars while at the same time giving new optimism on economic growth (Turco et al. 1983).

In addition, the world's population began to rise in an exponential manner after World War II attributable to the post-war baby boom and booming economies (refer to Fig. 2.3 in Chap. 2). This led many people to question whether the world can continue to feed its population given the limited resources, most notably, arable lands on the planet (Ehrlich 1968). At the same time, many developing and underdeveloped nations began implementing policy measures to contain the population increase (Repetto 1979).

Against this backdrop of the post-World War II societies and economies, a sustainable development critique was given birth. The scholars of this group asked the following core question: Is the economic growth sustainable (Meadows et al. 1972; Arrow et al. 1995)? Several global political events during the early 1970s appear to cap the birth of the sustainable development critique which has become ever more powerful since then. The most significant may have been the first of its kind the United Nations Conference on Human Environment held in Stockholm, Sweden, in June 1972 (UN 1972). At the conference, nations reached an agreement on the environmental concerns of economic development as well as the framework to help developing and underdeveloped nations financially and technically to address their pressing environmental problems in addition to poverty and hunger problems (Seo 2019, 2020).

The critique's intellectual layouts and specific agendas were also well expressed in and formed from the two highly advertised publications across the planet: the Rome Club report in 1972 entitled "The Limits to Growth" and the United Nations' World Commission on Environment and Development (WCED)'s report entitled "Our Common Future" in 1985 also referred to as the Brundtland Report (Meadows et al. 1972; WCED 1987).

Thenceforth, the sustainable development critique quickly became a major political force planetwide that would affect the global affairs. A series of major declarations by the United Nations epitomize the reach and influence of the critique: to name just some, the Agenda 21 at the Rio Earth Summit in 1992, the United Nations Framework Convention on Climate Change (UNFCCC) in 1992, the UN Millennium Development Goals (MDGs) in 2000, the UN 2030 Agenda for Sustainable Development in 2015 and the Paris Climate Agreement in 2015 (UN 1992, 2000, 2015; UNFCCC 1992, 2015). The 2030 Agenda, the latest of the UN declarations on sustainable development, has 17 goals and as many as 169 policy targets. The three UN declarations on sustainable development and their respective agendas will be analyzed in detail in Chap. 13 of this book.

To give readers a rough idea of what these declarations look like, let me briefly introduce the eight goals of the UN Millennium Development Goals (UN 2000, 2001). As will be discussed shortly, these agendas put forth by the UN are largely commensurate with the sustainable development framework or the theory if we may call it (Bartelmus 2012). The eight goals of the UNMDG are

(Goal 1) Eradicate extreme poverty and hunger
(Goal 2) Achieve universal primary education
(Goal 3) Promote gender equality and empower women
(Goal 4) Reduce child mortality rates
(Goal 5) Improve maternal health
(Goal 6) Combat HIV/AIDS, malaria, and other diseases
(Goal 7) Ensure environmental sustainability
(Goal 8) Develop a global partnership for development

Each of the eight goals has a list of policy targets. Under the Goal 7 of "Ensure environmental sustainability," for example, some of the specific policy targets are as follows:

Target 7A: Integrate the principles of sustainable development into country policies and programs; reverse loss of environmental resource.

Target 7B: Reduce biodiversity loss, achieving, by 2010, a significant reduction in the rate of loss.

Again, each of these policy targets is explained by a basket of indicators. For the targets 7A and 7B, the following indicators are relied upon (UN 2001):

(i)   Proportion of land area covered by forest
(ii) CO_2 emissions
(iii) Consumption of ozone-depleting substances
(iv) Proportion of fish stocks within safe biological limits
(v)   Proportion of renewable water resources used
(vi) Proportion of terrestrial and marine areas protected
(vii) Proportion of species threatened with extinction

As readers can verify and further discussed more thoroughly in Chap. 13, the sustainable development framework is nearly equivalent to an *ensemble* of policy goals. It is an *ad hoc* collection of policy goals and ideas by the committee at that time. The aforementioned three UN declarations are clearly in that defining characteristic. By and large, the works of the individual scholars in the sustainable development critique also follow the same characteristic, that is, an *ensemble* of *ad hoc* policy ideas (World Bank 1997; Munasinghe 2009; Bartelmus 2012; Sachs 2015).

As such, the sustainable development framework has been criticized for the lack of a consistent theory that is applied equally to the range of suggested policy goals. Further, critics leveled that the sustainable development critique lacks a conceptual framework for determining a policy priority. In other words, it is a collection of policy goals, but the priority of one policy goal over another among the declared policy goals and targets in the ensemble cannot be determined within this approach. Neither the ratio of tradeoff between the two policy goals nor two conflicting policy goals can be determined in the sustainable development framework itself.

These points were at the heart of the responses by Robert Solow himself to the sustainable development critique through a series of articles over time (Solow 1974a, b, 1993). In particular, Solow pointed out, if not directly, that the sustainable development theorists and enthusiasts do not define what a non-sustainable development is. Solow strived to explicate that, even with the environmental, natural resources, and other problems, the economy can and will still grow in a "sustainable" manner. That is, the society can spend resources and efforts to solve these problems, but at the same time manage the economy to grow in a "sustainable" manner (Solow 1993).

Following the lead by Solow, some economists offered a definition of a sustainable economic growth. For example, it may be defined as any growth path in which the amount of capital (K) in the economy continues to increase or alternatively any growth path in which the amount of consumption per capita continues to increase (Pearce and Atkinson 1993; Hartwick 1996; Hartwick and Olewiler 1997).

A notable work in the line of defense of economic growth was the article entitled "Is Growth Obsolete?" written by two eventual Nobel Prize winners of economics William Nordhaus and James Tobin (Nordhaus and Tobin 1972). The authors examined the empirical data on economic production, environmental damages, and natural resource uses to conclude that although the negative consequences of economic growth on environmental qualities and natural resources of the society are significant, they still amount to a small fraction of the gains (benefits) from the economic growth.

The emerging disputes during the 1970s led to a golden age of environmental economics whose goal was to quantify the damages in dollar terms that are created as side effects of economic growth (to name just some: Mendelsohn 1980, Smith and Huang 1995, Viscusi and Aldy 2003, Chay and Greenstone 2003, Maler and Vincent 2005, Mendelsohn and Olmstead 2009, Freeman III et al. 2014). The valuation studies, as this line of works is called, were centered on the human health impacts and the ecosystem impacts of the fossil fuel-fired powerplants' emissions of pollutants such as sulfur dioxide (SO_2), nitrogen oxides (NO_x), carbon monoxide (CO), carbon dioxide (CO_2), various fluorinated gases (CFCs), and fine particulate matter (PM_x) (Muller and Mendelsohn 2009; Muller et al. 2011; USEPA 2011).

The valuation studies of the past five decades revealed that the human health damages *via* pollution-caused mortality and morbidity of people account for a dominant fraction, specifically over 90%, of the total environmental impacts of pollution. Further, coal-fired powerplants are the most harmful source of air pollution while the particulate matter ($PM_{2.5}$ and PM_{10}) emissions is by far the most harmful pollutant to people. The utilities including the coal-fired powerplants account for about a third of the total pollution-caused damages. Adding up all the damages, the aggregate cost of all the pollutants on the economy is roughly 1% of the national GDP on an annual basis in the case of the United States (Muller and Mendelsohn 2009; Muller et al. 2011).

The valuation studies rely on an integrated assessment model (IAM) framework. It is an analytical method in which all the processes end-to-end in environmental pollution are linked *via* specified relationships by the modeler: for example, from a powerplant's emissions of a chemical, dispersion in the air, impacts on ecosystems and people, epidemiology of diseases, to valuation of the impacts (Mendelsohn and Olmstead 2009). This valuation method is referred to as a revealed preference method because it relies on the prices and costs in the markets, as such, revealed.

An alternative valuation method is referred to as a Contingent Valuation (CV) method which relies on stated preferences by survey respondents, for which reason it is called a stated preference method (Hanemann 1994). The stated preference-based valuation suffers, among other things, from strategic behaviors by respondents (Diamond and Hausman 1994).

The valuation studies are a critical input to designing an environmental policy and regulation (Montgomery 1972; Baumol and Oates 1975; Tietenberg 1980; Hahn and Dudley 2007). One of the most notable policy experiments was the SO_2 allowance trading system implemented in the northeast US (Stavins 1998; Schmalensee and Stavins 2013). As for the

SO_2 pollution, the valuation studies can point to an efficient price of the SO_2 permit as well as an efficient number of SO_2 permits in the economy. This and many other environmental policies in the US are implemented based on the environmental laws and regulations including the Clean Air Act (CAA), the Clean Water Act (CWA), and the Corporate Average Fuel Economy (CAFE) standards (Baumol and Oates 1975; USEPA 1990, 2008; Tietenberg 1999; Seo 2020).

The valuation studies also make it possible for the economists to build a novel national accounting system which incorporates the side effects of economic growth, specifically, pollution damages. This is commonly referred to as the Green GDP (Ahmad et al. 1989; World Bank 1997; Costanza et al. 1997; Uno and Bartelmus 1998; Nordhaus and Kokkelenberg 1999; Nordhaus 2000; Muller et al. 2011). The Green GDP is constructed from the conventional gross domestic product (GDP) by adding the negative consequences of environmental pollution caused by economic activities (Nordhaus 2000).

9.5   Conclusion

The Solow's neoclassical growth theory has been highly influential in the literature of economic growth on both its supporters and critics. In a highly abstract manner, it provides a lucid description of the nation's economic growth trajectory. It builds on the concept of capital, which is both an input into the model and the output of the model, and shows how the capital will accumulate over time in the economy by reinvesting a fraction of the economic output efficiently.

The Solow model's influence far exceeded the economic growth corpus. It spurred an emergence of the sustainable development critique. Further, it paved the way to a golden age of environmental economics whose chief focus was to quantifying in an economic manner the side effects of economic growth pursuits on the environment and natural resources. These efforts resulted in many notable achievements, some of which were mentioned in this chapter including valuation methods, market-based environmental policies and regulations, and a novel national accounting system such as the Green GDP.

The debates between the sustainable development proponents and the optimal economic growth proponents are still raging unrelented across the global communities. To elucidate these debates, the present author will need to clarify Koopmans's theory in Chap. 10 and Nordhaus's works in Chap. 11. The present author will come back to the question of sustainable development one more time in Chap. 13 where the tendencies to pursuing sub-optimal growth are explained.

References

Aghion, Philippe, and Peter Howitt. 1992. A Model of Growth Through Creative Destruction. *Econometrica* 60: 323–351.

———. 2009. *The Economics of Growth*. Cambridge, MA: MIT Press.

Ahmad, Yusuf J., Salah El Serafay, and Ernst Lutz, eds. 1989. *Environmental Accounting for Sustainable Development*. Washington, DC: World Bank.

Arrow, Kenneth, Bert Bolin, Robert Costanza, Partha Dasgupta, Carl Folke, Crawford S. Holling, Bengt-Owe Jansson, Simon Levin, Karl-Goran Maler, Charles Perrings, and David Pimentel. 1995. Economic Growth, Carrying Capacity, and the Environment. *Ecological Economics* 15: 91–95.

Barro, R.J., and X. Sala-i-Martin. 1992. Convergence. *Journal of Political Economy* 100: 223–251.

Bartelmus, Peter. 2012. *Sustainability Economics*. Oxfordshire, UK: Routledge.

Baumol, W.J., and O.A. Oates. 1975. *The Theory of Environmental Policy*. Upper Saddle River, NJ: Prentice Hall.

Carson, Rachel. 1962. *Silent Spring*. Boston, MA: Houghton Mifflin Harcourt.

Chay, Kenneth Y., and Michael Greenstone. 2003. The Impact of Air Pollution on Infant Mortality: Evidence from Geographic Variation in Pollution Shocks Induced by a Recession. *The Quarterly Journal of Economics* 118: 1121–1167.

Costanza, R., R. d'Arge, R. de Groot, et al. 1997. The Value of the World's Ecosystem Services and Natural Capital. *Nature* 387: 253–260.

Diamond, P.A., and J.A. Hausman. 1994. Contingent Valuation: Is Some Number Better Than No Number? *Journal of Economic Perspectives* 8: 45–64.

Ehrlich, Paul L. 1968. *The Population Bomb*. New York, NY: Sierra Club/ Ballantine Books.

Fisher, Irving. 1906. *The Nature of Capital and Income*. New York, NY: Macmillan.

———. 1930. *The Theory of Interest*. New York, NY: Macmillan.

Freeman, A.M., III, J.A. Herriges, and C.L. Cling. 2014. *The Measurements of Environmental and Resource Values: Theory and Practice*. New York, NY: RFF Press.

Hahn, R.W., and P.M. Dudley. 2007. How Well Does the U.S. Government Do Benefit-cost Analysis? *Review of Environmental Economics and Policy* 1: 192–211.

Hanemann, W.M. 1994. Valuing the Environment Through Contingent Valuation. *Journal of Economic Perspectives* 8: 19–43.

Hartwick, J.M. 1996. Constant Consumption as Interest on Capital. *Scandinavian Journal of Economics* 98: 439–443.

———., and N.D. Olewiler. 1997. The Economics of Sustainability. In *The Economics of Natural Resource Use*, 2nd ed. New York, NY: Pearson.

Hicks, John R. 1932. *The Theory of Wages*. London, UK: Macmillan.

Hulten, C.R. 2000. *Total Factor Productivity: A Short Biography*. National Bureau of Economic Research (NBER) Working Paper Series 7471, The NBER, Cambridge, MA.

International Institute of Applied Systems Analysis (IIASA). 2007. Probabilistic Projections by 13 World Regions, Forecast Period 2000–2100, 2001 Revision. http://www.iiasa.ac.at/Research/POP/proj01/.

Koopmans, Tjalling C. 1965. On the Concept of Optimal Economic Growth. *Pontificiae Academiae Scientiarum Scripta Varia* 28 (1): 1–75.

Likens, G.E., and F.H. Bormann. 1974. Acid Rain: A Serious Regional Environmental Problem. *Science* 184: 1176–1179.

Lutz, W., W. Butz, and K.C. Samir, eds. 2014. *World Population and Global Human Capital in the 21st Century*. Oxford, UK: Oxford University Press.

Maler, K.-G., and J.R. Vincent. 2005. *The Handbook of Environmental Economics, Valuing Environmental Changes*. Vol. 2. Amsterdam, NL: North-Holland.

Malthus, Thomas R. 1798. *An Essay on the Principle of Population*. London, UK: J. Johnson.

Mankiw, N. Gregory, David Romer, and David Weil. 1992. A Contribution to the Empirics of Economic Growth. *Quarterly Journal of Economics* 107 (2): 407–437.

Marx, Karl. 1867. *Das Kapital. Kritik der politischen Oekonomie*. Verlag von Otto Meisner, Germany.

Meadows, Donella H., D.L. Meadows, J. Randers, and W.W. Behrens III. 1972. *The Limits to Growth: A Report for the Club of Rome's Project on the Predicament of Mankind*. New York, NY: Universe Books.

Mendelsohn, R. 1980. An Economic Analysis of Air Pollution from Coal-fired Power Plants. *Journal of Environmental Economics and Management* 7: 30–43.

Mendelsohn, R., and S. Olmstead. 2009. The Economic Valuation of Environmental Amenities and Disamenities: Methods and Applications. *Annual Review of Environment and Resources* 34 (1): 325–347.

Molina, M.J., and F.S. Rowland. 1974. Stratospheric Sink for Chlorofluoromethanes: Chlorine Atom-catalysed Destruction of Ozone. *Nature* 249: 810–812.

Montgomery, W.D. 1972. Markets in Licenses and Efficient Pollution Control Programs. *Journal of Economic Theory* 5: 395–418.

Muller, N.Z., and R. Mendelsohn. 2009. Efficient Pollution Regulation: Getting the Prices Right. *American Economic Review* 99: 1714–1739.

Muller, N.Z., R. Mendelsohn, and W.D. Nordhaus. 2011. Environmental Accounting for Pollution in the United States Economy. *American Economic Review* 101: 1649–1675.

Munasinghe, M. 2009. *Sustainable Development in Practice: Sustainomics Methodology and Applications*. Cambridge, UK: Cambridge University Press.

Nordhaus, W.D. 1994. *Managing the Global Commons*. Cambridge, MA: MIT Press.

———. 2000. New Directions in National Economic Accounting. *American Economic Review: Papers and Proceedings* 90 (2): 259–263.

———. 2008. *A Question of Balance: Weighing the Options on Global Warming Policies*. New Haven, CT: Yale University Press.

———. 2014. The Perils of the Learning Model for Modeling Endogenous Technological Change. *The Energy Journal* 35: 1–13.

Nordhaus, W.D., and Edward C. Kokkelenberg. 1999. *Nature's Numbers: Expanding the National Economic Accounts to Include the Environment*. Washington, DC: The National Academy Press.

Nordhaus, W.D., and J. Tobin. 1972. *Is Growth Obsolete?* Cambridge, MA: National Bureau of Economic Research (NBER).

Pardi, N., M.J. Hogan, F.W. Porter, and D. Weissman. 2018. mRNA Vaccines—A New Era in Vaccinology. *Nature Reviews Drug Discovery* 17: 261–279.

Pearce, David W., and Giles D. Atkinson. 1993. Capital Theory and the Measurement of Sustainable Development: An Indicator of "Weak" Sustainability. *Ecological Economics* 8: 103–108.

Ramsey, F.P. 1928. A Mathematical Theory of Savings. *Economic Journal* 38: 543–559.

Repetto, R. 1979. *Economic Equality and Fertility in Developing Countries*. Baltimore, MD: Johns Hopkins University Press.

Romer, Paul. 1990. Endogenous Technical Change. *Journal of Political Economy* 98: S71–S102.

Romer, David. 2018. *Advanced Macroeconomics*. 5th ed. New York, NY: McGraw Hill.

Sachs, J.D. 2015. *The Age of Sustainable Development*. New York, NY: Columbia University Press.

Schmalensee, R., and R.N. Stavins. 2013. The SO2 Allowance Trading System: The Ironic History of a Grand Policy Experiment. *Journal of Economic Perspectives* 27: 103–122.

Schumpeter, Joseph A. 1942. *Capitalism, Socialism, and Democracy*. New York, NY: Harper & Brothers.

Seo, S.N. 2019. *The Economics of Global Allocations of the Green Climate Fund: An Assessment from Four Scientific Traditions of Modeling Adaptation Strategies*. Cham, CH: Springer Nature.

———. 2020. *The Economics of Globally Shared and Public Goods*. Amsterdam, NL: Academic Press.

———. 2022. *The Economics of Pandemics*. Cham, CH: Palgrave Macmillan.

Smith, Adam. 1776. *The Wealth of Nations*. London, UK: W. Strahan and T. Cadell.

Smith, V.K., and J.-C. Huang. 1995. Can Markets Value Air Quality? A Meta-analysis of Hedonic Property Value Models. *Journal of Political Economy* 103: 209–227.

Solow, Robert M. 1957. A Contribution to the Theory of Economic Growth. *Quarterly Journal of Economics* 70: 65–94.

———. 1974a. The Economics of Resources or The Resources of Economics. *American Economic Review* 64: 1–14.

———. 1974b. Intergenerational Equity and Exhaustible Resources. *Review of Economic Studies* 41: 29–46.

———. 1993. An Almost Ideal Step Toward Sustainability. *Resources Policy* 19: 162–172.

Stavins, R. 1998. What Can We Learn from the Grand Policy Experiment? Lessons from SO2 Allowance Trading. *Journal of Economic Perspectives* 12: 69–88.

Tietenberg, T.H. 1980. Transferable Discharge Permits and the Control of Stationary Source Air Pollution: A Survey and Synthesis. *Land Economics* 56: 391–416.

———. 1999. *Environmental & Natural Resource Economics*. Oxfordshire, UK: Taylor & Francis.

Turco, R.P., O.B. Toon, T.P. Ackerman, J.B. Pollack, and C. Sagan. 1983. Nuclear Winter: Global Consequences of Multiple Nuclear Explosions. *Science* 222: 1283–1292.

United Nations (UN). 1972. *Report of the United Nations Conference on Human Environment*. Stockholm, Sweden.

———. 1992. *Agenda 21*. Rio de Janeiro, Brazil: United Nations Conference on Environment & Development.

———. 2000. *United Nations Millennium Declaration*. New York, NY: UN.

———. 2001. *Road Map Towards the Implementation of the United Nations Millennium Declaration*. New York, NY: UN.

———. 2015. *Transforming Our World: The 2030 Agenda for Sustainable Development*. New York, NY: UN.

United Nations Framework Convention on Climate Change (UNFCCC). 1992. *United Nations Framework Convention on Climate Change*. New York, NY: The UNFCCC.

———. 2015. *The Paris Agreement. Conference of the Parties (COP) 21*. Paris, FR: The UNFCCC.

United States Environmental Protection Agency (USEPA). 1990. *The Clean Air Act Amendments*. Washington, DC: USEPA.

———. 2008. *Air Pollution Control Equipment. MACT (Maximum Achievable Control Technology) EEE Training Workshop*. Washington, DC: USEPA.

———. 2011. *The Benefits and Costs of the Clean Air Act from 1990 to 2020.* Washington, DC: USEPA.

Uno, Kimio, and Peter Bartelmus, eds. 1998. *Environmental Accounting in Theory and Practice.* Hingham, MA: Kluwer Academic Publishers.

Viscusi, W.K., and J.E. Aldy. 2003. The Value of a Statistical Life: A Critical Review of Market Estimates Throughout the World. *Journal of Risk and Uncertainty* 27: 5–76.

World Bank. 1997. *Expanding the Measure of Wealth: Indicators of Environmentally Sustainable Development.* Washington, DC: World Bank.

———. 2022. *World Development Indicators.* Washington, DC: World Bank.

World Commission on Environment and Development (WCED). 1987. *Our Common Future.* Oxford, UK: Oxford University Press.

CHAPTER 10

Tjalling Koopmans's Optimal Economic Growth

10.1 INTRODUCTION

A dynamic societal welfare optimization model of a national economy can be attributed to the Tjalling C. Koopmans's article entitled "On the Concept of Optimal Economic Growth" published in 1963 (Koopmans 1963, 1965). Koopmans was awarded the Nobel Memorial Prize in 1975, with Leonid V. Kantorovich, "for their contributions to the theory of optimum allocation of resources" (Koopmans 1975).

He was recognized during his time as a preeminent mathematical economist of the twentieth century for his contributions to the development of mathematical programming, along with Leonid Kantorovich (Koopmans 1949, 1951, 1957; Kantorovich 1939, 1959). The Nobel Prize citation quoted above refers to that contribution. The mathematical programming has become an important economic analysis tool ever since (Samuelson 1952; Uzawa 1960; Dorfman et al. 1987).

Koopmans's contribution to the dynamic welfare optimization model of economic growth might have been lost over the flow of time if it had not been pursued by one of his best students and later a colleague, William D. Nordhaus. Nordhaus, when giving the Nobel Memorial Prize Lecture in 2018, cited a single source for the inspiration of his much-famed climate and economy model, the Tjalling Koopmans's dynamic welfare optimization model (Nordhaus 1994, 2019).

S. N. Seo, *The Economics of Optimal Growth Pathways*, https://doi.org/10.1007/978-3-031-20754-9_10

William Nordhaus was a young college student at Yale University where he first met Tjalling Koopmans and became his colleague when returned in 1967 as an assistant professor after completing his PhD degree program at the Massachusetts Institute of Technology (MIT). His doctoral adviser at the MIT was Robert M. Solow whose contributions to the economic growth literature the present author reviewed in detail in the previous chapter (Solow 1957, 1974). His academic curiosities during that time lied in the economic problems of energy uses (Nordhaus and Tobin 1972; Nordhaus 1973).

Koopmans wrote, right at the top of his article, his motivation for writing the aforementioned 1963 article as follows (Koopmans 1963, 1965):

The search for a principle from which an "optimal" rate of economic growth can be deduced holds great fascination to economists. A variety of attitudes or approaches to this problem can be discerned in the literature.

His review of the literature in the article included, limiting to those actually described in the paper, Allais's *Economy and Interest* (Allais 1960), Harrod's *Towards a Dynamic Economics* (Harrod 1948), Tinbergen's *Optimum Savings and Utility Maximization over Time* (Tinbergen 1960), Frank Ransey's *A Mathematical Theory of Saving* (Ramsey 1928), Inagaki's *The Golden Utility Path* (1963), Bauer's *Economic Analysis and Policy in Underdeveloped Countries* (Bauer 1957).

10.2   Koopmans's Optimal Economic Growth: A Golden Rule of Accumulation

What is the most suitable mathematical formulation of the optimal economic growth? Koopmans's answer is that of a preference ordering of growth paths. He begins with the following continuous preference function, that is, the social utility function:

$$U = \sum_{t=1}^{\infty} \mathcal{F}^{t-1} u(x_t).$$ (10.1)

In Eq. (10.1), time is discrete and covers an infinite horizon. The utility in Eq. (10.1) is the discounted sum of future one-period utilities $u(x_t)$ over an infinite time horizon. The utility is a function of consumption at each period (x_t). The discount factor for each period is $\mathcal{F}^{t-1}$.

The economy is specified by a twice differentiable and concave production function, homogeneous of degree one, of the capital stock (K) and labor force (L), whose exact form will be specified in the next section. It is the same as the Solow growth model's simple specification: one sector model with one commodity, that is, the capital, to be produced:

$$F = F(K_t, L_t). \tag{10.2}$$

The output of the economy, that is, the capital, is allocated to consumption (X) and net investment (I):

$$X_t + I_t = F(K_t, L_t). \tag{10.3}$$

Since there is only one commodity that is produced in the economy and the capital stock of the economy at time t is the stock of the capital after consumption, the increase in the capital at each time period equals the net investment:

$$I_t = \dot{K}_t \tag{10.4}$$

To proceed further, we need to put several common restrictions on the production function. First, it is assumed that both capital and labor are essential for production. Second, the marginal productivity of each factor is positive. Third, the marginal productivity of each factor decreases for addition of each additional unit.

The labor force is assumed to grow exponentially at a constant rate (λ) from the initial population, that is, labor force (L_0), which differs in a major way from the Ramsey model with a constant population (Ramsey 1928; Lutz et al. 2014):

$$L_t = L_0 e^{\lambda t} \text{ with } \lambda > 0. \tag{10.5}$$

As in the Solow model, the production function can be written in a per-worker production form owing to the property of being homogeneous of degree one. With x consumption per worker (X/L), i ditto net investment (I/L), k ditto capital stock (K/L), and f ditto output (F/L):

$$f(k) = \frac{1}{L} F(K, L) = F\left(\frac{K}{L}, 1\right) = F(k, 1) \qquad (10.6)$$

The increase in the capital stock per period is then

$$K_t = \frac{d}{dt}(k_t L_t) = \dot{k}_t L_t + k_t \dot{L}_t = \left(\dot{k}_t + \lambda k_t\right) L_t \qquad (10.7)$$

With these rewriting in terms of per-worker variables, the feasible set in Eq. (10.3) can be written in the space of per-worker variables:

$$x_t + \dot{k}_t = f(k_t) - \lambda k_t, \qquad (10.8a)$$

$$x_t > 0, k_t > 0, k_0 \text{ given.} \qquad (10.8b)$$

The term λk is the needed net investment if the economy wants merely to provide the growing labor force, that is, the population, with the capital at the existing capital per worker ratio. In other words, the term represents the net investment needed to maintain the capital per worker ratio while the population continues to grow at the rate of λ.

For a clarification, the path (x_t, k_t) satisfying Eqs. (10.8a) and (10.8b) is referred to by Koopmans as the attainable set (for the given k_0). The feasible path is the attainable set for some k_0, as such, a wider sense of the attainable set.

The functions in Eqs. (10.8a) and (10.8b) are illustrated in Fig. 10.1. The assumptions on the production function, stated above, imply that $f(k)$ is strictly concave. It starts from the origin and rises at a decreasing rate. The λk is a straight line from the origin along the horizontal axis of k. The two lines intersect at $\bar{k}$. This is a steady state in the Solow model (Solow 1957).

More formally, any line λk through the origin with the slope λ such that $0 < \lambda < f(0)$ will ultimately intersect the production function at $\bar{k}$:

For any $\lambda > 0$ such that $0 < \lambda < f'(0)$, there is a $\bar{k} > 0$ such that

$$f(\bar{k}) = \lambda \bar{k}, \text{ with } f(k) < \lambda k \text{ for } k > \bar{k}. \qquad (10.9)$$

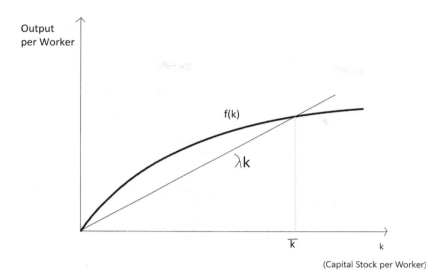

Fig. 10.1   Optimal economic growth path: production function

Here, λ is the rate of growth in labor force (population). The $\overline{k}$ is the level of the capital stock which is so large that the investment needed to keep it at the same level has to absorb all economic output, that is, leaving nothing for consumption.

In Fig. 10.1, the attainable set is defined, but the maximand, that is, the objective function, is not yet defined. To continue, we remove from the definition of the attainable set the restriction that k_0 is given. Let the initial capital be a free good. Instead, restrict the attainable set by an arbitrary stipulation that the consumption per worker and the capital per worker are to be held constant over time:

$$x_t = x,\, k_t = k, \text{for all } t \geq 0. \tag{10.10}$$

The new attainable set is given by the following, since there is no change in the level of capital:

$$x = f(k) - \lambda k,\, x > 0,\, k > 0. \tag{10.11}$$

Now, the problem is defined as follows: Choose k so as to maximize x, that is, the permanent level of consumption per worker subject to the attainable set thus defined:

$$\max_{k} x = f(k) - \lambda k. \tag{10.12}$$

This leads to the choice of $\hat{k}$ such that

$$f'(\hat{k}) = \lambda, \text{ so } \hat{x} = f(\hat{k}) - \lambda\hat{k}. \tag{10.13}$$

The $f(k)$ is a derivative of $f(k)$ with respect to k. It is the marginal productivity of capital, as shown in Eq. (10.14). With L held constant,

$$f'(k) = \frac{\delta F(K/L,1)}{\delta(K/L)} = \frac{\delta F(K,L)}{\delta K}. \tag{10.14}$$

Equation (10.13) is referred to as a golden rule of capital accumulation by Koopmans. It says that the marginal productivity of capital ($f(k)$) in producing capital should be equal to the rate of population (labor force) growth (λ) at all times. To emphasize, it is the golden rule of economic growth, in other words, the economic growth defined by the golden rate of capital accumulation. This is the simplest version which will be extended in this chapter to include rate of time preference as well as rate of technological growth.

This golden rule is illustrated in Fig. 10.2. The production curve, the λk straight line, and the steady-state $\bar{k}$ are all as before in Fig. 10.1. The golden rate of capital accumulation is at $\hat{k}$ where the slope of the production curve is equal to the growth rate of labor force, that is, the slope of the straight line.

At the golden rate of capital accumulation ($\hat{k}$), the golden consumption level (per worker) is marked in the figure as the thick gray vertical line on the vertical axis, $\hat{x}$. It is equal to the difference between the two curves at the golden rate of capital, as shown in Eq. (10.13): $\hat{x} = f(\hat{k}) - \lambda\hat{k}$.

To emphasize one more time, Eq. (10.13) is referred to by Tjalling Koopmans as "a prescription known as a golden rule of accumulation" (Koopmans 1963, 1965). The rule states that the capital of the economy should grow at the rate of population (labor) growth in the economy. To

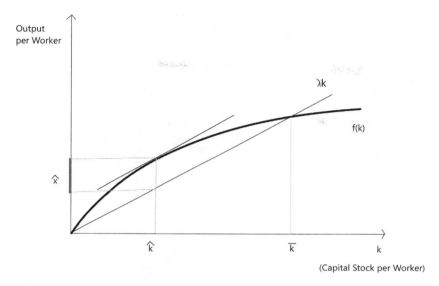

Fig. 10.2 The golden rule of capital accumulation

remind the readers once more, Eq. (10.13) has not yet incorporated consumers' preferences, nor the technologies.

Given these, do not miss the point that $\hat{k}, \hat{x}$ are not the fixed quantities in the model. The values for these variables will get larger continuously when the rate of population growth becomes lower and/or the rate of technological growth reduces the rate of diminishing returns in the production function. These two conditions tend to unfold in a growing economy.

10.3 Koopmans's Optimal Economic Growth: An Optimal Growth Path

Starting from the golden rule path $\left(\hat{x}, \hat{k}\right)$ as the baseline, let's return to the original problem where x_t and k_t vary over time and there is a historically given initial capital stock, k_0. To continue, the model needs to define a maximand, that is, an objective function that should be built on individuals' preferences.

Koopmans notes that there does not exist a utility function of all consumption paths, which satisfies all reasonable postulates on the utility function (Mas-Colell et al. 1995). To resolve this dilemma, Koopmans introduce an eligible set of consumption paths, that is, by eliminating ineligible sets of consumption paths which are clearly inferior. This elimination process is achieved through the golden rule path over a steadily increasing population.

The utility function is defined in a finite time horizon over a continuous time space, without the discount factor for the time being which is called the "timing neutrality" by him:

$$V_T = \int_0^T u(x_t)\, dt. \tag{10.15}$$

The instantaneous utility flow, $u(x_t)$, is a strictly concave function of the instantaneous consumption flow x_t. The former is an increasing and twice differentiable function of the latter. A strict concavity means that the society attributes greater importance or weight to the marginal unit of per capita consumption of a poor generation as compared with that of a rich generation. This is referred to in terms of a parameter of the degree of social inequality aversion in the economic growth literature, which the present author will come back to incorporate later in this chapter (Nordhaus 1991).

To avoid setting a subsistence minimum consumption, a boundary condition is introduced in the model: $\lim_{x \to 0} u(x) = -\infty$.

Let $\hat{u} = u(\hat{x})$ is the instantaneous utility flow derived from the consumption flow per worker on the golden rule path ($x_t = \hat{x}, k_t = \hat{k}$). With this set up so far, the process of finding a dynamically optimal path consists of measuring the difference between the utility in Eq. (10.15) obtained from any candidate feasible path and the utility obtained from the golden rule path. Koopmans explained the existence and characteristics of the optimal paths by way of the sequence of the eleven propositions, with a proof for each proposition provided in his article, which we will review presently one by one.

Proposition 10.1 There exists a number $\bar{u}$ such that

$$U_T = \int_0^T \big(u(x_t) - \hat{u}\big)\, dt \le \bar{u} \tag{10.16}$$

for all (x_t, k_t) and for all T, that is, time horizons.

Proposition 10.1 states that no path is "infinitely better" than the golden rule path. In particular, no feasible path x_t can indefinitely, that is, for all time horizons T, maintain or exceed a level of utility flow that exceeds $\hat{u}$.

Proposition 10.2 For every (x_t, k_t), either $\lim_{T\to\infty} U_T = c < \infty$ or $\lim_{T\to\infty} U_T \to -\infty$. Put plainly, for every feasible path, either $\lim_{T\to\infty} U_T$ is a finite number or diverges as T tends to infinity.

In the first case of Proposition 10.2, the path is eligible. In the second case, the path is ineligible. On the eligible set, the utility function is defined as follows:

$$U = \int_0^\infty \left(u(x_t) - \hat{u}\right) dt \tag{10.17}$$

The optimal path is defined as a path maximizing U in Eq. (10.17) on the set of eligible and attainable paths. Such an optimal path is defined in Propositions 10.3 and 10.4.

Proposition 10.3 For any starting-point capital stock, k_0, with $0 < k_0 \le \bar{k}$, there exists a unique optimal path $\left(\hat{x}_t, \hat{k}_t\right)$ in the family of eligible-attainable paths. For $k_0 \ne \hat{k}$, both $\hat{x}_t$ and $\hat{k}_t$ exhibit a strictly monotonic approach to $\hat{x}$ and $\hat{k}$, respectively. The former approaches the latter from below if $0 < k_0 < \hat{k}$ and from above if $\hat{k} < k_0 \le \bar{k}$. For $k_0 = \hat{k}$, the optimal path is the golden rule path, that is, $\hat{x}_t = \hat{x}$, $\hat{k}_t = \hat{k}$ for all t.

Proposition 10.4 In the optimal path $\left(\hat{x}_t, \hat{k}_t\right)$, the following condition holds:

$$u'(x_t)k_t = \hat{u} - u(x_t). \tag{10.18}$$

Proposition 10.4 says that at any time the net increase in capital per worker multiplied by the marginal utility of consumption per worker equals the net excess of the maximum sustainable "golden rule" utility level over the current utility level. The left hand size of Eq. (10.18) is the cost of delaying consumption for the sake of new investment. The right hand size is the utility difference between the golden rule consumption and the actual consumption on the optimal path.

Equation (10.18) is similar to the "Keynes-Ramsey" optimality condition, which was explained in Chap. 8, which states that the rate of saving multiplied by marginal utility of consumption should always equal "Bliss" minus the actual rate of utility enjoyed (Ramsey 1928). It reverts to the Keynes-Ramsey condition when the population growth rate is assumed to be zero, that is, $\lambda = 0$.

Up to this point, the social utility was defined as the undiscounted integral of future instantaneous utility flow, as in Eqs. (10.15) and (10.17). With a positive discount rate (ρ) introduced into the model, analogous optimality conditions are obtained, which are shown in the following propositions.

Proposition 10.5 The utility function, with discounting of future utilities,

$$V(\rho) = \int_0^\infty u(x_t) e^{-\rho t} dt, \text{ where } \rho > 0, \qquad (10.19)$$

is defined for all feasible paths for which $x_t \geq \underline{x}$ for all t, whenever $\underline{x} > 0$.

The restriction on consumption in Proposition 10.5, that is, $x_t \geq \underline{x}$ for all t, is to keep the consumption from becoming near zero, thereby to prevent a divergent path of $V_T(\rho)$ at large T. For the sake of an economy of notation and conformity with the formulation in the preceding section, let's define U instead of V using the distances from the utility level of the golden rule path:

$$U(\rho) = \int_0^\infty \left(u(x_t) - \hat{u}\right) e^{-\rho t} dt, \text{ where } \rho > 0. \qquad (10.20)$$

The discount rate in Koopmans's model is constant over time, as in Eqs. (10.19) and (10.20). As explained in the previous chapter, the constant discount rate is referred to as an exponential discounting in which the yearly discounting rate is kept unchanging over future periods. Koopmans's model is, however, applicable under a hyperbolic discounting in which the ratio of discounting rates in two periods remains constant over future periods (Ainslie 1991; Karp 2004; Nordhaus 2008; Seo 2020).

From this point on, an optimal economic growth path is searched, which maximizes Eq. (10.20), that is, by choices of $\left(\hat{x}_t, \hat{k}_t\right)$. Specifically, an eligible-attainable path $\left(\hat{x}_t, \hat{k}_t\right)$ which is given is investigated for optimality. Note that by now the Eqs. (10.19) and (10.20) are very similar to the objective functions of the dynamic optimization problems in the contemporary economic growth literature.

The optimality conditions to be described shortly are associated with implicit prices of the consumption good and the use of the capital good. These implicit prices are tentative until the optimality of the path is confirmed. When the optimality is confirmed, these prices are critically important in separating the optimal set from the attainable set. The price, p_t, of the consumption good at time t is the discounted marginal utility of consumption at that time:

$$p_t = u'\left(\hat{x}_t\right)e^{-\rho t}. \tag{10.21}$$

The price of the use of the capital good, q_t, is the present value of the marginal productivity of capital ($g'(\cdot)$) multiplied by the marginal utility of consumption at that time:

$$q_t = p_t g'\left(\hat{k}_t\right). \tag{10.22}$$

To proceed to Proposition 10.6, let's introduce a few additional notations to distinguish the objective functions. The first is for the attainable-eligible path and the second for the time horizon in the model:

$$\hat{U}_T\left(\rho\right) = \int_0^T \left(\left(\hat{u}_t\right) - \hat{u}\right)e^{-\rho t}\,dt \text{ for } T \leq \infty,$$

$$\text{and } \hat{U}\left(\rho\right) = \hat{U}_\infty\left(\rho\right). \tag{10.23}$$

The Propositions 10.6 and 10.7 are derived from the basic inequalities that arise from the concavity of the utility function and the concavity of the production function:

$$u(x) - u(x^*) \leq u'(x^*) \cdot (x - x^*) \forall x, x^*; \qquad (10.24a)$$

$$g(k) - g(k^*) \leq g'(k^*) \cdot (k - k^*) \forall k, k^*. \qquad (10.24b)$$

Proposition 10.6 If $(\hat{x}_t, \hat{k}_t)$ is an eligible-attainable path, and if (x_t, k_t) is any path, feasible or not, then the following inequality holds for all finite T, and for $T = \infty$ whenever the following integral converges:

$$U_T(\rho) - \hat{U}_T(\rho) \leq \int_0^T p_t(x_t - \hat{x}_t) dt \qquad (10.25)$$

Combining Eq. (10.24a) and Eq. (10.21) yields the Proposition 10.6. In the above proposition, if $x_t = \hat{x}_t$, both sides of Eq. (10.25) vanish. This means that the utility, $U_T(\rho)$, of the path (x_t, k_t) is maximized subject to the budget constraint, if $(x_t, k_t) = (\hat{x}_t, \hat{k}_t)$:

$$\int_0^T p_t(x_t - \hat{x}_t) dt \leq 0. \qquad (10.26)$$

If $x_t = \hat{x}_t$, this also means that the consumption expenditure at implicit prices, $x_t = \hat{x}_t$, reaches its minimum, on the set of paths with utility $U_T(\rho)$ equal to or exceeding that of the path $(\hat{x}_t, \hat{k}_t)$, if $(x_t, k_t) = (\hat{x}_t, \hat{k}_t)$.

Proposition 10.7 If $(x_t, k_t), (\hat{x}_t, \hat{k}_t)$ are two eligible-attainable trajectories, the following inequalities hold:

$$\int_0^T p_t(x_t - \hat{x}_t) dt \leq \int_0^T \left[q_t(k_t - \hat{k}_t) - p_t\left(\dot{k}_t - \dot{\hat{k}}_t\right) \right] dt$$

$$= \int (q_t + \dot{p}_t)(k_t - \hat{k}_t) dt - p_T(k_T - \hat{k}_T) \qquad (10.27)$$

for all finite T. In addition, the above inequalities hold for $T = \infty$ if the integrals converge and the last term is bounded.

Combining Eqs. (10.21), (10.22), (10.24a), and (10.24b) yields the Proposition 10.7. It states that, at prices implicit in the path $(\hat{x}_t, \hat{k}_t)$, revenue from "total output" minus rental cost of use of capital is maximized in that path, which can be read from rearranging Eq. (10.27):

$$\int_0^T p_t \left(x_t + k_t - \hat{x}_t - \hat{k}_t \right) dt - \int_0^T q_t \left(k_t - \hat{k}_t \right) dt \le 0 \qquad (10.28)$$

From Propositions 10.6 and 10.7, Propositions 10.8, 10.9, and 10.10 in the following are ensued. To understand Proposition 10.8, refer to Fig. 10.2 in which the relevant terms in the proposition are illustrated.

Proposition 10.8 Let $\hat{x}(\rho), \hat{k}(\rho)$ be the solution, x, k, to the following set of equations:

$$f'(k) = \lambda + \rho, f(k) - \lambda k = x, \text{where } 0 < \lambda \le \lambda + \rho < f'(0). \qquad (10.29)$$

Then if $k_0 = \hat{k}(\rho)$, the unique optimal path is defined by $\hat{x}_t = \hat{x}(\rho), \hat{k}_t = \hat{k}(\rho)$ for all $t \ge 0$.

The determination of $\hat{k}(\rho)$ is illustrated in Fig. 10.3. This can be compared with the determination of $\hat{k}$ in the figure. Owing to the strict concavity of $f(\cdot)$, it is the case that $\hat{x}(\rho)$ and $\hat{k}(\rho)$ exist and are unique. Further, with the choice of a lower discount rate (ρ^*), the capital accumulation is higher, which can be verified graphically from Fig. 10.3:

$$0 < \hat{k}(\rho) < \hat{k}(\rho^*) \le \hat{k}, \text{for } f'(0) - \lambda > \rho > \rho^* \ge 0. \qquad (10.30)$$

Moreover, since $f(k) - \lambda k$ increases over the interval $\left(0 \le k \le \hat{k} \right)$, the following holds with the choice of a lower discount rate (ρ^*), which again can be verified graphically from Fig. 10.3:

$$\hat{x}(\rho) \equiv f\left(\hat{k}(\rho) \right) - \lambda \hat{k}(\rho) < \hat{x}(\rho^*) \le \hat{x}, \text{for } f'(0) - \lambda > \rho > \rho^* \ge 0. \quad (10.31)$$

Proposition 10.9 The following holds for any starting-point capital stock, that is, $k_0 \ne \hat{k}(\rho)$. For all k_0 with $0 < k_0 \le \overline{k}$, the unique optimal

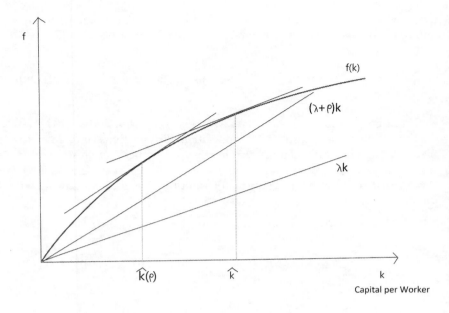

Fig. 10.3 Determination of $\hat{k}(\rho)$ with the discount rate ρ

economic growth trajectory $\left(\hat{x}_t, \hat{k}_t\right)$ is uniquely specified by the two conditions:

(a)
$$\lim_{T \to \infty} \hat{k}_T = \hat{k}(\rho), \tag{10.32}$$

(b) The prices, that is, the price of the consumption good (p_t) and the price of the use of the capital good (q_t), implicit in the trajectory $\left(\hat{x}_t, \hat{k}_t\right)$ satisfy the following differential equation:

$$q_t + \dot{p}_t = 0, \text{for all} \, t \ge 0. \tag{10.33}$$

Proposition 10.9(b) is interpreted as follows, which is illustrated as well in Fig. 10.4. The capital deviates for a short duration denoted as D in the figure, that is, $k_t > \hat{k}_t$. This deviation is marked in the figure as a thick

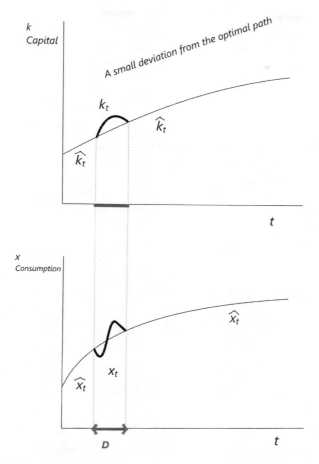

Fig. 10.4 The effects of a small deviation from the optimal path

black line in the top figure. The effects of this deviation on the consumption, which is marked as a thick black line in the bottom figure, occur through (i) an increase in capital investment inducing a decrease in consumption, (ii) an increase in capital investment inducing an increase in production. For an arbitrary small deviation, $x_t - \hat{x}_t$, of an arbitrary short duration, the utility effects of $x_t - \hat{x}_t$ must cancel out if the path ($\hat{x}_t, \hat{k}_t$) is to be the optimal path. This is depicted in the bottom figure as temporarily lower consumption in the initial phase and as temporarily higher consumption in the latter phase of the duration D.

If the condition (b) in Proposition 10.9 is satisfied, the inequality in Eq. (10.27) (Proposition 10.7) becomes the following inequality:

$$\int_0^T p_t \left(x_t - \hat{x}_t \right) dt - p_T \left(k_T - \hat{k}_T \right) \le 0. \tag{10.34}$$

What it says is that, in an economy that keeps its own capital accounts, the revenue from deliveries to consumption plus the value of the capital stock at the end of the planning horizon T are maximized in the optimal path ($\hat{x}_t, \hat{k}_t$).

From Eqs. (10.25) and (10.34), the following ensues,

$$U_T(\rho) - \hat{U}_T(\rho) \le \int_0^T p_t \left(x_t - \hat{x}_t \right) dt \le p_T \left(k_T - \hat{k}_T \right) \tag{10.35}$$

If condition (a) in Proposition 10.9 is also satisfied, Eq. (10.21) and Proposition 10.10 imply that the price p_t associated with the optimal path approaches zero as $t \to \infty$. In that case, $\lim_{t \to \infty} p_t \left(k_t - \hat{k}_t \right) = 0$. Then, the inequality in Eq. (10.35) becomes Eq. (10.36), which confirms the optimality of the path ($\hat{x}_t, \hat{k}_t$):

$$\lim_{T \to \infty} U_T(\rho) - \hat{U}_T(\rho) \le 0. \tag{10.36}$$

The middle member of the Eq. (10.35) converges and the following can be asserted: The revenue from deliveries to consumption $\int_0^\infty p_t x_t dt$ is maximized on the set of eligible-attainable paths if $(x_t, k_t) = (\hat{x}_t, \hat{k}_t)$.

Proposition 10.10 In the unique optimal path $(\hat{x}_t, \hat{k}_t)$ for any starting-point capital stock k_0 with $0 < k_0 \le \overline{k}, k_0 \ne \hat{k}(\rho)$, the following holds:

(i) $\hat{x}_t$ exhibits a monotonic and asymptotic approach to $\hat{x}(\rho)$, from above if $k_0 > \hat{k}(\rho)$, from below if $k_0 < \hat{k}(\rho)$;
(ii) $\hat{k}_t$ exhibits a monotonic and asymptotic approach to $\hat{k}(\rho)$, from above if $k_0 > \hat{k}(\rho)$, from below if $k_0 < \hat{k}(\rho)$.

10.4   TECHNOLOGICAL CHANGES AND A DISCOUNT RATE
IN KOOPMANS'S MODEL

Does the optimality of the path ($\hat{x}_t, \hat{k}_t$) hold if a negative discount rate were to be used in the model? The consequence of a negative discount rate can be examined from the afore-described model by setting $-\rho = \varphi$ with $\varphi > 0$. Koopmans wrote that the negative discount rate may be motivated if each generation is weighted by the number of its population in a gradually increasing population. The finite-horizon utility is written from a candidate optimal path (x_t, k_t):

$$V_T(-\varphi) = \int_0^T e^{\varphi t} u(x_t) dt \qquad (10.37)$$

If there exists an optimal path under the negative discount rate, we must be able to find a feasible path (x_t, k_t) such that

$$W_T^*(-\varphi) = \int_0^T e^{\varphi t} \left(u(x_t^*) - u(x_t) \right) dt \qquad (10.38)$$

is uniformly bounded from above for all feasible paths (x_t^*, k_t^*) and all values of T. However, no such path exists, which is the statement of Proposition 10.11.

Proposition 10.11 For a discount rate $\varphi > 0$, for each attainable trajectory (x_t, k_t), where $0 < k_0 \leq \overline{k}$, and for each arbitrary number $g > 0$, there exists another attainable trajectory (x_t^*, k_t^*) and a number T^* such that

$$W_T^*(-\varphi) > g, \forall T \geq T^*. \qquad (10.39)$$

The above proposition says that there is no upper bound to the range, on the feasible set, of a utility function. This was noticed also by the work of Tinbergen and Chakravarty in the context of a zero discount rate (Tinbergen 1960; Chakravarty 1962). This argument by Tinbergen, Chakravarty, and Koopmans with regard to a zero or negative discount rate is at the core of Nordhaus's response, known as a "hair-trigger" argument, to the near-zero discounting critics of global warming policy (Nordhaus 2007; Stern 2007; Weitzman 2007).

The reason for the absence of an optimal path for $\rho < 0$ is because a delay in consumption always increases the social utility. To elaborate, if the discount rate is zero ($\rho = 0$), then the implicit price of the consumption good per worker is constant, as per Eq. (10.21). In that case, a sacrifice of one unit of consumption (per worker) from the present period can be consumed by any period by the future generation, without affecting the utility. If $\rho < 0$, such a postponement of the time when the fruit of the sacrifice is reaped will always increase the utility. This is stated as Property 10.1 below.

If the same logic is applied to the negative consumption or damages caused by global climate change, readers will be able to get easily to the hair-trigger argument by Nordhaus (Nordhaus 2007).

Property 10.1 Let $\left(\hat{x}_t, \hat{k}_t\right)$ be an optimal path for a starting-point capital stock k_0. If $\rho = 0$, then, for any arbitrary T, the path $\left(x_t^*, k_t^*\right)$ constructed in the following way is optimal for $k_0^* = \hat{k}_T$:

$$x_t^* = \hat{x}_{T+t}, k_t^* = \hat{k}_{T+t} \qquad (10.40)$$

If the discount rate is negative, it is always better to put off the present generation's consumption to the future generation, more aptly, to the terminal generation T. In the model of infinite generations, that is, $T = \infty$, there is no generation to reap the benefits of the delay in consumptions. As such, preceding generations make indefinite and fruitless sacrifices, which is an indefensible economic argument.

A similar problem would occur if a technological progress factor is added to Koopmans's model in a certain way. The exogeneous technological progress function in the Solow model was explained in detail in Chap. 9 (Solow 1957). Let Koopmans's production function be written with an exogenous technological progress function A_t added multiplicatively which is assumed to grow at a constant rate of β:

$$F\left(K_t, L_t, A_t\right) = cA_t\, K_t^\alpha\, L_t^{1-\alpha}; \qquad (10.41a)$$

$$A_t = e^{\beta t}. \qquad (10.41b)$$

Notice in Eqs. (10.41a) and (10.41b) that the technological growth rate has the same effect on the model as the negative discount rate. To avoid the problem, the following Property 10.2 should hold (Inagaki 1963).

Property 10.2 With the assumptions of the technological growth at a constant rate of β, the discount rate ρ, and the capital elasticity of output α in the thus-far described Koopmans's model, for an optimal economic growth path to exist, the following inequality should hold:

$$\rho > \frac{\beta}{1-\alpha}. \tag{10.42}$$

Alternatively, to avoid this problem, the technological progress A_t can be modeled as a second-order process in which it grows over time but at a decreasing rate (Nordhaus 1994, 2002; Hulten 2000). Let $g_{A,\,t}$ be the growth rate function at time t of the total factor productivity (TFP), A_t. Assuming the growth rate declines exponentially at a constant rate (σ_A), we get the following TPF function:

$$A_t = A_{t-1}\left(1 + g_{A,t}\right) \text{ with } g_{A,t} = \frac{g_{A,t-1}}{1+\sigma_A}. \tag{10.43}$$

Summarizing Koopmans's model, we can draw a conclusion that in the societally welfare optimizing economic growth pathway, the growth rate of the economy will approximate the rate of population growth (Eq. 10.13) plus the rate of time preference (Eq. 10.29) plus the rate of unforeseeable technological growth (Eq. 10.43). This of course holds within the structure of Koopmans's model.

10.5   A Negative Externality Critique

A distinguishing aspect of Koopmans's model from the Solow model described in the previous chapter is that it explicitly defines the social welfare function whose maximization is achieved through the model. Koopmans succeeded in delivering the first exposition of a dynamic social welfare optimization model of economic growth.

Critics of the Solow model have leveled their criticisms on the possible unsustainability of the Solow growth model, which was explained at length in Chap. 9, considering the production focus of the model. Critics of

Koopmans's model tend to heed to externalities of the economic behaviors, especially negative externalities not accounted for by economic actors, considering the social welfare focus of the model. The two critiques are without doubt not unrelated.

The theory of negative externalities was first expounded by Arthur Pigou in his "Economics of Welfare" published in 1920 (Pigou 1920). Pigou argued that some economic production activities produce as a byproduct of producing the intended final goods unintended external effects. The external effects can be either harmful to the society or beneficial to the society. In the former case, they are called negative externalities while they are called positive externalities in the latter case.

The best example of the negative externalities, reviewing the investigations of the past hundred years since the Pigou's publication, is pollution caused by firms: air pollution, water pollution, vehicle pollution, noise pollution, and so on. To consider an example, let's assume that there is an apparel factory upstream a river. Its production activities discharge numerous pollutants including harmful chemicals into the river. Let's assume that there is a blueberry orchard downstream the river that utilizes the water in the river for irrigating the orchard.

The profit-maximizing production activities in the upstream factory result in harmful consequences on the downstream orchard. Relying on numerous examples such as this, Pigou argued that the utility and profit maximization activities by producers and consumers are in fact suboptimal from the society's welfare maximization standpoint (Pigou 1920).

An elegant response was offered by Ronald Coase from the Chicago School of Economics in his "The Problem of Social Cost" in 1960, which is known as the Coase theorem to economists (Coase 1960; Friedman 1962). Reviewing numerous examples that Pigou relied upon, Coase argued that there is a mutually beneficial bargaining that can take place between the two parties, that is, the polluter and the victim. The mutual bargaining will result in an agreement that will improve the welfare of both parties, as such, that of the society.

To continue with the above example, the downstream orchard can start by requesting the upstream apparel factory to stop its river pollution. The upstream apparel factory may respond by offering a compensation, considering the possibility of a string of lawsuits and governmental orders, of, say, 1 million US$ along with the installments of pollution-reducing technologies. Upon this, the downstream orchard may respond with a counter proposal. This process will ultimately result in a mutually agreed outcome.

Critics of the Coase's theorem of mutual bargaining, however, came forward in full force as soon as it took roots in economics. The Coase bargaining may not work in reality, they argued. To give you an example, there is not just one factory in the upstream, but a dozen factories. Then, the negotiation between the two parties would become drastically more difficult. On top of this, let's say that there are numerous factories and residential areas downstream the river. In such a case, the possibility of a mutually agreed outcome is quite slim, if any (Baumol and Oates 1971, 1975; Mendelsohn 1980).

Looking at the debates on the Coase theorem from another angle, it can be said that the Coase theorem does indeed address the Pigouvian externalities well. What it does not address is the problem of public consumption goods, public goods in short (Seo 2017a, 2020). A public good is a good, when produced, that is consumed jointly by a community of people (Bowen 1943; Samuelson 1954; Buchanan 1965). The opposite of it is a private good or a private consumption good.

When the good under consideration is harming the public collectively, it can be said a public bad. On the other hand, when the good under consideration is benefiting the public collectively, it can be said to be a public good.

Owing to the joint consumption, public goods are non-rivalrous as well as non-excludable in their consumptions (Bowen 1943). The non-rivalry means that a single individual's consumption of the public good does not decrease the amount available to the others, for example, lighthouse at a sea port. The non-excludability means that individual members cannot be excluded from the consumption of the public good once it has been provided to the public, for example, in the case of national defense.

Because of the unique characteristics of the public consumption goods, the term coined by Paul Samuelson, a provision of the public good is not achieved in the market at the efficient level. This means that policy interventions *via* various policy measures such as a public good tax or regulations should bring the efficient provision of the public good to the public (Samuelson 1954, 1955).

Of the range of the public goods, the biggest public good problem is that of a global public good (Nordhaus 1994; Seo 2020). The public goods can be classified into local public goods, state public goods, national public goods, multi-national public goods, and global public goods, based on the scope of the effects of the good under consideration (Samuelson and Nordhaus 2009). A global public good is a globally shared good by the planet's habitants (Seo 2020).

A representative globally shared good is global warming or climate change (IPCC 1990; UNFCCC 1992; Le Treut et al. 2007). The studies of global warming and climate change reveal that the policy efforts to deal with the problem have repeatedly failed during the past three decades, leaving each time frustrations as well as high cost to the global community (UNFCCC 1997, 2009, 2015; Seo 2012, 2017a, b, 2019; Nordhaus and Boyer 1999; Nordhaus 2010).

On the other hand, the societies are shown to have a wide range of options to adapt to the changing climate conditions of the planet including the mitigation options, that is, pollution reduction options, when it comes to the problem whose scale is as large as the entire planet (Seo 2015, 2016a, b, 2017c).

Summing up, the review of the literature on global warming reveals that there are market forces at work in this globally shared problem which render the global community's adaptation to climate change possible to a large extent. On the other hand, the multiplicity of powerful market forces at work makes it nearly impossible for a globally unified policy intervention to solve this grand problem (Seo 2019, 2020, 2021, 2022).

10.6   Conclusion

This chapter provided a comprehensive exposition of Koopmans's theory of optimal economic growth. This is the most refined and complete analysis on the problem that this book has taken on, that is, choosing an optimal economic growth pathway, if the society would aspire to choose such a one, from a wide range of possible pathways.

This book's scope is, however, far greater than Koopmans's theory introduced here, which the present author wants to emphasize one more time. This book integrates the theories of the economic growth such as Solow's and Koopmans's with the theories of the efficient resource uses and capital asset investments such as Ricardo's, von Thunen's, Faustmann's, Hotelling's, Fisher's, and so on (Faustmann 1849; Fisher 1906; Hotelling 1931). To put differently, while Koopmans's model describes the movement of the macro economy over a time horizon, this book also provides an exposition of the movements of the sectoral economies that constitute the macro economy.

Does Koopmans's model have any practical implication for the society and economic decisions, given that the society will not attempt to choose such an optimal growth pathway *via*, for example, pursuing a certain investment rate or a technological growth rate? Beating anyone's expectations, by the historic turn of events that Koopmans never foresaw, this highly conceptual model would be called upon three decades later to face the most practical, realistic, complex policy issue of the twenty-first century, that is, a warming planet. Koopmans's model was ideally situated to be a foundation for the global policy model, that is, the DICE model, by William Nordhaus and his presentation of the global carbon tax trajectory superbly entitled "An Optimal Transition Path of Controlling Greenhouse Gases," which was without doubt accomplished with intellectual force (Nordhaus 1992, 1994, 2008). That is the topic of the next chapter.

References

Ainslie, G. 1991. Derivation of 'Rational' Economic Behavior from Hyperbolic Discount Curves. *American Economic Review* 81: 334–340.

Allais, Maurice. 1960. *Économie & Intérêt; Présentation nouvelle des problèmes fondamentaux relatives au rôle économique du taux de l'intérêt et de leurs solutions.* Paris, FR: Imprimerie Nationale.

Bauer, P.T. 1957. *Economic Analysis and Policy in Underdeveloped Countries.* Durham, NC: Duke University Press.

Baumol, W.J., and W.E. Oates. 1971. The Use of Standards and Prices for Protection of the Environment. *The Swedish Journal of Economics* 73: 42–54.

———. 1975. *The Theory of Environmental Policy.* Upper Saddle River, NJ: Prentice Hall.

Bowen, H.R. 1943. The Interpretation of Voting in the Allocation of Economic Resources. *Quarterly Journal of Economics* 58: 27–48.

Buchanan, James M. 1965. An Economic Theory of Clubs. *Economica* 32: 1–14.

Chakravarty, S. 1962. The Existence of an Optimum Savings Program. *Econometrica* 30: 178–187.

Coase, Ronald. 1960. The Problem of Social Cost. *Journal of Law and Economics* 3: 1–44.

Dorfman, R., P.A. Samuelson, and R.M. Solow. 1987. *Linear Programming and Economic Analysis.* Mineola, NY: Dover Publication.

Faustmann, Martin. 1849. On the Determination of the Value Which Forest Land and Immature Stands Pose for Forestry. In *Martin Faustmann and the Evolution of Discounted Cash Flow*, ed. M. Gane. Oxford, England: Oxford Institute. [1968, Paper 42].

Fisher, Irving. 1906. *The Nature of Capital and Income.* New York, NY: Macmillan.

Friedman, Milton. 1962. *Capitalism and Freedom*. Chicago, IL: The University of Chicago Press.

Hotelling, H. 1931. The Economics of Exhaustible Resources. *Journal of Political Economy* 39: 137–175.

Hulten, Charles R. 2000. *Total Factor Productivity: A Short Biography*. National Bureau of Economic Research (NBER) Working Paper Series 7471, The NBER, Cambridge, MA.

Inagaki, M. 1963. *The Golden Utility Path*. Rotterdam, NL: Netherlands Economics Institute.

Intergovernmental Panel on Climate Change (IPCC). 1990. *Climate Change: The IPCC Scientific Assessment*. Cambridge, UK: Cambridge University Press.

Kantorovich, Leonid V. 1939. Mathematical Methods of Organizing and Planning Production. *Management Science* 6: 366–422.

———. 1959. *The Best Use of Economic Resources*. Cambridge, MA: Harvard University Press.

Karp, L. 2004. *Global Warming and Hyperbolic Discounting*. CUDARE Working Papers, #934, The University of California, Berkeley.

Koopmans, Tjalling C. 1949. Optimum Utilization of the Transportation System. *Proceedings of the International Statistical Conference* 5: 136–145.

———., ed. 1951. *Activity Analysis of Production and Allocation*. New York, NY: Wiley.

———. 1957. *Three Essays on the State of Economic Science*. New York, Toronto, and London: McGraw-Hill.

———. 1963. *On the Concept of Optimal Economic Growth*. The Cowles Foundation Discussion Paper # 163, Yale University, New Haven, CT.

———. 1965. On the Concept of Optimal Economic Growth. *Pontificiae Academiae Scientiarum Scripta Varia* 28 (1): 1–75.

———. 1975. *Concepts of Optimality and Their Uses*. Nobel Memorial Lecture, Stockholm, SE.

Le Treut, H., R. Somerville, U. Cubasch, Y. Ding, C. Mauritzen, A. Mokssit, T. Peterson, and M. Prather. 2007. Historical Overview of Climate Change. In *Climate Change 2007: The Physical Science Basis. The Fourth Assessment Report of the IPCC*, ed. S. Solomon et al. Cambridge, UK: Cambridge University Press.

Lutz, W., W. Butz, and K.C. Samir, eds. 2014. *World Population and Global Human Capital in the 21st Century*. Oxford, UK: Oxford University Press.

Mas-Colell, A., M.D. Whinston, and J.R. Green. 1995. *Microeconomic Theory*. Oxford, UK: Oxford University Press.

Mendelsohn, R. 1980. An Economic Analysis of Air Pollution from Coal-fired Power Plants. *Journal of Environmental Economics and Management* 7: 30–43.

Nordhaus, W.D. 1973. The Allocation of Energy Resources. *Brookings Papers on Economic Activity* 1973: 529–576.

————. 1991. To Slow or Not to Slow: The Economics of the Greenhouse Effects. *Economic Journal* 101: 920–937.

————. 1992. An Optimal Transition Path for Controlling Greenhouse Gases. *Science* 258: 1315–1319.

————. 1994. *Managing the Global Commons.* Cambridge, MA: The MIT Press.

————. 2002. Modeling Induced Innovation in Climate Change Policy. In *Technological Change and the Environment New York*, ed. A. Grubler, N. Nakićenović, and W.D. Nordhaus. NY: Routledge.

————. 2007. A Review of the Stern Review on the Economics of Climate Change. *Journal of Economic Literature* 55: 686–702.

————. 2008. *A Question of Balance: Weighing the Options on Global Warming Policies.* New Haven, CT: Yale University Press.

————. 2010. Economic Aspects of Global Warming in a Post-Copenhagen Environment. *Proceedings of the National Academy of Sciences* 107: 11721–11726.

————. 2019. Climate Change: The Ultimate Challenge for Economics. *American Economic Review* 109: 1991–2014.

Nordhaus, W.D., and J.G. Boyer. 1999. Requiem for Kyoto: An Economic Analysis of the Kyoto Protocol. *Energy Journal* 20: 93–130.

Nordhaus, W.D., and J. Tobin. 1972. *Is Growth Obsolete?* Cambridge, MA: National Bureau of Economic Research.

Pigou, Arthur C. 1920. *Economics of Welfare.* London, UK: Macmillan.

Ramsey, F.P. 1928. A Mathematical Theory of Savings. *Economic Journal* 38: 543–559.

Samuelson, P.A. 1952. Spatial Price Equilibrium and Linear Programming. *American Economic Review* 42: 283–303.

————. 1954. The Pure Theory of Public Expenditure. *Review of Economics and Statistics* 36: 387–389.

Samuelson, P. 1955. Diagrammatic Exposition of a Theory of Public Expenditure. *Review of Economics and Statistics* 37: 350–356.

Samuelson, P., and W. Nordhaus. 2009. *Economics.* 19th ed. New York, NY: McGraw-Hill Education.

Seo, S.N. 2012. What Eludes Global Agreements on Climate Change? *Economic Affairs* 32: 73–79.

————. 2015. Helping Low-latitude, Poor Countries with Climate Change. *Regulation* (Winter 2015–2016): 6–8.

————. 2016a. *Microbehavioral Econometric Methods: Theories, Models, and Applications for the Study of Environmental and Natural Resources.* Amsterdam, NL: Academic Press, Amsterdam.

————. 2016b. Modeling Farmer Adaptations to Climate Change in South America: A Microbehavioral Economic Perspective. *Environmental and Ecological Statistics* 23: 1–21.

———. 2017a. *The Behavioral Economics of Climate Change: Adaptation Behaviors, Global Public Goods, Breakthrough Technologies, and Policy-making*. Amsterdam, NL: Academic Press.

———. 2017b. Beyond the Paris Agreement: Climate Change Policy Negotiations and Future Directions. *Regional Science Policy & Practice* 9: 121–140.

———. 2017c. Measuring Policy Benefits of the Cyclone Shelter Program in the North Indian Ocean: Protection from Intense Winds or High Storm Surges? *Climate Change Economics* 8: 1–18.

———. 2019. *The Economics of Global Allocations of the Green Climate Fund: An Assessment from Four Scientific Traditions of Modeling Adaptation Strategies*. Cham, CH: Springer Nature.

———. 2020. *The Economics of Globally Shared and Public Goods*. Amsterdam, NL: Academic Press.

———. 2021. *Climate Change and Economics: Engaging with Future Generations with Action Plans*. Cham, CH: Palgrave Macmillan.

———. 2022. *The Economics of Pandemics: Exploring Globally Shared Experiences*. Cham, CH: Palgrave Macmillan.

Solow, Robert M. 1957. A Contribution to the Theory of Economic Growth. *Quarterly Journal of Economics* 70: 65–94.

———. 1974. The Economics of Resources or The Resources of Economics. *American Economic Review* 64: 1–14.

Stern, N. 2007. *The Economics of Climate Change: The Stern Review*. Cambridge, UK: Cambridge University Press.

Tinbergen, J. 1960. Optimum Savings and Utility Maximization over Time. *Econometrica* 28: 481–489.

United Nations Framework Convention on Climate Change (UNFCCC). 1992. *United Nations Framework Convention on Climate Change*. New York, NY: UNFCCC.

———. 1997. *Kyoto Protocol to the United Nations Framework Convention on Climate Change*. New York, NY: UNFCCC.

———. 2009. *Copenhagen Accord*. UNFCCC, New York.

———. 2015. *The Paris Agreement. Conference of the Parties (COP) 21*. New York, NY: UNFCCC.

Uzawa, Hirofumi. 1960. Market Mechanisms and Mathematical Programming. *Econometrica* 28: 872–881.

Weitzman, M.L. 2007. A Review of The Stern Review on the Economics of Climate Change. *Journal of Economic Literature* 45: 703–724.

CHAPTER 11

William Nordhaus's Optimal Carbon Tax Trajectory

11.1   Introduction

Koopmans's model described in the previous chapter laid out an analytical framework for addressing the question of how a nation may pursue an optimal economic growth path over a distant time horizon (Koopmans 1963, 1965). The model was carefully built after integrating his Nobel Prize winning works on optimal resource uses as well as his predecessors' works such as Fisher's theory of interest and capital, Ramsey's optimal saving rate, and Solow's growth model of capital accumulation (Fisher 1906, 1930; Ramsey 1928; Solow 1957).

From a bird's-eye view of what this book presents, Koopmans's optimal economic growth pathway can be interpreted as the envelope of the optimal growth pathways of the individual economic sectors and enterprises reviewed in this book such as crop agriculture, grasslands, urban land uses, forest harvests, energy generations, fish and marine resource harvests, and financial asset investments (Ricardo 1817; von Thunen 1826; Faustmann 1849; Hotelling 1931; Clark 1973; Fisher 1930; Samuelson 1947).

The flip side of that interpretation is that Koopmans's model is an abstract contribution to the theory of economic growth in that no national policy-maker would pursue an optimal economic growth trajectory as prescribed by Koopmans's model. Put differently, s/he would not attempt to achieve Koopmans's trajectory by choosing a set of variables such as population growth, technological progress, an interest rate, or a saving rate.

S. N. Seo, *The Economics of Optimal Growth Pathways,*
https://doi.org/10.1007/978-3-031-20754-9_11

By contrast, forest managers, for example, would actively endeavor to choose an optimal forest harvest rotation as prescribed by the Faustmann rotation (Faustmann 1849; Mitra and Wan Jr 1985; Newman 1988). Likewise, managers and policy-makers are easily observed to energetically pursue efficient land uses, optimal fossil fuel extractions, an optimal fish catch, and an optimal financial investment.

The abstract conceptualization of Koopmans's model, however, had turned out over time to lay a foundation for the economic analysis of global warming and climate change when this global level challenge surfaced to the world stage through the 1980s (WMO 1985; IPCC 1990; UNFCCC 1992). William Nordhaus revealed a highly practical meaning of Koopmans's optimal growth pathway for the global community in the context of the problem of global warming. The first paper by Nordhaus with an application and reinterpretation of Koopmans's theory of optimal economic growth was aptly titled "An Optimal Transition Path for Controlling Greenhouse Gases" published in Science in 1992 (Nordhaus 1992).

By what means and insights was William Nordhaus able to succeed in translating the highly abstract Koopmans's growth pathway into a highly practical transition pathway for the global community? One of them was the salient characteristics of a globally shared good that permeate the global warming challenges. A globally shared good is alternatively referred to as a global public good or the global commons in the literature with which many readers may be more familiar (Seo 2020a).

Let me elaborate this point. Owing to the predominant characteristics of global warming challenges as a globally shared good, scientists needed to resort to a single trajectory for the entire global community of one variable or another. Concretely, they started to build a highly abstract and simplified model of climate change to produce a single trajectory of global temperature change for the next 300 years (Manabe et al. 1965; Schneider and Thompson 1981; Schlesinger and Jiang 1990; Hansen et al. 1981; Mann et al. 1999) (refer to Fig. 11.1). Similarly, they produced a single global trajectory of atmospheric carbon dioxide concentration as well as that of carbon dioxide emissions (refer to Fig. 11.7) (Keeling et al. 2009; GCP 2017).

Like the simple trajectory of the global temperature change or the carbon dioxide concentration in the atmosphere, a highly abstract economic model of climate change was in need to match the scientific trajectories and to produce likewise a simple trajectory of an economic variable of vital

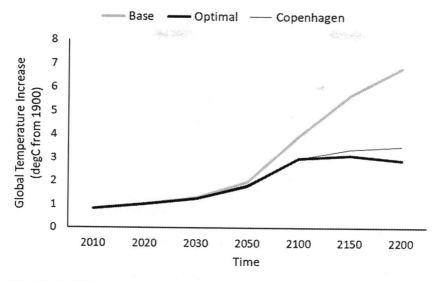

Fig. 11.1 Global temperature increase trajectories

importance. Koopmans's model was in the wait with all the basic theory and sophistications accomplished. William Nordhaus started his monumental work of developing the climate change economics model in the middle of 1970s, specifically, "Can We Control Carbon Dioxide?" in 1975 and "Economic Growth and Climate" in 1977, and was able to come up with the much-famed DICE model in the early 1990s (Nordhaus 1977, 2019). The DICE was short for the Dynamic Integrated Climate and Economy model, for a motivation of which he quoted "God does not play dice" by Albert Einstein (Nordhaus 1991, 1994).

The economist's trajectory that Nordhaus put forth was the trajectory of carbon tax or carbon price (refer to Figs. 11.4 and 11.5). It had an immediate appeal to economists and policy-makers. Like the tax instrument common in all major governmental policy areas, the carbon tax trajectory would tell policy-makers that the global efforts for controlling emissions of greenhouse gases and the planetary climate system shall simply follow the carbon tax pathway put forward by the DICE model such as the one in Fig. 11.4 of this chapter. A simple solution for a highly complex problem indeed!

By the time it dawned on policy-makers and economists that a globally harmonized carbon tax may not be a realistic policy option because of many barriers, they soon started to realize that the DICE trajectory is in fact the pathway of the true price of carbon dioxide emissions to the planet community, more rigorously referred to as the social cost of carbon (Pearce et al. 1996; Mendelsohn 2003; Nordhaus 2017; NRC 2017). The term refers to "The Problem of Social Cost" in Ronald Coase's seminal article which this book elaborated in Chap. 10 in the context of addressing negative externalities in the economy (Coase 1960).

11.2   THE DICE MODEL

The DICE model is an integrated assessment model (IAM) of climate change and policy options. It integrates all the processes end-to-end in the climate change geophysics and policy decisions (Nordhaus and Sztorc 2014). Specifically, it integrates the following five processes:

1. Carbon emissions generated by fossil fuel uses
2. Carbon cycle which redistributes carbon into atmosphere, plants, ocean, and so on
3. Climate system where changes in radiative forcing, temperature, precipitation, and so on occur
4. Impacts on ecosystems, agriculture, diseases, animals, humans, and so on
5. Policy measures to control carbon emissions such as tax, limits, emissions trading, and so on

11.2.1   *Objective Function*

Of a variety of integrated assessment models in the environmental literature, the DICE is uniquely a dynamic policy optimization model in which the social welfare function is optimized over a policy horizon, one of the legacies of Koopmans's model (Nordhaus 2013). The social welfare function of the model is defined by the following equations (Nordhaus 2008):

$$W = \sum_{t=0}^{T_{max}} U[c_t, L_t] \cdot R_t \qquad (11.1)$$

$$U[c_t, L_t] = L_t \cdot \left[\frac{c_t^{1-\alpha}}{1-\alpha}\right] \qquad (11.2)$$

$$R_t = \frac{1}{(1+\rho)^t} \qquad (11.3)$$

$$c_t = \frac{C_t}{L_t} \qquad (11.4)$$

In the DICE model, the world is assumed to have a well-defined social welfare function which ranks alternative paths of consumption (Koopmans 1965). The social welfare function, W, is defined as the sum of the present value of each period's population-weighted utility, U, of per capita consumption, c_t, over the policy time horizon T_{max}.

The social time preference discount factor in Eq. (11.1) is R_t which is defined by the pure rate of time preference, ρ. The form of Eq. (11.3) means that future discounting is modeled with an exponential discounting method, which will be clarified later in this chapter in the context of a hyperbolic discounting. A choice of the pure rate of time preference should depend on a market interest rate, a consumption growth rate, and an elasticity of marginal utility of consumption (Nordhaus 2007a, Weitzman 2009).

The utility function in Eq. (11.2) is of a Bernoulli utility function type (Bernoulli 1738). The critical parameter is α, which is mathematically the elasticity of marginal utility of consumption. Although many economists interpret it as a constant rate of relative risk aversion (CRRA) parameter (Stern 2007; Weitzman 2009), it is a social inequality aversion parameter as per different generations, more accurately (Nordhaus 2008). A high value of this parameter means that the social decisions place much importance on whether the future generations are richer or poorer than the present generations while a low value means that the social decisions place little importance on it. Put differently, $\alpha > 1$ means that the society prefers a more equal economic outcome while $\alpha < 1$ means that the society prefers a differential economic outcome.

The utility of each generation or period depends on the size of population, L_t. The size of population is external, that is, exogenous in the DICE model, whose growth path will be explained shortly (Solow 1957; Koopmans 1965). Along with the population size, the relative importance of different generations in the DICE model is determined by the two normative parameters explained above: the pure rate of time preference, ρ, and the social inequality aversion across different generations, α.

11.2.2   Economic Variables

The production function is specified with a constant-returns to scale Cobb-Douglas production function, as in Solow (1957) and Koopmans (1965):

$$Q_t = \xi_t \cdot \left[A_t K_t^{\gamma} L_t^{1-\gamma} \right] \qquad (11.5)$$

Equation (11.5) is the same as the one in the Solow model and Koopmans's model explained in the preceding two chapters. The labor force or, equivalently, population grows exponentially with a growth rate which is assumed to decline over time, as shown in Eq. (11.6). To stress, the population growth is exogeneous to the DICE model, whose growth trajectory is obtained in reliance on the projections from the reputed population study centers such as the United Nations Population Program or the International Institute of Applied Systems Analysis (IIASA 2007; Lutz et al. 2014):

$$L_t = L_{t-1} \cdot \left(1 + g_{L,t} \right), \text{where } g_{L,t} = \left. g_{L,t-1} \middle/ \left(1 + \delta_L \right) \right. \qquad (11.6)$$

The technological progress is also modeled exogenously, as shown in Eq. (11.7), captured by the Total Factor Productivity (TFP) function (Hulten 2000). It enters the production function as a Hicks-neutral process, that is, doesn't affect the ratio of capital and labor inputs (Hicks 1932). The growth of it is similarly modeled as the population growth trajectory:

$$A_t = A_{t-1} \cdot \left(1 + g_{A,t} \right), \text{where } g_{A,t} = \left. g_{A,t-1} \middle/ \left(1 + \delta_A \right) \right. \qquad (11.7)$$

The world output, Q, is the sum of the individual regions' productions. The summation is performed by a set of exchange rates, for which the purchasing power parity (PPP) exchange rates are used instead of the market exchange rates observed in the exchange markets (Nordhaus 2007b). The PPP exchange rates are available from the International Monetary Fund or the World Bank. The individual region's growth function is modelled with a partial convergence model of the regional economies of the planet (Barro and Sala-i-Martin 1992).

A distinct feature in the production function in Eq. (11.5) from the aforementioned models is that of ξ which is a function of the climate policy variables which are of primary concern to climate economists and policy-makers:

$$\xi_t = \frac{\text{Effects of GHG Abatement}}{\text{Effects of Climate Change}} = \frac{1 - \Lambda_t}{1 + \Omega_t} \tag{11.8}$$

It adjusts the Cobb-Douglas production function in a multiplicative manner. The numerator is the effect of abatement cost of the greenhouse gases (GHG), Λ, while the denominator is the effect (damage) of climate change, Ω. The damage function is specified as a quadratic function of the atmospheric temperature increase without an intercept:

$$\Omega_t = \varsigma_1 T_{A,t} + \varsigma_2 \left(T_{A,t} \right)^2 \tag{11.9}$$

The abatement cost function, Eq. (11.10a), is specified as a power function of the emissions control rate, μ_t, the exponent, θ_2, and the coefficient, $\theta_{1,t}$ (Nordhaus and Boyer 2000; Fischer and Morgenstern 2006):

$$\Lambda_t = \theta_{1,t} \left(\mu_t \right)^{\theta_2} \tag{11.10a}$$

$$\Lambda_t = \pi_t \theta_{1,t} \mu_t^{\theta_2}, \text{ where } \pi_t = \varphi_t^{1 - \theta_2} \tag{11.10b}$$

The cost of abatement (Λ_t) depends on how many countries participate in the abatement efforts for a certain global policy agreement/protocol, that is, a participation rate. The π_t in Eq. (11.10b) is a participation cost markup with φ_t, the participation rate which is defined as a fraction of world emissions included in the specific policy protocol (Nordhaus 2008, 2010).

The following are two accounting equations of the economy. In Eq. (11.11), the economy's production is either consumed or invested (I) for new production activities. In Eq. (11.12), the economy's capital stock increases with the new investment and decreases with a depreciation rate, δ_K.

$$Q_t = C_t + I_t \tag{11.11}$$

$$K_t = I_t + (1 - \delta_K) K_{t-1} \tag{11.12}$$

The size of industrial emissions of carbon, $E_{I, t}$, is determined by the level of production and a carbon intensity (σ_t) of the economy. If a climate policy is implemented with a target of a control rate (μ_t) of carbon emissions, the size of industrial carbon emissions is a direct function of a realized carbon control rate. Combining these factors yields Eq. (11.13):

$$E_{I,t} = \sigma_t (1 - \mu_t) A_t K_t^\gamma L_t^{1-\gamma} \tag{11.13}$$

$$\sigma_t = \sigma_{t-1}(1 + g_{\sigma,t}), \text{where } g_{\sigma,t} = {g_{\sigma,t-1}}\Big/{(1 + \delta_\sigma)} \tag{11.14}$$

The carbon intensity of the economy in Eq. (11.14) is expressed as the amount of carbon emissions per US\$ 1000 GDP produced. It is another variable in the DICE model that captures the technological progress of the economy. Especially, it measures the technological advances pertinent to carbon emissions reduction. Examples include a switch from incandescent lightbulbs to Light Emitting Diode (LED) lamps, a higher milage vehicle, better insulated buildings, and an improved power transmission and monitoring system. As presented in Eq. (11.14), the carbon intensity is assumed to decline with the rate of $g_{\sigma, t} < 0$ with a decreasing rate of δ_σ.

The carbon intensity is calibrated in the recent DICE model with $\sigma_{2010} = 0.489$. For each US\$ 1000 GDP, the global economy emits 0.489 ton of carbon in 2010. The growth parameters are set with $g_{\sigma, 2015} = -1\%$ per year, $\delta_\sigma = +0.1\%$ per five years, which are estimated from the empirical data (Nordhaus and Sztorc 2014).

The DICE model sets a limit on the total industrial emissions in reliance upon the total amount of carbon fuels in the world, heeding to the fact that fossil fuels are exhaustible resources, that is, limited resources. This is denoted as *CCum* in Eq. (11.15). It is calibrated to be 6000 GtC:

$$\sum_{t=0}^{T_{max}} E_{I,t} \leq CCum \tag{11.15}$$

11.2.3   Geophysical Variables

The DICE model links the economy described thus far to the geophysical variables of the planet which are condensed into the following three relationships: carbon cycle, radiative forcing, and the climate system. In a sense, the geophysical relationships to be explained in this subsection are the distinct contribution of the DICE modeling to the optimal growth theory expounded by Koopmans explained in the preceding chapter.

The task of developing a geophysical module for the integrated economy-geophysics model such as the DICE model poses major challenges. Consider the three sub-modules: carbon cycle, radiative forcing, climate system! Each of these modules is a complex system which is expressed by scientists with hundreds of equations and is solved only with a super computer whose price may exceed several billion US dollars. For reference, the weather/climate super computer is the most expensive asset of all the national government assets in developed countries. To verity, you may review the AOGCM climate models (Gordon et al. 2000; Schmidt et al. 2005; Taylor et al. 2012) or the carbon cycle models (Schlesinger 1997; Ciais et al. 2013).

The size of the aggregate carbon emissions is the sum of the industrial carbon emissions and the land use carbon emissions, $E_{L,t}$:

$$E_t = E_{I,t} + E_{L,t} \tag{11.16}$$

The size of the land use emissions is determined exogenously relying on the estimates from other sources (Houghton 2008; GCP 2017). In 2016, the size of the land use emissions was 12 GtCO$_2$eq, which is decomposed into the emissions from agriculture, forestry, and other land uses (6 GtCO$_2$eq), CH$_4$ emissions from agriculture (4GtCO$_2$eq), and N$_2$O emissions from agriculture (2GtCO$_2$eq) (IPCC 2019).

The carbon cycle module relies on the three reservoir model, displayed in Eqs. (11.17), (11.18), and (11.19) (Schneider and Thompson 1981; Schlesinger and Jiang 1990). $M_{A,t}$ is the carbon concentration in the atmosphere, which is the first reservoir. $M_{U,t}$ is the carbon concentration in the quickly mixing reservoir which are the upper oceans, which is the second reservoir. $M_{L,t}$ is the carbon concentration in the lower oceans, which is the third reservoir. The transfer parameter from reservoir i to reservoir j is denoted by ϕ_{ij}:

$$M_{A,t} = E_t + \phi_{11} M_{A,t-1} + \phi_{21} M_{U,t-1} \qquad (11.17)$$

$$M_{U,t} = \phi_{12} M_{A,t-1} + \phi_{22} M_{U,t-1} + \phi_{32} M_{L,t-1} \qquad (11.18)$$

$$M_{L,t} = \phi_{23} M_{U,t-1} + \phi_{33} M_{L,t-1} \qquad (11.19)$$

The accumulation of greenhouse gases *via* the three reservoirs increases the Earth's temperature by increasing the radiative forcing of the planet, F_t. The radiative forcing is defined as the radiative imbalance in the climate system on the top of the atmosphere caused by addition of greenhouse gases (Le Treut et al. 2007). The degree of radiative forcing is modeled by the following relationship in Eq. (11.20):

$$F_t = \eta \left\{ \log_2 \frac{M_{A,t}}{M_{A,1750}} \right\} + F_{EX,t} \qquad (11.20)$$

The total radiative forcing (F_t) is determined by the carbon dioxide content of the atmosphere relative to that in 1750 and the exogenous forcings ($F_{EX,t}$) by the other greenhouse gases. η is the temperature-forcing parameter expressed as °C per watts per meter squared (W/m^2). The radiative forcing caused by a doubling of carbon dioxide concentration in the atmosphere is estimated to be 3.8 W/m^2. In the recent DICE model, the radiative forcing from CO_2 is 6.1 W/m^2 by the year 2100 while the exogenous radiative forcing is 0.62 W/m^2 by the end of this century, both in the case of no policy interventions. The exogenous radiative forcing includes the effects of aerosols which have the cooling effects on Earth. The radiative forcing in 2010 was about 0.45 W/m^2 (IPCC 2019). For reference, the solar radiation falling on the top of the atmosphere is 1361 W/m^2 on average while it is about 1120 W/m^2 on average at the ground level (IPCC 1990).

A higher radiative imbalance warms the planet's atmosphere, which then heats the upper ocean and the deep ocean. The lags in the heat transfer among the layers are due to diffusive inertia of the layers. This climate change process is represented by the two equations in the DICE model, with $T_{A,t}$ atmospheric temperature and $T_{L,t}$ deep ocean temperature:

$$T_{A,t} = T_{A,t-1} + \tau_1 \left\{ F_t - \tau_2 T_{A,t-1} - \tau_3 \left[T_{A,t-1} - T_{L,t-1} \right] \right\} \quad (11.21)$$

$$T_{L,t} = T_{L,t-1} + \tau_4 \left\{ T_{A,t-1} - T_{L,t-1} \right\} \quad (11.22)$$

The DICE model sets the climate sensitivity to a doubling of carbon dioxide concentration to equal the center of the IPCC estimates, which is 3.2°C. This is referred to as the equilibrium temperature sensitivity. τ_2 is set to satisfy the following equation, with ΔT_A equilibrium temperature sensitivity and ΔF_t equilibrium radiative forcing sensitivity (Nordhaus 2008; Nordhaus and Sztorc 2014):

$$\Delta T_A = \frac{\Delta F_t}{\tau_2} \quad (11.23)$$

11.2.4 The RICE Model

The DICE model described thus far is a global optimization model by a hypothesized single economy of the planet which produces a single good. Soon after the DICE model became public, a regionally disaggregated model of the DICE was developed with 12 regions, that is, 12 regional economies (Nordhaus and Yang 1996; Nordhaus and Boyer 2000). These are US, EU, China, India, Japan, Russia, Eurasia, Middle East, Sub-Saharan Africa, Latin America, other high-income countries, and other developing countries. The model is named the Regional Integrated Climate and Economy (RICE) model.

The structure of the DICE model described above is carried over to the RICE model with a regional disaggregation. The geophysical module remains the same at the planet level. The preferences and the objective function in Sect. 11.2.1 must account for multiple regions, that is, multiple agents. The preference function in the RICE is a Bergson-Samuelson social welfare function over regions, $W = \mathcal{W}\left(U^1, U^2, \ldots, U^N\right)$ (Bergson 1938; Samuelson 1947, 1977) Specifically,

$$W = \sum\nolimits_{t=0}^{T_{max}} \sum\nolimits_{I=1}^{N} \omega_{I,t} \cdot U^{I}\left(c_{t}^{I}, L_{t}^{I}\right) \cdot R_{t} \qquad (11.24)$$

In Eq. (11.24), each region's utility is discounted with the same discount factor and weighted by region-time-specific weights, $\omega_{I, t}$, referred to as Negish weights. The Negish weights are set in a way that the marginal utility of consumption in each region and each time period is equalized in the RICE model, as per the maximization principle of the dynamic optimization program (Negishi 1960; Nordhaus and Yang 1996).

11.3   CALIBRATIONS OF THE DICE MODEL

To run the dynamic welfare optimization in the DICE and the RICE model, the parameters in the theoretical equations in the model need to be calibrated first. The ways many parameters are calibrated are already mentioned by the present author in the previous section. To highlight the calibration issues, this section focuses on the two critical parameters in the model: the discount rate and the damage function.

The discount rate is an important parameter in the objective function of the DICE model and any other dynamic optimization models. The discount rate is at the core tied to the interest rates traded upon in the market. The interest rate determination was explained in depth in Chap. 8 where Irving Fisher's theory of interest was analyzed (Fisher 1906, 1930). The other two economic parameters that affect the discount rate are the elasticity of marginal utility of consumption on the one hand and the consumption growth rate on the other, which was explained in the discussion of a "Ramsey equation" in Chap. 9 (Ramsey 1928; Stern 2007; Weitzman 1998, 2007). Using the notation of this chapter, with r real interest rate and g consumption growth rate in the model:

$$r = \alpha g + \rho. \qquad (11.25)$$

The calibration of the real interest rate in the DICE model in comparison with those from the other models is shown in Fig. 11.2. The DICE model calibrates the real interest rate in accordance with the market data ("Base" case in the figure) and assumes that it declines gradually over future time periods. Specifically, it sets the real interest rate at 5.1% per year in 2020, 4.4% in 2050, and 3.6% in 2100. This trajectory can be reconciled with the theory of hyperbolic discounting which assumes a

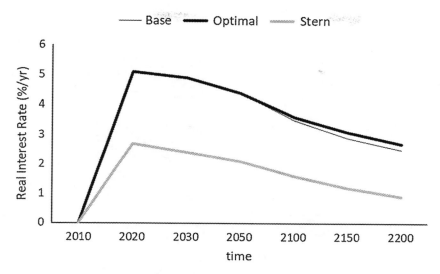

Fig. 11.2 A calibration of real interest rate in the DICE model

declining discount rate over time via a hyperbolic discounting function (Ainslie 1991; Laibson 1997; Seo 2020a).

As analyzed by Nordhaus, the Stern case in the figure sets the real interest rate (r in Eq. 11.25) implicitly at 2.7% in 2020, 2.1% in 2015, and 1.6% in 2100. This means that the Stern case sets the discount rate (ρ in Eq. (11.25)) nearly close to zero (Stern 2007; Weitzman 2007; Nordhaus 2007a; Nordhaus and Sztorc 2014).

Another key parameter in the DICE model is a climate change damage function, Ω_t, in Eq. (11.9). This measures the size of the economic damage at one time period caused by climate change as a percentage of the economic output of that time period. Among the economists, a specification of the climate damage function has been the most contentious of all economic debates (Mendelsohn et al. 1994; Pearce et al. 1996; Schlenker et al. 2006; Seo 2016a, 2016b, 2016c).

The DICE model calibration of the damage function is shown in Fig. 11.3 (Nordhaus 2013; Nordhaus and Sztorc 2014). It is a nonlinear, specifically, quadratic function of the temperature increase, as in Eq. (11.9). The damage function trajectory in the DICE model is roughly set to pass the averages of the point estimates of the climate change damage

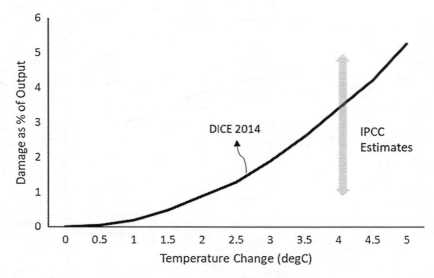

Fig. 11.3 The damage function calibration in the DICE model

made public in the literature (Tol 2009). Note that the trajectory in Fig. 11.3 passes through the range of the IPCC impact estimates at about 4.5°C warming, which is marked by a thick gray double-end arrow in the figure, at a slightly higher point than the mean estimate.

Concretely, the trajectory in the figure is drawn in such a way that the annual economic damage amounts to a 1.67% decrease in global economic output annually at 2.5°C warming and a 3.5% decrease annually from about 4°C warming. This means that the parameter of the quadratic term in Eq. (11.9) is set at $\varsigma_2 = 0.00238$ with the linear term parameter set at zero (Nordhaus 2008; Nordhaus and Sztorc 2014).

11.4   The Optimal Carbon Price Trajectory

The primary outcome of the DICE model is a societally optimal carbon price pathway for the planet. As explained before, it can be understood as the pathway of carbon tax to be imposed globally in a harmonized way in order to deal with the global warming challenges collectively. Alternatively, it can be interpreted as the social cost of carbon at each time period in the

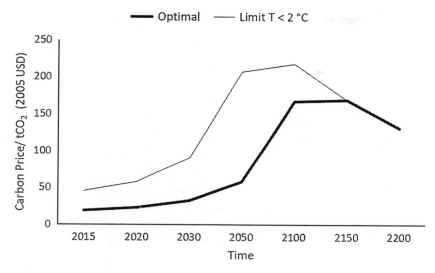

Fig. 11.4 A carbon price trajectory in DICE 2013

model. Therefore, it is a highly sought-after policy variable across the full spectrum of people who are concerned on the issue.

The carbon price trajectory from the DICE 2013 model is drawn in Fig. 11.4 (Nordhaus 2013; Nordhaus and Sztorc 2014). Under the globally optimal policy, the carbon dioxide price is US$ 23 per ton of carbon dioxide equivalent (tCO$_2$eq) in 2020, which increases to 32 US$/tCO2eq in 2030, 58 US$/tCO2eq in 2050, and 168 US$/tCO2eq in 2100. From that point on, the carbon price starts to fall.

The DICE model has the capacity for evaluating the impacts of alternative policy options. In the figure, a more stringent climate policy alternative of limiting global temperature increase absolutely under 2°C is evaluated. This policy has been a cornerstone of the international climate policy negotiations, including the Paris Agreement, since the Cancun Conference in 2010 when it was first proposed (UNFCCC 2010, 2015; IPCC 2018). Under this policy choice, the carbon dioxide price should be set at the levels in the near term three to four times the optimal level: 58 US$ per ton of carbon dioxide equivalent (tCO2eq) in 2020, which increases to 90 US$/tCO2eq in 2030, 207 US$/tCO2eq in 2050, and 218 US$/tCO2eq in 2100.

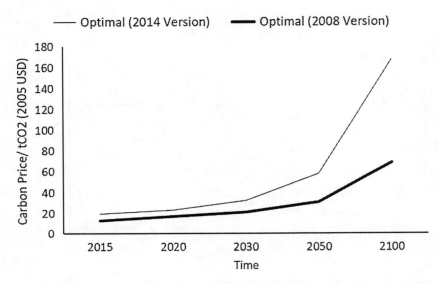

Fig. 11.5 Changes in the optimal carbon price trajectory in different DICE versions

Since the first version of the DICE model presented in the early 1990s, many revised versions of the DICE model have been put forth. Over the course of time, the carbon price trajectory has in general moved up, as demonstrated in the example of Fig. 11.5. The DICE 2008 version and the DICE 2014 version are presented in the figure with their respective carbon price trajectories. The carbon price pathway is significantly higher in the latter version of the model. This is attributable to changes in the parameter calibrations in the model. In particular, the changes in the damage function calibration and the intentional efforts to take into account the possibilities of catastrophic events were the primary reasons (Nordhaus 2013, 2017). The latter of the two is the topic of the next section.

The carbon price is calculated in the DICE model as the dual of the marginal cost of abatement at the socially optimal level of abatement at each time period. The optimal control rate trajectory, that is, μ_t in Eqs. (11.10a) and (11.10b), is drawn in Fig. 11.6. Under the socially optimal carbon policy, the globe should cut the greenhouse gases by 23% in 2020, 29% in 2030, 42% in 2050, 86% in 2100, and 100% in 2150 (Nordhaus 2013, Nordhaus and Sztorc 2014).

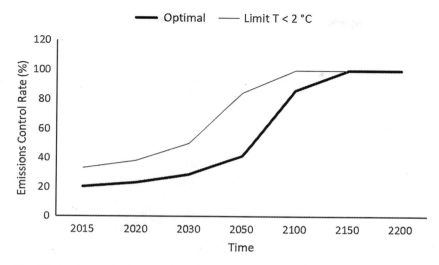

Fig. 11.6 An optimal control rate trajectory

Under an alternative climate policy that aims to limit the global temperature absolutely under 2°C in the most cost-effective manner, the carbon control rate should be set accordingly more stringently: 30% in 2020, 50% in 2030, 85% in 2050, and 100% in 2100. In other words, greenhouse gas abatement efforts should be set at nearly twice the levels of the optimal policy during the next three decades. This alternative trajectory is similar to the EU's mitigation goals from the European Union's climate policy (EC 2018).

What does the DICE model aim to achieve *via* the implementation of the carbon price trajectory? It aims to reduce the amount of carbon dioxide equivalent emissions by offering a policy recommendation, through which the global temperature rise can be controlled in a socially optimal manner. Figure 11.7 shows how remarkably the carbon price pathway of the DICE model will cut the amount of carbon dioxide equivalent emissions in the coming centuries.

Under the "Base" scenario where there is no climate policy intervention whatsoever anywhere around the planet, the carbon dioxide emissions are predicted to increase very significantly. From 40 GtCO$_2$eq per year in 2020, it nearly triples to 110 GtCO$_2$eq per year in 2100.

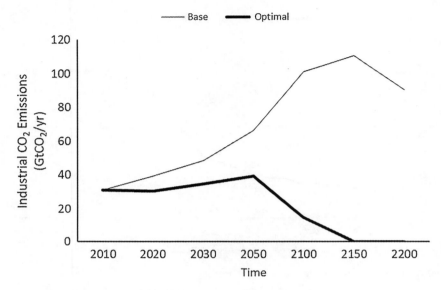

Fig. 11.7 The industrial CO_2 emissions trajectory

By taking and implementing an optimal climate policy according to the carbon price pathway suggested by the DICE model, the emissions trajectory will be astoundingly altered. From the 30 $GtCO_2eq$ in 2020, it increases to 40 $GtCO_2eq$ in 2050 and thenceforth falls rapidly to as low as 14 $GtCO_2eq$ by 2100.

Will this astounding course correction in the carbon dioxide equivalent emissions planetwide achieve the goal of "stabilizing" the global climate? It will, as depicted in Fig. 11.1 in the introduction section. Again, under the "Base" scenario, the global temperature increase reaches nearly 4°C by the end of this century and 7°C by the end of the next century. It is well documented that the planet cannot endure such an explosive temperature increase (Arrhenius 1896; Le Treut et al. 2007).

The socially optimal climate policy alters the uncontrolled "Base" climate trajectory dramatically. Under the DICE policy, the global temperature increase reaches gradually 3.0°C by around the early decades of twenty-second century, after which it declines in a gradual manner.

11.5   A FAT-TAIL CRITIQUE

The DICE model was challenged by many prominent critics, of which the fat-tail critique by Harvard economist Martin Weitzman was the most serious. According to what he called the dismal theorem (DT), the dollar amount the present generations are willing to sacrifice to prevent a climate catastrophe is infinite, he argued. Let me explain how he arrived at that conclusion.

The DT is succinctly expressed as:

$$\lim_{\theta \to \infty} E\left[M|\theta\right] = +\infty. \tag{11.26}$$

The stochastic discounting factor (SDF) as it was called by Weitzman, M in Eq. (11.26), is the dollar amount that the current time period is willing to sacrifice in order to secure a dollar in the future period. The theorem states that the SDF is infinite or unbounded under certain assumptions (Weitzman 2009). The θ is approximately the value of the statistical life for the entire civilizations on the planet (VSL-P). The VSL-P was assumed to be infinite because "the end of all civilizations on the planet as we know them" would be unbounded.

Weitzman proved Eq. (11.26) under a critical assumption on the tail distribution of a global warming realization, specifically, a fat-tail probability distribution (Schuster 1984, Nordhaus 2011). The equation does not hold under any other probability distribution, say, a Gaussian distribution.

In Fig. 11.8, the present author shows two tail distributions: a fat tail distribution on the top panel and a medium tail distribution on the bottom panel. The vertical axis is the probability of occurrence while the horizontal axis is the degree of global warming. In the fat tail distribution, the probability declines ever more slowly as the value in the horizontal axis gets larger. In the medium tail distribution, on the other hand, the probability declines at ever faster rates as the value in the horizontal axis becomes larger.

The consequence of the fat-tail distribution is illustrated by marking two threshold values on both tail distributions. The first corresponds approximately to a 10°C warming while the second to a 20°C warming in the Weitzman model. It is remarkable that the probability never approaches zero. Even more remarkably, the probability at the first critical value is nearly the same as the probability at the second critical value. In the

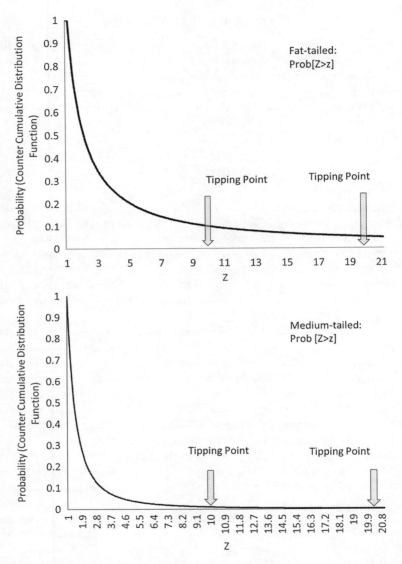

Fig. 11.8 A fat-tail distribution versus a medium-tail distribution in the dismal theorem

non-fat-tail distribution at the bottom panel, the probability is virtually zero at the first critical value, let alone at the second critical value. This graphic analysis makes it clear why the fat-tail distribution is at the core of the dismal theorem.

Let me explain the core of his mathematical proof. Let Z be a random variable which reveals the degree of global warming. The assumption of a fat-tail distribution of the random variable Z yields its probability density function (pdf) as follows, which was first defined by Vilfredo Pareto and as such known as the Pareto distribution in economics (Pareto 1896):

$$P[Z = z] = kz^{-(1+v)}. \tag{11.27}$$

The v (>0) is a shape parameter which determines the shape of the probability distribution of Eq. (11.27). If $v \to 0$, the distribution becomes a fat-tailed one. If $v \to \infty$, the distribution approximates a Gaussian distribution. The k is a constant.

The fat-tail distribution in Eq. (11.27) can be interpreted as a posterior-predictive distribution function in that the global warming uncertainty is so large that any amount of time and resources devoted to this could not reduce the fatness of the tail-distribution *ex-post* (Bayes 1763).

Given the assumption of VSL-P being infinite, the economic damage from a very high degree of global warming such as a 10°C increase or a 20°C increase in global average temperature from the preindustrial level, both of which were relied upon by Weitzman, would be extremely large. The damage function can be defined as an exponential function of Z with parameters m and ε:

$$D(z|\theta) = me^{\varepsilon z}. \tag{11.28}$$

Under the assumptions in Eqs. (11.27) and (11.28), the DT can be proved relying on the following. With z_0 being the degree of global warming that is irreversible:

$$\lim_{\theta \to \infty} E[D(z_0)|\theta] = \lim_{\theta \to \infty} P(z_0) * D[z_0|\theta] = +\infty. \tag{11.29}$$

From this point on, the present author will offer a succinct critique on the dismal theorem with a focus on the mathematical formulation as well as the proof of it, which was first elaborated in 2020 (Seo 2020b). First, let's assume that the global community is equipped with a range of climate control technologies, some of which are applicable today while the rest of which are expected to become applicable in a few decades. Such technologies would include solar radiation reflection technologies, carbon dioxide capture technologies, and ocean fertilization technologies (NRC 2015a, 2015b). In addition, there is a range of carbon dioxide mitigation technologies that are already widely available, which includes novel lighting technologies such as light emitting diodes (LEDs), Electric Vehicles (EVs), and solar photovoltaic (PV) energy technologies (Akasaki et al. 2014; MIT 2015).

The effect of the array of these technologies can enter the probability distribution in Eq. (11.27) as ψ which can be called a climate technology parameter as follows:

$$P[Z = z] = kx^{-(1+\upsilon+\psi)}. \tag{11.30}$$

The second parameter to introduce is a behavioral adaptation parameter. The possibility and experiences of adapting to changes in the climate and weather conditions have long been the subject of intensive research (Mendelsohn 2000; Seo 2015). A wide array of adaptation behaviors implemented in agriculture, natural resource industries, energy generations, civil engineering, natural disaster managements, and catastrophic events will make it possible for the planet to cope with the climate challenges at the least damages possible (Seo 2006, 2016a, 2016b, 2016c, 2017a, 2018).

We can include the effect of behavioral adaptations into the dismal theorem via a behavioral adaptation parameter χ in the damage function in Eq. (11.28):

$$D(z|\theta) = me^{(\varepsilon-\chi)z}. \tag{11.31}$$

With the reformulated model with Eqs. (11.30) and (11.31), the dismal theorem can be disproved if we can prove the following conclusion, with c being a constant:

$$\lim_{\theta \to \infty} E\left[D(z_0)|\theta\right] = c < +\infty. \tag{11.32}$$

The disproof in Eq. (11.32) holds generally because the following equality holds generally:

$$\lim_{\theta \to \infty} \frac{e^{\varepsilon z_0}}{\left(z_0^{1+\upsilon+\psi}\right)\left(e^{\chi z_0}\right)} = c.$$

(11.33)

The equality in Eq. (11.33) holds generally for the following reasons. First, the climate control technology parameter (ψ) has the definitive characteristic of making the tail probability of the distribution in Eq. (11.30) approaches zero. Alternatively stated, ψ is "meaningfully" large. Second, the behavioral adaptation parameter (χ) in the damage function in Eq. (11.31) has the definitive characteristic of making the damage function bounded by a limiting value. Alternatively stated, χ is "meaningfully" large.

Plainly stated, the dismal theorem will apply only when it is assumed that there are neither climate control technologies nor efficient behavioral adaptations. When both are introduced into the model, the dismal theorem does not hold (Seo 2020b).

11.6   Conclusion

The policy framework developed by William Nordhaus thus explained has increasingly faced the question of practicality since its first presentation. Specifically, is a globally harmonized carbon tax policy agreeable among a large number of parties and, if so, implementable at a global scale in a trustworthy way? The reality of global policy negotiations has demonstrated that the member countries of the United Nations Framework Convention on Climate Change (UNFCCC) have strong incentives to free ride on other countries' efforts and investments to reduce greenhouse gas emissions for the planet's wellbeing (Buchanan 1965, 1968; Seo 2012, 2017a, 2017b).

The recent remedies proposed to address the conundrum of free riding include a "climate club" approach in which non-club members are imposed trade penalties, for example, import and export tariffs (Nordhaus 2017). Another frontier in this line of research is a microbehavioral design of the global policy-making where a large array of behavioral incentives in people's actions are accounted for (Seo 2019). The resultant policy framework may be referred to as a shift from a mitigation paradigm to an adaptation paradigm for the planet's responses to climate challenges (Seo 2017a, 2020a, 2021, 2022).

With this prospective statement, the present author would like to conclude this chapter devoted to the William Nordhaus's theory of a globally and societally optimal carbon price trajectory. Also with this, individual chapters devoted to a specific theory espoused by an individual author are completed: a rent theory by David Ricardo in Chap. 2, a spatial land use theory by von Thunen in Chap. 3, a forest rotation by Martin Faustmann in Chap. 4, fossil fuel economics by Harold Hotelling in Chap. 5, a bio-economic fishery model in Chap. 6, a theory of capital and interest by Irving Fisher in Chap. 7, a national optimal saving by Frank Ramsey in Chap. 8, a modern growth theory by Robert Solow in Chap. 9, an optimal economic growth theory by Tjalling Koopmans in Chap. 10, and an optimal carbon tax trajectory by William Nordhaus in Chap. 11.

In the following two chapters, the present author will synthesize the discussions in the individual chapters from Chaps. 2, 3, 4, 5, 6, 7, 8, 9, 10, and 11 to offer an encompassing description of the economics of optimal growth pathways in Chap. 12, which will be followed in Chap. 13 by an exposition of the tendencies to pursue sub-optimal growth found in the economic growth literature. Chapter 13, which is the final chapter of this book, will deal with three intellectual traditions: a sustainable development critique, an ecological economics critique, and a degrowth critique. The sub-optimal growth theories will also be referred to as the post-growth theories, the reason for which will be clarified in Chap. 13.

References

Ainslie, G. 1991. Derivation of 'Rational' Economic Behavior from Hyperbolic Discount Curves. *American Economic Review* 81: 334–340.

Akasaki, Isamu, Hiroshi Amano, and Shuji Nakamura. 2014. *Blue LEDs: Filling the World with New Light. Nobel Prize Lecture.* Stockholm, SE: The Nobel Foundation.   http://www.nobelprize.org/nobel_prizes/physics/laureates/2014/popular-physicsprize2014.pdf.

Arrhenius, S.A. 1896. On the Influence of Carbonic Acid in the Air upon the Temperature of the Ground. *Philosophical Magazine* 41: 237–276.

Barro, R.J., and X. Sala-i-Martin. 1992. Convergence. *Journal of Political Economy* 100: 223–251.

Bayes, Thomas. 1763. An Essay Towards Solving a Problem in the Doctrine of Chance. *Philosophical Transactions of the Royal Society of London* 53: 370–418.

Bergson, Abram. 1938. A Reformulation of Certain Aspects of Welfare Economics. *Quarterly Journal of Economics* 52: 310–334.

Bernoulli, Daniel. 1738. Exposition of a New Theory on the Measurement of Risk. *Econometrica* 22: 23–36. (Translated in 1954 by Louise Sommer).

Buchanan, James M. 1965. An Economic Theory of Clubs. *Economica* 32: 1–24.

———. 1968. *The Demand and Supply of Public Goods*. Chicago, IL: Rand McNally & Co.

Ciais, P., C. Sabine, G. Bala, L. Bopp, V. Brovkin, J. Canadell, A. Chhabra, R. DeFries, J. Galloway, M. Heimann, C. Jones, C. Le Quéré, R.B. Myneni, S. Piao, and P. Thornton. 2013. Carbon and Other Biogeochemical Cycles. In *Climate Change 2013: The Physical Science Basis*. Cambridge, UK: Cambridge University Press.

Clark, C.W. 1973. The Economics of Over Exploitation. *Science* 181: 630–634.

Coase, Ronald. 1960. The Problem of Social Cost. *Journal of Law and Economics* 3: 1–44.

European Commission (EC). 2018. *EU ETS Handbook*. Brussels, BE: European Commission.

Faustmann, Martin. 1849. On the Determination of the Value Which Forest Land and Immature Stands Pose for Forestry. In *Martin Faustmann and the Evolution of Discounted Cash Flow*, ed. M. Gane. Oxford Institute: Oxford, England. [1968, Paper 42].

Fischer, C., and R.D. Morgenstern. 2006. Carbon Abatement Costs: Why the Wide Range of Estimates? *Energy Journal* 27: 73–86.

Fisher, Irving. 1906. *The Nature of Capital and Income*. New York, NY: Macmillan.

———. 1930. *The Theory of Interest*. New York, NY: Macmillan.

Global Carbon Project (GCP). 2017. Global Carbon Budget 2017. www.global-carbonproject.org/carbonbudget/index.htm.

Gordon, C., C. Cooper, C.A. Senior, H.T. Banks, J.M. Gregory, T.C. Johns, et al. 2000. The Simulation of SST, Sea Ice Extents and Ocean Heat Transports in a Version of the Hadley Centre Coupled Model Without Flux Adjustments. *Climate Dynamics* 16: 147–168.

Hansen, J., D. Johnson, A. Lacis, S. Lebedeff, P. Lee, D. Rind, et al. 1981. Climate Impact of Increasing Atmospheric Carbon Dioxide. *Science* 213: 957–966.

Hicks, J.R. 1932. *The Theory of Wages*. London, UK: Macmillan.

Hotelling, H. 1931. The Economics of Exhaustible Resources. *Journal of Political Economy* 39: 137–175.

Houghton, R.A. 2008. Carbon Flux to the Atmosphere from Land-use Changes: 1850–2005. In *TRENDS: A Compendium of Data on Global Change*. Oak Ridge, TN: Carbon Dioxide Information Analysis Center, Oak Ridge National Laboratory, U.S. Department of Energy.

Hulten, C.R. 2000. *Total Factor Productivity: A Short Biography.* National Bureau of Economic Research (NBER) Working Paper Series 7471, The NBER, Cambridge, MA.

Intergovernmental Panel on Climate Change (IPCC). 1990. *Climate Change: The IPCC Scientific Assessment.* Cambridge, UK: Cambridge University Press.

———. 2018. *Special Report on Global Warming of 1.5°C.* Cambridge, UK: Cambridge University Press.

———. 2019. *Climate Change and Land: An IPCC Special Report on Climate Change, Desertification, Land Degradation, Sustainable Land Management, Food Security, and Greenhouse Gas Fluxes in Terrestrial Ecosystems.* Cambridge, UK: Cambridge University Press.

International Institute of Applied Systems Analysis (IIASA). 2007. Probabilistic Projections by 13 World Regions, Forecast Period 2000–2100, 2001 Revision. http://www.iiasa.ac.at/Research/POP/proj01/.

Keeling, R.F., S.C. Piper, A.F. Bollenbacher, and J.S. Walker. 2009. Atmospheric CO_2 Records from Sites in the SIO Air Sampling Network. In *Trends: A Compendium of Data on Global Change.* Oak Ridge, TN: Carbon Dioxide Information Analysis Center, Oak Ridge National Laboratory. https://doi.org/10.3334/cdiac/atg.035.

Koopmans, Tjalling C. 1963. *On the Concept of Optimal Economic Growth.* The Cowles Foundation Discussion Paper # 163, Yale University, New Haven, CT.

———. 1965. On the Concept of Optimal Economic Growth. *Pontificiae Academiae Scientiarum Scripta Varia* 28 (1): 1–75.

Laibson, D. 1997. Golden Eggs and Hyperbolic Discounting. *Quarterly Journal of Economics* 112: 443–477.

Le Treut, H., R. Somerville, U. Cubasch, Y. Ding, C. Mauritzen, A. Mokssit, T. Peterson, and M. Prather. 2007. Historical Overview of Climate Change. In *Climate Change 2007: The Physical Science Basis,* The Fourth Assessment Report of the Intergovernmental Panel on Climate Change, ed. S. Solomon et al. Cambridge: Cambridge University Press.

Lutz, W., W. Butz, and K.C. Samir, eds. 2014. *World Population and Global Human Capital in the 21st Century.* Oxford, UK: Oxford University Press.

Manabe, S., J. Smagorinsky, and R. Strickler. 1965. Simulated Climatology of a General Circulation Model with a Hydrologic Cycle. *Monthly Weather Review* 93: 769–798.

Mann, M.E., R.S. Bradley, and M.K. Hughes. 1999. Northern Hemisphere Temperatures During the Past Millennium: Inferences, Uncertainties, and Limitations. *Geophysical Research Letters* 26: 759–762.

Massachusetts Institute of Technology (MIT). 2015. *The Future of Solar Energy: An Interdisciplinary MIT Study.* Cambridge, MA: MIT.

Mendelsohn, R. 2000. Efficient Adaptation to Climate Change. *Climatic Change* 45: 583–600.

————. 2003. *The Social Cost of Carbon: An Unfolding Value*. Presented at the Social Cost of Carbon Conference, London, UK.

Mendelsohn, R., W. Nordhaus, and D. Shaw. 1994. The Impact of Global Warming on Agriculture: A Ricardian Analysis. *American Economic Review* 84: 753–771.

Mitra, T., and H.Y. Wan Jr. 1985. Some Theoretical Results on the Economics of Forestry. *Review of Economic Studies* 52 (2): 263–282.

National Research Council (NRC). 2015a. *Climate Intervention: Reflecting Sunlight to Cool Earth*. Committee on Geoengineering Climate: Technical Evaluation and Discussion of Impacts, The National Academies Press, Washington, DC.

————. 2015b. *Climate Intervention: Carbon Dioxide Removal and Reliable Sequestration*. Washington, DC: The National Academies Press.

————. 2017. *Valuing Climate Damages: Updating Estimation of the Social Cost Of Carbon Dioxide*. Washington, DC: The National Academies Press.

Negishi, T. 1960. Welfare Economics and Existence of an Equilibrium for a Competitive Economy. *Metroeconomica* 12: 92–97.

Newman, D.H. 1988. *The Optimal Forest Rotation: A Discussion and Annotated Bibliography*. General Technical Report 48, Southeastern Forest Experiment Station, Forest Service, USDA.

Nordhaus, W.D. 1977. Economic Growth and Climate: The Carbon Dioxide Problem. *American Economic Review* 67: 341–346.

————. 1991. To Slow or Not to Slow: The Economics of the Greenhouse Effects. *Economic Journal* 101: 920–937.

————. 1992. An Optimal Transition Path for Controlling Greenhouse Gases. *Science* 258: 1315–1319.

————. 1994. *Managing the Global Commons*. Cambridge, MA: MIT Press.

————. 2007a. A Review of the Stern Review on the Economics of Climate Change. *Journal of Economic Literature* 55: 686–702.

————. 2007b. Alternative Measures of Output in Global Economic-Environmental Models: Purchasing Power Parity or Market Exchange Rates? *Energy Economics* 29: 349–372.

————. 2008. *A Question of Balance: Weighing the Options on Global Warming Policies*. New Haven, CT: Yale University Press.

————. 2010. Economic Aspects of Global Warming in a Post-Copenhagen Environment. *Proceedings of the National Academy of Sciences* 107: 11721–11726.

————. 2011. The Economics of Tail Events with an Application to Climate Change. *Review of Environmental Economics and Policy* 5: 240–257.

————. 2013. *The Climate Casino: Risk, Uncertainty, and Economics for a Warming World*. New Haven, CT: Yale University Press.

————. 2017. Revisiting the Social Cost of Carbon. *Proceedings of the National Academy of Sciences* 114: 1518–1523.

————. 2019. Can We Control Carbon Dioxide? (From 1975). *American Economic Review* 109: 2015–2035.

Nordhaus, W.D., and J. Boyer. 2000. *Warming the World: Economic Models of Global Warming.* Cambridge, MA: MIT Press.

Nordhaus, W.D., and P. Sztorc. 2014. *DICE 2013: Introduction and User's Manual.* New Haven, CT: Yale University.

Nordhaus, W.D., and Z. Yang. 1996. A Regional Dynamic General-Equilibrium Model of Alternative Climate Change Strategies. *American Economic Review* 86: 741–765.

Pareto, V. 1896. *Cours d'Economie Politique.* Geneva, CH: Librairie Droz.

Pearce, D., W.R. Cline, A. Achanta, S. Fankhauser, R. Pachauri, R. Tol, et al. 1996. The Social Costs of Climate Change: Greenhouse Damage and Benefits of Control. In *Climate Change 1995: Economic and Social Dimensions of Climate Change,* ed. J. Bruce, H. Lee, and E. Haites. Cambridge, UK: Cambridge University Press.

Ramsey, F.P. 1928. A Mathematical Theory of Savings. *Economic Journal* 38: 543–559.

Ricardo, D. 1817. *On the Principles of Political Economy and Taxation.* London, UK: John Murray.

Samuelson, P.A. 1947. *Foundations of Economic Analysis.* Cambridge, MA: Harvard University Press. [Enlarged Edition Published in 1983].

Samuelson, P. 1977. Reaffirming the Existence of 'Reasonable' Bergson–Samuelson Social Welfare Functions. *Economica* 44: 81–88.

Schuster, E.F. 1984. Classification of probability laws by tail behavior. *Journal of the American Statistical Association* 79 (388): 936–939.

Schlenker, W., M. Hanemann, and A. Fisher. 2006. The Impact of Global Warming on U.S. Agriculture: An Econometric Analysis of Optimal Growing Conditions. *Review of Economics and Statistics* 88: 113–125.

Schlesinger, W.H. 1997. *Biogeochemistry: An Analysis of Global Change.* 2nd ed. San Diego, CA: Academic Press.

Schlesinger, M.E., and X. Jiang. 1990. Simple Model Representation of Atmosphere-Ocean GCMs and Estimation of the Timescale of CO_2-induced Climate Change. *Journal of Climate* 3: 12–15.

Schmidt, G.A., R. Ruedy, J.E. Hansen, et al. 2005. Present Day Atmospheric Simulations Using GISS ModelE: Comparison to In-situ, Satellite and Reanalysis Data. *Journal of Climate* 19: 153–192.

Schneider, S.H., and S.L. Thompson. 1981. Atmospheric CO_2 and Climate: Importance of the Transient Response. *Journal of Geophysical Research* 86: 3135–3147.

Seo, S.N. 2006. *Modeling Farmer Responses to Climate Change: Climate Change Impacts and Adaptations in Livestock Management in Africa.* PhD dissertation, Yale University, New Haven, CT.

———. 2012. What Eludes Global Agreements on Climate Change? *Economic Affairs* 32: 73–79.

———. 2015. Helping Low-latitude, Poor Countries with Climate Change. *Regulation* (Winter 2015–2016): 6–8.

———. 2016a. *Microbehavioral Econometric Methods: Theories, Models, and Applications for the Study of Environmental and Natural Resources.* Amsterdam, NL: Academic Press.

———. 2016b. Modeling Farmer Adaptations to Climate Change in South America: A Microbehavioral Economic Perspective. *Environmental and Ecological Statistics* 23: 1–21.

———. 2016c. The Micro-behavioral Framework for Estimating Total Damage of Global Warming on Natural Resource Enterprises with Full Adaptations. *Journal of Agricultural, Biological, and Environmental Statistics* 21: 328–347.

———. 2017a. *The Behavioral Economics of Climate Change: Adaptation Behaviors, Global Public Goods, Breakthrough Technologies, and Policy-making.* Amsterdam, NL: Academic Press.

———. 2017b. Beyond the Paris Agreement: Climate Change Policy Negotiations and Future Directions. *Regional Science Policy & Practice* 9: 121–140.

———. 2018. *Natural and Man-Made Catastrophes: Theories, Economics, and Policy Designs.* Oxford, UK: Wiley-Blackwell.

———. 2019. *The Economics of Global Allocations of the Green Climate Fund: An Assessment From Four Scientific Traditions of Modeling Adaptation Strategies.* Cham, CH: Springer Nature.

———. 2020a. *The Economics of Globally Shared and Public Goods.* Amsterdam, NL: Academic Press.

———. 2020b. Appendix: A Succinct Mathematical Disproof of the Dismal Theorem of Economics. In *The Economics of Globally Shared and Public Goods.* Amsterdam, NL: Academic Press.

———. 2021. *Climate Change and Economics: Engaging with Future Generations with Action Plans.* Cham, CH: Palgrave Macmillan.

———. 2022. *Handbook of Behavioral Economics and Climate Change.* Cheltenham, UK: Edward Elgar.

Solow, R.M. 1957. A Contribution to the Theory of Economic Growth. *Quarterly Journal of Economics* 70: 65–94.

Stern, N. 2007. *The Economics of Climate Change: The Stern Review.* New York, NY: Cambridge University Press.

Taylor, K.E., R.J. Stouffer, and G.A. Meehl. 2012. An Overview of CMIP5 and the Experiment Design. *Bulletin of the American Meteorological Society* 93: 485–498.

Tol, R. 2009. The Economic Effects of Climate Change. *Journal of Economic Perspectives* 23: 29–51.

United Nations Framework Convention on Climate Change (UNFCCC). 1992. *United Nations Framework Convention on Climate Change.* New York, NY: UNFCCC.

———. 2010. *Cancun Agreements.* New York, NY: UNFCCC.

———. 2015. *Paris Agreements.* New York, NY: UNFCCC.

von Thunen, J.H. 1826. *The Isolated State* (C.M. Wartenberg, trans.). Oxford/New York: Pergamon. [1966].

Weitzman, M.L. 1998. Why the Far-distant Future Should be Discounted at Its Lowest Possible Rate. *Journal of Environmental Economics and Management* 36: 201–208.

———. 2007. A Review of The Stern Review on the Economics of Climate Change. *Journal of Economic Literature* 45: 703–724.

———. 2009. On Modeling and Interpreting the Economics of Catastrophic Climate Change. *Review of Economics and Statistics* 91: 1–19.

World Meteorological Organization (WMO). 1985. *Report of the International Conference on the Assessment of the Role of Carbon Dioxide and of Other Greenhouse Gases in Climate Variations and Associated Impacts.* Villach, Austria: WMO.

CHAPTER 12

The Economics of Optimal Growth Pathways with Managing Natural Resources Efficiently

12.1 Introduction

From Chaps. 2 to 11, with an introduction in Chap. 1, the present author gave an expansive exposition on the central question of this book: the optimal economic growth pathways. In this chapter, the present author will summarize and synthesize the discussions of the 11 preceding chapters with a goal to provide a condensed exposition regarding the central question.

The ten chapters from Chaps. 2 to 11 can be divided into two parts. The first part was concerned with individual natural resource sectors of the economy where individual resource managers search for the ways to maximize the net return from their decisions over a long planning horizon. The first part comprises Chaps. 2 to 7 where economic decisions in crop agriculture, grazing and other lands, forests, fossil fuel reserves, marine resources, and financial assets are described in respective chapters.

The second part was concerned with the economics of economic growth in a macro economy. The macro economy means the nation's economy in most cases in this book except for the chapter on climate economics. This comprises Chaps. 7 to 11. The book presented the concept of capital and the determination of market interest rates in Chap. 7, a theory of optimal national saving in Chap. 8, a modern economic growth theory in Chap. 9, a socially optimal economic growth pathway in Chap. 10, and a socially optimal carbon price trajectory in Chap. 11.

© The Author(s), under exclusive license to Springer Nature Switzerland AG 2023
S. N. Seo, *The Economics of Optimal Growth Pathways*,
https://doi.org/10.1007/978-3-031-20754-9_12

This is one of the unique features of this book from the other economic growth books and writings in the market (Solow 1957; Paul Romer 1990; Barro and Sala-i-Martin 1992; Mankiw et al. 1992; Aghion and Howitt 2009; David Romer 2018). Unlike these other publications, this book frames the answer to the central question on the basis of individual natural resource sectors' and enterprises' economically efficient and optimal decisions over respective planning horizons. The national economic decisions regarding how fast the economy should grow over an infinite time horizon are analyzed from the big picture in which numerous individual natural resource enterprises' decisions are efficiently managed.

This novel approach is taken by the present author for several reasons as it offers many theoretical advantages. First, it is often the case that a critique against the national economic growth falls flat when it is applied to the context of individual resource sectors. For example, a critic may argue for a zero growth rate or a negative growth rate in the national economy. The argument would be rather bland if applied to the standpoints of a natural resource manager such as a crop farmer, a forestland manager, a natural gas well manager, and so on.

Second, this fresh approach can bring out a critical feature in the national economic growth theories. That is to say, a national economic modeling cannot turn a blind eye on what goes on in individual resource sectors and enterprises. For example, let's say that a national economic growth model relies on a zero discount rate, that is, a zero social rate of time preference. The modeler, however, cannot be able to explain consistently any of the individual natural resource sector decisions which must rely inevitably on the cost of borrowing money or the price of lending money. Nearly all the individual resource sector decisions are dependent seriously on the interest (discount) rates in the market.

These examples are only a tip of the iceberg. A harmonization of the individual resource managers' decisions with the national economic decisions brings about many conceptual advantages and critical insights pertinent to the questions of economic growth, if such questions should be tackled consistently in a societally welfare optimizing manner. The analysis in this chapter will highlight many of these advantages and insights.

The exposition in this chapter will seamlessly lead to the discussions of the next chapter which clarifies a host of sub-optimal growth theories. The sub-optimal growth theories, which also can be referred to as the post-growth economic theories, are those that do not set the goal, either intentionally or unintentionally, of pursuing a societally welfare optimizing economic growth pathway for the economy. These include, to broadly encompass, a sustainable development proponent, an ecological economics proponent, and a degrowth proponent.

12.2 Decisions of Individual Natural Resource Managers

A national economy is composed of numerous economic sectors, each of which is in turn composed of a multitude of individual enterprises. The economic science has long been concerned with the ways each enterprise makes its decisions over a planning horizon as well as the ways the industry of these enterprises makes such decisions (von Neumann and Morgenstern 1944; Samuelson 1947; Friedman 1962; Mas-Colell et al. 1995).

The basic principle in their economic decisions as elucidated by economic theoreticians is a maximization of utility in the context of consumers and a maximization of profit in the context of producers (Mas-Colell et al. 1995; Samuelson and Nordhaus 2009; Mankiw 2020). This principle applies to all economic sectors and enterprises discussed in this book.

A unique feature of this book is an examination of the dynamic pathways of these decisions by producers and consumers over the course of a defined or infinite time horizon. As such, the value of time is a key dimension that is added to the aforementioned principle of economics in the economic analyses presented across individual resource sectors in this book. More strictly speaking, the cost of borrowing or lending 1 US dollar for a certain period of time is of critical importance (Fisher 1907, 1930). This loan can occur from one generation to another generation that is far apart from the former.

Even if well equipped with the two critical concepts, that is, the principle of profit maximization and the value of time, an analysis of an individual enterprise or an individual industry is a daunting task. This is due to many unique features that each of these enterprises possesses which determine jointly the value of the goods in the respective enterprise. This has led to the emergence of many fields and subfields of economic science.

This book has chosen the following six resource sectors and enterprises in order to make clear the economic principle of efficient and optimal uses and investments of resources, as summarized in Table 12.1. The first is David Ricardo's rent theory applied to crop agriculture (Ricardo 1817). The second is von Thunen's spatial land use theory that encompasses such

Table 12.1   Resource sectors and theories

Chapters	Individual resource sectors	Major theories
Chapter 2	Crop agriculture	David Ricardo's rent theory (Ricardo 1817)
Chapter 3	Land use, including grazing lands and urban lands	Von Thunen's spatial land use (von Thunen 1826)
Chapter 4	Forests	Faustmann's forest rotation (Faustmann 1849)
Chapter 5	Fossil fuels and other exhaustible resources	Harold Hotelling's resource rent theory (Hotelling 1931)
Chapter 6	Fisheries and open access resources	A bioeconomic model of fish catch (Clark 1973, 1985)
Chapter 7	Financial investments	Irving Fisher's theory of capital, income, and interest (Fisher 1906, 1930)

activities as grazing lands and urban land uses (von Thunen 1826). The third is Faustmann's forest optimal rotation (Faustmann 1849). The fourth is Harold Hotelling's optimal extraction paths of fossil fuels and other exhaustible resources (Hotelling 1931). The fifth is a bioeconomic model of fish catch attributable to Gordon, Clark, and others (Clark 1973, 1985). The sixth is Irving Fisher's theory of interest and investing financial assets (Fisher 1906, 1930).

Across all the theories included in Table 12.1 and beyond, a marginal revolution credited to David Ricardo remains still today an essential analysis tool for economics. He was the first economist to invent a marginal analysis. Ricardo clarified that the land rent, which was used for corn farming, is determined at the marginal land where there is no rent. The land doesn't demand the rent because of low fertility of the land. In the marginal land, the cost of farming is equal to the value of whatever the land earns (Ricardo 1817).

Let's consider the rent of a marginally more fertile plot of land next to the marginal plot of land. Fertility here means soil quality. Owing to a slightly higher fertility of the plot, the revenue earned from the plot will exceed the total cost of farming on that plot. This difference is the rent of the plot. The rent of the third plot of land which is again marginally better in terms of land fertility than the second plot of land will demand a slightly larger rent than that of the second plot.

Capturing Ricardo's concept, the rent at the farmland i at year t, for a fixed land size, is as follows:

$$\pi_{it} = TR_{it} - TC_{it}, \tag{12.1}$$

where TR is total revenue or total income and TC total cost of production which includes labor cost and the cost of capital employed.

Therefore, Ricardo's rent is determined by soil fertility, but the theory can be extended without a major modification to the other factors that affect the revenue, cost, and fertility, for example, chemical fertilizers, pesticides, and other technologies. He provided this analysis in response to the then highly contentious policy debate about corn imports from Europe, resulting in the Corn Law (Williamson 1990). More pertinent to this discussion is that his analysis was for the production of a single crop, corn.

A land use theory that describes changes in the land use from one type to another by a land owner on a concerned plot or across a larger landscape was put forth by a German economist von Thunen in his *The Isolated State* (von Thunen 1826). He might have or have not got into contact with Ricardo's Principle of Political Economy published a decade ago across the English Channel (Ricardo 1817). It is without doubts that the concept of rent also plays a central role in von Thunen's treatise.

Von Thunen imagined an isolated self-sufficient state where land use types are determined in concentric circles around the state's center. At the central smallest circle, the city and market are developed. At the next circle that surrounds the city center circle, an intensive farming such as a dairy farming is adopted as the land use type of choice. At the next circle that surrounds the intensive farming land, the forestlands for fuelwoods are adopted as the land use type. At the next larger circle, an extensive farming of field crops is adopted as the land use type. At the next larger circle, ranching or livestock management is adopted as the land use type of choice. Beyond the ranching circle, there lies the wasted land of the state which was called the wilderness.

In his spatial land use theory, a choice of one land use type over the other types by a land owner is determined by the rents that can be generated from a range of land use types. A land owner will choose the land use type that would earn her/him the largest rent.

Why would such rent-based choices by land owners end up with the land use pattern of concentric circles, more accurately semicircles, as imagined by von Thunen? It is attributable to the distances from production areas to the center market where whatever products the lands in the state produce should be brought for sale. The von Thunen model is an equidistance model coupled with the assumption of uniform soil quality. The distance that determines the cost of transportation plays a central role in the theory. Formally, the land rent per unit of land, say, an acre of land, in the plot i is defined as follows:

$$\pi_i = y_i \cdot (p - c_i) - y_i \cdot Fr_i \cdot D_i, \qquad (12.2)$$

where π is the land rent per acre of land, y the yield from the land, p the sale price of the yield at the market, c the production cost at the plot, Fr is the freight rate per unit of freight and unit distance, D is the distance from the land to the market.

Von Thunen's theory is important to the modern economics because it sheds light on the non-grain farming rural activities such as livestock management, dairy farming, vegetable production, tuber production, horticulture, and tree products (Seo 2016a, 2016b). From the other direction, it sheds light on the mechanism of urbanization via the values of urban land uses, including urban sprawls.

In both Ricardo's rent theory and von Thunen's spatial land use theory, it is implicitly assumed that the plot of land will generate the same rent year after year. Once the corn is planted in one year, for example, which results in the harvest in that year, the same will occur over and over again in the coming years. To put it differently, the two theories are a static model, that is, not a dynamic model.

The forest harvest modeling developed by Martin Faustmann deals with a very different economic problem in that regard. The profit that can be earned in a specific year varies widely from one year to another in the case of forest management. This is because trees or a forest stand will keep growing until its growth reaches a peak plateau from which it starts to shrink. As such, a forest modeling must account for the entire stream of profits, which vary year by year, that can be earned over the course of the forest stand over time.

The economic question boils down to what year the forest stand should be cut and sold in order to maximize the profit earned form the forest stand. Since the forest stand is cut at future time periods, an interest rate, which is the value of time, becomes an integral part of the modeling. Further, once the forest rotation is determined, the forest stand will be cut over and over again with the same rotation interval.

The maximization problem of the Faustmann model is as follows:

$$V^* = \max_{t}\left\{\left[pV(t)e^{-\gamma t} - \omega E\right]\left(1 + e^{-\gamma t} + e^{-2\gamma t} + e^{-3\gamma t} + \cdots\right)\right\} \quad (12.3a)$$

$$= \max_{t}\left\{\left[pV(t)e^{-\gamma t} - \omega E\right]/\left(1 - e^{-\gamma t}\right)\right\}. \quad (12.3b)$$

In the above equation, p is the price of timber per unit, $V(t)$ is the volume of tree at a specific time, γ is a discount rate, that is, an interest rate. The total effort, E, is a range of forestry efforts while ω is the cost of each unit of effort. The efforts and the cost of the efforts occur today and after a harvest while the income is earned at the time of harvest, t, whose process is repeated over and over again.

According to Faustmann, an optimal harvest rotation is determined when the following condition is satisfied:

$$pV_t = \gamma pV(t) + \gamma V^*. \quad (12.4)$$

Equation (12.4) tells that, at the optimal solution, the value of waiting for one more period (left hand side (LHS)) before the harvest by the forester is equal to the cost of waiting for one more period before the harvest (right hand side (RHS)). The left hand side (LHS) is the value of waiting one more period because the forest stand grows by V_t, with the subscript meaning a derivative, whose sale price is p per unit.

The right hand side (RHS) is the cost of holding the forest stand for one more period which has two components. The first component is the cost of holding the forest stand, which is the first term on the RHS, that is, $\gamma pV(t)$. This is the amount of interest that can be earned by cutting the trees today and investing the revenue at the market interest rate for one period. The second component is the cost of holing the land, which is the second component of the RHS. This is the rent you can earn by leasing the land in exchange for the land rent for one period, that is, γV^*, which is equivalent to selling the land and earning interests from the sale value.

A forest stand is a renewable resource, that is, forest harvests can occur indefinitely on the forestland. You would wonder what would happen to Eqs. (12.3a, 12.3b, and 12.4) if the resources under consideration are limited, as such, will be exhausted at some point in time. Fossil fuels such as coal, crude oil, and natural gas are one of such exhaustible resources.

The stocks of these fuels in the planet have respective limits owing to the biogeochemical processes involved in the generations of the fossil fuels (Ciais et al. 2013). Further, the economically recoverable reserves of these resources are also bounded, whose current projections of the years left are in the range of about five decades (for oil and gas) to about 15 (for coal) decades assuming the current levels of consumption of these fuels (BP 2021).

An owner of a coal mine or a petroleum well will desire to maximize the profit earned from the fossil fuel just like the afore-described forest owner, but saliently with a terminal date T in mind (Hotelling 1931):

$$\pi = \left[pq_0 - c(q_0) \right] + \left(\frac{1}{1+\gamma} \right) \left[pq_1 - c(q_1) \right] + \left(\frac{1}{1+\gamma} \right)^2 \left[pq_2 - c(q_2) \right]$$
$$+ \ldots + \left(\frac{1}{1+\gamma} \right)^T \left[pq_T - c(q_T) \right]. \tag{12.5}$$

In Eq. 12.5, p is the price of crude oil per unit and $c(q)$ is the total cost of extracting q amount of crude oil. The γ is again the interest rate. The maximand of the crude oil well owner is the sum of the present values of the stream of profits generated up to the terminal date.

From an intertemporal no-arbitrage condition, the solution to Eq. 12.5 is stated succinctly as follows (Hotelling 1931):

$$\frac{\left[p - c'(q_{t+1}) \right] - \left[p - c'(q_t) \right]}{\left[p - c'(q_t) \right]} = \gamma. \tag{12.6}$$

The intertemporal no-arbitrage condition says that the $p - c'(q_t)$ should increase at the rate of γ from one period to the next over the life of the well. This quantity, the difference between the price and marginal cost from one ton of oil, is called rent. The rent is also referred to in the literature by various names as user cost, royalty, dynamic rent, and Hotelling rent (Gray 1914; Hotelling 1931). So, the intertemporal condition is thus: the Hotelling rent should increase at the rate of γ, the market interest (discount) rate. This condition is called the γ percent rule or the Hotelling rule.

Note that p is taken as given by the well owner in Eqs. 12.5 and 12.6 and further is assumed to remain constant in the simple model. To explain the determination of the price of crude oil, we need to rely on the petroleum industry maximization problem, which was shown in Chap. 5. The industry level optimality condition is obtained similarly as above, which yields a price schedule $\{p_1, p_2, \ldots, p_t \ldots, p_T\}$. This price schedule then enters Eq. 12.6 for a more realistic optimality condition for the well owner.

The concept of a back stop energy emerged and was solidified during the latter half of the twentieth century. It is an energy source that replaces all existing energy sources including fossil fuels and that at the same time can provide energy to humanity indefinitely at a constant price of energy (Nordhaus 1973). The concept may have emerged from the optimism on nuclear fusion technology during the 1970s, whose optimism has not been realized five decades later since then as of 2022 (ITER 2022). Other than the nuclear fusion, a solar PV technology as well as a nuclear fission technology coupled with a secure storage still holds a promise as an eventual backstop technology.

With the inclusion of a backstop technology, the price of the backstop energy determines the terminal date T in the optimization problem in Eq. 12.5, that is, not the depletion date of the well. At the terminal date, the price of per unity energy supply from the fossil fuels exceeds the price of per unit energy supply from the backstop technology, which then causes the society's transition from fossil fuels to the backstop energy source.

For the resources described thus far, property rights are well defined in developed nations. In the case of forests, a large fraction is also owned by the public sector. For some resources, private property rights do not exist, the best example of which is marine resources such as fishes, especially remote ocean fishes. An analysis of fisheries needs to consider the characteristic of the fish as open access resources (Gordon 1954). Because of the open access characteristic, an over-exploitation of many fishes occurs, leading to in some cases the risk of extinction of some species. An over-exploitation or overfishing was frequent before the 200-mile offshore limit was established as the Exclusive Economic Zone (EEZ) by the United Nations Convention on the Law of the Sea (UNCLOS) during the mid-1970s (Clark 1973; UN 1982).

The economics of fisheries relies on a biological-economic analysis or a bioeconomic model in short (Clark 1973, 1985). The biological component is also important in managing other resources such as forest stands, but it is far more complicated in fisheries because fishes exhibit very different biological and growth patterns from one species to another, that is, across fish, mollusk, crustaceous, and sea mammals, while their biological characteristics are not determined by terrestrial and atmospheric conditions. Without careful understanding of the fish and marine biology, fishermen can easily over-exploit a certain species and in some cases to the degree that it cannot regenerate itself over time. On that note, fishes are also renewable resources.

The biological aspect of a fishery is captured by a fish growth function. With X_t being the stock of the fish, the instantaneous rate of growth of the fish population, $F(X)$, is:

$$F(X) = \frac{d}{dt}(X_t).$$ (12.7)

The most common fish growth function has a hill-shape relationship with the stock. In Phase I, the fish stock grows, measured as the stock of biomass, at each time period with an increasingly higher rate of growth. In Phase II, the fish stock still grows at each time period, however, with an increasingly lower rate of growth. In Phase III, the fish stock declines, that is, the rate of growth is negative. The stock level at which the growth rate is zero is the carrying capacity of the habitat.

The economic aspect of a fishery is captured by a harvest function (H) which is a function of fishing effort (E) and fish stock (X), at each time period t:

$$H_t = H(E_t, X_t).$$ (12.8)

The fishing effort is a composite of numerous factor inputs such as capital, labor, materials, and energy. That is, a variety of factor inputs are combined to yield a single measure of the fishing effort. In other words, it is an index for a bundle of fishing efforts. In the case of the lobster industry, for example, it can be thought of as the number of lobster traps set by fishermen (Hartwick and Olewiler 1997).

In the open access fishery, fishermen will enter the ocean to catch, for example, lobsters as long as there is profit to be earned, in other words, until Total Revenue (TR) equals Total Cost (TC). The TR is price per unit times the amount of harvest, that is, $TR = p * H$. The TC is the marginal cost of effort times the amount of efforts, that is, $TC = c * E$. The open access effort and fish catch are determined at the intersection of the TR curve and the TC curve.

In the private property fishery, an owner of the fish species will not catch the fish to such an extent because there is no reason to worry about other fishermen catching the fish on his/her property. The owner will equate the marginal cost (MC) of fishing to the marginal revenue (MR) of fish catch, that is, $MR = MC$ where the profit earned to the fish owner is maximized. At this point, an efficient fish catch is determined.

A core conclusion of the analysis is that the excess fishing effort is unavoidable under the open access fishery, leading to the problem of over-fishing. With E_{OA} the open access fishing effort and E^* the efficient fishing effort, it results in $E_{OA} > E^*$. To indue an efficient or socially optimal level of the fishing effort, a fishery tax can be levied on the harvest or on the fishing effort directly, which is one of the policy options. First, the effort tax can be imposed via a fee for a fishing license. With the license require-ment, the TC curve shifts upwards in parallel by the amount of the license fee: that is, the $TC = c * E + tax$. With the license fee, every fishing firm is required to purchase the fishing license, under which the efficient level of effort can be induced, that is, E^*. Second, the effort tax can be a uniform tax per unit of fishing effort, which rotates the total cost curve upwards. The new total cost curve is $TC' = (c + tax) * E$, which again can induce an efficient level of effort, E^*. Other policy options include individual trad-able fishing quota (Hartwick and Olewiler 1997).

For the financial assets, Irving Fisher defined the concept of capital and elucidated the mechanism through which an interest rate is determined. Fisher defined the capital to be any asset, whether it be a physical, finan-cial, natural, ecological, or technological asset, that generates a flow of income over time for the owner. The income is an earning by the owner of the asset at one point in time. So, the definition establishes the link between capital and income (Fisher 1906).

Then, Fisher defined the value of capital as the present value of the flow of net incomes that are generated from the asset. With π_t being net income at one point in time and γ being the interest rate, the value of capital (V) or the value of a financial asset that one holds is:

$$V = \int_0^\infty \pi_t e^{-\gamma t} dt;$$

$$\text{or} \sum_{t=0}^{\infty} \frac{\pi_t}{\left(1+\gamma\right)^t}. \tag{12.9}$$

What is the interest rate, γ in Eq. 12.9, and how is it determined? Fisher explained the concept of the interest rate in his magnum opus entitled the Theory of Interest in a lucid manner that any college student could understand it (Fisher 1930). He explained it via the mechanism in which individuals' preferences and the society's production technologies interact in a debt market.

As analyzed in Chap. 7, the interest rate arises most basically when an individual has to live more than two periods. It is determined by the intersection of the production possibility frontier (PPF) and the utility's indifference curve of the individual. In the single person economy, the interest rate is determined by the amount of the good the individual receives in the future period in return for the amount of the good s/he sacrifices in the present period.

In Fisher's Robinson Crusoe model, if the production technology is that of a constant returns to scale (CRS) technology, the interest rate is determined by the production technology alone, that is, the slope of the PPF. Specifically, it is the amount of the good that can be produced with the thus-described technology in return for the sacrifice of the amount of the good in the present period. The individual's preference does not matter in this Robinson Crusoe CRS model. In other words, whether s/he is a patient person or an impatient person does not affect the determination of the interest rate.

If the production technology exhibits a diminishing returns to scale (DRS), then the interest rate is determined by both the production technology and the individual's preference. At the tangency between the indifference curve and the production possibility frontier, the slope of the tangent line is equal to -(1 + γ). An impatient individual will decide to consume more at the present period, resulting in a higher interest rate. A patient individual will decide to consume less at the present period, resulting in a lower interest rate. Put differently, for an impatient individual, s/he would be willing to sacrifice one unit of consumption at the present period only if s/he would be rewarded in the next period with a significantly larger consumption. It would be the opposite for the patient individual.

In Fisher's two Crusoe model with a DRS technology, there are, say, Robinson Crusoe and Jane Crusoe who have different preferences, that is, characters of patience. Then, the interest rate is no longer determined by the joint force of the production technology and individuals' preferences. Enter the debt market! Each individual will soon find out that a trade via the debt market can be made in a way that is beneficial to both of them. A patient Jane Crusoe will attempt to lend the good in return for a considerable interest in the next period. An impatient Robinson Crusoe will attempt to borrow the good for an additional consumption in the next period after the interest payment to Jane Crusoe (Fisher 1930; Samuelson 1994; Shiller 2008). Readers who need to refresh may refer to Fig. 7.4 in Chap. 7 for a graphical analysis of this trade in the debt market.

It goes without saying that Fisher's two Crusoe model is extendable to an economy composed of a large number of agents. A critical insight from Fisher's theory of interest is that the debt market, which is equivalently called the lending market, improves the society's welfare. The institution of debt market is Pareto welfare improving to the society (Pareto 1896, 1906). This critical insight by especially Irving Fisher has led to an astonishing expansion of the debt economy, also called the credit economy, since the middle of the twentieth century. Individuals, institutions, as well as nations came to realize one after another the economic magic of borrowing and lending through the debt/credit market, based upon which countless economic growth initiatives can be pursued (Shiller 2004, 2005; Fabozzi et al. 2009).

Fisher also warned the risk of the debt market in his debt-deflation theory. When the debt economy driven primarily by a bubble bursts, Fisher predicted that the falls in the prices of goods and services in the market owing to the collapse of the economic bubble will raise the real value of the debt a borrower holds, which will make it harder for or even defeat the efforts by the borrower to pay off her/his debt (Fisher 1933). Through the hard times of the dot-com bubble crash and the sub-prime mortgage bubble crash during the first decade of the twenty-first century, the deb-deflation theory was revived among the economic thinkers as a theory that well clarifies the downside of the debt-driven bubble economy (Shiller 2000, 2004, 2009).

The interest rate in the Fisher model thus far described is, to clarify, a real interest rate. The real interest rate is a real return on an investment, in other words, a lending. This is defined as a nominal interest rate minus a rate of inflation. More formally, the real interest rate is determined in the following relationship which is known as the Fisher equation (Fisher 1920; Fabozzi et al. 2009):

$$(1+i) = (1+\gamma)(1+\varphi), \tag{12.10}$$

where i is the nominal interest rate, π the rate of inflation or price increase, and γ the real interest rate.

The theories of capital and interest elucidated by Fisher were fundamental and a harbinger to the emergence of financial economics, finance, and financial markets through the twentieth century in which, to name some of the most influential theories, a portfolio theory, a mutual fund theorem, a capital asset pricing model, an options pricing model, a futures market theory, an insurance theory, an efficient market hypothesis, behavioral finance, a speculative asset pricing model were put forth one after another (Markowitz 1952, Tobin 1958; Sharpe 1962; Fama 1970; Black and Scholes 1973; Ross 1976; Shiller 2004, 2005).

12.3   National Economic Decisions

It is clear that individual resource managers should manage their respective scarce resources for the goal of maximizing the profit to be earned over a time horizon of each of these resources. This should be accomplished by way of addressing the problem of social cost, that is, the external effects to their neighbors and society, which has been amply emphasized in the individual chapters of this book (Pigou 1920; Coase 1960; Nordhaus 1992b; Seo 2020).

It is not apparent to the observers whether a nation's economy should be managed similarly to achieve an optimal economic growth pathway. It appears to be a higher annual growth rate rather than an optimal growth pathway that is pursued by politicians. That is to say, even if they express in their policy agenda a clear goal of pursuing economic growth. However, if the individual sectors or enterprises that constitute the national economy each should pursue an optimal growth pathway, it is reasonable to speak of an optimal economic growth pathway at the national level.

The idea that the national economy should be managed in ways to achieve the highest social welfare over time or, put differently, should be developed along the optimal economic growth pathway was established conceptually as an economic theory by Koopmans (Koopmans 1963, 1965). Koopmans's "On the Concept of Optimal Economic Growth" was a theoretical masterpiece, drawing from the earlier works by Irving Fisher, Frank Ramsey, Robert Solow, Tinbergen, to name the most prominent, which put forth a social welfare optimizing dynamic economic growth model (Fisher 1906, 1930; Ramsey 1928; Solow 1957; Tinbergen 1960). The works by Koopmans and others that pertain to the national economic growth are summarized in Table 12.2.

The story of optimal economic growth theories can begin with the works of Irving Fisher where we left off in the preceding section. Fisher offered a succinct definition of capital (Fisher 1906). According to him, the capital can be any asset that generates a flow of incomes over time. It can be a physical asset such as factories, a machinery asset such as a tractor, a financial asset such as bonds and equities, a natural asset such as a crude oil reserve, or a technology asset such as a patent. The concept of capital has played a key role in the development of the economic growth theories thenceforth.

Ramsey, on the other hand, asked in his "A Mathematical Theory of Saving" whether there is an optimal rate of saving for the nation if the nation's economy should be managed in the best way: How much of the income earned by the present period should a nation save after spending on consumption for the present period (Ramsey 1928)? In tackling this question, Ramsey devised a model in which the society's utility is maximized over time with an imposition of a set of assumptions. The utility

Table 12.2 Theories on national economic growth

Chapters	National/global economic issues	Major theories
Chapter 7	Determination of interest rates	Irving Fisher's theory of capital, income, and interest (Fisher 1906, 1930)
Chapter 8	National saving rate	Frank Ramsey's theory of saving (Ramsey 1928)
Chapter 9	Economic growth	Robert Solow's modern growth theory (Solow 1957)
Chapter 10	Optimal economic growth pathway	Tjalling Koopmans's optimal growth pathway (Koopmans 1965)
Chapter 11	Climate change	William Nordhaus's optimal carbon tax trajectory (Nordhaus 1994)

function was a constant rate of relative risk aversion (CRRA) type, which is widely used by today's analysts (Hope 2006; Stern 2007; Weitzman 2007).

The Ramsey rule, sometimes referred to as the Ramsey-Keynes rule, for an optimal rate of national saving which was the answer to his aforementioned question was stated as follows:

$$\begin{bmatrix} \text{The rate of saving multiplied by the marginal utility of money} \end{bmatrix}$$
$$= \begin{bmatrix} \text{the amount by which the total net rate of enjoyment of utility} \\ \text{falls short of the maximum possible rate of enjoyment} \end{bmatrix}. \quad (12.11)$$

The Ramsey model assumed a fixed population, as such, the maximum rate of enjoyment which he called "bliss" was fixed as well. Further, it assumed a constant technology in the economy without growth. In the Ramsey equation in Eq. 12.11 as well as in his model, technological development and population growth are therefore absent.

Just as importantly, the Ramsey model was intentionally *sans* a discount rate. He stressed that his model "does not discount later enjoyments in comparison with earlier ones" and emphatically argued that the practice of discounting future enjoyments is an "ethically indefensible" practice that arises "merely from the weakness of the imagination." This view has influenced the writers and modelers that followed (Hope 2006; Stern 2007).

The Solow growth model addresses the two problems in the Ramsey model. The capital accumulation model of economic growth formulated by Robert Solow relies, in contrast to Ramsey, on the production function of the national economy which encapsulates the changes in labor (population) as well as technological progress (Solow 1957).

In "A Contribution to the Theory of Economic Growth," Solow explains the process of economic growth as an increase in the sole economic output (Y) in the model which adds to the economy's total capital stock, using the following extended Cobb-Douglas production function (Mankiw et al. 1992):

$$Y(t) = K(t)^{\alpha} \left(A(t)L(t) \right)^{1-\alpha}. \quad (12.12)$$

In Eq. 12.12, K is capital, L is labor, and A is technological progress. The α, $1 - \alpha$ are elasticities of output with regard to the capital input and the effective labor input, respectively.

In the Solow growth model, the optimal capital accumulation of the national economy occurs when, from his simple model version, the following equation holds:

$$\dot{r} = sF(r,1) - nr. \tag{12.13}$$

In the above, $sF(r,1)$ is the output per worker $F(r,1)$ multiplied by the saving (investment) rate s. r is the capital labor ratio (K/L). n is a constant, specifically, the growth rate of population. When Eq. 12.13 is satisfied, the optimal capital-labor ratio is determined, which is denoted as r^*. At this point, a steady state of the economy is achieved.

Tjalling Koopmans integrates the relevant theories to the conceptualization of economic growth that preceded him including Fisher, Ramsey, Solow, Tinbergen, Inagaki (Koopmans 1963, 1965). He devised a generalized social welfare function, instead of a CRRA utility function, which is maximized in the model. Future utilities and consumptions are discounted in the model. A production function was incorporated to the model in a generalized manner. That is, a rising population was incorporated over an infinite time horizon. A changing technology was incorporated with a regularity condition as an exogenous technological change.

With this setup, Koopmans devised "the most suitable" mathematical formulation of the concept of optimal economic growth via a preference ordering of alternative growth paths. The utility or societal welfare function to be maximized over an infinite time horizon is written in general:

$$U = \sum_{t=1}^{\infty} \chi^{t-1} u(x_t). \tag{12.14}$$

In Eq. 12.14, Koopmans's model covers an infinite time horizon in discrete time. The utility is the sum of the present values of one-period social welfares $u(x_t)$ over the time horizon. The social utility is a function of consumption at each period (x_t) but does not have to be a CRRA type. The discount factor for each period is χ^{t-1}.

The economy's production is specified as a twice differentiable and concave production function, homogeneous of degree one, of the capital stock (K) and the labor force (L):

$$F = F(K_t, L_t). \tag{12.15}$$

The labor force, which is equivalent to population in the model, is assumed to grow exponentially at a constant rate (λ) of growth from the initial population (L_0) (Eq. 12.16):

$$L_t = L_0 e^{\lambda t} \text{ with } \lambda > 0. \tag{12.16}$$

As in the Solow model, he defined $k = {}^K\!/_L$, the capital stock per worker. Then, the golden rule of capital accumulation ($\hat{k}$) occurs when

$$f'\left(\hat{k}\right) = \lambda. \tag{12.17}$$

The golden rule of capital accumulation in Eq. 12.17 states that the marginal productivity of capital ($f(k)$) in producing the capital should be equal to the rate of population (labor force) growth (λ) at all times.

At the golden rate of capital accumulation ($\hat{k}$), the golden consumption level (per worker) is as follows:

$$\hat{x} = f\left(\hat{k}\right) - \lambda\hat{k}. \tag{12.18}$$

After describing the golden rule of capital accumulation and the golden consumption level relying on the simplest model, Koopmans provides an extensive analysis of why and how the economy can reach that point by choosing an optimal economic growth pathway by extending it to ever more complex models.

Let ($\hat{x}_t, \hat{k}_t$) be a feasible and attainable economic growth path. Then, Koopmans showed that:

For any initial capital stock, k_0, with $0 < k_0 \leq \overline{k}$, there exists a unique optimal path $\left(\hat{x}_t, \hat{k}_t\right)$ in the set of feasible and attainable paths. For $k_0 \neq \hat{k}$, both $\hat{x}_t$ and $\hat{k}_t$ exhibit a strictly monotonic approach to $\hat{x}$ and $\hat{k}$,, respectively.

Further, with the integration of a discount rate ρ in the model, he proved that: Let $\hat{x}(\rho), \hat{k}(\rho)$ be defined as the solution x, k of

$$f'(k) = \lambda + \rho, f(k) - \lambda k = x, \text{ where } 0 < \lambda \leq \lambda + \rho < f'(0). \tag{12.19}$$

Then if $k_0 = \hat{k}(\rho)$, the unique optimal path is $\hat{x}_t = \hat{x}(\rho), \hat{k}_t = \hat{k}(\rho)$ for all $t \geq 0$.

In the Koopmans's growth theory where the discount rate is accounted for, the stock of capital in the economy which is managed in a socially welfare optimizing manner should grow at the rate that equals the rate of population growth plus the discount rate, which is what Eq. 12.19 states.

Furthermore, embedding technological progress to the model as an exogeneous factor of production, the production function is rewritten with an exogenous technological progress function A_t which is assumed to grow at a constant rate of β over time (Inagaki 1963; Hulten 2000):

$$F\left(K_t, L_t, A_t\right) = cA_t K_t^\alpha L_t^{1-\alpha};\tag{12.20}$$

$$A_t = e^{\beta t}.\tag{12.21}$$

With the technological progress assumed at a constant rate of β, the discount rate of ρ, and the capital elasticity of output α in the model, the following regularity condition should be satisfied for an optimal growth pathway to exist:

$$\rho > \frac{\beta}{1-\alpha}.\tag{12.22}$$

In the most realistic Koopmans's growth theory where both a discount rate and technological progress are accounted for, the stock of capital in the economy which is managed in a socially welfare optimizing manner should grow at the rate that approximates the rate of population growth (λ) plus the discount rate (ρ) plus the rate of unforeseeable technological growth ($h(\beta)$).

The abstract theory of the Koopmans's optimal growth path came to light with strong force when William Nordhaus developed a global climate policy model named the Dynamic Integrated Climate and Economy (DICE) model (Nordhaus 1991, 1992a, 1994). The first global climate conference at Villach, Austria, coincided accidentally with Koopmans's death in 1985, which subsequently led to the formation of the Intergovernmental Panel on Climate Change (IPCC) in 1988 and of the United Nations Convention on Climate Change (UNFCCC) in 1992, the two foundational institutions of climate change policy-making (WMO 1985; IPCC 1990; UNFCCC 1992).

The DICE model relied on Koopmans's afore-described model as its foundation and then merged it with the modules that describe the biogeochemical processes of global warming. The DICE model has the two components seamlessly integrated: an economic system and a geophysical system.

Like Koopmans's model, the societal welfare to be maximized over the course of a policy horizon (T_{max}) is, with c per capita consumption, L labor (population), R social time preference discount factor for each time period:

$$W = \sum_{t=0}^{T_{max}} U[c_t, L_t] \cdot R_t \qquad (12.23)$$

In the production function, Nordhaus incorporates two climate change policy variables, carbon dioxide abatement cost and climate change damages, into the Solow production function endogenously:

$$Q_t = \xi_t \cdot \left[A_t K_t^{\gamma} L_t^{1-\gamma} \right] \qquad (12.24)$$

$$\xi_t = \frac{\text{Effect of CO2 Abatement}}{\text{Effect of Climate Change Damages}} = \frac{1 - \Lambda_t}{1 + \Omega_t} \qquad (12.25)$$

The numerator is the effect of carbon dioxide abatement cost, Λ, while the denominator is the effect of climate change damages, Ω. The damage function is specified as a quadratic function of the atmospheric temperature increase from the pre-industrial average global temperature ($T_{A,t}$):

$$\Omega_t = \varsigma_1 T_{A,t} + \varsigma_2 \left(T_{A,t} \right)^2 \qquad (12.26)$$

The abatement cost function is specified as a power function of the emissions control rate, μ_t, the exponent, θ_2, and the coefficient, $\theta_{1,t}$ (Nordhaus and Boyer 2000; Fischer and Morgenstern 2006):

$$\Lambda_t = \theta_{1,t} \left(\mu_t \right)^{\theta_2} \qquad (12.27)$$

$$\Lambda_t = \pi_t \theta_{1,t} \mu_t^{\theta_2}, \text{ where } \pi_t = \varphi_t^{1-\theta_2} \qquad (12.28)$$

The global cost of abatement depends on how many countries participate in the abatement efforts, that is, a participation rate. The π_t in Eq. 12.28 is a participation cost markup which depends on φ_t, the participation rate. The participation rate is defined as the fraction of the world's total emissions that a climate treaty addresses directly, which is in turn defined as the sum of the emissions of the treaty participants (Nordhaus 2008, 2010).

The carbon dioxide equivalent emissions (CO_{2eq}) is the sum of industrial emissions and land use emissions. The industrial emissions of carbon, $E_{I,t}$, is determined by the production level of the economy, carbon intensity (σ_t) of the economy, an emissions control rate (μ_t):

$$E_{I,t} = \sigma_t \left(1 - \mu_t\right) A_t K_t^{\gamma} L_t^{1-\gamma} \qquad (12.29)$$

A unique contribution of the DICE model is that it builds a dynamic societal welfare optimization model after linking the economic system to the nature's processes. The carbon dioxide emitted from the economic activities, as in Eq. 12.29, mixes in the atmosphere with other chemicals, which then is absorbed into the oceans. This cyclic process is referred to as a carbon cycle (Schlesinger 1997; Ciais et al. 2013). Nordhaus simplifies this complex biogeochemical process with a three-reservoir model in which a set of transfer coefficients link one reservoir to another (Schneider and Thompson 1981). The three reservoirs are the atmosphere, upper ocean, and deep ocean.

Let $M_{A,t}$ be the amount of carbon dioxide equivalent emissions in the atmosphere, which is the first reservoir; $M_{U,t}$ that in the quickly mixing reservoir which is the upper oceans, which is the second reservoir; $M_{L,t}$ that in the lower oceans, which is the third reservoir. With the transfer coefficients from reservoir i to reservoir j denoted by ϕ_{ij}, the carbon cycle is succinctly written as the following three equations:

$$M_{A,t} = E_t + \phi_{11} M_{A,t-1} + \phi_{21} M_{U,t-1} \qquad (12.30)$$

$$M_{U,t} = \phi_{12} M_{A,t-1} + \phi_{22} M_{U,t-1} + \phi_{32} M_{L,t-1} \qquad (12.31)$$

$$M_{L,t} = \phi_{23} M_{U,t-1} + \phi_{33} M_{L,t-1} \qquad (12.32)$$

The accumulation of carbon dioxide equivalent emissions in the planet's atmosphere increases the Earth's temperature by way of increasing the radiative forcing of the planet, F_t, which is the imbalance in the solar radiation flow that is received by the planet directly and indirectly (Le Treut et al. 2007). The degree of radiative forcing is modeled by the following relationship:

$$F_t = \eta \left\{ \log_2 \frac{M_{A,t}}{M_{A,1750}} \right\} + F_{EX,t} \tag{12.33}$$

The total radiative forcing is determined by the carbon dioxide content of the atmosphere relative to that in 1750, which is at the heart of climate science (Arrhenius 1896). Further, there is an exogenous radiative forcing ($F_{EX, t}$), that is, by other greenhouse gases as well as the aerosols which cause a negative radiative forcing. The η is the temperature-forcing parameter expressed in °C per watts per meter squared (W/ m^2).

An increase in the radiative forcing alters the planet's climate system. It warms the planet's atmosphere, which then warms the upper oceans and subsequently the deep oceans. The heat transfers among the layers are determined by the diffusive inertia of the layers, which is captured by the transfer coefficient, τ_i, in the following equations. With $T_{A, t}$ an atmospheric temperature anomaly and $T_{L, t}$ a deep ocean temperature anomaly, the Earth's climate system is represented by the following equations:

$$T_{A,t} = T_{A,t-1} + \tau_1 \left\{ F_t - \tau_2 T_{A,t-1} - \tau_3 \left[T_{A,t-1} - T_{L,t-1} \right] \right\} \tag{12.34}$$

$$T_{L,t} = T_{L,t-1} + \tau_4 \left\{ T_{A,t-1} - T_{L,t-1} \right\} \tag{12.35}$$

In the DICE model, the temperature increase in the atmosphere via the carbon cycle is linked back to the macro economy by the climate change damage function as specified in Eq. 12.26. The larger the temperature anomaly, the larger the climate damages on the economy gets. The larger the damages, the higher the optimal control rate of carbon dioxide emissions generated by the model, that is, called for by the model.

Nordhaus acknowledges on numerous occasions the great challenges of integrating the biogeochemical processes of the planet into the economic decision module. The challenges are severe because there is large uncertainty in many aspects of these biogeochemical processes, across the available climate change prediction models as well as within a specific climate change prediction model (Le Treut et al. 2007; Taylor et al. 2012).

Nordhaus calibrates these geophysical modules in such ways that the DICE model predictions of the biogeochemical variables lie in the middle of the ranges of the estimates put forth by the relevant scientific communities.

12.4 Conclusion

Should a nation manage its economic path in a way that maximizes the societal welfare over an infinite time horizon? If anyone would try to answer this question, s/he would be daunted by the abstract nature of the answers s/he might have to give. That is to say, even if s/he would be certain that the answer should be positive.

This chapter provides a condensed synthesis of a historical series of the works by economists, based on an extensive exposition of each of them throughout this book, devoted to this question for the past 120 years: from Irving Fisher, to Frank Ramsey, to Robert Solow, to Tjalling Koopmans, and to William Nordhaus. This literature shows how the theoretical foundation for the optimal economic growth has been established over the course of time as well as how the question of optimal economic growth has evolved in a gradual fashion into a concrete highly debated issue across the global community.

Equally importantly, the question of economic growth can be looked into from the perspective of individual sectors and enterprises that constitute the macro economy, especially those that manage highly valuable natural resources on the planet. That an individual enterprise or industry's objective in managing such a resource is to achieve an optimal dynamic trajectory in its utilizations has been clearly expounded by the economists for the past two centuries since David Ricardo in 1817: Ricardo for crop agriculture, von Thunen for spatial land uses, Faustmann for forest harvests, Hotelling for fossil fuels, Gordon and Clark for fisheries, Irving Fisher for financial assets.

The review of the literature in this book reveals that the greatest challenge to the economics of optimal growth pathways is how the society can provide public goods efficiently, that is, optimally (Samuelson 1954, 1955). The ways economists have dealt with this problem have been amply addressed in this book. Readers can refer to the discussions of the open access fishers in Chap. 7 (Gordon 1954; Ostrom 1990) as well as the expositions of the climate change economics in Chap. 11 (Nordhaus 1994, 2008).

At the heart of the economists' solutions to the public good problems is a creation of the efficient price for the utilization of a public good or commons. A trajectory of carbon price, which may be implemented nationally with a globally harmonized carbon tax scheme, places the efficient price on the emissions of carbon dioxide by individuals, that is, all individuals on the planet without exception.

An emerging literature, on the other hand, puts forth a different policy solution. It demonstrates that the problem of a globally shared good should be addressed by reliance on the microbehavioral incentives and actions that people are faced with because of the concerned problem (Seo 2020, 2021, 2022a). As for the problem of global climate change, people have ample incentives to adapt to changes in the climate system over the long term in order to maximize the benefits and minimize the losses, which may call for a large array of efficient micro adaptations (Mendelsohn 2000; Hanemann 2000; Seo 2006). Some of the efficient microbehavioral adaptations by people will be directed to carbon dioxide and other greenhouse gas emissions reduction efforts including renewable energy, novel lighting, and battery revolutions, some of which will call for forward-looking and foresighted adaptations. Further, technological possibilities exist to contain the temperature anomalies of the planet via either solar radiation reflection technologies or carbon dioxide capture and storage technologies (Seo 2020, 2021, 2022b). This literature may be referred to as microbehavioral economics.

The microbehavioral economics whose unit of analysis is micro decision-makers has been applied to tackle the issues of globally shared goods such as climate change and worldwide pandemics (Seo 2022a, 2022b). Similarly, it can be aptly applied to the economics of optimal economic growth, the topic of this book, whose possibility and reality can also be gleaned with little effort from this book's overarching structure as well as the expositions of individual sectors and enterprises. To put this most succinctly, the economics of optimal economic growth of the national economy must be supported by the respective economics of individual sectors and enterprises each of which pursues an economically optimal pathway for the utilization of the concerned resource.

REFERENCES

Aghion, P., and P. Howitt. 2009. *The Economics of Growth*. Cambridge, MA: MIT Press.

Arrhenius, S.A. 1896. On the Influence of Carbonic Acid in the Air upon the Temperature of the Ground. *Philosophical Magazine* 41: 237–276.

Barro, R.J., and X. Sala-i-Martin. 1992. Convergence. *Journal of Political Economy* 100: 223–251.

Black, F., and M. Scholes. 1973. The Pricing of Options and Corporate Liabilities. *Journal of Political Economy* 81: 637–654.

Ciais, P., C. Sabine, G. Bala, L. Bopp, V. Brovkin, J. Canadell, A. Chhabra, R. DeFries, J. Galloway, M. Heimann, C. Jones, C. Le Quéré, R.B. Myneni, S. Piao, and P. Thornton. 2013. Carbon and Other Biogeochemical Cycles. In *Climate Change 2013: The Physical Science Basis*. Cambridge, UK: Cambridge University Press.

Clark, C.W. 1973. The Economics of Over Exploitation. *Science* 181: 630–634.

———. 1985. *Bioeconomic Modelling and Fisheries Management*. New York, NY: Wiley.

Coase, Ronald. 1960. The Problem of Social Cost. *Journal of Law and Economics* 3: 1–44.

Fabozzi, F.J., F. Modigliani, and M.G. Ferri. 2009. *Foundations of Financial Markets and Institutions*. 4th ed. Hoboken, NJ: Prentice-Hall.

Fama, Eugene F. 1970. Efficient Capital Markets: A Review of Empirical Work. *Journal of Finance* 25: 383–417.

Faustmann, Martin. 1849. On the Determination of the Value Which Forest Land and Immature Stands Pose for Forestry. In *Martin Faustmann and the Evolution of Discounted Cash Flow*, ed. M. Gane. Paper 42, 1968. Oxford, England: Oxford Institute.

Fischer, C., and R.D. Morgenstern. 2006. Carbon Abatement Costs: Why the Wide Range of Estimates? *Energy Journal* 27: 73–86.

Fisher, Irving. 1906. *The Nature of Capital and Income*. New York, NY: Macmillan.

———. 1907. *The Rate of Interest*. New York, NY: Macmillan.

———. 1920. *The Purchasing Power of Money: Its Determination and Relation to Credit, Interest and Crises*. New York, NY: Macmillan.

———. 1930. *The Theory of Interest*. New York: Macmillan.

———. 1933. The Debt-deflation Theory of Great Depressions. *Econometrica* 1: 337–357.

Friedman, Milton. 1962. *Capitalism and Freedom*. Chicago, IL: The University of Chicago Press.

Gordon, H.S. 1954. The Economic Theory of a Common-Property Resource: The Fishery. *The Journal of Political Economy* 62: 124–142.

Gray, L.C. 1914. Rent under the Assumption of Exhaustibility. *Quarterly Journal of Economics* 28: 466–489.

Hanemann, W.M. 2000. Adaptation and Its Management. *Climate Change* 45: 571–581.

Hartwick, J.M., and N.D. Olewiler. 1997. Ch. 4. *The Economics of the Fishery: An Introduction & Ch. 5. Regulation of the Fishery. In: The Economics of Natural Resource Use*. 2nd ed. New York, NY: Pearson.

Hope, C. 2006. The Marginal Impact of CO2 from PAGE2002: An Integrated Assessment Model Incorporating the IPCC's Five Reasons for Concern. *Integrated Assessment Journal* 6: 19–56.

Hotelling, H. 1931. The Economics of Exhaustible Resources. *Journal of Political Economy* 39: 137–175.

Hulten, C.R. 2000. *Total Factor Productivity: A Short Biography.* National Bureau of Economic Research (NBER) Working Paper Series 7471, Cambridge, MA: The NBER.

Inagaki, M. 1963. *The Golden Utility Path.* Rotterdam: Netherlands Economics Institute.

Intergovernmental Panel on Climate Change (IPCC). 1990. *Climate Change: The IPCC Scientific Assessment.* Cambridge, UK: Cambridge University Press.

International Thermonuclear Experimental Reactor (ITER). 2022. *ITER: The World's Largest Tokamak.* https://www.iter.org/proj/inafewlines

Koopmans, Tjalling C. 1963. *On the Concept of Optimal Economic Growth.* The Cowles Foundation Discussion Paper # 163, Yale University, New Haven, CT.

———. 1965. On the Concept of Optimal Economic Growth. *Pontificiae Academiae Scientiarum Scripta Varia* 28 (1): 1–75.

Le Treut, H., R. Somerville, U. Cubasch, Y. Ding, C. Mauritzen, A. Mokssit, T. Peterson, and M. Prather. 2007. Historical Overview of Climate Change. In *Climate Change 2007: The Physical Science Basis*, ed. S. Solomon et al. The Fourth Assessment Report of the Intergovernmental Panel on Climate Change. Cambridge: Cambridge University Press.

Mankiw, N. Gregory. 2020. *Principles of Economics.* 9th ed. Stamford, CT: Cengage Learning.

Mankiw, N. Gregory, David Romer, and David Weil. 1992. A Contribution to the Empirics of Economic Growth. *Quarterly Journal of Economics* 107: 407–437.

Markowitz, Harry M. 1952. Portfolio Selection. *Journal of Finance* 7: 77–91.

Mas-Colell, A., M.D. Whinston, and J.R. Green. 1995. *Microeconomic Theory.* Oxford, UK: Oxford University Press.

Mendelsohn, R. 2000. Efficient Adaptation to Climate Change. *Climatic Change* 45: 583–600.

Nordhaus, W.D. 1973. *The Allocation of Energy Resources.* Brookings Papers on Economic Activity 1973: 529–576.

———. 1991. To Slow or Not to Slow: The Economics of the Greenhouse Effects. *Economic Journal* 101: 920–937.

———. 1992a. An Optimal Transition Path for Controlling Greenhouse Gases. *Science* 258: 1315–1319.

———. 1992b. The Ecology of Markets. *Proceedings of the National Academy of Sciences* 89: 843–850.

———. 1994. *Managing the Global Commons.* Cambridge, MA: MIT Press.

———. 2008. *A Question of Balance: Weighing the Options on Global Warming Policies*. New Haven, CT: Yale University Press.

———. 2010. Economic Aspects of Global Warming in a Post-Copenhagen Environment. *Proceedings of the National Academy of Sciences* 107: 11721–11726.

Nordhaus, W.D., and J. Boyer. 2000. *Warming the World: Economic Models of Global Warming*. Cambridge, MA: MIT Press.

Ostrom, E. 1990. *Governing the Commons: The Evolution of Institutions for Collective Action*. Cambridge, UK: Cambridge University Press.

Pareto, V. 1896. *Cours d'Economie Politique*. Geneva, CH: Librairie Droz.

———. 1906[2014]. In Montesano, A., A. Zanni, L. Bruni, J.S. Chipman, M. McLure. (eds.). Manual for Political Economy. Oxford, UK: Oxford University Press.

British Petroleum (BP). 2021. *Statistical Review of World Energy 2021*. London, UK: The BP.

Pigou, Arthur C. 1920. *Economics of Welfare*. London, UK: Macmillan.

Ramsey, F.P. 1928. A Mathematical Theory of Savings. *Economic Journal* 38: 543–559.

Ricardo, D. 1817. *On the Principles of Political Economy and Taxation*. London, UK: John Murray.

Romer, Paul. 1990. Endogenous Technical Change. *Journal of Political Economy* 98: S71–S102.

Romer, David. 2018. *Advanced Macroeconomics*. 5th ed. New York, NY: McGraw Hill.

Ross, Stephen A. 1976. The Arbitrage Theory of Capital Asset Pricing. *Journal of Economic Theory* 13: 341–360.

Samuelson, P.A. 1947. *Foundations of Economic Analysis*. Cambridge, UK: Harvard University Press. [Enlarged edition published in 1983].

———. 1954. The Pure Theory of Public Expenditure. *Review of Economics and Statistics* 36: 387–389.

Samuelson, P. 1955. Diagrammatic Exposition of a Theory of Public Expenditure. *Review of Economics and Statistics* 37: 350–356.

Samuelson, P.A. 1994. Two Classics: Böhm-Bawerk's Positive Theory and Fisher's Rate of Interest Through Modern Prisms. *Journal of the History of Economic Thought* 16: 202–228.

Samuelson, P.A., and W.D. Nordhaus. 2009. *Economics*. 19th ed. New York, NY: McGraw-Hill Education.

Schlesinger, W.H. 1997. *Biogeochemistry: An Analysis of Global Change*. 2nd ed. San Diego, CA: Academic Press.

Schneider, S.H., and S.L. Thompson. 1981. Atmospheric CO_2 and Climate: Importance of the Transient Response. *Journal of Geophysical Research* 86: 3135–3147.

Seo, S.N. 2006. *Modeling Farmer Responses to Climate Change: Climate Change Impacts and Adaptations in Livestock Management in Africa.* Ph.D. dissertation. Yale University, New Haven, CT.

———. 2016a. *Microbehavioral Econometric Methods: Theories, Models, and Applications for the Study of Environmental and Natural Resources.* Amsterdam, NL: Academic Press.

———. 2016b. The Micro-behavioral Framework for Estimating Total Damage of Global Warming on Natural Resource Enterprises with Full Adaptations. *Journal of Agricultural, Biological, & Environmental Statistics* 21: 328–347.

———. 2020. *The Economics of Globally Shared and Public Goods.* Amsterdam, NL: Academic Press.

———. 2021. *Climate Change and Economics: Engaging with Future Generations with Action Plans.* Cham, CH: Palgrave Macmillan.

———. 2022a. *The Economics of Pandemics: Exploring Globally Shared Experiences.* Cham, CH: Palgrave Macmillan.

———. 2022b. *Handbook of Behavioral Economics and Climate Change.* Cheltenham, UK: Edward Elgar.

Shiller, R.J. 2000. *Irrational Exuberance.* 1st ed. Princeton, NJ: Princeton University Press.

———. 2004. *The New Financial Order: Risk in the 21st Century.* Princeton, NJ: Princeton University Press.

———. 2005. *Irrational Exuberance.* 2nd ed. Princeton, NJ: Princeton University Press.

———. 2008. Financial Markets: Open Yale Courses. New Haven, CT: Yale University.

———. 2009. *Subprime Solution: How Today's Global Financial Crisis Happened and What to Do About it.* Princeton, NJ: Princeton University Press.

Solow, R.M. 1957. A Contribution to the Theory of Economic Growth. *Quarterly Journal of Economics* 70: 65–94.

Stern, N. 2007. *The Economics of Climate Change: The Stern Review.* New York, NY: Cambridge University Press.

Taylor, K.E., R.J. Stouffer, and G.A. Meehl. 2012. An Overview of CMIP5 and the Experiment Design. *Bulletin of American Meteorological Society* 93: 485–498.

Tinbergen, J. 1960. Optimum Savings and Utility Maximization Over Time. *Econometrica* 28: 481–489.

Tobin, James. 1958. Liquidity Preference as Behavior Towards Risk. *Review of Economic Studies* 25 (2): 65–86.

United Nations (UN). 1982. *United Nations Convention on the Law of the Sea.* New York, NY: UN. https://www.un.org/depts/los/convention_agreements/texts/unclos/unclos_e.pdf.

United Nations Framework Convention on Climate Change (UNFCCC). 1992. *United Nations Framework Convention on Climate Change.* New York, NY: UNFCCC.

von Thunen, J.H 1826 [1966]. *The Isolated State.* Trans. C.M. Wartenberg. Oxford/New York: Pergamon.

Von Neumann, J., and O. Morgenstern. 1944. *Theory of Games and Economic Behavior.* Princeton, NJ: Princeton University Press.

Weitzman, M.L. 2007. A Review of The Stern Review on the Economics of Climate Change. *Journal of Economic Literature* 45: 703–724.

Williamson, J.G. 1990. The Impact of the Corn Laws Just Prior to Repeal. *Explorations in Economic History* 27: 123–156.

World Meteorological Organization (WMO). 1985. *Report of the International Conference on the Assessment of the Role of Carbon Dioxide and of Other Greenhouse Gases in Climate Variations and Associated Impacts.* Villach, Austria: WMO.

CHAPTER 13

Tendencies for Sub-optimal or Post-growth Pathways

13.1 INTRODUCTION

This is the final chapter of this book. All the things that needed to be explained regarding the economics of optimal economic growth pathways have been explained in the previous 12 chapters. Before finally closing this book, however, the present author will give a brief exposition of the theoretical tendencies that intentionally pursue a socially sub-optimal growth pathway, synthesizing the host of critiques presented in individual chapters of the book.

The sub-optimal growth proponents are those who set aside as unimportant the pursuit of a societally optimal economic growth pathway in managing the nation's economy. They propose a palette of different goals other than the societally optimal economic growth. In that sense, it seems also apt to call them post-growth theorists, as in the "Manifesto for a Post-growth Economy" (Speth 2012; Paech 2012).

The post-growth proponents are many and diverse groups of people, although they appear to share many ideas as well. This chapter classifies them into three most prominent groups. The first is a sustainable development group. The second is an ecological economics group. And, the third is a degrowth group.

For the past five decades since the 1970s perhaps around the first United Nations' Conference on Human Environment, they emerged one after another and have grown gradually but markedly in their influence on the

S. N. Seo, *The Economics of Optimal Growth Pathways*, https://doi.org/10.1007/978-3-031-20754-9_13

economics literature as well as the major policy debates (UN 1972). By the second decade of the twenty-first century, they individually have become a prominent player in the policy debates on economic growth and other social and environmental issues in nearly all countries around the planet.

The main arguments put forth by these groups have already been clarified throughout this book. In each chapter, the present author introduced at least one of them as a prominent critique against the main theory thereof. The critiques scattered across the preceding twelve chapters are in most cases coming from the post-growth or sub-optimal growth theorists. This will be briefly summarized in the next section.

In addition, the present author's analyses and responses to each of these critiques were given in the relevant individual chapters throughout this book. That being the case, there is no need to repeat those analyses and responses in this chapter. This chapter instead can be understood as a presentation of the three overarching theories of the more than a dozen critiques introduced in the preceding twelve individual chapters.

13.2   Sub-optimal or Post-growth Tendencies Introduced in the Book

Table 13.1 summarizes the sub-optimal or post-growth critiques introduced in the individual chapters of this book, along with the primary theories against which these critiques were leveled. In total, there are 10

Table 13.1   Sub-optimal growth critiques in individual chapters

Chapters	Primary theories	Primary critiques
Chapter 2	Ricardo's rent in corn land	The Rome Club critique (a limits-to-growth critique)
Chapter 3	Von Thunen's spatial land use	A wasteland critique
Chapter 4	Faustmann's forest rotation	A deforestation critique
Chapter 5	Hotelling's fossil fuel extractions	A peak oil critique; an environmental and health critique
Chapter 6	A bioeconomic fish catch model	A species extinction critique
Chapter 7	Fisher's capital and interest	A zero discounting critique
Chapter 8	Ramsey's theory of saving	A Ramsey discounting critique
Chapter 9	Solow's modern growth theory	A sustainable development critique
Chapter 10	Koopmans's optimal economic growth path	A negative externality critique
Chapter 11	Nordhaus's carbon price trajectory	A fat-tail critique

primary theories and 11 individual critiques that were presented from Chaps. 2 to 11.

Chapter 2 presented the theory of rent in corn farming according to David Ricardo (Ricardo 1817). A critique against the theory was presented with the Rome Club Report widely known as a limits-to-growth critique (Meadows et al. 1972).

Chapter 3 presented the spatial land use theory by von Thunen (von Thunen 1826). A critique against the theory was given by a so-called wasteland critique (Rosenzweig and Parry 1994; Schlenker and Roberts 2009). The term refers to an implicit assumption that the land uses other than the target land use of an analyst, for example, croplands, are wastelands, that is, of no value.

Chapter 4 presented the forest economics by Martin Faustmann that determines the optimal forest rotation and subsequently the value of a forestland (Faustmann 1849). A critique against the optimal harvest rotation was given with a deforestation problem of the world's forests (Myers 1979; Repetto and Gillis 1988; Pearce 1998; Curtis et al. 2018).

Chapter 5 explained the economics of optimal fossil fuel extractions by Harold Hotelling and others (Hotelling 1931). A critique of the theory was offered with a peak oil theory and an environmental and health critique (Hubbert 1956; Likens and Bormann 1974; Molina and Rowland 1974).

Chapter 6 explained the bioeconomic model of fisheries and fish catch (Gordon 1954; Clark 1973). A critique against the fishery's bioeconomic model was offered with a concern on species extinction (Reid and Miller 1989; IUCN 2021).

Chapter 7 described the theories of capital and interest rate set forth by Irving Fisher (Fisher 1906, 1930). A critique against the theory of interest was presented with a zero-discounting argument for a long-term public policy design (Weitzman 1998; Stern 2007).

Chapter 8 described the mathematical theory of optimal national saving by Frank Ramsey (Ramsey 1928). A critique was presented with a focus on the Ramsey equation in support of no discounting whatsoever of future consumptions for any dynamic economic policy consideration (Arrow et al. 1996; Weitzman 2007).

Chapter 9 clarified the modern economic growth theory by Robert Solow which is a theory of capital accumulation (Solow 1957, 1974). A critique of the chapter was presented with a host of critiques put forward from the sustainable development viewpoint as well as the responses to them by Solow himself (UN 1992, 2000, 2001, 2015).

Chapter 10 elucidated the theory of optimal economic growth path put forth by Tjalling Koopmans (Koopmans 1965). A critique of the chapter was presented with a host of critiques from a negative externalities standpoint (Pigou 1920; Coase 1960; Carson 1962; Baumol and Oates 1975).

Chapter 11 elucidated the theory of a dynamic carbon dioxide price trajectory or the social cost of carbon dioxide set forth by William Nordhaus (Nordhaus 1991, 1994). A critique against the theory was presented by a theory of a fat-tail distribution which emphasizes an exceptionally extreme event whose probability of occurrence is very slim but uncertain (Weitzman 2009).

13.3   A Sustainable Development Critique

From this point on, the three overarching theories will be presented in order: the sustainable development critique, the ecological economics critique, and the degrowth critique. First, the sustainable development critique was introduced in Chap. 9 as a response to the modern economic growth theory by Robert Solow and others. This group's core criticism was that the economic growth as explained by the optimal capital accumulation in the economy is not sustainable.

The group's intellectual foundations were laid out and widely spread by the notable publications such as the Rome Club Report in 1972 entitled "The Limits to Growth" and the United Nations' World Commission on Environment and Development (WCED)'s report entitled "Our Common Future" in 1985 (Meadows et al. 1972; WCED 1987).

The sustainable development critique has become a powerful political force in world affairs via the United Nations and related international organizations. The conceptualization and framework espoused by this group can be well gleaned from a series of United Nations' declarations over the past 30 years: the Agenda 21 at the Rio Earth Summit in 1992, the UN Millennium Development Goals (MDGs) in 2000, and the UN 2030 Agenda for Sustainable Development in 2015 (UN 1992, 2000, 2015).

The group's intellectual foundation was laid as a response to the range of problems that the world has increasingly faced since World War II, including toxic and hazardous chemicals; environmental pollutions such as acid rain, smog, water pollution, particulate matter pollutions; a global ozone layer destruction; nuclear disasters and wars; poverty, hunger, malnutrition, especially of children and mothers, in the least developed countries (Carson 1962; Likens and Bormann 1974; Molina and Rowland 1974, Turco et al. 1983; Byerlee and Eicher 1997; Evenson and Gollin 2003).

The conceptual framework which is proposed to tackle these issues by the supporters is an ensemble of policy interventions (Bartelmus 2012; Speth 2012). It puts together a large number of suggested remedies in a way that each of these remedies is directed to a corresponding single perceived problem only. For example, the 2030 Agenda for sustainable development, the latest of the series of UN declarations, has 17 goals and as many as 169 policy targets.

In Chap. 9, the present author described the UN Millennium Development Goals (MDGs) as a representative sustainable development agenda (UN 2000, 2001). A more detailed description is given in Table 13.2 with its policy targets and indicators. There are eight goals in an ensemble which covers a wide range of concerns which the proponents regard as comprehensive: poverty and hunger; primary education; gender; child mortality; maternal health; HIV/AIDS, malaria, and other diseases; environmental sustainability; a global partnership for development. Under these eight goals, 21 policy targets are suggested, some of which are included in the table. For each of these targets, there are again relevant indictors based upon which a progress in achieving each policy target is assessed.

Let's give it a closer look. Under the Goal 1 of "Eradicate extreme poverty and hunger," there are three policy targets: (1) Halve, between 1990 and 2015, the proportion of people living on less than $1.25 a day; (2) Achieve decent employment for women, men, and young people; (3) Halve, between 1990 and 2015, the proportion of people who suffer from hunger.

Of particular interest to this book is the Goal 7 of "Ensure environmental sustainability." To achieve the goal, there are four suggested policy targets: (1) Integrate the principles of sustainable development into country policies and programs and reverse loss of environmental resource; (2) Reduce biodiversity loss, achieving, by 2010, a significant reduction in the rate of loss; (3) Halve, by 2015, the proportion of the population without sustainable access to safe drinking water and basic sanitation; (4) By 2020, to have achieved a significant improvement in the lives of at least 100 million slum-dwellers.

Table 13.2   UN Millennium Development Goals, targets, and indicators

ID	Goals	Policy targets (selected)	Indicators (selected)
1	Eradicate extreme poverty and hunger	Target 1A: Halve, between 1990 and 2015, the proportion of people living on less than $1.25 a day Target 1B: Achieve decent employment for women, men, and young people Target 1C: Halve, between 1990 and 2015, the proportion of people who suffer from hunger	
2	Achieve universal primary education		
3	Promote gender equality and empower women		
4	Reduce child mortality rates		
5	Improve maternal health		
6	Combat HIV/AIDS, malaria, and other diseases		
7	Ensure environmental sustainability	Target 7A: Integrate the principles of sustainable development into country policies and programs; reverse loss of environmental resource Target 7B: Reduce biodiversity loss, achieving, by 2010, a significant reduction in the rate of loss Target 7C: Halve, by 2015, the proportion of the population without sustainable access to safe drinking water and basic sanitation Target 7D: By 2020, to have achieved a significant improvement in the lives of at least 100 million slum-dwellers	[Pertains to Target 7A and 7B] i) Proportion of land area covered by forest ii) CO_2 emissions iii) Consumption of ozone-depleting substances iv) Proportion of fish stocks within safe biological limits v) Proportion of renewable water resources used vi) Proportion of terrestrial and marine areas protected vii) Proportion of species threatened with extinction
8	Develop a global partnership for development		

The progress in each of these policy targets is assessed by a batch of indicators. For the Goal 7, the indicators relied on by the UN MDG annual report to assess Targets 7A and 7B are (1) Proportion of land area covered by forest; (2) CO_2 emissions; (3) Consumption of ozone-depleting substances; (4) Proportion of fish stocks within safe biological limits; (5)

Proportion of renewable water resources used; (6) Proportion of terrestrial and marine areas protected; and (7) Proportion of species threatened with extinction (UN 2001, 2015).

In 2015, the United Nations reached a new agreement adopting the 2030 Agenda for Sustainable Development entitled "Transforming Our World: The 2030 Agenda for Sustainable Development" (UN 2015). It replaced "Development" in the 2000 UN MDG declaration with "Sustainable Development." It comprises a far longer list of goals and policy targets. In total, there are 17 goals and 169 policy targets. Notice that the number of policy targets jumped from 21 in the UN MDG in 2000 to 169 in the 2030 Agenda in 2015, nearly an 800% increase. The list of policy goals is summarized in Table 13.3.

Table 13.3   UN 2030 Agenda for sustainable development

ID	Sustainable development goals
1	End poverty in all its forms everywhere
2	End hunger, achieve food security and improved nutrition, and promote sustainable agriculture
3	Ensure healthy lives and promote wellbeing for all at all ages
4	Ensure inclusive and equitable quality education and promote lifelong learning opportunities for all
5	Achieve gender equality and empower all women and girls
6	Ensure availability and sustainable management of water and sanitation for all
7	**Ensure access to affordable, reliable, sustainable, and modern energy for all**
8	**Promote sustained, inclusive and sustainable economic growth, full and productive employment, and decent work for all**
9	Build resilient infrastructure, promote inclusive and sustainable industrialization, and foster innovation
10	Reduce inequality within and among countries
11	**Make cities and human settlements inclusive, safe, resilient, and sustainable**
12	**Ensure sustainable consumption and production patterns**
13	**Take urgent action to combat climate change and its impacts**
14	Conserve and sustainably use the oceans, seas, and marine resources for sustainable development
15	Protect, restore, and promote sustainable use of terrestrial ecosystems, sustainably manage forests, combat desertification, and halt and reverse land degradation and halt biodiversity loss
16	**Promote peaceful and inclusive societies for sustainable development**, provide access to justice for all and build effective, accountable, and inclusive institutions at all levels
17	Strengthen the means of implementation and revitalize the global partnership for sustainable development

If you read through the list of 17 goals in Table 13.3, you will realize that it is a remarkable update to the UN millennium declaration in 2000. It contains such remarkable and ambitious goals as "affordable energy for all," "full employment for all," "ensure sustainable consumption," "make cities inclusive," "peaceful and inclusive societies," and "water and sanitation for all."

The United Nations' declarations in 2000 and 2015 came into reality as a consequence of the adoption of Agenda 21 at the Rio Earth Summit in 1992, more formally, the United Nations Conference on Environment and Development (UN 1992). The agenda items are listed in Table 13.4, which totals 38 items and covers all the policy areas pursued in the MDGs in 2000 and the SDGs in 2015.

13.4   An Ecological Economics Critique

An ecological economics critique is the second post-growth tendency we review which has become increasingly influential in the economics literature and policy debates. This group's critique on the traditional environmental economics, natural resource economics, and economic growth literature in general is rooted most fundamentally on the concept of ecological limits. Because of the ecological limits which are unavoidable, they argue, a continued economic growth is not possible and will even be catastrophic for humanity.

The ecological economics critique is anchored by related concepts such as a steady-state economy, carrying capacity, biophysical limits, ecological footprints, and environmental justice (Arrow et al. 1995; Daly and Farley 2003; Costanza 2010; Nelson and Coffey 2019). The International Society of Ecological Economics (ISEE) was established during the late 1980s, whose founders have played a central role in the development of ecological economics.

One of the founders defines the ecological economics as a transdisciplinary field for "a more integrated picture of how humans have interacted with their environment in the past and how they might interact in the future," or "an attempt to look at humans embedded in their ecological life-support system, not separate from the environment" (Costanza 2010).

Ecological economists do not think that the field is a sub-discipline of economics. Protagonists argue that the field is different from "mainstream economics" which largely focused on markets and does not address the

Table 13.4 The Agenda 21 in 1992

Sections	Agenda 21
1. Social and economic dimensions	International cooperation to accelerate sustainable development in developing countries and related domestic policies Combating poverty Changing consumption patterns Demographic dynamics and sustainability Protecting and promoting human health conditions Promoting sustainable human settlement development Integrating environment and development in decision-making
2. Conservation and management of resources for development	Protection of the atmosphere Integrated approach to the planning and management of land resources Combating deforestation Managing fragile ecosystems: combating desertification and drought Managing fragile ecosystems: sustainable mountain development Promoting sustainable agriculture and rural development Conservation of biological diversity Environmentally sound management of biotechnology Protection of the oceans, all kinds of seas, including enclosed and semi-enclosed seas, and coastal areas and the protection, rational use, and development of their living resources Protection of the quality and supply of freshwater resources: application of integrated approaches to the development, management, and use of water resources Environmentally sound management of toxic chemicals, including prevention of illegal international traffic in toxic and dangerous products Environmentally sound management of hazardous wastes, in hazardous wastes Environmentally sound management of solid wastes and sewage-related issues Safe and environmentally sound management of radioactive wastes

(*continued*)

Table 13.4 (continued)

Sections	Agenda 21
3. Strengthening the role of major groups	Global action for women toward sustainable and equitable development
	Children and youth in sustainable development
	Recognizing and strengthening the role of indigenous people and their communities
	Strengthening the role of non-governmental organizations: partners for sustainable development
	Local authorities' initiatives in support of Agenda 21
	Strengthening the role of workers and their trade unions
	Strengthening the role of business and industry
	Scientific and technological community
	Strengthening the role of farmers
4. Means of implementation	Financial resources and mechanisms
	Transfer of environmentally sound technology, cooperation, and capacity-building
	Science for sustainable development
	Promoting education, public awareness, and training
	National mechanisms and international cooperation for capacity-building in developing countries
	International institutional arrangements
	International legal instruments and mechanisms
	Information for decision-making

externalities, even if recognized by economists. Ecological economics studies "everything outside the market as well as everything inside the market," they argue.

Protagonists further argue that the mainstream economics does not recognize biophysical, ecological limits and thinks in a misguided manner that "technology can solve any resource constraint problems." They argue "the environment creates certain limits and constraints," which is recognized by ecological economics (Costanza 2010).

For the ecological economists, a pursuit of economic growth is misguided as well as dangerous. A key concept on this regard is a steady-state economy (Georgescu-Roegen 1971a, 1971b; Daly 1973). The steady-state economy is characterized by a fixed stock of capital and a fixed stock of population. These stocks are maintained by the flow of natural resources to the human system. The constant, non-growing economy is the best of all systems, according to the protagonists, because the economic system is a sub-system of the natural environment with scarce resources and the ecosystems which are fragile (Daly 1973).

Protagonists argue that the mainstream economics views the economy as an isolated circular system where goods and services are exchanged among the players in the system, without any physical contact to the natural environment (Daly and Farley 2003). This is not a fair description of the economics literature on these issues (Nordhaus 1992a, 1992b; Seo 2020, 2021).

As these protagonists expressed, the concept of a biophysical or ecological limit is the core of this group's critique (Arrow et al. 1995). There are many such limits of concern to them, one of the most hotly debated of which is the planet's climate threshold (Weitzman 2009). Beyond the climate threshold or the threshold global temperature, if it were to be proven, the planet's human and other civilizations may not survive. Another such biophysical limit exists in the fish stock, which was referred to in Chap. 6 as the carrying capacity of the habitat. An over-exploitation of the fish stock owing to open access will lead to an extinction of the fish species (Clark 1973). Other than fish, many marine and terrestrial species may go extinct beyond certain thresholds in either a habitat's carrying capacity, or ocean temperature, or atmospheric temperature, or chemical concentrations (Reid and Miller 1989). For example, coral reefs may not survive beyond an ocean temperature increase threshold (Kleypas et al. 1999). In Chap. 5, fossil fuels were discussed as exhaustible resources whose stocks are limited. This is another biophysical limit (Hotelling 1931; Hubbert 1956).

There are many biophysical and ecological limits. What is critical is how these limits are defined and then measured by ecological economists. One of the most popular indicators used by this group is an ecological footprint (GFN 2022). There are other similar footprint indicators including carbon footprint, water footprint, land footprint.

Let me explain, for the sake of evaluation by readers, how the ecological footprint is defined and used. It is defined by the two statistics: (1) The size of the biologically productive areas people use for their consumption and (2) The size of the biologically productive areas available on Earth (Rees 1992; Wackernagel 1994). The first is referred to as the ecological footprint and the latter is referred to as biocapacity. Both are measured in hectares per person.

An ecological deficit is the difference between the ecological footprint of a population, for example, a nation or a globe, and the biocapacity of the area available to that population, that is, when the difference is positive. The concept of an ecological deficit is illustrated in Fig. 13.1, which depends on the ecological footprint and the biocapacity.

How are the "productive" areas defined? How are human consumptions associated with the productive areas? Briefly speaking, researchers simply add up the relevant areas. These questions have long remained a gray area to ecological economists, although pivotal to the validity and applicability of these measures. This issue was highlighted in Chap. 3 as a wasteland critique (Seo 2006, 2016, 2019). The upshot is that the today's wastelands or wilderness may become valuable or productive when people's land uses are shifted.

Another key concept in the ecological economics critique is environmental justice whose concept is widely appropriated by many groups of people concerned with policy interventions. This concept focuses on the conflicts among groups of people with regard to ecological and environmental benefits and damages, especially among the rich and the poor (Martinez-Alier 2002).

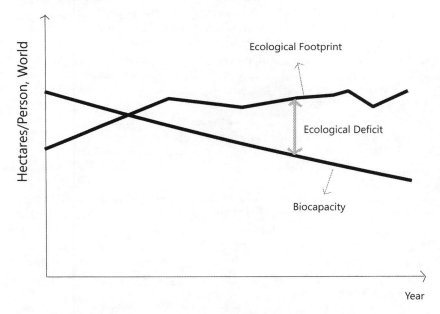

Fig. 13.1 An illustration of the concept of ecological footprint

It may turn out to be discomforting to the ecological economists to come to realize that the environmental justice is often in conflicts with the economic justice. Further, it is often not in sync with the society's justice system. Moreover, it is often in troubles with the racial justice and others. In plain terms, a policy intervention to improve the ecological health or the global climate can in reality turn out to harm the poor or enrich the rich over a long term (Seo 2015, 2019, 2020).

13.5   A Degrowth Critique

A degrowth critique is the third of the three post-growth theories. When it comes to the opposition against the concept of economic growth, it is the most direct counterforce. Protagonists of this group explicitly reject the merit of economic growth and publicly advocate zero or even negative economic growth. A zero or negative economic growth is referred to as degrowth by this group (D'Alisa et al. 2014; Kallis et al. 2018).

The first international conference convened by this movement was held in Paris in April 2008, which was entitled "The Conference on Economic Degrowth for Ecological Sustainability and Social Equity" (PDED 2008). The conference produced the Paris Declaration on Economic Degrowth (PDED).

In the PDED, the participants diagnosed that the economic growth in the past has not reduced poverty substantially while the global economy is already beyond the ecologically sustainable limits (PDED 2008):

> The best available scientific evidence indicates that the global economy has grown beyond ecologically sustainable limits, as have many national economies, especially those of the wealthiest countries.
>
> There is also mounting evidence that global growth in production and consumption is socially unsustainable and uneconomic (in the sense that its costs outweigh its benefits).

Based on this diagnosis, they called for a paradigm shift from a pursuit of economic growth to a "right-sizing of the global and national economies," which involves degrowth in the wealthy parts of the world as well as the global economy as a whole (PDED 2008):

> The process by which right-sizing may be achieved in the wealthiest countries, and in the global economy as a whole, is "degrowth".

We define degrowth as a voluntary transition towards a just, participatory, and ecologically sustainable society.

An academic description of the degrowth critique, as far as the economics is concerned, is found in the article which includes the section entitled "Managing without growth: the economics of degrowth" most recently published by a group of scholars (Victor 2008; Kallis et al. 2018). The present author summarizes some major arguments from this article presently.

Degrowth proponents argue that classical economists such as Adam Smith and David Ricardo "considered" a stationary state where economic growth ends owing to a limit to division of labor as for Smith or a limit to land supply as for Ricardo (Smith 1776; Ricardo 1817). They further believe that zero or negative growth is not incompatible with full employment in the neoclassical economic models, although we can easily glean, based on the exposition of the economic theories in this book, that such is not the case in a growing population or a declining natural resource stock (Koopmans 1965; Solow 1974).

According to the degrowth protagonists, the conditions for "stable degrowth" that are suggested by one or another are as follows, as reviewed by Kallis and coauthors (Kallis et al. 2018):

A decline in the supply of production inputs (such as labor, natural resources) and a reduction of working hours (Lange 2018);
A decrease in labor supply;
A constant aggregate demand;
A decrease in firm investments;
A nonincreasing demand by households and government, resulting in lower firm investments. Specifically, zero net investments and savings, a fixed total of consumption and government spending (Lange 2018);
The distance between producers and consumers is shortened via 'regionalized' economic structures; working hours are reduced; consumption is reduced by repairing, sharing, and downscaling (Paech 2012);

The degrowth protagonists espouse strong governmental policy interventions to force degrowth of economy, which includes:

To simulate low or negative growth paths, initiate a set of economic policies including carbon taxes, reductions in average working hours, and a combination of progressive taxation and social spending (Victor 2008);

Policy packages such as green taxes, caps, and eliminating fossil fuel subsidies;

Minimum and maximum income and wealth levels imposed (Kallis et al. 2012);

To counter a monetary imperative for growth to pay back interests, bank profits are socialized or distributed to savers;

Preventing economic actors from accumulating interest *via* a combination of policy interventions such as collective firm ownership, prevention of economies of scale, and limits on the exploitation of fossil fuels. (Lange 2018)

It is not hard to see that many of these suggested interventions are radical measures in a capitalist economy. The policies such as imposing a maximum wealth level, socializing all bank profits, preventing interest earnings/payments, preventing economies of scale would surely be very destructive for the economy and people on the planet. As far as the economics is concerned, these policies are medieval economic concepts (Shiller 2004).

13.6   Conclusion

This final chapter introduced the three post-growth theories which pursue non-optimal, sub-optimal, or even negative economic growth pathways. These critiques have been thoroughly addressed throughout this book in this chapter as well as in the preceding individual chapters, which patient readers will come to grasp at this point.

In the societally welfare optimizing trajectory of economic growth, according to Tjalling Koopmans, the macro economy will grow at the rate that approximates a rate of population growth plus a rate of discounting plus a rate of unexpected technological growth, all of which depend on such variables as the society's time preference as well as individuals' preferences (Koopmans 1965). The economy thus managed will be on the growth pathway by efficiently managing natural and ecological resources as well as by addressing the problems of negative consequences of economic activities such as environmental pollution and climate change (Nordhaus 1992b, 1994, 2008; Seo 2020, 2021).

An ad hoc approach, that is, a by-the-committee approach, to the question of economic growth will result in a mismanagement, if not a mess-up, of the priorities in the society and people (Seo 2019). The ecological limits set by theoreticians have turned out and will turn out to be over and over again that the humanity and the planet are in fact already past such presumed thresholds and limits (Seo 2020, 2021). Researchers and policymakers should heed to Irving Fisher's advice that when people can exchange goods and services freely, they will always find ways to better manage the problems at hand, improving the welfare to both parties and therefore society (Fisher 1930).

With this, the book entitled "The Economics of Optimal Growth Pathways: Evaluating the Health of the Planet's Natural and Ecological Resources" is concluded.

References

Arrow, Kenneth, Bert Bolin, Robert Costanza, Partha Dasgupta, Carl Folke, Crawford S. Holling, Bengt-Owe Jansson, Simon Levin, Karl-Goran Maler, Charles Perrings, and David Pimentel. 1995. Economic Growth, Carrying Capacity, and the Environment. *Ecological Economics* 15: 91–95.

Arrow, K.J., W. Cline, K.G. Maler, M. Munasinghe, R. Squitieri, and J. Stiglitz. 1996. Intertemporal Equity, Discounting, and Economic Efficiency. In *Climate Change 1995: Economic and Social Dimensions of Climate Change, Intergovernmental Panel on Climate Change*, ed. J.P. Bruce, H. Lee, and E.F. Haites. Cambridge, UK: Cambridge University Press.

Bartelmus, Peter. 2012. *Sustainability Economics*. Oxfordshire, UK: Routledge.

Baumol, W.J., and O.A. Oates. 1975. *The Theory of Environmental Policy*. Upper Saddle River, NJ: Prentice Hall.

Byerlee, D., and C.K. Eicher. 1997. *Africa's Emerging Maize Revolution*. Boulder, CO: Lynne Rienner Publishers.

Carson, R. 1962. *Silent Spring*. Boston, MA: Houghton Mifflin Harcourt.

Clark, Colin W. 1973. The Economics of Over Exploitation. *Science* 181: 630–634.

Coase, R.H. 1960. The Problem of Social Cost. *Journal of Law and Economics* 3: 1–44.

Costanza, R. 2010. *What Is Ecological Economics? Yale Insights*. New Haven, CT: Yale School of Management. https://insights.som.yale.edu/insights/what-is-ecological-economics

Curtis, P.G., C.M. Slay, N.L. Harris, A. Tyukavina, and M.C. Hansen. 2018. Classifying Drivers of Global Forest Loss. *Science* 361 (6407): 1108–1111.

D'Alisa, Giacomo, Federico Demaria, and Giorgos Kallis. 2014. *Degrowth: A Vocabulary for a New Era*. Oxfordshire, UK: Routledge.

Daly, Herman E. 1973. *Toward a Steady-state Economy*. New York, NY: W.H. Freeman and Company.

Daly, Herman E., and J. Farley. 2003. *Ecological Economics: Principles and Applications*. 1st ed. Washington, DC: Island Press.

Evenson, R., and D. Gollin. 2003. Assessing the Impact of the Green Revolution 1960–2000. *Science* 300: 758–762.

Faustmann, Martin. 1849. On the Determination of the Value which Forest Land and Immature Stands Pose for Forestry. In *Martin Faustmann and the Evolution of Discounted Cash Flow. Paper 42*, ed. M. Gane. Oxford, England: Oxford Institute; 1968.

Fisher, Irving. 1906. *The Nature of Capital and Income*. New York, NY: Macmillan.

———. 1930. *The Theory of Interest*. New York, NY: Macmillan.

Georgescu-Roegen, N. 1971a. *The Entropy Law and the Economic Process*. Cambridge, MA: Harvard University Press.

———. 1971b. The Steady State and Ecological Salvation: A Thermodynamic Analysis. *BioScience* 27: 266–270.

Global Footprint Network (GFN). 2022. Ecological Footprint. https://www.footprintnetwork.org/our-work/ecological-footprint/

Gordon, H.S. 1954. The Economic Theory of a Common-Property Resource: The Fishery. *The Journal of Political Economy* 62: 124–142.

Hotelling, H. 1931. The Economics of Exhaustible Resources. *Journal of Political Economy* 39: 137–175.

Hubbert, M. King. 1956. *Nuclear Energy and the Fossil Fuels*. San Antonio, TX: Presented at the Spring Meeting of the American Petroleum Institute.

International Union for Conservation of Nature (IUCN). 2021. IUCN Red List Summary Statistics. https://www.iucnredlist.org/resources/summary-statistics

Kallis, G., C. Kerschner, and J. Martinez-Alier. 2012. The Economics of Degrowth. *Econ. Degrowth* 84 (Suppl. C): 172–180.

Kallis, G., V. Kostakis, S. Lange, B. Muraca, S. Paulson, and M. Schmelzer. 2018. Research On Degrowth. *Annual Review of Environment and Resources* 43: 291–316.

Kleypas, Joan A., Robert W. Buddemeier, David Archer, Jean-Pierre Gattuso, Chris Langdon, and Bradley N. Opdyke. 1999. Geochemical Consequences of Increased Atmospheric Carbon Dioxide on Coral Reefs. *Science* 284: 118–120.

Koopmans, Tjalling C. 1965. On the Concept of Optimal Economic Growth. *Pontificiae Academiae Scientiarum Scripta Varia* 28 (1): 1–75.

Lange, S. 2018. *Macroeconomics Without Growth. Sustainable Economies in Neoclassical, Keynesian and Marxian Theories, Vol. 18*. Marburg, DE: Metropolis.

Likens, G.E., and F.H. Bormann. 1974. Acid Rain: A Serious Regional Environmental Problem. *Science* 184: 1176–1179.

Martinez-Alier, J. 2002. *The Environmentalism of the Poor: A Study of Ecological Conflicts and Valuation*. Cheltenham, UK: Edward Elgar.

Meadows, D.H., D.L. Meadows, J. Randers, and W.W. Behrens III. 1972. *The Limits to Growth; A Report for the Club of Rome's Project on the Predicament of Mankind*. New York, NY: Universe Books.

Molina, M.J., and F.S. Rowland. 1974. Stratospheric Sink for Chloro fluoromethanes: Chlorine Atom-catalysed Destruction of Ozone. *Nature* 249: 810–812.

Myers, Norman. 1979. *The Sinking Ark: A New Look at the Problem of Disappearing Species*. Oxford, UK: Pergamon Press.

Nelson, A., and B. Coffey. 2019. What is 'Ecological Economics' and Why Do We Need to Talk About It? The Conversation. *Published on November* 4: 2019.

Nordhaus, W.D. 1991. To Slow or Not to Slow: The Economics of the Greenhouse Effects. *Economic Journal* 101: 920–937.

———. 1992a. Lethal Model 2: The Limits to Growth Revisited. Bookings Papers on Economic Activity 1992: 1-59.

———. 1992b. The Ecology of Markets. *Proceedings of the National Academy of Sciences* 89: 843–850.

———. 1994. *Managing the Global Commons*. Cambridge, MA: MIT Press.

———. 2008. *A Question of Balance: Weighing the Options on Global Warming Policies*. New Haven, CT: Yale University Press.

Paech, N. 2012. *Befreiung vom U¨ berfluss: Auf dem Weg in die Postwachstumso¨konomie*. Mu¨nchen: Oekom Verlag.

Paris Declaration on Economic Degrowth (PDED). 2008. Degrowth Declaration of the Paris 2008 Conference. In *The Conference on Economic Degrowth for Ecological Sustainability and Social Equity, on 18–19 April 2008*. Paris: FR.

Pearce, D. 1998. Can Non-market Values Save the Tropical Forests? In *Tropical Rain Forest: A Wider Perspective*, ed. F.B. Goldsmith. Dordrecht, DE: Springer.

Pigou, A.C. 1920. *Economics of Welfare*. London, UK: Macmillan and Co.

Ramsey, F.P. 1928. A Mathematical Theory of Savings. *Economic Journal* 38: 543–559.

Rees, William E. 1992. Ecological Footprints and Appropriated Carrying Capacity: What Urban Economics Leaves Out. *Environment & Urbanization* 4: 121–130.

Reid, Walter V., and Kenton R. Miller. 1989. *Keeping Options Alive: The Scientific Basis for the Conservation of Biodiversity*. Washington, DC: World Resources Institute.

Repetto, R., and M. Gillis. 1988. *Public Policy and the Misuse of Forest Resources*. Cambridge, UK: Cambridge University Press.

Ricardo, D. 1817. *On the Principles of Political Economy and Taxation*. London, UK: John Murray.

Rosenzweig, C., and M. Parry. 1994. Potential Impact of Climate Change on World Food Supply. *Nature* 367: 133–138.

Schlenker, W., and M. Roberts. 2009. Nonlinear Temperature Effects Indicate Severe Damages to Crop Yields under Climate Change. *Proceedings of the National Academy of Science USA* 106: 15594–15598.

Seo, S.N. 2006. *Modeling Farmer Responses to Climate Change: Climate Change Impacts and Adaptations in Livestock Management in Africa.* Ph.D. dissertation,. New Haven: Yale University.

———. 2015. Helping Low-latitude, Poor Countries with Climate Change. *Regulation Winter* 2015–2016: 6–8.

———. 2016. *Microbehavioral Econometric Methods: Theories, Models, and Applications for the Study of Environmental and Natural Resources.* Amsterdam, NL: Academic Press.

———. 2019. *The Economics of Global Allocations of the Green Climate Fund: An Assessment from Four Scientific Traditions of Modeling Adaptation Strategies.* Cham, CH: Springer Nature.

———. 2020. *The Economics of Globally Shared and Public Goods.* Amsterdam, NL: Academic Press.

———. 2021. *Climate Change and Economics: Engaging with Future Generations with Action Plans.* Cham, CH: Palgrave Macmillan.

Shiller, Robert J. 2004. *The New Financial Order: Risk in the 21st Century.* Princeton, NJ: Princeton University Press.

Smith, Adam. 1776. *The Wealth of Nations.* London, UK: W. Strahan and T. Cadell.

Solow, R.M. 1957. A Contribution to the Theory of Economic Growth. *Quarterly Journal of Economics* 70: 65–94.

Solow, Robert M. 1974. The Economics of Resources or the Resources of Economics. *American Economic Review* 64: 1–14.

Speth, G. 2012. Manifesto for a Post-growth Economy. *YES! Magazine,* WA. Accessed from https://www.yesmagazine.org/new-economy/Manifesto-for-a-post-growth-economy-james-gustavesspeth

Stern, N. 2007. *The Economics of Climate Change: The Stern Review.* Cambridge, UK: Cambridge University Press.

Turco, R.P., O.B. Toon, T.P. Ackerman, J.B. Pollack, and C. Sagan. 1983. Nuclear Winter: Global Consequences of Multiple Nuclear Explosions. *Science* 222: 1283–1292.

United Nations (UN). 1972. *Report of the United Nations Conference on Human Environment.* Sweden: Stockholm.

———. 1992. *Agenda 21.* Rio de Janeiro, Brazil: United Nations Conference on Environment & Development.

———. 2000. *United Nations Millennium Declaration.* New York, NY: UN.

———. 2001. *Road Map Towards the Implementation of the United Nations Millennium Declaration.* New York, NY: UN.

————. 2015. *Transforming Our World: The 2030 Agenda for Sustainable Development*. New York, NY: UN.

Victor, P.A. 2008. *Managing Without Growth: Slower by Design, Not Disaster.* Cheltenham, UK: Edward Elgar.

von Thunen, J.H. 1826 [1966]. *The Isolated State.* Trans. C.M. Wartenberg. Oxford/New York: Pergamon.

Wackernagel, M. 1994. *Ecological Footprint and Appropriated Carrying Capacity: A Tool for Planning Toward Sustainability.* (Ph.D. Thesis). Vancouver, CA: School of Community and Regional Planning. The University of British Columbia.

Weitzman, M.L. 1998. Why the Far-distant Future Should be Discounted at Its Lowest Possible Rate. *Journal of Environmental Economics and Management* 36: 201–208.

————. 2007. A Review of The Stern Review on the Economics of Climate Change. *Journal of Economic Literature* 45: 703–724.

————. 2009. On Modeling and Interpreting the Economics of Catastrophic Climate Change. *Review of Economics and Statistics* 91: 1–19.

World Commission on Environment and Development (WCED). 1987. *Our Common Future.* Oxford, UK: Oxford University Press.

INDEX